The Art of Music Production

U.C.B.
LIBRARY

The Art of Music Production

THE THEORY AND PRACTICE

FOURTH EDITION

Richard James Burgess

OXFORD
UNIVERSITY PRESS

OXFORD
UNIVERSITY PRESS

Oxford University Press is a department of the University of Oxford.
It furthers the University's objective of excellence in research, scholarship,
and education by publishing worldwide.

Oxford   New York
Auckland   Cape Town   Dar es Salaam   Hong Kong   Karachi
Kuala Lumpur   Madrid   Melbourne   Mexico City   Nairobi
New Delhi   Shanghai   Taipei   Toronto

With offices in
Argentina   Austria   Brazil   Chile   Czech Republic   France   Greece
Guatemala   Hungary   Italy   Japan   Poland   Portugal   Singapore
South Korea   Switzerland   Thailand   Turkey   Ukraine   Vietnam

Oxford is a registered trademark of Oxford University Press in the UK and certain other
countries.

Published in the United States of America by
Oxford University Press
198 Madison Avenue, New York, NY 10016

Library of Congress Cataloging-in-Publication Data
Burgess, Richard James.
[Art of record production]
The art of music production: the theory and practice/Richard James Burgess.—Fourth edition.
pages cm
Includes bibliographical references and index.
ISBN 978–0–19–992172–0 (hardcover: alk. paper)—ISBN 978–0–19–992174–4 (pbk.: alk.
paper)   1. Sound recordings—Production and direction.   2. Sound recording industry—
Vocational guidance. Title.
ML3790.B84 2013
781.49023—dc23
2013000203

9 8 7 6 5 4 3 2 1
Printed in the United States of America
on acid-free paper

To my sons Ace and Blaze for making every day an adventure and for bringing even more music and words to our house and my life than I imagined possible. And to my parents who gave me freedom of mind and whom I miss.

CONTENTS

PREFACE

I have spent my working life in music, most of it in the recording industry. Recordings entranced me as a child. I was fortunate to work as a studio musician and recording artist, with many talented and successful producers to whom I am indebted. In 1980, I struck gold with my first production of Spandau Ballet's debut album. I subsequently produced, engineered, and mixed or remixed hundreds of recordings for many major-label artists on both sides of the Atlantic. Fortunately, a good number were successful and certified gold, platinum, or multiplatinum. Writing a book had not been my goal but, in 1994, I could not find one giving an inside perspective on the non-technical aspects of record production, so I naïvely set about writing one. Producers are diverse and production is complicated and ever-changing, so each edition remains challenging. I am humbly grateful that enough people read the first three editions that I was invited to write a fourth. Writing the book purely from my experience would have been easier, but the research was an opportunity to deconstruct the lives, careers, and thought processes of producers that I admire from all periods and styles.

This book does not recommend equalization (EQ) settings, microphone (mic) placements, or compression ratios; there are other books that explain these things well. This book attempts to identify the essence of music production, the skills, philosophies, and methodologies of successful producers, along with timeless ingredients, ways to enter the business, and a sense of how the job evolved. I touch on interactions with labels, artists, managers, and attorneys, as well as contracts, budgets, and pitfalls. I parse some fundamentals to give insights into various genres, as well as success and money, and what the future might hold. There are some stories and, I hope, a few moments of fun.

I wrote so that producers might see their lives reflected while gaining inspiration from the careers and thoughts of others. There are no position descriptions for producing work; I presume to outline one. I would like to play my part in stimulating discourse and furthering academic research and publication on the topic. Above all, I wrote to learn and to share my realizations.

Producers rarely work alone, and I have been fortunate in the substantiation I have received. I am extremely grateful to Norm Hirschy for his enthusiasm in bringing the book to Oxford University Press and his expert guidance throughout. Chris Charlesworth encouraged me to write the first edition and lent his wisdom through the second and third. I am forever indebted and grateful to him. My deepest thanks go to the many artists who trusted me with their music, their hopes, dreams, and futures, and who unknowingly sowed the seeds that flower here. I cannot forget the many producers, engineers, managers, musicians, label staff, colleagues, employees, band members, friends, and gloriously crazy people I know, and with whom I have created music. It would be impossible to thank my sons Ace and Blaze enough for challenging my every thought and notion, and for never allowing me the luxury of assumptions. Special thanks for contributions: Chuck Ainley, Marcella Araica, Benny Blanco, Ace Elijah Burgess, Blaze Burgess, Lauren Christy, Mike Clink, Peter Collins, Ros Earls, Cathy Fink, Pete Ganbarg, Richard Gottehrer, Jim Hall, Bruce Iglauer, Katia Isakoff, Andy Jackson, Don Kaplan, Joanna Kelly, Kip Lornell, Anna Loynes, Manfred Mann, Arif Mardin, Marcy Marxer, Caroline Morel, Alan Moulder, Dennis Muirhead, Kaitlyn Myers, Hugh Padgham, Wendy Page, Tim Palmer, Kevin Parme, Linda Perry, Marlene Plumley, Perry Resnick, Sandy Roberton, Alison Rollins, Danny Saber, Daniel Sheehy, Katrina Sirdofsky, Robin Su, and Minna Zhou.

Comments, corrections, or casual conversation can be sent to Richard James Burgess at rjb@burgessworldco.com. For further information, please go to www.burgessworldco.com.

The Art of Music Production

Introduction

I began writing the first edition of this book, then entitled *The Art of Record Production*, in 1994. The second and third editions, published in 2001 and 2004, were renamed *The Art of Music Production,* at the (previous) publisher's request. Throughout the history of record production, there have been many developments—cylinders, acoustic recording, electric technology, 78s, magnetic tape, multitrack recording, LPs, mono, stereo, quadraphonic, eight-tracks, cassettes, digital multitrack, random access, CDs, SACD, surround, and digital delivery—these and other technological advancements were all part of the evolution of the recording industry and production. Technological and social change caused the industry to expand and contract several times. Most of the major labels changed their names from "Something Records" to "Acronym Records" and then to "Something Music Group." Many people still refer to them as record companies or labels. The term "record producer" is problematic; some contracts refer to the label as the record producer or the producer, and the term "record" became erroneously associated with vinyl discs, which is odd because the term precedes them. Record producers, as discussed here, are rarely involved in manufacturing, typically delivering a final mix or master of the music in the prevailing professional format. The label then manufactures any physical product and sets up digital delivery and distribution. Music production is thus a less ambiguous term because it references the thing we produce, irrespective of its ultimate encoding as grooves on a cylinder or disc, pits and land on a CD, or ones and zeros in a digital file.

Nevertheless, the word "record" can still apply in the context of documenting or recording music. If you record something, the product would be a record. If you write down (record) a thought, what you wrote would be a record of that thought; it is similarly so with music. Whatever form or formlessness recorded music takes, it is a record of an event or series of events. All of which may explain the term's persistence as being more than nostalgia or habit. There is a vernacular use of the word, as in "sounds like a record," signifying completion. This is the satisfying moment when you lean back in your chair knowing the whole finally transcends the parts.

I use the terms "record producer," "audio producer," "music producer," and "producer" interchangeably. Nonetheless, the producers discussed here record music mostly for distribution to consumers but also for film, television, electronic games, commercials, and more. Dissemination and monetization through multiple channels are now common.

As a child, vinyl discs intrigued me—the music visibly shimmered in the grooves. I pored over the label and the liner notes, wanting to know who wrote the song, which musicians played on it, and what a producer did. How special it is to be able to capture creative moments in time and then fashion them to excite and inspire others using musical, managerial, and technical skills. The term "art" is in the title rather than skill, craft, trade, musicology, ethnomusicology, or profession, and the Oxford Dictionary defines art as:

> The expression or application of human creative skill and imagination...producing works to be appreciated primarily for their beauty or emotional power...works produced by human creative skill and imagination...skill at doing a specified thing, typically one acquired through practice.[1]

My hope here is to offer glimpses into how producers capture, compile, and mold creative moments so others are compelled to press "play" again.

The term "producer" is overarching like "doctor," "pilot," or "architect," each of which encompasses specializations that determine their exponents' particular expertise, and so it is with producers. I was initially motivated to write this book because I felt that the art of music production was poorly understood, even within the industry. At that time, the demise of the commercial studio system was underway along with its apprenticeship system, which developed so many successful producers. The responsibility for training shifted to individuals and the education system. An abundance of information was available, but the preponderance of it focused on technical topics rather than the art of music production.

Consequently, this is an auto-ethnographic work combining qualitative research from an insider's perspective while connecting to broader participatory cultural understandings. By this means, I hope to provide some cultural contextualization of the art, craft, business, and lifestyle of music producers. In each edition, I attempted to spotlight contemporary production environments while documenting the diversity of past methodologies. The foundational material originates from living and working in this setting for most of my life. Nonetheless, I endeavor to extend my perspective and demythologize my assumptions through interviews and extensive research. These made the writing of each edition an exciting journey of affirmation and discovery.

The loss of traditional, cultural frames of reference, such as studio protocols and etiquette in the transition from an apprenticeship system to educational programs, draws comment from many longtime engineers and producers. Assistant engineers and fledgling producers come into the studio with ample technical knowledge but lacking an understanding of the interpersonal dynamics that facilitate successful sessions and elicit great performances. Additionally, production today is often fragmented, less concerned with managing group performance, and more reliant on digital manipulation or creation. As we see with every technological change, the recording medium and the shift of philosophy and focus in training skew the methodologies and the character of recorded music. Newer generations of engineers and producers typically have more experience editing elements in a digital audio workstation (DAW) than coaxing better performances out of artists and musicians. Thus we have the relatively recent emergence of specialist credits such as "vocal producer," "vocals recorded by," "orchestra recorded by," and "strings recorded by." These increasingly disassociated traditional production and engineering roles require specialized training, experience, skills, and mindsets involving complex relational and psychological interaction with the participants.

Much of what is taught today under the rubric of production would, historically, have been considered engineering, which is an integral part of production but not its entirety. A quick review of some course titles is illustrative: Audio Music Technology, Music and Audio Technology, Music Recording, Recording engineer, Recording Arts Degree, Audio Engineering Diploma, Certificate in Audio Engineering, Music Production and Engineering Major, and Audio Design Technology. The emphasis is on recording, editing, mixing, and operating a DAW—invaluable skills in today's production environment. My concern is the minimization of the broader range of essential musical, interpersonal, behavioral, managerial, legal, financial, and business skills. As Hugh Padgham (Phil Collins, the Police, Sting, Genesis) said to me, "50-percent of being a producer is being able to manage the band." A cursory review of some of the most successful producers (such as George Martin, Quincy Jones, Mutt Lange, Rick Rubin, etc.) shows evidence of critical contributions that far exceed their ability to operate machinery. Most producers have a working knowledge of the technology of their era, but operation of the machinery is a means to achieve a musical and performative result. Alan Lomax transported and set up his equipment for field recordings, but he also fulfilled the role of producer, as well as being a folklorist and ethnomusicologist. The same is true for Frances Densmore in the early 20th century. Similarly, Fred Gaisberg sourced the artists, played accompaniments, and ran the recording machines at the very beginnings of the recording industry.

Most art forms encompass technical components—painters choose, mix, and apply paint, sculptors use tools of the period, and so on. Just as a high degree of skill in mixing and applying paint does not define a great painter, adeptness with recording technology does not make a great producer. Notwithstanding, the history of record production is inseparable from the development and use of technology. In effect, the first record producers were the inventors of sound recording, Édouard-Léon Scott de Martinville and Thomas Alva Edison. As far as we can tell, all the parameters of production were present in those sessions—the organization of the session, including selection of material, place, and performers, as well as the choice of technology and techniques to be used. There is little doubt that they directed the recording of the performances. The demarcation is often unclear, but the titles of "engineer" and "recorded by" exist for those who specialize in the technological aspects of capturing the recording and do not, for the most part, venture into the directorial role that we regard as music production.

This book, therefore, is not a study of music technology. This reflects my view that there is an abundance of this requisite material but a scarcity of the conceptual, theoretical, musical, interpersonal, directorial, managerial, and organizational. I am gratified that the academic study of record production now appears to be on a stronger footing than when I wrote the first edition. Many scholars are presenting and publishing insightful work, much of it at the Art of Record Production Conference[2] and in the *Journal on the Art of Record Production*.[3] There is also the Association for the Study of the Art of Record Production, and all three international organizations have their base at the London College of Music in the United Kingdom.

I quote a great number of producers and experts in this book. Many are friends whose work I respect; quite a few are people I have long admired; and I present conflicting viewpoints for balance. I try to avoid lists of the greatest, the most innovative, the first, and so forth that, in my opinion, err toward celebrity rather than innovation—perhaps a case of the victors writing history. My observation is that many true innovators, in any field, appear to pass into history with inadequate or no credit. Others who contributed to technological or conceptual progress almost invariably precede most inventions and innovations, so when I refer to firsts or innovations, prior contributions are implied.

The book is in two parts, the first of which covers the theory of producer typologies, which I modified significantly from the first three editions. In part two, I address the practical considerations of being a music producer, including the responsibilities and day-to-day tasks. This section is also extensively revised to reflect shifts in musical and technical trends. I attempt to describe deliverables and obligations in broad-enough terms that they apply to any genre and highlight idiosyncrasies where generalizations do not apply. My intention was that the book could be read in any order; however, clarifying examples are interwoven throughout, so some context may be missed by starting part way through.

SECTION ONE

The Theory

Music production is the technological extension of composition and orchestration. It captures the fullness of a composition, its orchestration, and the performative intentions of the composer(s). In its precision and inherent ability to capture cultural, individual, environmental, timbral, and interpretive subtleties along with those of intonation, timing, intention, and meaning (except where amorphousness is specified), it is superior to written music and oral traditions. Music production is not only representational but also an art in itself.

1

Types of Music Producers

The ability to deal with people is as purchasable a commodity as sugar and coffee. And I pay more for that ability than for any other under the sun.
—John D. Rockefeller

This chapter examines classifications or categorizations of producers. I only discuss the producer, co-producer, and "produced by" credits here; executive producer, associate producer, and additional production credits are dealt with in chapter 11.

Why do we need classifications? Record production as a practice is little more than a century old and responds to societal and technological shifts. It is only in the past two decades or so that a theoretical analysis of production (independent of technical considerations) has emerged as a field of academic study within the broader disciplines of ethnomusicology, musicology, and anthropology. Classification is an ancient practice and perhaps the most fundamental of scientific interpretive tools, although it is complex, ever changing, and sometimes controversial with regard to common criteria chosen for inclusion in a category.[1] In applied production, categorizing producers by functionality can help labels and artists choose appropriate producers and vice versa. Understanding requirements for the functional classifications can help aspiring producers develop necessary skills. The producer credit in the field of recorded music is a catchall term, describing a range of skills, responsibilities, and functions. Different genres and subgenres of recorded music have their own production requirements, and the relationship between producer and artist varies accordingly. For instance, a suitable producer for bands such as Metallica, Disturbed, or Slipknot is, in general, unlikely to be a good fit for pop artists like Katy Perry, Justin Bieber, or Britney Spears. Variances in approach are even more pronounced if we consider styles outside of popular music, such as traditional musics, classical, and jazz. Furthermore, the breadth of each genre means that genre alone is not the determinative factor; outwardly similar artists may require different functional classes of producer. For instance, two groups both considered stylistically pop punk might require, in one instance, a producer who can help them strengthen their songs for radio and, in another, someone who can optimize their own material and performances. The results may sound similar but the required producers' skills and creative relationships with the artist are quite different. A system of classification such as this may help in matching producers to artists and in developing a theory of music production that can guide students in acquiring the required skills. Just as some producers cross genres, bifunctionality and polyfunctionality are possible for those who acquire the necessary skills and can mentally shift into appropriate roles.

It is important to note that there is no hierarchy implied in the classification. There is no "best" type of producer. Different artists and projects have different production needs, and the best producer is the one that fits those requirements most closely. Like the blank tile in Scrabble that can substitute for any letter, music producers have to be versatile and supply the missing elements to make a great recording. Furthermore, when a producer and artist work together on successive projects, their creative relationship will evolve. Referring to his changing role over four successful Simply Red albums, Stewart Levine said,

> [a]s a producer, you have to be prepared to adapt to the circumstances. . . . Mick [Hucknall] wanted to take a larger role on the fifth album. When you have a situation where the artist is growing, if you are wise, you help him to do just that.

Paul McCartney, in an interview with Mark Lewisohn, spoke of the Beatles' growth in their relationship with George Martin from the first session in 1962:

> George [Martin] was the mastermind then. But as it went on, the workers took over the tools more, and we started to say, "We're coming in late, and we might not need you, George. If you can't make it, we'll go in on our own."[2]

No two producers or production teams have identical skill sets or ways of working, but commonalities do exist. There are many useful criteria for classifying producers, among them current success, musical genre, training, studio ownership, price, location, and methodologies. On these bases, you could select someone who recently had a big hit, a heavy metal producer, an engineer/producer, a studio owner, someone who works at cheaper rates, or a person who programs everything using a digital audio workstation and synthesizers. I have been in A&R meetings where some or all of these criteria have been discussed. Nonetheless, this list is incomplete for matching the complexity of a specific artist's needs with a producer in order to achieve an optimal result. Thus, I choose to classify producers primarily by their functional interaction with the featured artist, the material, and the studio environment. I view background (engineer, musician, songwriter), methodology (records the band live, uses only computer-programmed parts, etc.), genre, success, studio ownership, price, location, and so forth as subsets of functionality. A modest budget may make studio ownership imperative, but not just any studio owner will do. Similarly, if prior success is crucial (it often is—major labels value hits) and becomes the initial filter, functionality will still need to be the ultimate criterion for a successful outcome. Identifying producers by background or training—engineer/producer, songwriter/producer, musician/producer, and so on—omits other critical considerations. Engineer/producers often discontinue engineering and contribute to arrangements, song doctoring, and performance coaching. Likewise, songwriter/producers nowadays often engineer and do not always insist on writing the material they produce. Even one of the first producers, Fred Gaisberg, is difficult to classify by background. He was a musician; he played accompaniments on his early recordings; and the designers and builders of the equipment trained him extensively in its use; at the same time, he exhibited management skills and the ability to identify talent at an early age.

I have not attempted an exhaustive or broad classification of producers although the six categories here are derived from observed working practices of successful producers. I extended, refined, and renamed these from the four in the first three editions of this book, but the overarching point remains the same: that function in the studio does not consistently align with background skills. Furthermore, these classifications may not apply to the person of the producer exclusively but rather to the techniques he or she applies to a particular production. As described earlier, some producers have bi- or polyfunctionality and can switch roles from project to project. Moreover, a producer can be a team or an individual, although I use the term "production team" when it is clear that two or more are formal partners. It is worth noting that established production teams generally interact with each other and the artist differently than individuals who co-produce with the artist in what is, frequently, an ad hoc working relationship.

Functional Typologies

ARTIST

This is the simplest of all categories—artists who produce themselves. This is a growing class of producer, and it will continue to grow significantly in the foreseeable future because of the democratizing effect of digital recording technology. Examples go back many decades: Ben Selvin, Les Paul, Stevie Wonder (starting with "Where I'm Coming From") Mike Oldfield, Prince, and so on. At the time of writing, there are two *Billboard* Top Ten hits, Gotye's "Somebody I Used to Know" and Calvin Harris's "Feel So Close," both of which were written, produced, and performed by the artist. Anecdotally, when I teach classes on production, a significant portion of the class identifies themselves as artists who are studying to develop the skills to produce themselves.

AUTEUR

This category describes a music producer (or team) who is audibly the primary creative force in the production. The word is French for author and, in this context, derives from the term "auteur theory," originated by French film critics when referring to directors who express their unique personality through their films,

observable "in a thematic and/or stylistic consistency in all (or almost all) the director's films."[3] This style is not without its detractors, but it is widely accepted to
the extent that screen credits have indicated "a film by (director's name)" since the
1950s. (Previously, the scriptwriter, star, or producer was credited in that manner.)[4]

In music production (at the time of writing), many, but not all, auteur producers write the songs, play instrumental parts, lay down guide vocals, engineer,
edit, and perhaps even mix as well. In any event, the defining factor is the unique
personal identity with which they infuse their productions. The *Billboard* Hot 100
has seen a gradually increasing trend over the past 50 years to the current situation
where auteur producers are generating most of the top ten hits.

Successful auteur producers are musically, technically, and commercially
strong. Their songs, arrangements, orchestrations, sounds, and vocal parts are
often recognizable, even though the artist may be unfamiliar. They may also
have a sonic imprint or character that is distinct. Auteurs are not a natural
choice for a band that writes and wants to play everything on their record. They
are perfect for non-writing artists or those who need a co-writer. In demand by
record companies, these producers solve an A&R person's problem of finding a
song and a producer, and they tend to focus on producing hits—something that
bands often find difficult to do. Successful auteurs' names carry weight with the
media, which can make a difference in the struggle to make a breakthrough for
an unknown artist.

Historically, certain formats, such as pop and R&B or urban, have favored
auteur producers, though in the late 1990s and early part of the 21st century,
those distinctions eroded. R&B has long had producers such as Holland, Dozier,
and Holland, Gamble and Huff, L.A. and Babyface, and Jam and Lewis who fit
this category. Hip hop producers such as the Neptunes, Timbaland, and Kanye
West generated hit singles for many artists. In pop music, Max Martin, Red
One, Dr. Luke, Benny Blanco, and Stargate have charted productions for many
artists, as did the British team of Stock, Aitken, and Waterman in the '80s and
'90s. The Matrix penetrated the rock-pop crossover market with their production of "Complicated" for Avril Lavigne. With the music industry diminished
(as it has been since the early 2000s), the necessity for hit singles, and the difficulty of getting untested artists on the radio, all formats now seem susceptible
to the auteur approach. Train's productions by Stargate are a contemporaneous
example of a rock group that has changed its sonic identity, becoming somewhat subjugated to that of the production team's.

Self-contained auteur producers often own a production company or label.
With their comprehensive skills, it makes sense to apply their time, expertise, and
energy in building a catalog of valuable copyrights, perhaps producing for other
labels under only the most favorable terms and for substantial artists. Auteurs often
enjoy a sustained period of success once established. Those with a distinctive style
can become influential and even create a sub-genre. This was true with Holland,
Dozier, and Holland's remarkable series of '60s hits, which formed the backbone of

the "Motown Sound," and similarly, Gamble and Huff created the "Philadelphia Sound" in the '70s.

When auteurs fall from favor or fashion, it can be hard for them to recover because their recognizable sound is strongly associated with a period or trend. In consolation, a few big hits as producer and writer can generate considerable income, and the skills are transferable. Testimony to that is L.A. Reid who, after producing distinctive hits for many artists (with the L.A. and Babyface team) went on to run Arista Records, Island Defjam, and Epic Records in addition to becoming a judge on "The X Factor."

Auteurs require diverse skills, and teams rather than individuals are common to the typology. In the case of a team, one of the partners may be musically creative, with the other being a sounding board: the "big picture" person and/or the business brains. An example of this is Stock, Aitken, and Waterman where Stock and Aitken were the primary writers who were active in the studio and Waterman supplied the business and A&R expertise. Even when this is not the case, there is usually some division of labor. I asked Lauren Christy from the three-person production team The Matrix how they define their roles. She said, "People see Scott in front of the recording equipment, Graham with a guitar, and me with a book, and they think 'that's what they do.'" In fact, the lines are blurred. Graham might sing some words that Lauren will like and write down, and then Scott might add to that. Every idea goes in her book. When Scott starts to lay drums, Lauren might say, "Uh uh, I'm not feeling that groove against the vocal, the kick pattern is wrong." Meanwhile Graham is working on the melody with Scott suggesting that the top line of the chorus swoop up so that it starts higher than the last note of the verse. As Christy said, "That's what makes the partnership great. We're kind of like a monster with three heads."[5]

The Holland, Dozier, and Holland writing and production team split up their responsibilities differently. In an interview with Dale Kawashima, Brian Holland explained,

> Lamont and I would start writing the songs on piano. Eddie would also be there early on, and we would discuss what the melody and structure should be. Lamont and I would then start recording the tracks, which would be the actual tracks for the master (not just demo tracks).[6]

Despite the fact that this was 50 years ago, this writing to tape technique is functionally similar to the methodology of many auteurs today. Lamont Dozier continued,

> In the recording studio, Brian and I would split the room. Brian would work with the drummer (usually Benny Benjamin). I would get with the keyboard players (usually Earl Van Dyke or Joe Hunter) and show them how to play the track and chords. I would also give the bass lines to James Jamerson; then he would inject his own bass ideas to make it stronger. We wanted to guide the musicians, so we could create our own sound. We would never let the band just go in and play the chord sheets. We were very focused on what we had in mind for these productions.[7]

Brian Holland elaborated:

> We would record the full track, which would include the melody with a scratch vocal, without lyrics yet, although sometimes we would have the title, and some of the chorus lyrics [such as "Baby Love" and "I Hear a Symphony"]. Then we would give the track to Eddie, who would go off and write the lyrics.[8]

Eddie Holland would then take the track to his Detroit townhouse, close the curtains and shades, and lock himself away to write. He added, "There was no telephone. I didn't go out much; most of my life was devoted to writing lyrics".[9]

Walter Afanasieff produced Mariah Carey and Michael Bolton, and wrote hits such as Kenny G's "Don't Make Me Wait for Love" and Gladys Knight's "Licensed to Kill." He often likes to play everything on a track, and when he uses musicians, he tightly controls their parts and performances as an arranger does. On the track "Hero" for Mariah Carey, he performed all the instrumental parts saying,

> I tried to simulate an orchestral sound with my synthesizers. There's a huge timpani roll, a swell of strings, and French horns, which were all done on keyboards. In the back of my mind, I thought we might have an orchestra recreate the string parts. However, when Mariah completed her vocals, she said the recording sounded fine just the way it was, and that we didn't need to bring in an orchestra[10]

"Hero" became the second single from her album *Music Box*, reaching number one on the *Billboard* Hot 100. Afanasieff, in a *Mix* interview with Brad Leigh Benjamin, said,

> I like to do everything. I'll create the rhythm, the drum parts, the bass lines, the keyboard parts, the string arrangements, the horn arrangements, and the vocal arrangements. Even when the guitar players are in doing their parts, I'll be in their face every minute, every second, making sure they're giving me exactly what I want them to play. I like being responsible for every note on the record, which I suppose classifies me more as a producer/arranger.[11]

Arif Mardin mentioned the term "arranger/producer" to me, and certainly many of the most successful producers such as Mardin, George Martin, and Quincy Jones are formally trained arrangers who specifically define musical parts in their productions. Clearly, Afanasieff is functioning as an arranger (and performer) and, in the case of "Hero," also as the songwriter. To a greater and lesser extent, most producers contribute to arrangements and sometimes they perform. However, the term "arranger/producer" does not well delineate the producer's relationship to the track or the artist. Afanasieff, like all auteur producers, employs a level of control that creates a signature identity, whereas Mardin's and George Martin's work tends to emphasize, adopt, or complement and adapt to the identity of the artist. The level of control and the signature sound are the characteristic qualities of the auteur producers who commonly take complete command of the production, building from the composition up. As Max Martin said,

> I want to be part of every note, every single moment going on in the studio. I want nothing forgotten; I want nothing missed. I'm a perfectionist. The producer should decide what kind of music is being made, what it's going to sound like—all of it, the why, when and how.[12]

Benny Blanco said something similar to me as well.[13]

In the 1960s, Phil Spector, using very different technology, techniques, and many musicians, exercised this level of mastery over his signature productions. As with film directors, people often refer to his productions as "Phil Spector records." Mitch Miller also imbued his productions from the 1950s with his own identity, rather than the artist's.

Very often, the only thing the auteur producer requires of the artist is that he or she sing or rap. Teddy Riley says this about his work with Michael Jackson and Bobby Brown:

> Most of the vocal tracks were completed on the first or second try....If you can't come into the studio and sing a song the way it's supposed to be sung, then you don't need to be working with me....If the singer feels the music, and you've got the melody recorded beforehand, you're going to get the vocals down cold.[14]

Timbaland has worked with Missy Elliott, Jay Z, Memphis Bleek, Ludacris, Justin Timberlake, Ginuwine, and many others. Timbaland was explicit in a January 2004 interview with *Billboard* when he said, "My producing style is this: 'I am the music.' The artist is the front man for the producer."

In the U.K. success of Stock, Aitken, and Waterman (SAW), even the artists' singing ability was secondary to factors such as prior fame. SAW laid the foundations for an empire by writing and producing a run of hits for the previously nonsinging but famous soap actors Kylie Minogue and Jason Donovan, triggering a decades-long recording career for Minogue.

Nowadays, inexpensive digital technology makes it easier, and more practical, to develop impressive studio skills at an early age. The influence of artists and producers like Prince, Jam and Lewis, Timbaland, Calvin Harris, and so forth may inspire more kids to become proficient writers, arrangers, and multi-instrumentalists. Those who choose not to become recording artists in their own right may develop into the next generation of auteur producers.

Like Holland, Dozier, and Holland, working as a team helps Jam and Lewis handle several projects simultaneously. They have a saying, "We have no slack," which helps them come up with a solution to any musical or technical problem. If one of them is experiencing a creative block, the other one can take over. Jimmy Jam calls Terry Lewis "vocal master," and Terry Lewis calls Jimmy Jam "track master," loosely defining the roles they play in productions.[15]

Although L.A. and Babyface have not produced as a team for many years, when they were collaborating, Reid said he liked having "someone to bounce ideas off." He felt that it kept them from getting "stale" and kept up "the inspiration level." He quoted Babyface as saying: "By working as part of a team, one always has the benefit of a second opinion."

FACILITATIVE

Often credited as a co-producer, this category of producer commonly starts out as an engineer, programmer, musician, or co-writer. The artist is the primary creative force in the recording, and the role is to support, facilitate, and maximize the recording of the artist's ideas.

This person may connect with an artist early in his or her career by making the production process seamless. If the artist becomes successful, he or she may see no need to change the formula, and the facilitative producer can become indispensable. Success with one artist can lead to parallel relationships or full production credits with others if recording and touring schedules can be coordinated. The facilitative role meshes well with confident, self-directed artists who need a motivated, capable, and supportive person to keep the production process moving forward smoothly. The facilitative producer takes care of tasks that the artist does not have the time, expertise, or inclination to handle; these are often centered on the engineering and technical aspects but they may include musical and administrative functions. Facilitative producers generally do not want to be highly visible, or be the driving force behind the artist, or dictate every note recorded, and for that reason, they are not ideal for artists who do not have a strong vision and creative compass.

An artist may want to work with a facilitative producer who has a music background for his or her formal or extended understanding of music, or for help with arrangements, song doctoring, or organizing and rehearsing the band. Facilitative producers who are engineers enjoy considerable room for personal creativity with regard to technical matters. These relationships can become long-standing, fulfilling, and lucrative, even though the royalty rate may be relatively low. The role is typically hands-on, detail-oriented, and comfortable. As Andy Jackson said, "You can roll into the next album and it's like riding a bike. You pick it up where you left off, and you haven't got to reinvent the wheel."[16]

COLLABORATIVE

It is my observation that a significant percentage of producers characterize themselves as collaborative. The role is akin to coauthors of a literary work or screenplay where collaborators may contribute in different ways but, overall, they share the creative load. The result has a fresh identity that may be an extended or expanded version of the artist's but not one that is overtly distinctive of the producer. Collaborative producers can come from any background: engineering, arranging, songwriting, DJing, or from a band. Collaborative producers do not attempt to control every detail of a recording; they bring an extra-band-member mentality to their productions. Often described as the fifth Beatle, George Martin's contributions to their many productions are undeniably considerable. Nonetheless, in contrast to auteur producers, he invariably allowed artists to have the predominant voice or stylistic fingerprint on their recordings. Whatever their background skills, the best collaborators fit in, contributing as they deem necessary to gently steer the artist in the right direction, using their casting vote sparingly. They exhibit flexibility and a desire to extract maximum value from the artist's ideas. The collaborative producer maintains a minimal sense of hierarchy in the studio, throwing his or her ideas into the creative stew along with everyone else's. In some cases, they allow creative, organizational, or technical leadership to shift, recognizing good ideas from any source and encouraging their exploration. This relationship works well with a musically self-contained artist who has a vision and an identity but who wants a seasoned professional challenging and extending him or her daily. The collaborative producer's objective is to elevate the recording and the artist's career by optimizing the artist's identity.

When well matched to the artist, a collaborative producer's experience can save an artist time, money, and frustration. There are times when seemingly absurd ideas can produce positive results, but unmediated groups of musicians can waste valuable creative energy exploring dead-end ideas and processes that a studio veteran can avoid. A consummate collaborative producer carefully guides the workflow around creative, technical, interpersonal, and logistical blockages.

ENABLATIVE

Technology has been the driving force behind the history and techniques of record production. Before Jack Mullin brought magnetic tape-recording technology back from Germany in 1945, the final recording, including all its parts and any effects, was best captured in a single, simultaneous performance. The term "producer" did not come into general use for decades; the director of recording, recorder, or technician performed the various roles, through the first half of the twentieth century, without credit on the recordings. Thus, the art of music production lay in finding talent and material, and creating conditions in which a successful recording could take place. These skills form a large part of what I call the enablative role. In the very early days, the role that we now think of as A&R was conflated with that of producer. Fred Gaisberg was a talent scout, musician, music director, and engineer. A documented division began at Victor, with their A&R committee identifying talent. Employees such as the Sooys performed the technical act of recording and probably some of the functions of a producer.

Proto-producers, such as Fred Gaisberg, John Lomax, Ben Selvin, Ralph Peer, and John Hammond, had limited control once the cutting head was lowered, and so they specialized in discovering and capturing the essence of new acts. However, from what we know, they did not simply record the acts as they were, and there were differences in the way these producers contributed to the recordings. Gaisberg often accompanied artists on their recordings, and Selvin was an accomplished arranger. Lomax was interested in documentation, but was also known to have manipulated material and artistic direction to suit his preferences. Hammond would influence the choices of musicians and material.

As it is today, early producers brought their expertise and methodologies to their productions and learned additional skills when necessary. John Lomax (and later his son Alan) made many field recordings, which required mechanical expertise, in locations where there was no technical backup. Selvin recorded under so many guises and for so many labels that we may never know how many recordings he made, but it is alleged to be in the tens of thousands. Credited with founding the country music genre, Peer recorded Fiddlin' John Carson and later the famous Bristol sessions through which he introduced the Carter Family and Jimmy Rodgers to the world. Hammond, a Vanderbilt, initially financed his own sessions in professional studios with the best technical expertise and placed the recordings with major labels. Hammond's skill undoubtedly lay in identifying talent—he played some role in the discovery or exposure of many classic American artists, such as Fletcher Henderson, Count Basie, Billie Holiday, Benny Goodman, Gene Krupa, Bob Dylan, Aretha Franklin, Bruce Springsteen, and Stevie Ray Vaughan, to name a few. He persuaded Goodman to hire Krupa, a relationship that, despite later tensions, turned out to be one of the most successful musical and commercial partnerships of the 20th century.

These were fertile times (early in the history of the music industry, when much talent remained unrecorded and artists had no easy ways to record and distribute their music). Nonetheless, the number and stature of the artists Hammond discovered and produced with consistency across four decades and various styles of music is impressive. An accomplished classical violinist with a passion for music rooted in African-American traditions, he allowed the talent of the artist to shine through. He found and signed artists, chose the material, recording location, and personnel, and then largely allowed artists to be themselves. Miles Davis's producer, Teo Macero, who was a colleague of Hammond's at Columbia Records, was critical of Hammond's approach: "It was the artist who was really controlling things...it was the artist who decided what the take was."[17]

Hammond certainly did not perform the active creative and collaborative role that Macero did in Davis's '60s fusion recordings. Additionally, as is common in the industry, Hammond may have exaggerated some of his "contributions"; Billie Holiday said in her autobiography that it was "not John Hammond" but another Columbia executive "who really went to bat for me" and "almost lost his job at Columbia fighting for me."[18] He was not the producer who defined Aretha Franklin's sound. Nevertheless, Hammond's contribution to 20th-century American music is undeniable. It is clear that he had a strong vision and a passion for the kinds of artists he wanted to sign, as well as the greatest of respect for their talent. That his low level of creative and technical intermediation in the studio was a conscious technique is borne out by his publicly expressed disapproval of highly processed pop production styles as exemplified by another Columbia colleague, Mitch Miller.[19] In this respect, Hammond models the enablative role.

The enablative producer stands distinct from the next category, the consultative producer, insofar as they are often responsible for the first recordings by acts previously known only regionally or locally. These producers, though not highly controlling in the studio, are usually present during the recording process. Characteristic of some early producers, this is still an active methodology used in recording traditional artists from all over the world and some jazz.

CONSULTATIVE

The consultative producer performs the role of a mentor in a production, garnering loyalty from appropriate artists even though he or she may spend little time in the studio. Though closely related to the ideal A&R role in representing the high-altitude or big-picture perspective with "fresh ears," they are generally on location more than most A&R people. The term "Svengali" has been used to describe this role, but it is inappropriate because of its negative implications of manipulation, domination, and selfish intent. That role does exist, but it is associated more with the owners and/or managers of put-together groups who may also produce the act. Those individuals control the direction, membership, material, and all decisions, retaining most or all of the revenue and rights. In contrast, the consultative producer counsels, coaches, advises, guides, and provides conceptual, psychological, and visionary alignment for the project.

Talking about his approach to producing, Rick Rubin said, "My goal is to just get out of the way and let the people I'm working with be their best."[20] This comment might sound like that of an enablative producer, but the consultative producer, though often not present for the entire production, is highly integrated into the creative process, especially in choosing and shaping the material. Nonetheless, their records tend to be characterized by the identity of the artist. Rubin reputedly spends little time at the studio. The consultative producer is not a micromanager and fits well into Theodore Roosevelt's dictum: "The best leader is the one who has sense enough to pick good men to do what he wants done, and the self-restraint to keep from meddling with them while they do it."[21]

Chili Peppers guitarist John Frusciante said of Rubin, "I love the working relationship we have. [He] makes everybody comfortable and . . . lets things be when they are fine."[22] Singer Anthony Kiedis enjoyed working with Rubin and said of him, "He's very intelligent, very emotionally in tune with hardcore, soulful music."[23]

On the other hand, Slipknot front man Corey Taylor was critical of Rubin's lack of presence. He said Rubin was there only "45 minutes a week" and would "lay on a couch, have a mic brought in next to his face so he wouldn't have to f***ing move. . . . And then he would be, like, 'Play it for me.'" Taylor noted his respect for

Rubin's past work but said, "He is overrated, he is overpaid, and I will never work with him again as long as I f***ing live."[24] He added, "I only saw him about four times," and "Rubin is a nice man" who has "done a lot of good for a lot of people," but "he didn't do anything for me...if you're going to produce something, you're f***ing there. I don't care who you are."[25] Other band members were apparently happier than Taylor was with Rubin's work on the album.

There is a distinction between a consultative producer and those who simply put their name on a record and are paid without showing up. This syndrome seems to be more common in America than in Europe. Producer manager Ros Earls of 140dB Management who represents Flood (P. J. Harvey, U2, Depeche Mode, and Nine Inch Nails) thinks that Americans might be "more honest about it." Nonetheless, she said that

> Flood is adamant that he won't lend his name to something. He gets really angry about the way a name becomes public property, the way a name can help get a record on the radio. They're not really listening to [the work].

Earls said she represents "very hands-on" producers, although she does not disapprove of the "managerial approach."[26]

Successful Los Angeles-based engineer John X (Black Grape) had the experience of working on a four-month album project with a famous producer who, X says, appeared for about half an hour in the entire four months. Despite this, when the band was out at night, after the session, when asked what they were up to, they said they were recording with the absentee producer. Seemingly, the producer's reputation was such that association by name was sufficient. This is not consultative production. In order to fit this typology, there must be sufficient investment of time and expertise that contribute to the direction, sound, and success of the record. True consultative producers do not simply rent their names and their choices of studios and personnel.

When the consultative producer is in the studio, the guidance he or she gives can range from specific and detailed to vague, philosophical, and sometimes obscure. Brian Eno rejects the notion that there are "correct" ways to do things. In 1975, he developed his "oblique strategy" cards. They feature more than one hundred ideas for alleviating uncertainty and creative blockages in the studio. Tony Visconti showed them to me in the '70s after he had worked with Eno on a Bowie album. Somewhat like the *I Ching*, you choose a card if you are unsure what to do next. It might advise you to "Consider different fading systems" or "Remove specifics and convert to ambiguities."[27] Producers often have to find ways to disrupt unproductive states. Eno says this about his own role:

> Normally I don't stay with the project for the whole time. I deliberately keep out so I can come back in and hear things with fresh ears. Some things will seem completely obvious to me straight away. Like "that doesn't work, that works brilliantly, this is confused." I can very quickly, within an hour's listening, set

up an agenda which says, "This we must talk about philosophically, we have to look at that structurally, we have to look at this in terms of whether it's going anywhere like the direction of the rest of the record." I set agendas like that, to the extent that I will say that I want to take control of this song for, say, half a day. For half a day, I'll say what to do and we'll see if it works. Sometimes it doesn't. And of course any other participant can take the same role... It's very good if you can be in a working relationship with people and you can say, "OK, I tried it and it doesn't work," and they say "Yep, fine." Fortunately, most of the relationships I am in are like that. You have to have the respect for people who say, "Look you're grown up, you can take an option and not pretend that it's interesting when it isn't."[28]

David Bowie once said about working with Eno, "It was a bit like being four years old again and having a rather fun uncle who could produce coins out of his ear."[29] Flood, who worked with Eno on the U2 project, said of him,

His psychological approach is something that very much influenced me—the way that people can be encouraged, and how to judge a situation and discover what's happening, why it's happening and what its possible outcomes could be.[30]

Clearly, the role is not a good fit for every producer or with every artist, and success depends very much on the individual producer, the simpatico with the group, and perhaps the timing within that producer's career cycle. It is difficult to start out as a consultative style of producer; most artists would not accept the lack of presence from an unproven unknown. Being detail oriented and needing a high degree of control are barriers to being comfortable in this role. Specific musical and technical content may need to be considered. Nevertheless, the primary considerations are conceptual issues of direction, material, mood, energy, appropriateness, and other intangibles, as well as larger considerations that drive an artist's career forward. Consultative producers have to identify and harness talent, relying heavily on their team and the artist for day-to-day processes.

Subset Typologies

The preceding six functional typologies are broadly generalized groupings of functionality. They are not buckets within which all producers are identical, but rather a continuum with six methodological peaks that fade in and out like six stations on a radio dial. Some producers are bifunctional or polyfunctional and can operate in more than one mode. Certainly, each individual brings his or her unique combination of skills, talents, and relationships to bear on their work in the studio, in preproduction, and even in acquiring work. These six categories describe metafunctions focusing on the interpersonal, musical, technical, and (to some extent) business relationship of the producer with the artist throughout the production process. The nature of these artist-producer relationships can and will evolve project by project as relationships mature, and throughout the course of the producer's career.

It is common to describe producers by their base, source, or background skills. Arif Mardin illustrated three such categories, as he saw them:

> There is the songwriter/producer—who is in control of his or her composition and records the song with an artist. We are talking about Gamble and Huff, Lamont Dozier, Leiber and Stoller—songwriter/ producers. Or you have music-lover producers, like Ahmet Ertegun, Jerry Wexler, the Chess brothers, Berry Gordy. They don't have music training, but they love music and they have a song sense, they know lyrics and things like that, they can analyze a song. Then the other would be engineer/producer; Hugh Padgham, Tom Dowd, they sit behind the controls and help shape the sessions.[31]

I pointed out to Mardin that, according to this schema, he had missed his own category, arguably the most successful one of all that he shared with Quincy Jones and George Martin—the arranger/producer. All three trained in music, arrangement, and orchestration, equipping them to produce diverse acts and maximize the musical and commercial potential of the material. Other common source skills for successful producers are musician, artist, and DJ (which could fit under Mardin's music-lover category). Especially today, many producers and aspiring producers have several highly developed skills—Dr. Luke trained at the Manhattan School of Music, played guitar in the "Saturday Night Live" band, was a DJ in New York City clubs, and co-writes the songs that he produces. Although these source skills tell us something about a producer, they do not explain how that person functions in the studio or in relation to the artist and the material. Background skills are most usefully considered as a subset of functional typologies.

For example, most would agree that George Martin is one of the most successful producers of all time, not just in commercial terms, but because of the diversity of his contributions to the various records he produced, and to the Beatles' records in particular. It is hard to imagine how differently "Eleanor Rigby" might have sounded if someone other than Martin had produced it. Despite the magnitude of his talent and contributions, Martin never took the auteur role with the artists he produced. He did not write the songs; he did not play much on the recordings; and he did not try to control all parameters. From the early to the late Beatles, to America, the Mahavishnu Orchestra, and Jeff Beck—each production had its own sound and musical identity. Martin represented the artists, framing them beautifully with his contributions. He fits best in the collaborative typology. He adapted his abilities to the artist's needs, which enabled him to work with powerful and opinionated artists on an equal footing.

On the other hand, Quincy Jones is also an arranger; he does not usually write the songs for his artists, and he does not play a significant number of parts on the recordings. He often brings in other arrangers, and he uses the best studio musicians.

Those parameters do not immediately add up to an auteur typology. Regardless, his work has a distinctive identity, characteristics of which you can trace back to albums and soundtracks he made under his own name. Listen to any of his Michael Jackson albums and then George Benson's "Give Me the Night." Jones controls the parameters of his recordings very tightly; he mostly works with singers rather than bands; and he uses a small pool of carefully selected writers, musicians, background singers, arrangers, and engineers who fit his sensibility. Quincy Jones's unmistakable identity makes him an auteur producer.

Similarly, Phil Spector did not write "Unchained Melody," and he always used studio musicians, but he powerfully stamped that track, like most of his work, with his unique sonic identity.

I am sure that the artists who worked with Quincy Jones and George Martin are comparably satisfied. There are no better or worse ways of working, just different approaches that are most successful when matched appropriately to an act.

It is possible to repeat this exercise, comparing pairs of producers with similar background typologies who would be categorized in different functional typologies, making them ideally matched for different kinds of artists and projects.

It is worth asking why categorizing producers like this might be useful. For an artist, producer, or A&R person who has an intuitive grasp of how the artist, producer, and label are likely to fit together, understanding the underlying theory may not seem important. Unfortunately, mismatches of producers with artists happen too often and at all levels of the industry. I have been offered work with artists for whom I would not be the ideal choice. I have often heard A&R people say that a band just needs an engineer/producer to make a good-sounding record, when in fact engineers come in all six colors. One engineer will record the band as they come, capturing their sound as well as he or she can; another will deconstruct and reconstruct the music according to his or her vision rather than the group's; and there are all shades in between.

I experienced the latter situation as an artist. In this case, it was a bait-and-switch tactic, where the A&R person agreed to a successful producer who was acceptable to us, but the album wound up being produced by his engineer who was trying to launch his own production career. The deal imperceptibly morphed from the producer we wanted, to him acting in a consultative role. As it transpired, he never did show up at the studio, and the album was produced entirely by the engineer who received the producer credit. We continued recording because the studio time was booked; we were excited to be recording for a major label; and although we were uncomfortable with the situation, we were too inexperienced to know how to resolve it.

Based on abilities, the engineer should have assumed an assistive role, allowing the band to be the primary producer. Instead, he was aggressively proactive in defining the studio methodologies, deconstructing and reconstructing our music, and divisively conquering interpersonal relationships in the band. The result was a commercial failure and an album of some of my favorite material that I still cannot listen to because of its poor production values.

As a producer gets busier and more expensive, it's common for labels to turn to that producer's engineer or Pro Tools operator, apparently thinking that they can get the same result for less money. It can work out well sometimes, but a positive result is not a given; there may be radically different skill sets and philosophies at work. There are producers from an engineering background who are wonderful song doctors and who have all the required interpersonal abilities, and there are others who don't. Raising the question of subtle differences between a producer's functionality versus the needs of the artist might be critical in making a correct creative match and achieving the desired result.

As mentioned at the beginning of this chapter, there are many other subset typologies, such as success, musical genre, training, studio ownership, price, location, and methodologies. These categories can be useful as subsets of the primary functional typology. There is one subset typology that is significant enough to point out, and that is the entrepreneurial producer. Any of the six classes can also be entrepreneurial. An entrepreneur is someone who organizes and manages an enterprise or business, with initiative and risk. Examples of entrepreneurial producers are Moses Asch (Folkways Records), Sam Phillips (Sun Records), the Chess brothers (Chess Records), and Bruce Iglauer (Alligator Records). There are many more, but each of these has actively produced recordings while owning their own studio and record label. Moses Asch was an electronics engineer by trade, but his preference was to use a single microphone directly recorded to disc or tape with no processing and very little intervention on his part. Asch was an enablative producer; he would find an artist he liked and let them record what they wanted, sometimes recording dozens of tunes in a single session with artists such as Woody Guthrie, Lead Belly, and Pete Seeger. Sam Phillips was more of a collaborative producer with auteur leanings, intermediating musically and technically. The Chess brothers maintained the individuality of their artists even though they were operating within a limited number of genres. Bruce Iglauer specializes in blues at his Alligator Records, which he has run for more than 40 years in Chicago. A non-musician whose respect for the artist's identity comes through in his productions, his intermediation with regard to choice and refinement of material and performance positions him as a collaborative producer.[32]

In Summation

On a sliding scale of control from absolute to advisory, music producers actively direct the creative process of recording. My observation is that producers' personal philosophies and beliefs about making records combined with their interpersonal skills and toolkit of methodologies—largely independent of source skills—will cause them to gravitate toward one of the six functional typologies on the continuum. Their place on that continuum will have a greater and more predictable impact on their working relationship with the artist and the outcome of the production than will their source skills.

Analogous Structures

There is another way we can express the functionality continuum, and that is by using the well-established corporate leadership model as a metaphor. The term "analogous structure" comes from biology, in which it describes features that perform similar functions in two separate species that did not develop from a common ancestry. Given the roots and development of the recording industry, it seems unlikely that the various production roles were inherited or transferred from corporate or organizational structures. It is more likely that they evolved independently in response to need. If we think of the project as the corporation and analogize producers within that context, the producer's range of roles could look something like owner, chairperson, chief executive officer, chief financial officer, chief operating officer (the "C-suite"), president, and consultant. These positions are all accountable to the board, which represents the shareholders, and we could think of the board as representing the record label.

We can superimpose these roles over the six functional typologies' continuum with the artist on the right and consultative producer on the left. We start with the owner on the far right, which corresponds to self-producing artists—they are beholden to no one other than themselves (except perhaps the record label- -if there is one). To the left of him or her, the auteur producer would hold the roles of chairperson, chief executive officer, and president—a combined position that corrals most of the institutional governance and day-to-day decision-making power. The middle position is the facilitative producer, which correlates to the chief operating officer in greasing the wheels and keeping operations running smoothly. The collaborative producer can equate to the commonly combined position of CEO and president, one that is responsible for all operations and implementation of strategic decisions throughout the organization. This person communicates with the chairperson (the artist) and the board (the record label—as the primary stakeholders). On the far left, the consultative producer aligns with the outside consultancy firm brought in to analyze the performance of the organization and to give counsel. These consultants have no daily operational responsibilities; rather they observe and report on strengths, weaknesses, opportunities, and threats, offering possible solutions or provoking discussion that leads to them.

Leadership Styles

Many people in C-suite and equivalent positions hold advanced degrees such as an M.B.A., a law degree, or perhaps even a Ph.D. They may have undergone additional leadership training, as well as having proven themselves at each step up the organizational ladder. Producers rarely underwent formal training (for production) historically, but they nonetheless have to demonstrate leadership ability in each of their roles. Most learn these skills by trial and error in the studio or in a related position such as leading a band. Some learn directly from a mentor or by assimilation through working with experienced producers.

With the possible exception of the assistive typology, the primary task of a producer is to provide leadership. There are many definitions of leadership, but Peter Northouse has a concise one: "Leadership is a process whereby an individual influences a group of individuals to achieve a common goal."[33] This is the most fundamental aspect of what producers do—inspiring and enabling others toward a common vision. The producer may set the goal, stimulate others to set it, or lead the team to determine one jointly, sometimes in combination with others. There are many styles of leadership, some more productive, appropriate, or necessary under various circumstances.

In "Leadership that Gets Results," Daniel Goleman describes six styles of leadership: visionary, affiliative, democratic, coaching, pacesetting, and commanding. These can be epitomized in the following ways:

"Come with me." (visionary)
"People come first." (affiliative)
"What do you think?" (democratic)
"Try this." (coaching)
"Do as I do, now." (pacesetting)
"Do what I tell you." (commanding)[34]

Goleman characterizes the last two as tending to create a negatively charged climate because of poor execution or misuse. Alan Murray in a *Wall Street Journal* article suggested that the best leaders move among these six styles.[35]

Goleman defines the visionary as articulating goals but not the details of how to achieve them, which can be liberating for an innovative and self-motivated team. The affiliative style creates harmony in a team but has the disadvantage that it can allow for mediocre performance. Democratic leaders tap the collective wisdom of the group, but the style does not work well in a crisis when decisive action is required. The coach focuses on developing individual performance, which works with self-motivated people but can seem like micromanagement to some, undermining self-confidence. Pacesetters work to a very high standard themselves and expect everyone to strive to do things better and faster. Goleman's research shows that pacesetting often "poisons the climate," undermining morale. A commanding style derives from the military and is very common but often ineffective, again undercutting morale. However, this style works well in a crisis when a fast, decisive response is required. Murray makes the point that the best leaders understand what motivates the individuals being led.[36]

This underlines a difficult aspect of production, which is that producers mostly lead ad hoc teams, substantial parts of which change from project to project. Even within the same musical genre, personalities run the gamut. This necessitates rapidly assessing the new cohort (artist/band, engineer, manager, A&R person, etc.)

and adjusting leadership techniques for each new team and, in some instances, for individual personalities.

Nevertheless, what most artists and labels are paying for is an effective producer: one who produces a positive and successful result. What might be regarded as a negative leadership style—one that is not enjoyable to work under—can produce success. For instance, Phil Spector's style could be described as autocratic or commanding, but he was also visionary. His results were frequently commercially successful; consequently, artists clamored to work with him. I have seen an instance of a band requesting to work with a well-known producer based on his undeniable results, but then only recording one track with him because the producer's leadership style was autocratic and unacceptable to the group. Relying on creating a hit to make everyone happy is not a strategy that leads to a long and happy career. The best leadership strategy is to make the artist and label feel confident and engaged in the process. Mature artists and self-contained groups develop their own methodologies and studio culture and are less likely to be tolerant of abrasive or mismatched styles.

SECTION TWO

The Practice

Like all artistic endeavors, the successful pursuit of music production requires the development of practical skills. Producers live around the junction where technology, music, art, culture, innovation, business, and management meet. Each producer develops his or her unique combination of skills, but even with their different emphases, all are balancing creative ambition with the pragmatic constraints of technology, time, budget, and their ability to inspire people. Consciously or otherwise, it is out of the convergence of theory and practice that the art of music production emerges.

2

Becoming a Music Producer

Nothing in the world can take the place of persistence. Talent
will not; nothing is more common than unsuccessful men with
talent. Genius will not; unrewarded genius is almost a proverb.
Education will not; the world is full of educated derelicts.
Persistence and determination alone are omnipotent.

—Calvin Coolidge

How Do You Become a Music Producer?

Successful producers come from diverse backgrounds and seem to travel down one
of about seven paths. As we have seen from the discussion of typologies in the previous chapter, background skills may not define the role the producer plays in the
studio. Nevertheless, certain background skills provide an entrée, and the presence
or absence of a skill affects how a producer interacts with the artist, technology,
musicians, and other contributors, including the record label. Experienced producers often manifest multiple skill sets accumulated over time. With the ubiquity of
digital audio workstations (DAWs), most producers, since the turn of the century,
have been capable of recording and manipulating audio in their workstation of
choice. This further blurs the distinction between audio engineering and production. In this context, the eight habitually used routes to becoming a music producer represent centers of ability rather than clear demarcations. Many producers
develop multiple skills on the winding road to success, but leading music producers'
beginnings are traceable to one or more of these eight core routes:

Musician or artist
Audio engineer
Songwriter
DJ
Self-taught/school-trained
Discoverer
Entrepreneur
Multipath

THE MUSICIAN OR ARTIST

Producing uses many of the same skills as running rehearsals and participating in the standard creative practices of any music group. Writing songs and playing music with other people is an organic way of learning to be at ease giving guidance and being sensitive to creative moments—skills producers use everyday. Developing a solid musical reputation, as an arranger, musical director, musician, or artist can lead to opportunities for production work, but it is most likely that you will have to be self-motivated and produce some high-quality work of your own before a label or artist will trust you with their music and money. It used to be that producing demos was a low-risk way to begin, but the distinction between demos and a self-released or small indie production has all but disappeared. Today, in order to move up the ladder, anything you produce has to compare favorably with currently successful recordings.

Producing your own music is a tried and tested route for musicians and artists, but it requires some startup capital to hire a studio or buy your own recording equipment. Even with the low price of digital equipment, cost can be a barrier. Beginners often seem to suffer from the impression that an extensive professional setup is required, and that is not the case. Depending on the kinds of productions you wish to make, inexpensive or free software with a low cost interface and microphone can be sufficient to start with. Books, magazines, DVDs, and free online videos can be helpful in learning good engineering and production practices. Developing your "ear" by listening analytically to the best recordings from your target market, as well as recordings from other genres and eras is imperative.

Certain techniques commonly understood by experienced producers may appear arcane when you are locked in your bedroom with your, so-far disappointing, first production and big ambitions. It is worth remembering that learning to produce and engineer a recording takes as much practice as learning to play an instrument. According to K. Anderson Ericsson et al.'s research cited in Malcolm Gladwell's book *Outliers*, you have to invest 10,000 hours in order to become expert at any complex cognitive skill.[1]

There are distinct advantages in coming to producing from a music background. You can speak to musicians and artists in terms that they understand and sense any difficulties they may be having in the studio. It is useful to gain experience recording yourself for this reason. I recall the frustration of standing in the studio having given my all on a take, watching the producer through the glass chatting on the phone or talking to someone in the control room.

THE AUDIO ENGINEER

The traditional recording studio apprenticeship system was predicated on starting at the bottom, in the mailroom, setting up and breaking down the studio, sweeping floors, and making tea and coffee. This phase could extend for years going from tape op to assistant engineer and eventually engineer. This thorough if somewhat tortuous training system barely exists anymore. With the demise of so many professional studios and particularly the large complexes, opportunities to assist without prior experience or training are limited.

The advantages of this system lay in working in the best studios with world-class engineers and producers who let you literally look over their shoulders, study their techniques, write down their EQs and reverb settings, and observe the qualities of the interpersonal relationships that create great records. Assistants participated in the most intimate studio moments and could study in a Zen-like manner the almost unteachable secret of the record producer—how to get the best out of the artist. The assistants I knew who became successful producers did not regard the job as beneath them. They recognized their essential role in the production team as the lubricant that kept projects running smoothly.

This is Chris Lord-Alge's (Green Day, Madonna, Dave Matthews, Bruce Springsteen) recommendation for getting started as an engineer:

> Find the best studio in town and fight your way in. Get a job, whether you're pushing a broom or cleaning the toilets, and work your way up from there. Don't be scared to take a chance on anything. The only way you are going to learn is by watching the best at what they do.[2]

This may seem like archaic advice in today's environment, but Benny Blanco did this with Disco D, and Max Martin did it with Denniz Pop at Cheiron Studios.[3] Working with the best producers, engineers, and artists is the nascent producer's equivalent of a Harvard or Oxford education.

Moving from engineer to producer can be gradual and organic. Going from gofer to assistant to engineer typically takes many sessions with different artists and producers. Observing various creative styles techniques and approaches develops a broad perspective on the processes. As Mitchell Froom (Sheryl Crow, Crowded House, Paul McCartney) says, "Good engineers contribute a lot to the production. People need titles, but every record has production suggestions from other people."

Today, in place of the severely diminished apprenticeship system, there is a spectrum of audio engineering and production courses and programs in schools, colleges, and universities. Many are excellent and are taught by experienced producers and engineers. A student can come out of such programs with a more complete and formal understanding of the technology and the business of audio production than they might get from a hands-on environment. But the studio etiquette and the subtle interpersonal techniques that producers and engineers acquire from experience are more difficult to teach in college.

A common complaint from producers and engineers regarding assistants who recently graduated from a college program is that they are sometimes overconfident, have unrealistic expectations, and can be insensitive in a production environment. If someone has spent a lot of time and money to complete a course or degree in audio production, music technology, or the like, it is understandable that they may be frustrated making tea and coffee, and not getting their hands on the equipment or having their opinions considered.

Based on the principle of supply and demand, the producer of a successful record becomes desirable and more expensive. This can open up an opportunity for an engineer to get his or her break into production. A new group discussing who they would like to produce their first record will probably suggest a producer who has current hits. The A&R person may say something like, "Well, I just spoke to her yesterday and she is not available for at least twelve months." If the A&R person is being honest, he or she might say, "She's going to cost you at least X thousand dollars per track, and that's not in your budget." It is not uncommon for them to suggest using someone who works with the requested producer, and this can be an entrée into a production career.

THE SONGWRITER

Some of the most enduring productions have come from producers or teams who produce material they have written. It may be that a songwriter is not necessarily eager to become a producer, but experiencing poorly produced versions of your songs is sufficient to convince some writers that they can do a better job. Wendy Page, who has produced songs she wrote for Hilary Duff and Lulu, said she got into production, "Because I wanted to make the songs I wrote sound how I wanted to hear them."[4] I had the same experience: I would submit a good demo of a song and when the album came out, the producer had not only ignored the positive qualities of the demo but also missed the essence of the song.

The line between writing and producing has blurred in recent years. Writers began producing demos that were more sophisticated. Publishers, artists, producers, and A&R people became used to hearing high-quality song demos and now, unless you are a very successful songwriter, the opportunity no longer exists to play your song on a piano to an artist, publisher, or A&R person. Labels and publishers want high-quality demos in the style of the target artist. If you are looking for songs for a less famous artist during the six months after, say, Beyoncé, Christina Aguilera, Britney Spears, or Katy Perry finish an album, publishers will send you a collection of highly produced demos that sound like these artists. These are songs that have been released after being "on hold" for the past six, 12, or 18 months, waiting for one of the coveted slots on those artists' albums.

Additionally, many of the songs that make it onto these albums are co-written with the artists. Collaborating with artists on songs is a more reliable way of getting the production job. You have the opportunity to build a relationship with the artist and establish your production abilities in his or her mind. They now have a stake in the song, and if they like it and found the writing process enjoyable, continuing on to finish the production is a likely outcome.

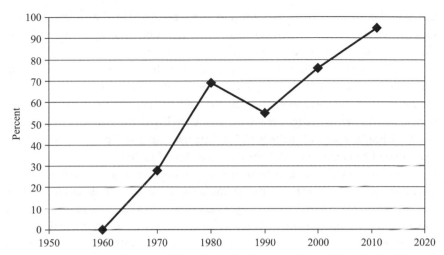

FIGURE 2.1 Percentage of Producer/Writers in the Top 10 of the *Billboard* Hot 100, First Week of September each decade since 1960.

The consistently successful songwriter/producer is in a strong position and typically becomes the auteur type of producer. In the first week of September 2011, auteur producers who wrote or co-wrote the songs they produced commanded more than 90 percent of the top ten tracks on the *Billboard* Top 100. This contrasts with 0 percent in 1960 and, apart from a small decline in the '80s, the trend toward songwriter/producers has steadily increased each decade (see figure 2.1).

THE DJ

Producers who start out as DJs have been increasingly prevalent since the early '80s. They became fixtures in club and hip hop production, eventually spilling over into R&B, pop, and most other genres. Base genres for producers with a DJ background are often dance or hip hop because those are the most common forms of music played by DJs in clubs. At the time of writing, the top hits on the *Billboard* Hot 100 chart are predominantly dance-inflected pop, with producers such as French DJ David Guetta. Being a successful music producer has a great deal to do with understanding how music affects people, and DJs get direct feedback from the dance floor when they are spinning. DJs pace their programming to keep the flow going on the dance floor. They learn how the dynamics of a set and a song, and certain beats, tempos, artists, and song types affect the audience. They become experts in certain genres and subgenres of music. The DJs that scratch are using basic production techniques in a live forum. Turntablists beatmatch, beatmix, and beatjuggle, blending tracks, samples, and beats together. Remixers use similar conceptual arrangement techniques to make loop- or beat-based tracks, particularly in the hip hop, dance, and pop genres. Most DJs now mix from laptops loaded with tens of thousands of tracks, but the sophisticated conceptual and physical techniques they use via software date back to early hip hop.

Producers need an intuitive understanding of how successful records work emotionally on an audience. DJs who experience this nightly often continue to spin after it ceases to be an economic necessity in order to maintain that connection and remain on the cutting edge. French DJ/producer David Guetta underscored this point: "I headline concert halls for 20,000 people, but I still play smaller venues. Everything I do comes from the clubs. If I lose that, I'm done."[5]

DJs develop technical and musical skills, an understanding of repertoire, and something about the history of their genre, being dedicated fans with large collections of music. They learn how to ramp up excitement in a club in a similar way that live musicians do. Although Jack Douglas came up through the traditional tape op/assistant route, he said, "There's guys out there that just walk into a studio from a club where they're DJing and they sound phenomenal." He attributed this to the fact that DJs spend so much time listening to records.

SELF-TAUGHT/SCHOOL-TRAINED

More than a century ago, John Philip Sousa perceptively pointed out that "[t]he tide of amateurism cannot but recede until there will be left only the mechanical device and the professional executants."[6] This was Sousa's way of saying that recording technology would be the death of amateur musicianship.[7] In many ways, he was correct; not only recording technology, but also film, radio, and TV ushered in a century of passive entertainment. It is easy to forget that Edison's machine was a recording device not intended just for playback, and once he gave up on the idea of it being strictly for dictation, there was still the thought that people would (and they did) record themselves and others.

Emile Berliner, inventor of the gramophone and the flat disc, did away with the recording aspect, but with motion pictures taking hold, radio about to start, and TV in development, a period of passivity in entertainment was assured. The wheel turns of course, and entertainment is becoming progressively more interactive via computers, electronic games, and mobile devices. There are increasingly powerful programs and apps for recording, providing a host of ways to experiment with recording inexpensively with little expertise. In the same way that still and video cameras have become ubiquitous, so too has audio recording technology.

Access is no longer a significant factor; preteens can have recording technology on a number of devices that are more powerful than professional equipment of 50 years ago. This has become a DIY route for the curious. There are a plethora of free samples and MIDI files online and many more to buy. Musical parts can be constructed by dropping colored blocks onto a grid with a finger or mouse. Musical training and experience still help, but neither is required. Music software can appear complex, and input cables, output cables, and connectors intimidate some, but these apps and programs present much like electronic games, and the millennial generation is at ease in this world.

Books, magazines, Google, and YouTube, along with trial and error, provide a massive instructional resource, not all of which is reliable but still generally helpful for the discerning. This is where schools and colleges help, although courses do not instantly generate a professional. Nonetheless, combined with a proactive DIY approach, a good school program can fill in knowledge gaps and instill a deeper understanding of the fundamentals while increasing awareness of best practices. It is oxymoronic to expect to learn interpersonal skills from a book or a course without real-life practice. Without an internship or apprenticeship, it is necessary to be self-aware in dealing with the various personalities during sessions and to be self-analytical afterward. This means mentally rerunning the session and asking yourself, "what happened and could I have handled that better." Good interpersonal skills for a session are fundamentally similar to those used in any organization, but they become more critical in a creative environment. Recording, being a process of group creativity, tends to create or exacerbate tension, and a significant part of the producer's job is to reduce or eliminate it.

DIY is a proactive self-learning approach to the production art and craft that can make you aware of the questions and problems that all producers face daily. With more than a century of well-tested production skills and techniques, any opportunity to work with or observe successful professionals can speed the path to the solutions. Confucius (551–479 B.C.E.) appeared to know a thing or two about producing when he said,

> By three methods we may learn wisdom: first, by reflection, which is noblest; second, by imitation, which is easiest; and third, by experience, which is the bitterest.[8]

Reflection and experience are essential, but save yourself the agony and learn as much as you can by imitation from the most experienced people who are available to you.

DISCOVERER

A successful production career is inseparable from the producer's ability to find the very best and most appropriate acts. The answer to the question "How do you produce a great record?" may be "Find a great artist and great material." Of course, there are other elements, but without those two, the chances of success are slim—at any level and in any genre. At the height of a successful career, it is a matter of using your time most productively. This is the concept of opportunity cost—once you embark on a production, you block out time that might be better spent finding or producing a superior project.[9] Discovering a talented new act can launch a career and revive a moribund one.

George Martin signed the Beatles; Tony Visconti discovered Marc Bolan; and John Kurzweg produced Creed's multiplatinum album *My Own Prison* for $6,000 in his home studio before they had a record deal. My first real production opportunity came from seeing very early Spandau Ballet gigs before labels had heard of them. Being there early, watching them play, getting to know them, and understanding their tastes, concerns, and ambitions enabled our relationship to develop before the industry feeding frenzy happened. I had no sole producer credits on hit records, but when it came time for them to choose a producer, they chose me over established names. Labels often like to think that they choose the producer, and certainly they can influence or block a choice, but very often the artist's opinion holds sway. Discovery is what Fred Gaisberg and all the early recorders did. It is part of the essence of production. John Lomax, John Hammond, Ralph Peer, Sam Phillips, and the Chess Brothers did it. Being able to pick the best acts out of various offers from labels is a facet of this ability.

ENTREPRENEUR

There are successful producers who did not start out as engineers, musicians, songwriters, singers, DJs, DIYers, or discoverers. They are usually entrepreneurial, good leaders, often charismatic, with deal-making ability, who understand how to muster the necessary help to get the job done. Sometimes these producers persuade a label to fund the production (even though the musical and technical skills may come primarily from others), and sometimes they finance projects themselves. The tradeoff for the programmers, musicians, engineers, songwriters, and singers who actually make the record is that this person will pay the recording costs and generate the success and revenue to do it again. As in any entrepreneurial venture, there are many who try but fail. On the "nothing down" principle, sometimes these producers ask the creative team, and the studio, to give their time "on spec," meaning that they pay them only if the project earns revenue. Most experienced musicians, engineers, and studios learn the pitfalls of these deals and decline or demand a written contract. There are entrepreneurial producers who will promise to pay contributors on invoice, knowing that they do not have the funds to pay but hoping they can place the project with a label before the invoice comes due. This does not necessarily reflect a lack of scruples; some entrepreneurs have a high degree of optimism and tolerance for risk. Some become rich and successful when the risks pay off, and others leave a trail of disgruntled musicians, studios, and engineers behind them. The latter generally become personae non gratae. No deal is certain without a signed contract and a cleared check. Deals that fail to happen or fall through snag overeager impresarios in their pursuit of success. Entrepreneurs can be impatient, but it is wise to plan for the long term and preserve valuable relationships. The music industry is surprisingly small, and a reputation is a hard thing to rebuild once it is damaged.

MULTIPATH

The preceding paths into production are not exclusive or always clearly demarcated. Very few producers only have one set of background skills, but in many cases, there are clear areas of emphasis. Commonly, producers play a little bit of guitar, piano, or other instrument and by osmosis or necessity learn enough engineering skills to run a DAW and route an audio signal. However, some develop multiple competencies, sequentially or in parallel, approaching the 10,000 hours required for the mastery of a complex cognitive skill as outlined in K. Anders Ericsson's et al.'s research.[10] It is my unscientific observation that doing so can increase the chance of success.

Examples of Producers from Different Backgrounds

MUSICIAN

Many of the best-known popular music producers of the 20th century trained and/ or worked as musicians and/or arrangers: Fred Gaisberg, John Hammond, Mitch Miller, George Martin, Quincy Jones, Arif Mardin, Mutt Lange, Dr. Luke, and most classical producers. Of course, songwriters are usually musicians too (some lyricists are not in the strict sense), and many musicians write songs or compose music. Nonetheless, here we are talking about producers who are primarily players or arrangers rather than composers.

Dann Huff was one of the most sought-after session guitarists in Los Angeles in the '80s. He played sessions for me and would show up with another studio's worth of equipment in rolling racks, but what made him so valuable was his musicality, sense of the appropriate, and remarkable versatility. He flips from one style to another always sounding authentic. While playing on Shania Twain's album, her producer Mutt Lange told him, "You are a producer in guitarist's clothes." He had no idea how to start, so Lange introduced him to Faith Hill. Known primarily for producing country artists such as Martina McBride, Keith Urban, and Rascal Flatts, he maintains his versatility, working across genres from time to time with groups such as Megadeth. He attributes his ability to do that to his experience as a session player and having to embrace many musical styles.[11]

Bill Appleberry played organ as a child and then drums in the U.S. Marine Drum and Bugle Corps, training at the School of Music in Norfolk, which he said was one of the best decisions he ever made. Artists he has worked with include the Stone Temple Pilots, Joe Walsh, the Wallflowers, 311, Puddle of Mudd, the Used, Macy Gray, the Fugees, Adam Levine, Cee Lo Green, Christina Aguilera, Jermaine Paul, and many more. Since 2011, he has produced and mixed every song by every artist on every episode of the NBC TV show "The Voice." Various singles sales have reached multiplatinum status with many number-one hits on iTunes and entries into the *Billboard* Hot 100. Appleberry frequently works a seven-day a week production schedule with little or no sleep.[12]

Walter Afanasieff played keyboards for jazz-fusion violinist Jean Luc Ponty and Bay Area producer Narada Michael Walden. He stepped into the producer role in 1991, producing and writing a run of hits with Mariah Carey and others such as Barbra Streisand, Kenny G, Marc Anthony, Ricky Martin, Babyface, and Savage Garden. Afanasieff won the best producer Grammy in 2000.

ENGINEER

Flood got his nickname when he was assisting at Morgan Studios in London because he was so timely with tea-making, a vital function in U.K. studios. At that time in commercial studios, the first few years learning the craft were considered vital. As it did for Flood, the process could take more than five years to graduate from tea boy to tape op/assistant to house engineer and eventually to working free-lance. "When Flood was head engineer, the tape op to assistant to engineer process was very strict," says his manager Ros Earls. Earls looked for people who could move through the ranks, such as dance producer Paul Oakenfold's engineer Steve Osborne, who she employed as a "tea boy." She pointed out that they have to "be easy to have around, be intelligent, have musical taste and personal creative ambition, while being willing to make tea and good at filling out track sheets."[13]

She thinks that there has been an increasingly unhealthy pressure to move up through the ranks with some looking for a manager after only a year's studio experience. She said,

> Engineers have always been regarded [in England] as "just" an engineer, which they aren't in America. People there may be engineers for [40] years and they are formidable talents.[14]

Engineer and mix engineer Marcella Araica (Missy Elliott, Timbaland, Britney Spears, Mariah Carey) graduated with honors from the Full Sail Recording and Production program in Florida. She said that once she began working in studios, she wished she had started as an intern because the actual studio experience was so different from school. The pace of a professional session can swing from frustratingly slow to impossibly fast. Missy Elliott was initially impatient with her because of her lack of speed with Pro Tools. Araica knew she had to step it up or she would be off the session, so she spent a couple of weeks with a friend who was a more experienced Pro Tools operator and long hours practicing so that she could handle the real-world pace. Her conscientiousness and hard work paid off, and she built a successful working relationship with Elliott, who became a significant figure in Araica's career.[15]

Andy Jackson came up through the ranks at Utopia Studios in London, which was new at the time and expanding quickly. He was engineering demos and jingles within a year, which was "good discipline because you had to work very quickly."

He thinks that he would have had to wait two or three years before "engineering something" at another studio.[16] Jackson subsequently engineered several Pink Floyd and Roger Waters albums. He commented that a period of assisting in a major studio is valuable because "you see good practice." When he did encounter bad engineers, it "reinforced the good techniques you learned." Perhaps most important, he noted that "it's not just the engineering tricks you pick up on, but the way the producer handles the session in general."[17] He gave the example of Bob Ezrin, who "has a little saying, which is 'Do anything even if it's wrong.'" He can then react to what he did and if it is wrong, say, "This isn't right and I can see why this isn't right, so it gives me an insight into what would work."[18]

Smashing Pumpkins' producer and mixer for the Foo Fighters, Alan Moulder, started as an assistant engineer at the famed Trident Studios in London. He describes how he moved from engineering to producing by building a relationship with artists. "They decide to bypass their producer to do some B-sides so you get to do some tracks on your own with them." He adds, "It's mainly from co-production, where bands want to do the record and have a big input themselves."[19] To some extent, you can predict an assistant's future in the business by the way he or she deals with the menial tasks. The assistants I worked with who consistently messed up the lunch orders did not translate into successful producers. The ones who got them right, including Tim Palmer (mixed Pearl Jam's first album *Ten*) when he first started at Utopia, Alan Moulder at Trident, Pete Walsh at Utopia (produced Simple Minds) and Flood at Morgan Studios, were always there when you needed them. They read the "vibe" in the room. Teas and coffees arrived at the right moments, food orders were correct, and if you turned your head, they knew what you needed; they kept up with the session. More than 30 years later when I talk to Tim Palmer, he asks me if I still like Earl Grey tea, weak with a little honey in it (I do). These are all extremely intelligent people capable of complex tasks, as they subsequently proved, but they understood their roles as assistants. They were pleasant, helpful, and fit in seamlessly without being overly familiar.

Alan Parsons parlayed a background of engineering acts such as the Beatles and Pink Floyd into a successful career as a producer and subsequently as an artist. Working with bands and producers of the Beatles and Pink Floyd's magnitude not only instills an innate sense of how a successful record is constructed, but it also builds a formidable network of industry decision-makers. Like many engineers, he began contributing to productions with other producers, built a good network of A&R people from being in the studio with the bands he was engineering, and the word spread. Not coincidentally, his first two projects as a producer were Pilot and Cockney Rebel, both on EMI—the label of both the Beatles and Pink Floyd and Parsons's employer as the owner of Abbey Road Studios. Parsons's progression from assistant to producer took about five years.

After engineering successful records for bands like Whitesnake, Mike Clink produced Guns N' Roses' *Appetite for Destruction* for the same label. Brendon O'Brien went on to produce Stone Temple Pilots and Pearl Jam after engineering for Rick Rubin. Hugh Padgham's engineering career included Peter Gabriel's seminal, third solo album. That project introduced the Phil Collins drum sound, and Padgham went on to co-produce Phil Collins, the Police, Sting, and Genesis. He subsequently commanded production credits of his own.

"Flood developed from engineer to co-mixer to 'recorded by' credit, which implies a better position than just engineer," says his manager Ros Earls. With Depeche Mode, he began by engineering, but by the second album, "he was co-producing with the band and on the third one, he was producing."[20]

Jack Douglas's discography includes six Aerosmith albums, three with Cheap Trick, John Lennon's *Double Fantasy* and Alice Cooper's anthem "School's Out." Douglas started out in bands, but while recording at A&R Recording, found the other side of the glass more fascinating. An engineer told him about a new studio opening up, called The Record Plant, where "everyone was going," including Shelley Yakus, Roy Cicala, and Jay Messina. Douglas started out cleaning toilets and moving Hendrix tapes around, while they were working on the *Woodstock* soundtrack. He worked his way up to tape librarian and eventually assistant engineer. His leap to engineering was sudden and dramatic during some sessions intended for The Who's *Who's Next* album.[21] Douglas was assisting an engineer called Jack Adams who primarily worked with R&B acts and did not like rock music. Adams told Douglas to go to another room and call to say Adam's houseboat was on fire. Adams allegedly started screaming, telling Kit Lambert (the producer) and Pete Townshend that his boat was on fire and that Douglas was "a great engineer" who could take over the session.[22] In fact, Douglas had done only jingle dates and a Patti LaBelle session. A number of other successful engineers and producers have had lucky breaks that were also sudden and nerve-wracking, if less histrionic.

SONGWRITERS

The Neptunes, The Matrix, Scott Storch, Timbaland, Max Martin, L.A. and Babyface, Jam and Lewis, Narada Michael Walden, Walter Afanasieff, Gamble and Huff, Holland, Dozier, and Holland, Benny Blanco, Shellback, Stargate, the Smeezingtons, Red One, and many more producers made their names primarily due to their skills as songwriters. As mentioned earlier, most songwriters are musicians in that they play instruments and have some arranging skills, formal or otherwise. Songwriters are not necessarily skilled instrumentalists, and writing a song requires related but different skills than deconstructing and editing someone else's material.

Benny Blanco had produced 13 U.S. number-one songs by the age of 24. He has worked with Dr. Luke and many of the most successful pop writers and producers of recent times including Shellback and Max Martin. Although he took music lessons on various instruments from the age of four, he claims that he is barely mediocre on any instrument and that recording a part takes him a long time, to the extent that he builds chords for guitar parts by playing one note at a time. Nonetheless, he plays many of the parts on his productions, writes as part of a team, and reputedly has an innate sense of when a song is complete and ready to be a hit. Dr. Luke calls it "Benny-proofing" a song, saying, "If Benny doesn't get it, America won't get it."[23]

DJ

From the South Bronx and temporarily transplanted to Atlanta as a teenager, Swiss Beatz produced tracks for DMX, Jay Z, Bone Thugs-n-Harmony, Chris Brown, T.I., Li'l Wayne, Beyoncé, and Drake. He made beats and was sneaking into clubs to DJ by age 17. He established his production career when he sold a beat through his uncles' Ruff Ryders label that became DMX's last hit single, "Ruff Ryder's Anthem."

David Guetta is the French house music DJ who changed the sound of the American pop charts. For nearly two decades, dance music topped the charts in Europe but remained a niche genre in the United States. American labels told him he would have to adapt his style to succeed in America:

> When I recorded "Sexy Bitch" with Akon, [Akon's] label said: "You're going to have to adapt yourself to the American market. What we've done won't work in the U.S. because of the style of the beat." I told them they were wrong.

Guetta did not compromise; the track hit number five on the U.S. charts and within 12 months, he had produced Black Eyed Peas, Madonna, and Kelis. Guetta triggered the vogue for strong four-to-the-bar, bass-drum grooves in the U.S. charts. This pattern had rarely been heard in the U.S. charts since disco died. As all DJ producers must, Guetta recognizes the difference between a successful club track and one that works on the radio:

> The more melodies and chord changes, the less good it is for the clubs, but the better it is for radio, because it makes it really emotional. Yet, what gives dance music energy and drive is that it's hypnotic and repetitive. My battle is to find the balance between the two.[24]

Rick Rubin began producing with no training or background in bands or studios while he was still in college. He had been DJing at clubs and found rap fascinating, realizing it was a new approach. He said,

> Being a fan and understanding what rap was really about, I just tried to capture that on record, and, ironically, part of the answer was not knowing anything about the technology and what was considered right or wrong in the studio. It was about capturing some really awkward sounds at times. Looking back, they're pretty funny-sounding records, but that was what was going on.

Part-time DJ and record storeowner Shep Pettibone capitalized on the '80s remix craze by rebuilding tracks for dance artists such as Gloria Gaynor, Alisha, and Loleatta Holloway. Pettibone was remixing British acts such as the Pet Shop Boys, Thompson Twins, New Order, and Erasure when U.K. radio discovered dance music, and remixes became "the sound." Janet Jackson, Paula Abdul, MC Hammer,

Lionel Richie, Prince, Cyndi Lauper, and Madonna were all recreated for clubs by Pettibone. He said,

> By the time I worked on "Like a Prayer" and "Express Yourself," it looked as if Madonna liked the remixed versions better than the ones that were on the album. That was great, but producing was still at the top of my wish list.[25]

Finally, she asked him to write and produce a B-side for the single off her *Breathless* album. That B-side was "Vogue," which became the biggest selling single of 1990 and introduced Pettibone as a producer. Madonna encouraged him to continue writing, and a single evolved into the album *Erotica*.

Shep Pettibone was able to make the move from being Madonna's remixer to her co-producer on the *Erotica* album by collaborating with her at the writing stage. Obviously, they already had a good working relationship because of the remixes he had done for her. Had he simply tried to submit songs to her, he would have been competing with many professional songwriters for every song on the album. Instead, he did what he does best: built tracks in the style of his remixes for which she could write the lyrics and melodies. The nature of dance music is such that the production ideas, the parts, and the sounds almost inextricably intertwine with the song itself. Once Pettibone and Madonna had written and demoed the songs together, not only was there little point in bringing in an outside producer, but they wound up transferring most of the stuff they had recorded on the eight-track demos over to 24-track tape and onto the final record.

Arthur Baker worked in a Boston record store. He went on to spin records at a local club, where he met Tom Silverman of Tommy Boy Records. Baker moved to New York City in 1980, producing electro-dance for Emergency Records and working with some of the early hip hop artists such as Afrika Bambaataa and Soul Sonic Force for Tommy Boy. His work as a producer and writer led to remix work with artists such as David Bowie, Mick Jagger, and Cyndi Lauper.

Cypress Hill's DJ Muggs has written, produced, and mixed tracks for the Beastie Boys, Ice Cube, House of Pain, Funkdoobiest, Daddy Freddy, YoYo, and Mellow Man Ace. He did remixes for Janet Jackson and U2. His own band's "Black Sunday" went straight to number one on the *Billboard* charts. His real name is Larry Muggerud, and he grew up in Queens, New York, moving to Los Angeles during high school. It was his love of rap music and break-dancing that led to DJing. He began producing his own tracks using a pair of Technics SP1200s while in tenth grade. In the mid-1980s, he formed the "Spanglish" rap group DVX with B-Real and Sen Dog, the three of whom would eventually become Cypress Hill. When DVX broke up, he joined forces with the rappers 7A3, released an album on Geffen, and got a song on the *Colors* soundtrack. Muggs decided to get back with B-Real and Sen Dog to form Cypress Hill, sending the early demos to Joe "The Butcher" Nicolo, a young engineer from Philadelphia who he had connected with on the 7A3 album. Nicolo signed the band to his newly formed Ruffhouse Records and got distribution through Columbia.

SELF-TAUGHT

Jack Endino, the "Godfather of Grunge," used a home studio to develop a unique style and to create a place in rock and roll history. He was instrumental in shaping the early Seattle sound, having recorded over 80 albums, 110 seven-inch singles, and 300 EPs, from more than 200 bands, including Soundgarden, Mudhoney, Screaming Trees, Afghan Whigs, L7, Babes In Toyland, and, perhaps most famously, Nirvana. Endino talked to Daniel House about getting started:

> The first band I was in I played drums and from the first time we jammed I had a cassette deck with two microphones right behind me at the drum set. I was making these little stereo recordings and I thought, well, this is really easy and it didn't sound too bad . . . and for a few seconds it actually sounded like a band, and there was a potential of not sucking. Recording was always a mirror for me that allowed me to gain confidence in my playing. I was recording myself right from the very beginning, from when I first started playing music. Some of the first multitracking I did was with cassette decks bouncing back and forth from one deck and then playing live on top of the previous track. Then I had a roommate who had a [four]-track reel-to-reel that I bought. I was thinking, "This is what I've been waiting for my whole life." After that, I was always recording.[26]

He began recording his own band in his basement using a TEAC quarter-inch, four-track machine. Then around 1983, he started recording other bands for five dollars an hour. A track he recorded that went on a seminal proto-grunge compilation called *Deep Six*, led to a job engineering in a new local recording studio, Reciprocal Studios, where he recorded the first Soundgarden album in 1986 on an eight-track machine. Many of the clients followed him to the new studio. Endino said,

> During '85 and '86 there was nobody in Seattle who was good at recording grungy rock bands, and especially for cheap. It's a small town and when people found out I was making decent sounding recordings for next to nothing, they beat a path to my door. I was recording frantically—about a single a week. It seemed like everybody was coming to me with or without Sub Pop, with or without a record deal.[27]

Tucker Martine has worked with an unusual lineup of artists: Wayne Horvitz, Bill Frisell, Eyvind Kang, John Zorn, Mudhoney, the Decemberists, My Morning Jacket, and many others. Originally from Nashville, a drummer and the son of a successful songwriter, he began by recording his own bands. He moved to Seattle as grunge was beginning and scraped together the money for recording equipment by bartending, which also served as an excellent networking tool. He bought a half-inch, eight-track tape recorder, one of the first Mackie 24 x 8 consoles, and an SM57 or 421 microphone here and there whenever he could afford them. He began in his home studio by recording bands for nothing so that he could gain experience and learn how to make a great record. Eventually he started charging five dollars, then seven dollars an hour and was able to work with artists of the caliber of Bill Frisell and Wayne Horvitz whose chamber ensemble, Four Plus One, he recorded. He tried to get a job at a Seattle recording studio. In an interview with Blair Jackson, he said, "I was ready to take out the garbage and stuff, but no one was calling me back, so I thought, 'That route's not going to work. I just need to learn by doing it.'" He read a lot, asked many questions and, he says, "Made a million mistakes." The democratization of production was beginning with the advent of the modular digital multitrack ADAT machines and Mackie consoles. Martine thinks that if his timing had not coincided with inexpensive equipment, he might not have had these opportunities. He has subsequently developed longstanding working relationships with some artists and occupies an interesting niche with his flexible and transparent approach that demonstrates a preference for the unusual.[28]

With the equipment price implosion since the early 1990s, it seems as if every band and artist now has a home recording setup and knows something about the process. Previously, production and engineering were somewhat of a mystery to artists, but the many books, magazines, DVDs, and YouTube features on the topic have created a much greater awareness, which can be helpful or challenging from a producer's perspective—a little knowledge being a dangerous thing at times.

DISCOVERER

John and Alan Lomax, Ralph Peer, and John Hammond all built their careers primarily because of their abilities to discover and document or develop talent. Among many others, the Lomaxes discovered Lead Belly; Peer found both the Carter Family and Jimmy Rodgers in one trip; and John Hammond's list ranges from Fletcher Henderson to Bob Dylan and beyond. This is where the definition of producer becomes somewhat fuzzy. It is one thing to find a great talent and even to develop it musically, but having the business ability to either place the artist with a label or release it yourself lies outside of what many consider to be production. Often thought of as what A&R people, talent scouts, or managers do, in practice, those distinctions did not exist in the early days of the recording industry, and many producers have subsequently operated across those lines. In the post-millennial music industry, to be willing and able to discover, develop, and place artists may be necessary to survive.

Russ Titleman began his career by finding an artist. He produced his first album in 1969 after taking a musician friend's band over to another friend, Lenny Waronker, who happened to be at Warner Bros. at the time. The musician friend was Lowell George, and the band was Little Feat. Lowell and Bill Payne (Little

Feat's keyboardist) played a couple of songs and Lenny said, "Great. Go talk to Mo (Ostin) and let's make a record."[29]

These days, deals are rarely done that easily; it is not 1969, and most people do not have friends like Lowell George and Lenny Waronker. The principle, however, remains the same. Find an artist that you believe in, record them, and convince a label to put it out or release it yourself. If it sells, you establish credibility as a producer. If not, repeat the process until you find the right artist and can make a record that attracts enough attention. Producers who take this route, especially early in their careers, can do well in the music business. Finding unknown talent and developing it into a successful act is the core function of the industry.

One bona fide superstar can lift you to the higher echelons. Of course, this is easy to say and yet difficult to do, but having an area of focus and becoming a subject matter specialist helps, whether philosophical, geographical, or genre-specific. By this I mean knowing everything that is going on in your town or state, or focusing on one genre, for instance, hip hop, dance, or jazz, or taking a more generalized approach, such as only looking at artists who tour a lot (which could encompass acts from anywhere and in multiple genres).

Peter Asher is a producer who has inhabited the upper regions of the music business for many years because of his production skills and his ability to discover, sign, and develop artists who became stars. He has produced 28 gold albums, 18 platinum, and won two Grammy awards, 21 years apart. His introduction to the music business was as a member of the pop duo Peter and Gordon. After nine top 20 records, he moved into A&R for the Beatles' Apple label. He credits Paul Jones, Manfred Mann's ex-lead singer, with giving him his break into production. "I owe him a lot because he was the first person who said he liked my ideas and asked if I would produce his record.[30] It was a bold step on his part, for which I am grateful."

Right after Asher started working for Apple, he discovered a significant artist. Danny Kortchmar, who also went on to a successful production career, had played in Asher's backing band. Kortchmar's childhood friend and partner in another band called the Flying Machine was James Taylor. When the Flying Machine broke up, Taylor decided to move to London. Danny Kortchmar had given Peter Asher's number to Taylor. They met, and Taylor played a tape for Asher, who immediately understood the magnitude of his find and said, "Listen, it so happens I've just started working for this new label—I'd like to sign you to the label and produce your new record. It all fell into place very easily."

ENTREPRENEUR

Leonard and Phil Chess owned the Macamba Lounge nightclub on Chicago's Southside before buying into Aristocrat Records in 1947. The brothers bought out their partners in 1950 and founded Chess Records. Initially, they identified and serviced a local niche market for jazz and blues, and in so doing, produced and built one of the finest collections of internationally influential electric blues music.[31] Decades later, Bruce Iglauer started Alligator Records in Chicago, also focusing on the blues genre. Bruce did not classify himself as a musician or an engineer, but he was a blues enthusiast who worked for the acclaimed independent jazz and blues label Delmark Records. Iglauer brought Hound Dog Taylor to the attention of Bob Koester (the owner of Delmark). Koester declined the act, so Iglauer formed his own label, Alligator Records, and financed, produced, and released the record himself. Iglauer found more artists and produced recordings, as his resources would allow. He told me that, in the early days, each record he produced had to sell enough to finance his next production. Forty years on, Iglauer has built a significant collection of blues recordings, created a respected independent record label, and sustained an enviable production career.

MULTIPATH

It is important to emphasize that having multiple background skills does not necessarily translate to doing everything yourself, as is demonstrated by my first example.

Dr. Luke (Kelly Clarkson, Katy Perry, Pink, Ke$ha) has scored many number-one hits. His break as producer came via his 2004 composition for Kelly Clarkson, "Since You Been Gone." Most songwriters are also musicians to some degree, but Lukasz Gottwald (his real name) studied music formally at the Manhattan School of Music, which he left to begin a ten-year stint with the "Saturday Night Live" house band. He concurrently worked as session guitarist, remixer, and DJ in New York City until 2007, when he turned his attention to fulltime producing. His career is a textbook example of how to proactively increase the probability of success. He simultaneously used at least four of the eight routes: musician, songwriter, engineer, and DJ. Additionally, he widely networked in one of the world's most active music industry scenes, New York City. On a chance meeting with Max Martin, during one of his DJ gigs, he seized the opportunity to give Martin a tour of New York's club scene; he built a friendship and eventually collaborated with Martin, producing several hits. Although not responsible for his breakthrough as a producer, Luke discovered, developed, and broke Ke$ha as an artist and writer.[32] Despite Luke's consummate musicianship and multipath abilities, he chooses to work with a large team of the most successful writers and producers.

Albhy Galuten produced hits with the Bee Gees, Andy Gibb, Samantha Sang, Barbra Streisand, Kenny Rogers, Diana Ross, and Dionne Warwick. He went from guitarist and keyboard player to string arranging and songwriting to assistant engineer, eventually becoming a producer. His studio experience began at Ardent Studios in Memphis. He landed a job assisting Tom Dowd at Criteria in Miami by hanging out there with friends in the Atlanta Rhythm Section. He learned his craft on records such as Eric Clapton's *Layla* and the Allman Brothers' *Eat a Peach*. Assisting led to a staff producer position with Atlantic. His musical training began with piano lessons in high school and continued for a couple of years at the Berklee College of Music in Boston, as well as playing in several bands. He distinguishes between learning theory, notes, and technique and "the development of the ears," which he "discovered in the studio with Tommy Dowd and Jerry Wexler."[33]

Tony Visconti's first opportunities in production came about because of his abilities as a musician and arranger. He moved from the United States to the United Kingdom in 1967, eventually working with Procol Harum, the Move, T. Rex, Joe Cocker, David Bowie, Marc Bolan, Badfinger, Gentle Giant, Thin Lizzy, Boomtown Rats, and the Stranglers, among many others. American studios were still making albums very quickly, "six to twelve hours for recording, three hours to mix it." His New York publishing company assigned budgets and trained him as a record producer. He also did some talent scouting. He said he "was fired as a songwriter and hired as a record producer because my demos were good."

> I would read articles about how the Beatles took one week per song to make *Revolver*—like thirteen weeks on an album—and I thought, "just give me two weeks and I'll make a great album!" Then, through very lucky circumstances, I met Denny Cordell who was the producer of Procol Harum and Joe Cocker and the Move and Georgie Fame. He had come to New York to make a record with Georgie Fame called "Because I Love You" and he was hiring all these good players like Clark Terry to play on it, but he didn't have a chart. He thought he was just going to play them the demo, and then they'd write their own charts. So I said, "That's going to cost you a fortune in New York City." So I wrote a quick arrangement and copied out the trumpet line from the demo, and then the session went very well, and he hired me to be his assistant in London. . . . I worked for Denny Cordell for two years and through him, I made a lot of contacts. I met both David Bowie and Marc Bolan during those two years. I met Bowie through his publisher, and Marc Bolan I found on my own—I went talent scouting and found him playing in a club one night. Then, through having hits with those two guys, people came to me.[34]

I have worked with Visconti, and he is not only an excellent producer but also a very capable musician, arranger, and engineer—and, clearly, Marc Bolan was a significant discovery.

Qualifications and Training

ARE QUALIFICATIONS NECESSARY?

Benjamin Franklin said, "An investment in knowledge pays the best interest." This is true, and there is a distinction between knowledge and qualifications. Qualifications may substantiate ability and/or knowledge and are worthwhile for career backup, should plan A fail. Nonetheless, qualifications are rarely a factor in finding production work. Many producers are highly trained musicians and/or engineers, but there are far more graduates of music and audio engineering schools than there are working musicians, engineers, and producers. Even in classical music production, where conservatory music degrees are necessary, experience and exceptional achievements are required in addition to a degree and can sometimes substitute for the qualification.

In the commercial music and major label arena, Atlantic Records executive VP Pete Ganbarg said that if an "unemployed high school dropout" produced a great record, "everyone's going to want that guy. You could be musically illiterate as long as the record sounds great." He said it is the "magic" that "people are looking for."

Assuming that qualifications are irrelevant, what training would be most useful? A music degree with a concentration in arranging and composition would definitely help. A certificate or degree from a reputable school in music/audio technology, music production, or recording or audio engineering would reduce trial-and-error learning. Some courses (such as Tonmeister) are highly regarded by studios and have good job placement results. Some producers suggest that psychology credits would be advantageous.

Producers today rely on discography and reputation. Mitch Miller (Tony Bennett, Rosemary Clooney, Johnny Mathis)[35] and Goddard Lieberson (*Pal Joey*, *Porgy and Bess*, studio revival recordings) graduated from the Eastman School of Music. Teo Macero (Miles Davis) earned a master's degree from Juilliard, and many other successful producers were highly qualified musicians. In 1960, Columbia Records in New York City ran an A&R training course. Goddard Lieberson, the president of the company, took a great personal interest in it. Mike Berniker qualified for the program after passing aptitude tests, such as following an orchestral score while keeping up with a conductor of the stature of Leonard Bernstein.[36] Berniker went on to produce Barbra Streisand, Eydie Gorme, Brenda Lee, Perry Como, many jazz artists including Irakere, and Grammy award-winning Broadway shows.

Peter Collins spoke to me about starting as a producer trainee at Decca studios in North London:

> In those days, labels owned their own studios and they groomed people to become staff producers. Gus Dudgeon, John Burgess, and George Martin, all those guys came through the studio systems. And I was destined to become a staff producer when it all started going pear shaped for Decca financially.

Labels no longer seek trained musicians, nor do they develop staff this way. Producers' educations can be oblique. Jerry Harrison took a course at Harvard that could have led into either painting or filmmaking. He joined Jonathan Richman's Modern Lovers, taught a little at Harvard, worked for a computer company, and was eventually asked to try out for Talking Heads.

WHAT IS HELPFUL?

Having an opinion without being dogmatic is an important quality for success as a producer. (Although one of the many answers to "How many record producers does it take to change a lightbulb?" is "I don't know, what do you think?") Neil Finn of Crowded House said about producer Mitchell Froom, "In some cases he does hardly anything, but he's got a solid opinion all the time. In the studio, when everyone else is wavering, he's good for a consistent opinion." Neil's brother Tim adds, "Even if you don't agree, it's good to have someone who is clear, someone you can bounce ideas off."

The reason why some producers earn more than others is market validation. A successful producer's choices jibe with many consumers. No amount of education matters if a production does not resonate with the target audience. An appropriate network and strong interpersonal skills are necessary, as is perseverance. School can establish the basics but you still have to put in the hours in a studio. Tom Lord-Alge said,

> Recording schools can't teach you how to hear, how to mix. They can only teach you how the equipment runs. I learned in the studio, under pressure: deal with the people, sit in the chair, you sink or swim. You don't learn until you're put under that pressure and you learn from someone who is great.[37]

He then added, "Music is hell."[38]

Based on Confucius's formula for the acquisition of wisdom—reflection, imitation, and experience, working with and learning from established and successful producers can offer all three of these methods. This is a rich and well-proven path to success. Formal knowledge is necessary in certain situations; Alan Moulder told me he wishes he could read music at times: "[w]hen I'm recording an orchestra and trying to follow the score blindly." However, orchestral sessions are hardly a daily occurrence for him, and he added, "I wouldn't say it was too much of a hindrance....I was lucky in that I got into an area of music that I've always been interested in." Some think that formal training is disadvantageous. Moulder said, "Having worked in America, I can see that sometimes having a formal engineering training can cause people to get hung up on what is 'good' and 'bad.'" Alan worked with me at Trident when he was starting out as an assistant, and he was one of the most knowledgeable assistants I ever had. However, the Trident way was to use your training as a tool, not a rule. As he said, "Sometimes it's just better to get it on tape than to worry about the technicalities too much."

The best assistants are helpful, remain invisible, and do no harm to the session. This was true for Moulder at Trident and both Andy Jackson and Tim Palmer who worked with me in their early days at Utopia.[39] This balance of formal and practical knowledge along with the ability to blend in while being positive and not overbearing or interruptive is not easy to teach or achieve. Qualifications and knowledge must be tempered with wisdom, sensitivity, and humility to maintain a healthy dynamic in the studio. Jackson recalled assistants with substantial knowledge who were confrontational to the engineer: "That's an appalling situation." There is such a thing as too much confidence coming into the studio. Being "somewhat overawed makes you mind your P's and Q's."[40]

Wendy Page learned most of what she knows "sitting with other people watching them do their jobs and looking, listening, and learning." Page was in the British band Skin Games and has written and produced for Hilary Duff and Lulu, among others. From producing their own demo recordings, Wendy and her producing partner Jim Marr learned to "comp" vocals and guitars, record drums, and position microphones by trial and error. Along with the experimentation, and what she calls "studio patience," they were also lucky enough to work with other professionals. Page says, "Necessity is the mother of invention. You need to make your demos compete with records, so you have to learn." She likes taking her time learning new software and speculates that this creative freedom is the reason home studios are so popular. A combination of self-experimentation and apprenticeships or relationships with talented and experienced professionals who act as de facto mentors is a good way to develop skills.

Although the industry may not value qualifications, it is notable that some of the most consequential producers of recent times have been highly trained musicians. George Martin studied music at Guildhall School of Music and Drama in London. Arif Mardin won a scholarship to the Berklee College of Music. Quincy Jones abandoned his music scholarship at Seattle University to study at Berklee (then called Schillinger House). He left Berklee to play with Lionel Hampton, later studying with French composer and teacher Nadia Boulanger in Paris. Much of his early education came from working alongside some of the greatest jazz and R&B musicians of the mid-20th century. He said,

> I devoted 28 years of my life developing my core skills and learned all of the principles of music. You have to develop your skills until you really know what you're talking about—really know deep down inside.[41]

Martin, Mardin, and Jones all had considerable life experience and practice working with musicians and artists in addition to knowledge and qualifications before they began producing, which is undoubtedly an optimum combination. The formal qualifications will not result directly in production work, but the knowledge acquired does influence production capabilities and styles. Producing is a complex combination of science, art, and interpersonal skills. Combining all three Confucian methodologies (reflection, imitation, and experience) is worthwhile and is evident in the backgrounds of the most successful producers.

HOW MUCH TECHNICAL KNOWLEDGE DO YOU NEED?

It all depends on what kind of producer you want to become (see chapter 1). The full spectrum of possibilities is available, ranging from technophile to technophobe, although producers who have very limited technical capabilities are increasingly rare.

Lack of technical ability will not prevent someone from producing a hit, but it calls for a managerial approach, which means hiring or collaborating with someone who has the missing skills. Your ideas will be filtered through your engineers and DAW operators.

George Martin produced many hits, yet he does not consider himself to be a technical producer. Talking about communication with the engineer, he said,

> You might say that the drum sounds a bit dull or [you'd] like it to be "snappier." When it comes to other sounds, like horns and orchestral sessions, then I will be very particular about the kind of sound I want. The engineer has to realize the kind of sound you're looking for, in [terms] of clarity and good "liquid" sound from the strings.

Producers who work this way are usually not micromanagers when it comes to technical considerations; they choose their technical staff carefully and give them latitude in sonic decision-making.

Prior to the mid-1960s, recording engineers often needed to design, build, and repair their own equipment (including consoles). Equipment today is significantly more complex in its principles and construction, and it is rare to find a producer (even one with an audio engineering background) who can repair a piece of recording equipment. With the increasing miniaturization and integration of components, most modern electronic equipment is no longer fixed with a soldering iron and discrete components—the board, module, or even the entire piece of equipment is simply swapped out. This is the societal progression of specialization in technology.

However, underlying complexity creates greater ease of operation. Although many producers used to work with engineers who operated the equipment and understood how best to manipulate the audio, producers who can run the machinery themselves are now common. Of course, producers running equipment is nothing new. Pioneers such as Fred Gaisberg, Frances Densmore, and the Lomaxes did so, as did Les Paul, Moses Asch, Sam Phillips, and newer generations of producers from an engineering background such as George Massenburg and Hugh Padgham. The current merging of roles is partly a function of the new music industry economics taking advantage of the Moore's law-like rule of ever-decreasing cost and ever-increasing power. This, combined with the universality of computer technology and the graphical user interface (GUI) since the '80s, has increased ease with technology. Now most people (in countries with relatively affluent populations) are comfortably operating computers, relatively complex software, and smart phones or other software and menu-driven devices on a daily basis.

This now-essential everyday equipment is no longer considered technically complex enough to require specialist skills. Similarly, the level of technical knowledge required to run the most sophisticated DAW is not significantly greater than that of most other software. Nevertheless, the particularities can present a learning curve that forms a psychological barrier for some. A high-altitude understanding of functionality helps in optimal operation of complex equipment. Equipment design and repair has been a separate specialization for the past 40 years or so, with a few notable exceptions such as Tom Dowd, Roger Nichols, and George Massenburg.

Grammy-winning mixer Chris Lord-Alge's attitude to technology is "Give us the toys, and we will play with them. We take the manual and throw it in the garbage and turn the knobs until it blows up."[42]

Classical producers usually use their equipment within its technical specifications because their primary objective is to capture the natural sounds of the instruments and the acoustic performance space. Even so, most classical producers do not need advanced technical skills, focusing instead on the musical performance, overseeing and critiquing articulation, timing, pitch, and interpretive qualities. Generally, if classical producers think the sound quality needs adjusting, they communicate their ideas to the engineer, who will make the appropriate adjustments. There are exceptions, 2012 Grammy winner (producer, classical) Judith Sherman was trained as an engineer.[43] She chooses the microphones and sets them up with what she refers to as her "engineer hat on." Then she reverts to her producer role, which she defines as being "in charge of what notes go on the CD" and "capturing it before everyone falls off their chairs with fatigue."[44]

This touches on another dichotomy that all producers face, which is how to manage and even micromanage musical and technical details while guiding the project toward the wider creative vision. Some producers (even those with technical skills) still do it by outsourcing the detailed technical work. Others constantly flip back and forth from detail to overview, analytical to creative, technical to musical— a difficult skill for some. New generations of producers are, as Marc Prensky puts it, "digital natives" who speak the language of technology fluently. Many older producers have also become fully conversant with digital production—in Prensky's terms, these are "digital immigrants."[45]

Digital technology has lessened the technical responsibilities during a take, allowing an operator/producer to concentrate on performance qualities rather than watching levels and thinking about balances, EQ, and compression. Bit depth that exceeds the dynamic range of human hearing decreases concern about the noise floor and overloads, reducing the need to ride levels, and unlimited tracks allow instruments to be recorded flat. Compression, EQ, and other treatments can be added and changed throughout the project in non-real time. Of course the undo and redo function, along with the ability to save multiple versions, allows for a more relaxed approach to decisions made on the fly. If the producer is a sole operator, setup still falls under the analytical/logical mindset, but it can be time-separated from the creative elements of the production, making the mental switch from the engineer to producer role less challenging.

Producers who also engineer need to beware of allowing technical considerations to override musical ones. Performance qualities generally take precedence over sonics: Think about old jazz, traditional music, or any recordings prized for their performance values. They are noisy with limited bandwidth, both of which qualities aficionados overlook. Perhaps the producer's most important technical consideration is to make sure the technology is transparent to the artist. Tinkering with equipment when an artist has a creative spark or is "on a roll" can miss the moment of a great performance or idea. Producers need to have or hire enough technological expertise to use the equipment as an invisible means to the most creative end.

I learned engineering skills in order to have more control in the studio. It is frustrating to fall short of a creative goal because the person in charge of the machines cannot or will not maintain an open-enough mind to reach for objectives outside of the norm. Producers have made many wonderful recordings with very little technical knowledge. However, the less technically inclined you are, the more you depend on your engineer for all sonic aspects of the production. You need to be confident that he or she is capable of meeting your needs.

Different types of records require different skills. What a producer does need to know about technology is how it can best serve the music and how to not allow the medium to dictate the methodology. For example, a live recording of a blues band to a DAW does not necessarily need to be tweaked, tuned, and aligned any-more than it would if it was being recorded on analog tape. For some people, being able to see those infinitesimal discrepancies on a screen and easily (if laboriously) fix them is impossible to resist.

Producers who are not strong technically need good managerial and commu-nications abilities. They must explain what they want in terms that engineers and operators can comprehend. The economic realities of today's music industry tend to favor producers who operate with smaller teams. Directly controlling the tech-nology cuts at least one link out of the production chain.

HOW MUCH MUSICAL KNOWLEDGE DO YOU NEED?

How you produce is defined in large part by your combination of musical and technical ability. If you sing, write, play, and arrange, you will most likely gravi-tate toward the auteur typology. At the very least, you will be contributing to the arrangements, possibly playing parts and singing backgrounds on the album as well. Perfect pitch and a degree in music are not necessary to be this type of producer, but those attributes are likely to cause you to become frustrated when persuading bands to play in time and in tune. A self-contained world in which you have direct musical control will probably be more enjoyable.

Conversely, if you have minimal musical knowledge, you will depend on others for musical input. This can include working with bands that are musically self-contained but need technical, logistical, or philosophical guidance. Should the need arise, you can contribute musical input by hiring musicians, arrangers and/or com-posers. Communication can be a binary "yes/no, I like it/I do not like it" process.

Interestingly, certain genres such as dance music, hip hop, and dubstep, all of which have crossed over into pop music, require little formal knowledge of music in order to be an auteur-style producer. In a world of samples and beats where everything is programmed into a DAW, it is no longer necessary to have a strong grasp of music theory. If you have a reasonable ear and can pick out what you want to hear on a keyboard, beat out a rhythm on some MPC style pads, or drop blocks onto a grid with a mouse, controlling the entire production can again become a "like it/don't like it" process between the producer and the computer. Even a strong sense of pitch and timing is becoming less necessary because of the visual tools now available.

As discussed in this chapter, familiarity with music in the genre being produced is indispensable as is listening to music in different environments and observing how people react. Just as producers who engineer have to maintain the detail-versus-overview perspective, so do musicians who produce. They tend to focus on musical details and occasionally need to zoom out from the specifics to serve the generality. Some producers have to hear every note as they envision it, and others prefer to choose musicians whose ideas they like. This is somewhat like a systems analyst who thinks in block diagrams, as opposed to a programmer who focuses on each line of code.

Producing has much to do with choices. Many of the producers I worked with as a studio musician used this binary "yes/no" basis. They might occasionally offer a suggestion, such as "a bit more punk," "a little less fancy," or "open up more at the chorus," but few of them precisely specified parts for us to play. Even on sessions where parts are written out, rhythm section players are mostly expected to extrapolate and interpolate—to inject life into the "dots" on the page.

Using musicians in this way is not a lot different from sampling. In both cases, the track acquires not only the notes played but also the ambience of that sample or those musicians' years of experience. The producer, in turn, needs to know when they have captured something that works for the track. The diversity of production today is staggering. At one end of the spectrum is electronica and electronic dance music entirely constructed from synthetic sounds. There is hip hop, which may combine synthetic sounds with samples and performances. At the other end are classical music and jazz. Classical music production is a complex cocktail of musicianship, technology, and acoustics and, as with jazz, the performance usually prevails and the producer selects.

Producers are the artists in the art of music production (hence the title of this book). The producer's tools and materials are recording and sound generating technology, instruments, acoustics, arrangers, musicians, singers, samples, sounds, and most important, his or her own judgment. These tools and materials are ultimately subject to the producer's judgment or "ear" as the critical factor in selecting and blending the component parts and could be thought of as a progressive, post-1877 extension of music theory and practice.

WHAT IF YOU HAVE NEITHER MUSICAL NOR TECHNICAL SKILLS?

It is possible to produce records with limited musical and technical expertise and never more so than today with software and hardware that allow construction of tracks using point-and-click techniques. Most people seem to have some innate musical ability, and it is difficult to live in the 21st century without developing technological capability. Nevertheless, it is clear that many successful producers working today have a less formal grasp of music than, say, the '50s Columbia producers, most of whom were consummate conservatory-trained musicians. As previously stated, the less musical and technical knowledge a producer has, the more the execution of the tasks will rely on leadership and management skills. Most CEOs of large organizations could not step onto their company's production line and successfully perform the tasks, nor could they directly correct a line employee; they lead the organization and directly and indirectly manage layers of middle managers, supervisors, and employees. Similarly, producers who operate this way have to develop systems and a vocabulary to communicate their ideas to and through the musicians, engineers, and programmers.

Most producers use some degree of leadership and management skills. This continuum has the producers who do everything themselves at one end and those who run large teams of musicians, writers, arrangers, programmers, engineers, administrators, and so forth at the other. The most leadership- and management-oriented producers choose musicians, engineers, and even administrative people whose intuitions and abilities align with the producer's objectives. If the producer fails to achieve the envisaged results, he or she must convey what is needed to the musicians and/or technical crew or modify the team. This method can be advantageous in allowing the producer to work on diverse projects by bringing in team members with experience in various genres. Even producers with musical and technical skills change the musicians and technical staff they use depending on the needs of the project. As a successful production career develops, most producers tend to reduce their hands-on involvement and move toward a managerial style, which improves objectivity and makes for a less frenetic lifestyle.

Among others, Joe Boyd produced Pink Floyd, Nick Drake, REM, and Billy Bragg, and he did this without being a musician or an audio engineer. With a "profound feeling for music" and without the "slightest desire to play an instrument," he embarked on his career in the 1960s with the thought of becoming a latter-day Ralph Peer. Boyd said in an interview for the *Financial Times*, "A producer should be able to listen so acutely that musicians really feel heard." He compares production to writing, describing it as a process of "paring, reshaping, eliminating excess, repositioning, knowing when to obsess over details, knowing when to stop."[46]

When I asked Danny Saber about the musical or technical qualities a producer needs, he said, "That's a tough one. For everything I name, there's someone producing who doesn't have that. There are no rules." He recounts the story of a famous producer who, while doing a track for TV, kept saying, "I want it to be sharp." It turned out that what he really wanted was distortion. "He turns out excellent records," said Saber, but "he doesn't have a clue" about the specifics.

Mostly, even nonmusical, nontechnical producers acquire some musical and technical vocabulary from spending time in studios around other producers, engineers, and musicians. Recording is like looking at a performance through an audio microscope, but even the musically educated can be challenged in hearing whether the end of word drifts sharp or flat or whether the acoustic guitar is ahead of or behind the hi hat. In my first few months as a studio musician, I would hear the producers talk about timing and tuning problems that I had difficulty hearing. Gradually, these nuances became obvious to me, until I could not bear to work with producers who seemed oblivious to such discrepancies.

"I guess my parents didn't know how often you were supposed to tune a piano," says Albhy Galuten,

> In the studio, while tracking, we tune the piano every day, but in suburban middle America you, maybe, tuned the piano every couple of years. I didn't really know what "in tune" was, and here I was in the studio, never having played guitar, and just took tuning for granted. Jerry Wexler was saying something to Aretha during the session for "Spanish Harlem" about her pitch being a little flat, and I was thinking, "I didn't even hear it." Today's technology has made it much easier to hear, so contemporary records are much more in tune and much more in time. The pitch microscope was not so finely tuned back then, and we've learned over the years to look carefully at pitch, make adjustments with harmonizers, look at the meter, use razor blades, and delay lines. But around 1970, it was a new world to me—suddenly hearing careful tuning. If you listen to records from that era, many of them are way out of tune. The opening chord comes in, they're singing, the choir comes in and hits that chord, and you go "Ow!" But back then it sounded normal. To be in this environment with Jerry Wexler, Arif Mardin—their ears were fabulous, well educated, and well tuned.[47]

These are instructive comments because, in terms of musical and technical training, Mardin had extensive conservatory training, but Wexler was a journalist for *Billboard* before he bought into Atlantic Records. Mardin worked with him for decades and described Wexler as a "music-lover producer."[48] Like Joe Boyd, Wexler was able to acquire on-the-job skills to translate that "profound feeling for music"[49] into his own hit records without formal training.

MAKING THE TRANSITION TO MUSIC PRODUCER

In chapter 1, we discussed the background skills that offer proven ways into music production, but making the transition remains individual and enigmatic. It is rare for artists or labels to offer a production to someone who has little or no practical experience. I grew up in New Zealand, which was a wonderful place to live but, in the 1960s, it was not an international music business hub. I wish I could have enjoyed my career from my hometown, but with the state of communications at the time, it seemed impossible. The local knowledge base from which to develop the various skills I needed was limited, so I sought opportunity elsewhere. I studied music in Sydney, Australia, Boston, Massachusetts, and London, England; I lived and worked in many parts of the world, eventually spending most of my time working in London, New York City, and Los Angeles. I learned new skills and broadened my network everywhere I went: a different approach here, an alternative technique there, and new ways of dealing with similar problems. The growth of communications technology has subsequently transformed the ability of people far from internationally acknowledged music centers to acquire knowledge without physically leaving town. In an entirely different discipline, New Zealanders in New Zealand produced and directed *The Lord of the Rings*. Director Peter Jackson's career and the spectacular success of this movie are an example of how people living far away from previously accepted industry centers can acquire and evolve the expertise, experience, and equipment to compete internationally in the entertainment industry.

Success happens when opportunity meets preparedness. For several years, along with being a studio musician, I had been recording and co-producing my own demos and albums, including some for major labels. Through networking and by making a social connection, Spandau Ballet asked me to produce their first album, which gave me my first full production and first gold album as a producer. The music industry knew me from being a studio musician for more than a decade and from being signed to several labels as an artist. Additionally, I was fascinated by and well connected inside the nascent New Romantic scene in London. I knew Spandau Ballet and their manager from seeing their first gigs and chatting with them at clubs and parties.

Dr. Luke had played in the "Saturday Night Live" band for ten seasons and was doing remixes and DJing on the side when he met Max Martin. He took him on a tour of the New York City club scene, built a relationship, and wound up writing and producing with him.

Martin himself got his entrée into producing while playing in a Swedish rock band. He snuck into Cheiron's studio to write pop songs, and the owner of Cheiron and internationally successful producer of Ace of Base, Denniz PoP, saw potential. He asked him to come and be a writer/producer, leading to co-production on Ace of Base's second album and subsequently the Back Street Boys' first album, which opened all the doors for Martin.[50] Engineers in professional studios often record bands on the side, and like those who own their own studios, get their break with a band for which they made early recordings. DJs often specialize in a narrow niche of dance music and get to know both label people and artists through which opportunities arise.

The more careers you examine, the clearer it becomes that it takes a considerable amount of drive and initiative to kick-start a production career—or any entertainment career. It requires development of ability, the creation of something tangible that can be heard and liked, and an influential business network. Max Martin built his career out of Stockholm, hardly the center of the entertainment industry, and there are now many examples of successful producers who broke through outside of the familiar music centers. Influential and successful scenes have emerged within the last 25 years or so, in cities not historically associated with the music business. Producers often drive these centers of influence. Jam and Lewis developed out of Minneapolis; there are many hip hop producers and artists in Atlanta and St. Louis. Grunge put Seattle at the forefront in the '90s; a production enclave developed in Virginia Beach with Teddy Riley, the Neptunes, and Timbaland. Gotye produced an international hit while based in Australia, featuring the New Zealand singer Kimbra.

For some time now, communications technology has allowed an enterprising kid from an out-of-the-way place to launch him or herself into the international music arena without getting on a plane. Location is no longer a determinant. Personal connections and the ability and determination to build observable success (even in a limited market or niche) can be parlayed into national and international hits. Similarly, in other formats such as classical, jazz, and traditional music, a strong personal network along with demonstrable ability in the genre will lay the stepping stones that lead to the next level.

THE DOOR IS OPEN, YOUR FOOT IS IN, NOW WHAT?

Being proactive in controlling the shape and direction of your career is imperative and requires research, planning, and work. Some producers wait for work to come to them; this can be fine in a successful period, but not when beginning in the industry or if a career is fading. Most producers move mountains to get their first project. Ideally, we should pursue our entire careers with the same vigor and enthusiasm, though it is tempting to become comfortable and tire of constantly hustling.

A good manager can help with planning and implementation, but it is difficult to find a manager to represent you at an early stage of a production career. Managers are businesspeople, and in order for them to be interested in representing you, they need to believe that the time they invest in your career will provide a positive cost–benefit to them. For most producers, like artists, this leaves them in the position of having to develop their own careers until they are successful enough to attract a competent manager. It is common to have to produce a hit first.

Strategic intent is important to a career. Things rarely go according to plan, but clearly stated written goals should lay out benchmarks and milestones by which to measure progress and the impact of career decisions. Goals should be specific and include action steps with a timeline. Your plan can change at any time, to suit new circumstances, needs, or desires. Strategic plans define objectives and measure progress by asking, "Will this action or choice move me closer to my goal?" The efficacy of written goals has been urban legend for decades, with the most cited source being a 1953 Yale study that allegedly did not take place. A later study by Dr. Gail Matthews of Dominican University in California, however, did produce solid evidence showing that people with written goals that were shared with a friend and updated weekly were, on average, 33 percent more successful in accomplishing their stated goals than those who merely formulated them.[51]

The first edition of this book evolved from a set of written goals. I made a list of possible objectives; the action item for this particular objective was to write a synopsis and send it to publishers. I wrote a one-and-a-half-page synopsis, sent it to five publishers, and the first one I approached offered me a book deal. Things went similarly with my production career, except that there was a six-month-or-so gap between deciding that producing was my primary goal and receiving an offer for my first production. My first producer advance was considerably less than the session fees I was making as a studio musician (until royalties started to flow). Despite the fact that I would make less money producing than I could doing sessions, accepting the production job was an easy decision because that choice moved me closer to my stated objective.

I attribute no mystical power to lists or goals. It seems likely that documenting objectives forces you to focus on desired outcomes and then aligns and drives subsequent actions toward them. Sharing goals with others creates a sense of personal obligation. Professional athletes use visualization along with rigorous training to achieve their goals. Prioritized lists narrow your attention so you can visualize only what will make your goals materialize. Quincy Jones said, "When you start dreaming and visualizing, you've got to be very specific or it won't happen."[52]

3

Being a Music Producer

The Day-to-Day Responsibilities and Process

As outlined previously, using the metaphor of the corporate management structure, there are many tasks for which the producer is responsible. Some are not creative and not what most people would consider enjoyable. The fun parts of record production fall under the CCO or chief creative officer role. Nonetheless, the producer's objective is to realize the vision for the artist, manager, and label. This is true whether the vision is commercial (to go to number one on the *Billboard* Hot 100) or mission-driven (to capture the nuances of traditional music from a community in Venezuela, New Guinea, etc.). Some of what a producer does is audibly manifested in the final product, and much is not. Regardless, everything a producer does affects the resultant recording and the impact it will have on the target audience.

Irrespective of cost or success, there is no audience or accolade for budgeting, administration, booking of musicians and studios, completing union contracts, liaising with the label, preproduction, travel, setting up the studio, renting equipment, cataloguing metadata, backing up the recordings, ensuring there is sufficient digital storage space, and so on. However, if these tasks are not completed properly and on time, the project becomes chaotic. These elements, and more, are part of the position description and have an effect on the final sound people will hear. These responsibilities can be delegated, but the producer remains accountable for their completion.

People decide whether a record is satisfying or stimulating to them in some way. A track succeeds because enough people invest in it. The investment can be a radio program director assigning it one of his or her coveted rotation slots, or a consumer spending time listening to it and attaching his or her credibility to it by sharing it with friends. However, before any of this can happen, a label must commit marketing dollars for promotion through the media and distribution channels. If a producer makes a record that meets enough market criteria, he or she increases the likelihood that the label will promote it or that the track will go viral on YouTube and so forth.

Producers hold sway over whether the song is memorable, attractive, or stimulating. They can influence the intuitiveness of the arrangement so it flows naturally, is appealing on a first listen, creates a desire to be heard again, and holds the listener's interest through repeated plays. They control the quality of the performances and make sure the melody, lyrics, supporting harmonies, and rhythmic parts are well balanced. They shape the sonic qualities for clarity and punchiness, making sure that the highs are smooth and the lows are rich. Producers consider the end users and construct the track to survive its competition. Although the criteria are different, this is as true for a Smithsonian Folkways traditional world-music recording as it is for a Katy Perry single.

So how do you achieve all of this? A successful outcome begins long before the mix sessions. It includes the administrative work, without which the project will fall apart. Depending on the project, preproduction may be critical. But, before any of this can take place, early meetings with the label and the artist are important in matching personalities, expectations, and abilities.

THE FIRST MEETING

Ideally, these meetings should be in person, but they could be done on the phone, by e-mail, or Skype. They may be less critical for the auteur-type producer, because of the amount of control the auteur exercises over the musical result. Nonetheless, the artist is the central part of a project, and this meeting is a firsthand opportunity to assess the interpersonal chemistry and the artist's commitment to both the production and the promotion. The producer's objective should be to ferret out any mismatched expectations and take a reading of the personalities and dynamics involved. The assessment should encompass the A&R person, manager, and the artist, as well as influential friends and any entourage. The first meeting is an opportunity to clarify everyone's views on how the recording will be made. When I hear about and reflect on productions that went wrong, it seems to me that more due diligence in the first meeting might well have exposed some critical factors. The roots of a failed production can often be traced to problems such as taking on an ill-fitting project, perhaps for the money (to fill a gap in the schedule), or ignoring early signs of personal, musical, creative, or philosophical incompatibilities. The first meeting should occur before any commitment to produce and is an opportunity for the producer to vet the artist, label, and manager, and vice versa. This is no trivial matter because the producer, artist, manager, and A&R people generally think and speak about a project in different terms. The onus falls on the producer to translate the expectations of the creative and business partners into the tangibles that will comprise the record.

It is easy for misunderstandings to arise that can result in an unhappy ending. I had one album fail early in my production career, and I was concerned that it would put a chill on it. The primary stakeholder for this album was the owner of the group. This person was not in the studio at all times but was present at various stages in several studios all over the world, including for the mix in London. After I delivered the mixes, the A&R person called me to say that "they" were not happy with the result. I was blindsided because there had been enthusiasm and no indication of a problem right through the mixing, which had only ended a couple of days before. In retrospect, I realized that the relationship of the most influential stakeholder to the project was significantly different and more complex than usual. The label and the owner seemed unwilling to negotiate a solution and, several months later, they released a completely remade album that failed to chart. In any event, the very expensive and traumatic disconnect can be traced to my lack of understanding of the complex relationships and thus a protracted communications failure, both of which I subsequently made every effort to avoid. On reflection, I should have declined this project.

Hugh Padgham introduced Sheryl Crow and her material to A&M, resulting in her long-running deal and ultimate success. However, the recording process was fraught with problems. Padgham co-produced Crow's first album (with her) and had a contractual commitment to do more, but she was unhappy with the results they were getting, saying that they were too slick. Despite attempts at remixing with her boyfriend of the time, Kevin Gilbert, and Jay Oliver who co-wrote and co-produced the original demos, she remade the album completely. The new producer was her friend Bill Bottrell, who introduced a set of writers they called the "Tuesday Night Music Club," the name they entitled the new album. As reported in Richard Buskin's book, with reference to Padgham, she told the *Chicago Tribune* that "[w]e never had a common mindset on what kind of album it should be." This occurred at a peak time in Padgham's career and turned out to be a $450,000 miscommunication.[1]

In both cases, given the personalities and circumstances, it is possible that these problems were unavoidable, but all parties would have been happier if everyone's intentions and needs had been better understood from the beginning, culminating in less distressing conclusions.

In addition to aligning expectations, the early meetings are opportunities to begin making the artist feel at ease and testing your comfort level with him or her. No artist will perform well unless he or she is content and confident in themselves, as well as the production team. There needs to be mutual respect, and the artist should feel that the producer understands and believes in them.

ADMINISTRATION

Doing administrative work is less fun than watching paint dry for many producers. Ideally, before doing anything, you will have a fully executed (signed by all parties) producer contract. It is common to begin projects before the contract is completed and signed, but if the deal goes awry before it is signed, you are at risk of not being paid for any work done. Your production contract needs to be carefully read (preferably by you, as well as your lawyer and manager) to make sure that it reflects your understanding of what was agreed verbally and in the headings agreement (which it sometimes does not). Unless you are on an "all-in deal," working on "spec," or have the artist signed to your production company/label, you cannot begin until you submit a budget.

If it is an all-in, spec, or own-label deal, a budget is the only way to ensure that you do not wind up working for nothing. As discussed earlier, if you are successful and a good delegator, someone else will most likely put the budget together for you. Unless you have a person who knows your working habits very well, you will have to answer a multiple-choice quiz about studios, dates, times, hard drives, musicians, arrangers, and equipment rental packages. Peter Collins opts for a Q&A phone session with his management company, but it is easy enough to create a modifiable spreadsheet template that transfers from one project to the next. The budget needs to align with any contractual requirements, irrespective of what the A&R person says to you. If there is any variance from the contract terms, it must be approved in writing by the contractually authorized parties. Once you are on the project, you may have to sign studio invoices and rental bills, and complete, sign, and submit union forms and rights clearances. Once the budget is approved, it must be monitored throughout the production, comparing actual with projected expenditures. Some producers handle this, some managers do, and others hire a production coordinator. Setting measurable milestones maintains confidence that the money will last until the project is complete.

In the '70s and '80s, large budgets were common. Most budgets have shrunk considerably since the year 2000, and overage clauses still hold the producer responsible for any costs incurred above the agreed amount.[2] For a time, many producer deals were "cost-plus," meaning that there was a recording budget and a separate producer advance, which was recoupable against the producer's royalties. Nonetheless, if producers ran over budget they were charged the additional costs when the contract contained an overage clause and the overrun was not authorized in writing. In a cost-plus deal, there are no bonuses for completing a project under budget. Overage clauses have a tendency to inflate recording budgets because producers, not wanting to pay for part of the album, pad their budget projections.

"All-in" funds are now common, where all recording costs, including the producer's advance or fee, are paid from a contractually agreed amount. These deals help contain costs for labels and are good for producers who are adept at controlling expenses. The producer spends down the fund and keeps the remainder at the end. Auteur producers, especially the ones who play most of the instruments, write the songs, and own their own studio, can often retain more of the budget for themselves because they tightly control all aspects of the production process. The more reliant you are on outside studios, engineers, programmers, musicians, singers, arrangers, etc., and/or the more say the artist has, the more risky all-in deals become for the producer. For instance, if an artist decides that he or she needs more recording days, rental equipment, or additional musicians not accounted for in the initial budget, these expenses will reduce or eliminate the producer's margin. All-in deals can create tension between the producer and artist. Producers sometimes have to rein in spending to stay within budget. With an all-in fund, the artist may think that the recording budget is being held back for the producer's financial gain. Producers are usually much wealthier than first-time recording artists; this can exacerbate the perception of self-interest.

With the plethora of information available about 360 deals and the pros and cons of "free agency" versus being with a label, signed artists are realizing that most expenses will be deducted from any royalties generated. Some acts behave as though they will generate so much income that advances and costs will become insignificant. In fact, a million units sold may not recoup costs. A three-minute video can easily exceed the recording costs for the album, and so might tour support. This knowledge does nothing to incentivize artists to save money during recording. Sheryl Crow did not receive her first royalty check until she sold three or four million units.[3] It can be fun to go wild with what seems like corporate money, but there are many ex-artists who would be having a much better time now if they had conserved more during the good times.

Once a budget is approved, the other administrative work begins. The planning and setup of the sessions can be thought of as part of preproduction, although the term is usually used to mean the creative development phase that precedes the recording sessions.

PREPRODUCTION

Preproduction is a preparatory, decision-making phase. It is when material is chosen, arranged, and refined. Performances may be rehearsed in this period. The purpose is to sort through options and make choices before they become difficult or expensive to make or change. Decision-making has been increasingly deferred since Les Paul began making sound-on-sound and then multitrack recordings. The sequencing and MIDI era introduced flexibility right up to the moment when parts were dumped to tape for completion with live overdubs. Before affordable digital recorders, recording the live elements usually entailed a professional studio. The expense and difficulty of making changes to parts recorded to linear tape made a preproduction phase financially wise. Yogi Berra summed up the creative necessity for preproduction when he said, "If you don't know where you're going, you'll end up somewhere else." Without a preproduction phase, all fundamental creative decisions have to be made in the studio. Those kinds of choices, when working in commercial studios, can make maintaining a high-altitude perspective and staying within budget difficult.

There are exceptions to every rule, and for some records—particularly ones involving much improvisation (as in jazz)—the completely spontaneous capturing of creativity may be the best option. Nonetheless, within the exceptions, there is a range of opinions and approaches to recording improvised music. Some producers feel that preparation compromises the spontaneity, and others do not. Blues and jazz producer Bob Porter reflected this dichotomy in his comment, "The difference between Blue Note and Prestige was two days' rehearsal." Blue Note paid for a couple of day's preparation while Prestige chose the immediacy of interaction on the session.[4]

Preproduction can be quite brief in the case of improvised music, when recording a working group's material, or if all parties have worked together extensively. It can entail a few phone calls or e-mails to discuss material, personnel, choice of studio, schedule, and so forth. If there are studio musicians and written parts, the writing of the arrangements or discussions with an outside arranger may constitute preproduction.

On recordings that do not rely so heavily on spontaneity and live interaction between the musicians, key creative and administrative decisions are often made at the preproduction stage. Thorough preproduction makes cost and time projections more accurate and reduces project creep and disappointing results. When musicians perform together, having distinct preparation and capture (or preproduction and production) phases limits uncertainty on recording days.

Preproduction is not necessarily for locking down fine details, but rather for making sure that the band is familiar with the arrangements and the attitude or feel of the tracks. In the studio, the band should not have to worry whether the next transition is to another chorus or the bridge. The cut, paste, and edit functions can be used to solve exceptional problems rather than as a modus operandi.

Selection of material is part of the preproduction process. With artists who write, this means listening to their material, and it is often necessary to ask if they have more. Artists frequently hold back material, and the big hit can be the song they were not intending to record—maybe an unfinished or older song. Artists often tire of their older songs and can be poor judges of their material. There can be rivalries within groups that lead to the exclusion of potential hit material from the selection process. The producer can better lobby for a song than a band member who wrote it. With a non-writing artist, unless you are writing for them, preproduction entails soliciting material and listening through many demos or old albums.

With artists' demos, it is necessary to take into account the conditions under which they were made. A lack of money and experience can make for poor choices. A band with a strong rhythm section might use a drum machine on the demo because they could not record live drums in their apartment. Artists often record demos soon after writing the songs and a year later, with 200 live shows behind them, the arrangements and performances are tighter. When producing an artist who developed through playing live, I consider it imperative to see at least one performance if not several. In the case of the most poorly produced album I made as an artist, the producer never saw the band live, and there was no preproduction period. Consequently, the album lacks the vitality or interactivity the band had in that period.

Preproduction is when you decide how to make the record—whether it will be overdubbed, performed live, programmed, or a combination. On occasion, I have changed my intended methodology based on observations from early rehearsals. Some producers only work one way, and the artist must conform. In any event, some early decisions are difficult to reverse or change later. Recording basic tracks without a click track will affect the process and final sound of the recording. Beginning by laying computer parts or a click track allows for flexibility in the recording process, but imparts a distinct quality to the final track that may or may not be desirable.

Whether the band records together in the studio or by overdubbing one part at a time, preproduction is the time to advance, if not finalize, the arrangements. The musicians rehearse the material until they know it well. Deciding whether a song is better with or without two extra bars after the chorus while you are tracking in the studio can sap musicians' energy. It is better to resolve structural arrangements in a rehearsal space and create a sense of event in the studio to capture the performance. If live musicians are overdubbing to a click track, preproduction is the opportunity for the band to play the songs through together, ensuring that the parts are complementary, to avoid surprises as the track builds up. Inexperienced bands often need to rehearse with a click so they become accustomed to playing the song at a single, steady tempo. Introducing a click track to a drummer for the first time in the studio can make him or her nervous and produce a stilted feel.

Producers frequently need to improve arrangements, identifying, creating, and organizing elements that will comprise the finished record. Artists commonly underemphasize the best parts of a song, create convoluted structures, and fail to mark transitions clearly. They sometimes emotionally attach to their arrangements; this requires diplomacy on the part of the producer. Preproduction helps bands settle into the recording process, allowing the producer to assess personalities and gently introduce the changes he or she thinks necessary. Strengths and weaknesses in the material become apparent, and this is the time to fix any problems, including writing or acquiring any new material, if needed.

No battle plan survives contact with the enemy, and so it is with preproduction. Once recording commences and you play back the first take, your approach can change. It may be that the "extra two bars after the bridge" do have to come out. Nevertheless, the increased comfort level with the material and between the producer and artist (that develops in the lower-pressure preproduction environment) tends to reduce the stress of any necessary restructuring in the studio.

The ubiquity of digital audio workstations (DAWs) has changed the relationship between preproduction and production. The differentiation between the two phases has diminished since the '70s, when preproduction was the rehearsal and preparation phase during which nothing was recorded that would be usable on the final master. Production was the capture phase (using multitrack tape at the time). This remained true throughout the '80s for projects using only live musicians. Of course, successful artists with multitrack studios could write and mock up their albums to 16- or 24-track tape, and groups such as Pink Floyd did.

For most artists, the erosion of the boundary between the preproduction and production phases began with the introduction of inexpensive four- and eight-track tape recorders and with sequenced and MIDI-based recording. Each of these technologies meant that parts and sounds prepared during the writing or rehearsal stage could be transferred over to the master multitrack.

The digital-tape-based Alesis ADAT was a higher-quality solution than semi-professional analog machines. Inexpensively capturing live parts at master quality and mixing from ADAT or transferring to a professional multitrack format reduced the need to recreate everything in an expensive studio. ADATs could synchronize with sequencers and MIDI devices, but DAWs merged the recording of MIDI events with that of sounds, extending the possibility of a continuously iterative creative process of refinement, until the recording became the final master. As a result, many productions now have no line between preproduction and production. The distinctions now are of place, equipment, and expertise, such as needing a large live area for a big ensemble or orchestra. In order to minimize cost, sessions in commercial rooms require some form of preproduction, if only for booking the room and personnel, determining arrangements, and agreeing on conceptual parameters.

Creative need drove the development of multitrack recording and the trend toward an iterative continuum. Producers attempted to retain special performances and sounds from demos and preproduction work long before it was a simple matter. Prior to DAWs, producers used modular digital machines to preserve unique performances or sounds, but the synchronization of these machines was not seamless. Before that, producers had bumped tracks over to the multitrack master from substandard analog formats for at least a decade, one of the most famous examples being Phil Collins's debut album *Face Value*, featuring the hit single "In the Air Tonight." Collins recorded the demos over a period of more than a year on his home one-inch, eight-track analog tape recorder. When Atlantic wanted him to finish the album, he did not want to recreate what he had already recorded. Collins's engineer and assistant producer Hugh Padgham bounced the tracks over to the master, and they added the compressed and gated drums complete with the famous fill. They then added other parts, as well as rerecording Collins's vocals. This process of transferring the demos formed the basis for the way Collins would work on his solo recordings thereafter.

Musicians usually enjoy working at their own pace in their own environment, but the equipment of that time presented qualitative technical challenges for producers and engineers. It is difficult to express the extent to which the digital revolution has transformed the work process for most producers, saving time and frustration. Now, if you can capture an idea or a sound at any phase of the production, technical or quality parameters are unlikely to prevent the part from making it into the final mix. It used to be commonplace to spend time trying to reproduce timbral or performance qualities from a part on a demo that was unusable because of technical inadequacy.

The ubiquity of the DAW and consequent diminution of the transitions from writing to preproduction to production has made the necessity for a distinct preproduction phase a genre- and producer typology-dependent viewpoint. The defining conditions are: When resources need to be amassed and hard costs are time-related, a preparatory phase, or preproduction, makes creative and financial sense.

THE PRODUCTION PHASE

Understanding the needs of the artist is paramount in production. Making artists comfortable in the studio and with the creative team is essential. As discussed, creating this comfort level begins well before the production phase with the first meeting and through preproduction. Even so, tensions can ramp up at critical points. Throughout the production, knowing when to push, when to back off a little, and when to take a break can be crucial to capturing special performances. As Nashville veteran Barry Beckett says, "I wish I had taken Psychology 101 in college instead of making music. It would have helped me out a great deal."[5] Benny Blanco said in an interview with *Sound On Sound*, "Producing is about making everyone feel comfortable and making them feel that their ideas matter and are being used. It is all about setting the ambience."[6]

Good producers think about creating the right ambience for a particular artist. Each requires a different approach, but there are universal working practices that typically make the recording process more enjoyable. Preparing the studio before the artist and/or musicians arrive lubricates the proceedings. Experienced engineers and producers set up the room, including putting out chairs, drinks, and pre-positioning gobos and booths as necessary. (Gobos are acoustically treated, movable screens usually about eight feet high and four feet wide). They pre-set mic levels, EQs, compressors, reverbs, and foldback (the mix of music sent to the performers' headphones or speakers) before the musicians and singers walk through the door. Headphone balances are critical to a great performance. The best producers check and double-check everything to avoid technical problems and delays during a take. The less inconvenience you put the performer through, the more likely you are to elicit great performances. It can be demoralizing for a performer to lay a great take only to have to do it again because the levels were not correct or other such problems.

If you have worked with a particular singer before, then you should know which mic they like, their favorite headphones, where in the room they like to be, what kind of balance they prefer to hear, and at what levels they are likely to sing. If you have never worked with the person before, you can set everything up based on general experience. It is much quicker and easier to make minor adjustments once a singer begins than it is to set up levels from scratch. Sometimes artists' requirements can be idiosyncratic. I worked with a singer who would not allow a smidgen of reverb on his voice in the final mix, but who nevertheless needed a Taj Mahal-like reverb in his headphones when he was laying his vocal tracks. The odd part was that he did not appear to know what reverb actually was. He would not ask for reverb on his voice when he was singing but would say, "They (the headphones) sound flat," which, of course, has another well-defined musical meaning. Likewise, if there was the slightest amount of effect on his voice in the final mix he would say, "...[it] sounds like I'm in a tunnel, Rich." Interpreting non-technical and non-musical language is part of the challenge of being a producer.

Lack of preparation can cause unusable takes because levels, EQs, or compressors were not set correctly or conservatively enough. Almost all singers and musicians generate more level when they are performing a take than when they are rehearsing or warming up. EQ and compression can be added later, but it is impossible to clean up distorted vocals and difficult to expand over-compressed signals. Digital recording has a wide dynamic range, and it is safer to leave some headroom on a first take than to generate "overs" that render sections unusable. I have seen singers lose their confidence (and patience) while the engineer "gets a sound." The hackneyed studio joke cracked at the end of a brilliant take is "OK—let's record." Sometimes, unfortunately, the engineer or producer is not joking. Always be "in record" when anyone is performing, even for a run-through. There is a psychological factor: Lost takes tend to assume perfect proportions in a performer's mind. If you capture a take, complete with technical deficiencies, close listening usually reveals some performance issues, and everyone happily resolves to do another, rather than begrudgingly thinking that you or the engineer are incompetent.

Good engineering practices minimize problems. I like to set up, plug up, check phase, and get levels on everything that might be used so that each instrument is ready to capture a spontaneous creative moment. Every microphone, cable, and channel needs to be auditioned before any performers arrive, and multi-mic setups should be checked for phase, especially if they are being combined onto a track with other mics. It is very difficult to make a great sounding record if you do not record tracks at good levels with well-balanced sonic properties. "Fix it in the mix" should be a philosophy of last resort, reserved for performances that you cannot reproduce. Many mixers complain about having to "rescue" badly recorded tracks. It is easier to know when a recording is complete if the daily working balance sounds close to a final mix. Conversely, it is an act of faith to say, "It sounds like a mess, but when it's mixed it'll be fine." Sending un-compiled vocals and un-rationalized tracks to an outside mixer is unlikely to produce the result you intended. Delete everything that you did not intend for the mix and compile all solos and vocals so that hitting play approximates the sound of the finished record. The mix should be a process of optimization or enhancement of what was recorded, not an organizational conundrum.

Producer and engineer Val Garay (Kim Carnes, James Taylor, Queensrÿche) records everything at the correct relative levels so, as he is working on overdubs, he can set the faders in an almost straight line and, without rides, hear something close to the envisaged mix. As he put it, "At that point my mother could mix it."[7]

In any human interaction, there are at least two points of view, which can bring a session to an irresolvable impasse or argument. William Wrigley Jr. said, "When two men in business always agree, one of them is unnecessary." Different perspectives expressed in a civil and collegial way can produce excellent results, but all too often bands become like dysfunctional families, lacking respectful boundaries and becoming argumentative or disparaging. Ideally, the producer does not become the judge and jury but mediates to bring everyone to the higher viewpoint of the "best solution for all."

The producer who knows when to contribute and when to sit back on the couch is the best kind. In *Rolling Stone* magazine, Jerry Wexler (Allman Brothers, Aretha Franklin, Wilson Pickett) said of the late Ray Charles,

> ...I was very happy this time when he said, "Pardner"—he always called me that—"those were my best years, with you and Ahmet." But when people say, "You and Ahmet produced Ray Charles," put big quotation marks around produced. We were attendants at a happening. We learned from Ray Charles. My dear friend (writer) Stanley Booth once remarked, "When Ahmet and Jerry got ready to record Ray Charles, they went to the studio and turned the lights on, Ray didn't need them."[8]

Of course, one of the hallmarks of greatness is modesty.

W. Somerset Maugham was not talking about a record producer when he said, "Like all weak men he laid an exaggerated stress on not changing one's mind." When all eyes are on the producer for the next idea, the first utterance need not be immutable, especially if it stimulates a better one from someone else. Linus Pauling emphasized the merits of not being precious when he said, "The best way to have a good idea is to have lots of ideas." Industrialist John D. Rockefeller stressed the benefits of reaching for the stars by saying, "Don't be afraid to give up the good to go for the great." Jim Collins in his book *Good to Great* rephrased that, saying, "Good is the enemy of the great," which means that good may disincentivize the search for the great.

Some producers do almost everything. In the case of the auteur type, the producer may be the songwriter, orchestrator, engineer, producer, and vocal arranger. All the artist has to do is sing the song, and occasionally they don't even do that (remember Milli Vanilli?). With less experienced singers, it is very common for them to copy every note and inflection of the producer's guide vocal or guidance during the recording of the vocal. The producer may also structure or restructure the part by editing and using vocal tuning software.

Sometimes producers act as a stimulant or catalyst. Bands and artists fall back on their clichés (or, worse, someone else's). Sometimes artists get creatively tired and settle for mediocre ideas. At times the first idea is the best, sometimes it is not, and frequently it represents a good starting point. Having someone in the room who rejects the good and reaches for the great can be enough to turn on the creativity faucet. The producer can be the bit of grit that irritates and stimulates the artist to create the pearl.

Producers are required to moderate and nurture the full range of the creative process, and sometimes this means protecting the democratic or participative environment and other times allowing someone (including the producer) to be autocratic. "Usually what people are practicing is not democracy, but cowardice and good manners," says Brian Eno,

> Nobody wants to step on so-and-so's toes, so nobody wants to say anything. The valuable idea of democracy is that if there are five people in the room

and one of them feels very strongly about something, you can trust that the strength of their feelings indicates that there is something behind it. My feeling about a good democratic relationship is the notion that it's a shifting leadership. It's not, "We all lead together all the time," it's "We all have sufficient trust in one another to believe that if someone feels strongly then we let them lead for that period of time."[9]

This is consistent with the idea of blending or transitioning through all six leadership styles as circumstances demand.

We book session musicians for their strengths. That is not to say they do not need guidance or cannot be stretched, and a producer should certainly never be intimidated by any musician's reputation. The best players are very good at taking direction, but it is possible to disempower even the greatest musicians and get lackluster performances by not allowing them the space to contribute. If a session with a studio musician becomes too much of a struggle, then you may have the wrong musician, or someone or something might be interfering with the creative flow.

Excitement and passion are more likely to produce a great record than conciliation and compromise. It is important to negotiate for the best possible outcome rather than settle for the least objectionable solution. Sometimes producers need to protect vulnerable, sensitive, or introverted members of the band while they experiment with ideas. Creative notions and moments are fragile. It is rare that creative ideas emerge fully formed. They often begin as a vague sense of possibility, and are realized only by actively exploring in a nonjudgmental environment. One disparaging retort or facial expression from another band member can shut down a creative moment before it fully manifests. Bands are often hotbeds of politics, jealousies, and cliques. Part of the producer's job is to understand the interpersonal dynamics so he or she can correctly interpret attitudes and comments.

Sometimes producing is about defining parameters, sketching out boundaries, or as Eno puts it, "establishing the cultural territory." There are times in a band's career when they are at the center of what is happening; they intuitively understand who they are, what they represent, and how they relate to what is going on around them culturally. Usually this is early in their career. They have grown up at one with the influences of their generation; they may be influential themselves; they are buoyed by youthful confidence and unburdened by conflicting perspectives. This enables them to generate relevant music for their time that may be trend-setting, trend-related, trend-following, or beyond trend.

Even artists who broke on the forefront of a trend are not always excited about change. Many want to keep doing what has worked for them when they should change, and vice versa. If change is necessary, what form should it take, why, how, and to what degree? It is best if the answers come from the artist, and the producer may need to focus the artist's attention on the relevant questions. Eno does it by asking, "Where are we culturally? What are we trying to be? What books? What films?"[10] From there he eliminates possibilities to "narrow the field" not to limit creativity but to focus "a meaningful amount of attention on something, rather than a small amount of attention on everything."[11]

Andy Jackson thinks that good producers can liberate artists, allow them to do what they believe in, and break through their inhibitions, fears, or preconceptions to fulfill what they had the potential to do anyway. Almost like a therapist, they help "the artist to zero in on what they really want to do, rather than what they imagine they want to do—to free up their creativity."[12] Artists are more likely to embrace solutions that they develop. Jackson believes a producer who can do that no longer needs to be there, adding, "It's something I have a tremendous amount of respect for."[13]

Tom Dowd was a highly influential engineer and producer for Atlantic Records who covered much of the '60s and '70s rock and soul spectrum. Trained as a nuclear physicist (he contributed to the development of the first atomic bomb), he started in the music industry as an audio engineer. His responsibilities at Atlantic were very wide- ranging. He built and repaired much of the early equipment on which he engineered and produced sessions, and he encouraged Atlantic to move up to Ampex eight-track recorders. In a particularly intense and creative period in the '60s, he was commuting several times a year from his home base in New York to Memphis, Muscle Shoals, and Macon.

> Sometimes I was needed for updating facilities, or for engineering, suggesting arrangement changes or conducting, you name it. Whatever had to be done, had to be done.[14]

Roles in the industry have become more specialized since then. It is uncommon now for someone to be so adept at both the musical and the technical sides.

George Martin got to the nub of the skill most essential for all producers when he said,

> You've got to get on with people and you've got to lull them into a kind of sense of security and you've got to get rid of their fears. You've got to relate to people.[15]

This statement holds true for any of the producer typologies. Whether you are getting a kick-drum sound, suggesting an overdub, arranging a string part, trying to get the artist to consider an outside song, hiring a studio musician, recording a vocal or talking high-concept with the artist, they must feel that they can trust you.

The production phase can be tense for artists; this is when the creative vision becomes reality and either succeeds or fails. They may have had negative studio experiences, and they might have concerns about this juncture in their career. Empathy for their situation and quiet, confident guidance help to reduce anxiety and create happy sessions.

THE MIX

Mixing has many connotations and is now a postproduction function thanks to overdubbing and multitrack recording. At its most basic, the function of a mix is to balance and optimize the components of the production for the maximum musical impact so that the creative team hears them as they intended. Mixing (or balancing) was initially done to a mono master (disc or tape) as the recording was taking place. Mixing to mono continued through the late 1950s and into the '60s both as a live technique during recording and as a postproduction process after the introduction of multitrack recording and stereo mastering. Mono mixing adjusts relative loudness and orchestrates perceived placements in a single, front-back dimension (depth) by microphone placement, frequency choice and modification, and the use of compression and effects.

The popularity of acoustically dead (lacking reverb time) recording spaces was an effort by engineers and producers to gain more control over individual sounds, so that individual equalization, compression, effects, and the illusion of space could be added creatively, either as the track was being recorded or in postproduction mixing. It is possible using a combination of compression and expansion to make something recorded with a distant mic sound close, by fusing any ambience with the original sound source. But, this is more difficult than making a close mic'd sound appear to move to the rear on the front-back axis by using an effect. Perception of distance is a psychoacoustic mélange of early reflections (or lack thereof), frequencies or timbre, and phase and expectation. Simply reducing the relative level of an instrument or voice does not necessarily make it recede in the mixed image.

Stereo recording and mixing uses the second axis of width or side-to-side positioning that creates a perceived two-dimensional soundstage for the listener. Front-back and side-to-side placement in the stereo image is achieved with microphone technique or electronic panning/placement within the binaural field. Whether mixing in mono or stereo, during recording or in postproduction, the mixer's primary objective is to focus the listener's attention on the most compelling elements. Mixing extends all the musical techniques that precede it, strengthening the perception of the song by reinforcing the structure, orchestration, and emotional affect for the intended audience. There are other factors, such as making the track sound current or appropriate for a particular audience and accommodating stakeholder priorities. Ultimately, a good mix is one that appeals to the desired audience.

An exciting mix may use a combination of static and dynamic balance, equalization, compression, limiting, expansion, gating, reverbs, delays, and other effects to optimize the sounds, increase their impact, and ensure they occupy their own space in the audio spectrum. Equalization or EQ affects the tone color or timbre of a sound making it, among other things, brighter, duller, harsher, smoother, fatter, richer, bigger, or smaller. Generically referred to as dynamic control, compression, limiting, expansion, and gating can be used in a number of different ways to affect the shape, impact, length, or apparent loudness of a sound or combination of sounds. Additionally, one or more sounds can trigger or key these treatments to shape another.

Mixing can involve riding the levels of the instruments and vocals. This changes comparative loudness by moving faders relative to time and the other audio material. Fader rides can improve the dynamic flow of the track, drawing attention to various facets of the orchestration over time. They can also prevent part of the orchestration from overwhelming another and compensate for unwanted variations in recorded levels, as well as build the overall excitement of the mix. Semantics are never more fraught than during the mix. I once worked with an artist who kept saying he wanted the snare drum to be bigger. I was fattening it up using EQ and compression so that it occupied more space in the track. When it became clear that was not what he meant, I asked him to play me something that had a "big" snare drum on it, and it transpired that he wanted what I would have described as a small, distant snare drum in a great deal of reverb.

OTHER PERSPECTIVES

Aerosmith's lead guitarist Joe Perry says that every band has a different style and a different relationship with their producer. In working with Bruce Fairbairn, on their albums *Permanent Vacation*, *Pump*, and *Get a Grip*, the group groomed their songs to the point where they liked them. Then they brought Fairbairn in to bring a fresh perspective. Perry thinks that having a producer is very important, but that it is a difficult job:

> I don't want to get any closer to producing Aerosmith than I am right now. Everybody in the band has strong feelings about it too. I don't think it's wise for us to get to the point where we don't have someone to act as a mediator.[16]

Validating Perry's point, Aerosmith's singer Steven Tyler finds it difficult to work with a producer, particularly in accepting another perspective and the changes the producer wants to make:

> You've got to decide whether you take a hard-nosed stand and say, "No way, man, this is me and this is the way it stays," or take chances. . . . With each album it gets harder and harder to listen to other people, but every album gets better and better, so a producer is definitely necessary.[17]

This is the dichotomy producers often face: Artists become attached to their perspectives, but personal insecurities, tensions within the band, and differences between the band and label necessitate a mediator. Acting as a peacemaker or intermediary is part of the job. With experienced artists, there are usually enough ideas flying around the studio that the last thing they need is an autocratic producer. In those situations, the producer's role is to ensure that the best ideas make it to the final mix while maintaining civil and collegial interpersonal relationships between the decision-makers. Producers also have to resolve any conflicts between commercial and artistic needs that sometimes surface as an external pressure to be current versus allowing artists to follow their muses. When the push is coming from A&R or marketing people (whose job it is to get radio, TV, and press coverage), artists are often not sympathetic. Some artists seem to have an internal compass that guides them to where they need to be artistically and commercially, and others do not (even when they are successful).

Juggling these considerations requires experience and strong interpersonal skills. Sam Phillips learned about the latter while working for a country funeral parlor:

> I was very sensitive to the things I heard, saw and felt around me....Those times, working with the country mortician, made me very aware of how to handle people and their problems later on.[18]

Beyond the actualities of day-to-day life in the studio and the commercial realities we all face, there can be a deeper inspiration and methodology for the producer. Jim Dickinson summed this up in his production manifesto, which says, "Music has a spirit beyond notes and rhythm. To foster that spirit and to cause it to flourish—to capture it at its peak—is the producer's task." He elaborated:

> I try to remain aware and attuned to the peculiar harmonic properties of the events as they unfold. This is not just musical. I'm talking about how the balance is gonna change in the room constantly during the process, just because of the process itself. It's in the life of the event where you find the soul, and that's what you are trying to capture. This becomes a moral responsibility for the producer.[19]

It is never easy to make a great record that stands in sharp relief above contemporaneous releases. Nevertheless, the quality of the result relevant to the artist's needs must be the objective in every step of the process, refining and distilling each aspect to avoid a rote production and colorless result.

"The vast majority of records are driven by a very fearful thing of not doing something wrong rather than doing something right," says Andy Jackson. "We don't let things go. We're striving for perfection, which is actually just avoiding the possibility of someone saying 'Ooh, that's weird.'" Producers and artists have painstakingly micromanaged some very successful albums, but the ability to create circumstances in which something special can happen is a desirable production skill. Jackson recorded with Tony Visconti a few years ago. The album "only took about two and a half weeks," and he found it "interesting to watch him function." When he analyzed what Visconti contributed, he observed "a very easy atmosphere to work in" where "things could happen very easily and quickly."[20] I witnessed this effect many times in my years as a studio musician; the best producers make the process effortless for everyone, and it is hard to parse what it is they are doing that makes it so.

Some Session Specifics

RECORDING MUSICIANS LIVE IN THE STUDIO

Any time there is a musician in the studio performing, the intensity level of the session rises. As the producer you have to assume, at all times, that the upcoming performance may be the best one, and if you fail to record it properly, a great performance will be lost forever.

It is bad enough if you miss a flawless overdub, but the stakes are higher when a group of musicians records together. With multiple possibilities for mistakes, the perfect performance becomes very precious. The chemistry that occurs between musicians playing together can create a whole performance that transcends the sum of the parts. When this chemistry happens, it is dramatic and can be unrepeatable. It is a bad day for the producer or engineer who fails to capture such moments.

Kevin Shirley produced Iron Maiden's *Brave New World* album and suggested that they record it live in the studio. The band was skeptical at first; they had made their previous albums by overdubbing. In any event, the live recording worked well, and they recorded their next album the same way. Shirley said, "You get things very quickly this way and you get a real sense of whether things are happening.... By recording them live I could really capture their sound."[21]

It sometimes seems as though recording a band live in the studio or at least recording the basic rhythm section live is becoming a lost art. The reason often cited for recording by overdub is to have more control in the mix because of the total separation, which is a valid argument. Nonetheless, many of the best-sounding albums in the history of recorded music had substantial parts or all of the tracks recorded with the players in the studio at the same time. Jazz is an obvious example; *Kind of Blue* comes to mind as do any of the Rudy Van Gelder recordings for Blue Note or Impulse!. The Beatles played together in the studio, as did Led Zeppelin and The Band. Lack of separation is sonically manageable in many ways: isolation booths with good foldback and sightlines, and strategically placed screens or gobos to reduce spill to the degree that it will not compromise the mix. Sometimes it is better to set everyone up close together and let the spill happen. If everyone plays well, and at roughly the same volume in a complementary acoustic environment, the spill will actually enhance the recording. Of course, breakdowns (cutting out several instruments for sections of the mix) and remixes that leave out played parts become difficult or impossible when there is leakage on other instruments or vocals.

Recording musicians together with any significant amount of leakage between the instruments requires good musicianship. They have to get it right because it may be impossible to replace parts that were not DI'd or recorded in iso booths. Recording this way requires engineering expertise that is becoming harder to find. Mic'ing a group of musicians (and/or singers) is conceptually different than mic'ing them individually. Each mic cannot be optimized for that instrument without considering its effect on the overall mix. The phase relationships of the mics to each other become critical. The group sound has to be considered as a whole, and some decisions made at the time of recording are irreversible. It is not impossible to repair mistakes in a live recording, but it is often preferable to fix them by editing between takes or from a different part of the same take in order to maintain a consistent ambience on all tracks.

Overdubbing works well sonically, but most of the great jazz albums could not have been made that way. Neither could many of the classic electric blues albums, because the interaction between the musicians is an integral part of the value of the recording. Even with a rock band that is playing already agreed-upon parts, when the musicians play together, there is an extra presence, which we can think of as the whole being greater than the sum of the parts. Carefully controlled spill can make a track sound larger than one with total separation. When musicians play together, there is a far greater differential between "the take" and the "outtakes" than when tracks are layered by overdub. As Kevin Shirley indicated, if the musicians are good, the recording process can be fast and at the end of the session, you can hear whether everything works together.

The result is what counts, and when we agonize over every detail, it is worth reminding ourselves that the first Beatles' album was largely recorded in one day, and Jimi Hendrix's *Axis: Bold as Love* was completed in 72 hours.

RECORDING AN ORCHESTRA OR BIG BAND

Recording an orchestra, big band, or any large ensemble raises the stakes in many ways. The microphone techniques are different because, even with multi-mic setups, the objective is to capture the group as a whole rather than the individual players. The dynamic range is usually greater than that of a rock group or an electronic recording. Orchestral musicians are often musicians' union members, and producers have to observe union rules. A few minutes of overtime at the end of the session can cost a great deal more than was budgeted for. There is not much room for error and consequently the atmosphere is electric before and during a take. This can be simultaneously exhilarating and terrifying, especially the first few times. There is no good way to ease into the experience; the first time you are in charge, you realize that a mistake will be very expensive and embarrassing.

Bruce Swedien (Michael Jackson, Duke Ellington, Barbra Streisand) was Quincy Jones's engineer, right-hand studio person, and friend for four decades and went on to produce tracks for Michael Jackson. He recorded many of the great artists of the '50s, '60s,'70s, '80s, '90s, and on. Swedien spoke about recording Count Basie at Universal Studios in Chicago during the 1950s. As was customary at the time, the whole band was set up in the 80 x 50 x 30 foot room. The singer Joe Williams was in the room facing the band with gobos behind and on both sides of him. Swedien set up the room with the brass on a riser, the drums and bass as close as possible to each other, and the trumpets facing the saxophones, which were on the floor, playing into two mics. He recalled, "There was a lot of talking, foolishness and messing around," and there was no opportunity to "get a good level." This session had begun at 2 a.m. after the Basie band finished their club date, and much of their audience had followed them to the studio, so there was a sizable party crowd in the room. Swedien rolled tape, hit record, Teddy Reig slated, and as Basie gave the downbeat, the audience fell silent. Swedien's thought at that moment was, "Boy, that tape had better be rolling, because the performances were incredible!"[22]

With large groups, preparation is of the essence. By the time the musicians arrive, everything must be ready. The microphones should be set up, plugged up, line checked, phase checked, and rough levels set. Chairs and music stands should be set out, coffee made, and, with a little tweaking, you will be ready to roll.

OVERDUBBING LIVE MUSICIANS

Overdubbing usually involves one musician performing over previously recorded material or to a click track. The challenges are blending the overdubbed performance with the already recorded track and anticipating what remains to be recorded so that the part being overdubbed does not compete or clash with future parts. If a group of musicians performs together in the studio, even if they cannot see each other, they seem to feel the natural dynamic and tempo fluctuations that happen as they play. They can perform tightly as an ensemble even through tempo changes. However, once recorded, that communication between musicians—during a simultaneous performance—no longer exists. For overdubbing musicians, the task is to learn any idiosyncrasies of the already recorded tracks—particularly in the case of tempo shifts. Discrepancies tend to be additive, and an otherwise-tight track can be ruined by a single sloppy overdub.

Les Paul was a pioneer of the technique and had many hits overdubbing his own guitar parts and Mary Ford's vocals during the '40s and early '50s. Since the mid-1960s, it has become a standard way to make records outside of the jazz and classical fields. The process offers many advantages, not least of which is the opportunity for one musician to play several or all of the instruments. Collaborators can be time- and space-shifted to make an apparently simultaneous performance. It is relatively easy to change an arrangement or orchestration with overdubbed instruments because of the complete separation from other tracks. Additionally, the engineer's control over the sonic qualities of each instrument is much greater. The disadvantage is that results can be stiff or sterile because of the lack of interaction between the musicians. The response is one way—each subsequent player follows the earlier ones.

The band that honed this way of working to perfection was Steely Dan. Walter Becker noted:

> Back in the '70s, our big problem was trying to get the tracks with live musicians to be steadier and more mechanically perfect and so on. Whereas now, the big problem is trying to get the machine tracks to be more natural sounding and have more of the feel and variation of tracks played by real musicians.[23]

There are two basic approaches to overdubbing an album. One typical method is to lay, say, the drums for all tracks, then the bass parts, guitars, and vocals, with any additional instrumentation such as percussion, strings, horns, or whatever being recorded after the basic band tracks. The other method is to try to complete the instrumentation and vocals on each track before moving on to the next. In either case, instruments and vocals can be recorded in whatever order makes sense to the band and producer. The advantages to building complete tracks as you go include a greater sense of satisfaction in hearing a nearly complete track, and the musicians pace themselves better and become less fatigued. Singers especially need breaks, and with the instrument-by-instrument method, they often have several consecutive days of vocals, which can tire their voices, increase psychological pressure, and produce substandard performances. Singers usually perform better for short periods later in the day; completing tracks as you go naturally enables that.

Sometimes, the budget and availability of musicians dictate that basic tracks be recorded first, especially if an expensive studio is needed for the drum or rhythm section tracking. It is undoubtedly easier to lay all the drum tracks one after another—once the mics and channels are set up—than it is to keep changing from one instrument to another. To that end, some producers like to set up all the channels for all instruments so that they can add a vocal or an instrument to any track at any time. This is a musical and inspiring way of building a track, enabling some spontaneity and everyone to hear the song develop quickly. It also gives the musicians an interesting schedule and tends to produce more varied sounds and performances than the first method.

THE PROGRAMMED SESSION

If a single factor distinguishes programmed sessions from those with musicians playing live, it is the absence of adrenalin. There may be excitement in the musical or technical ideas, but there is no "red light fever"—that sense of elation in capturing the creative moment. Programming parts is more akin to data entry; it is a process rather than a real-time performance. I noticed this immediately in the '70s when we began recording using the MC-8 MicroComposer; the process is more like writing notes on a page as in composition, arranging, and orchestration than performance. Programming is a progressive, cerebral and creative act that embodies its own sense of excitement and anticipation at the growing construction, but one that is distinctly different from performance. All options, including key and tempo changes, remain open until the final mix; this encourages procrastination and mind-changing, but it also provides a powerful tool to the decisive. As with many areas of production, DAWs have all but removed the distinction between the programmed and the performed, in that any performance can now be restructured to almost the same extent as step-entered data. Even when parts are played or sung, they can so easily be quantized, tuned, modified, edited, and corrected that the stress on accuracy during performance disappears. Producers can now make creative or necessitated choices as to how to record. Frank Zappa reputedly said, "The computer can't tell you the emotional story. It can give you the exact mathematical design, but what's missing is the eyebrows." However, he said this at an early stage in the development of music computing, and as it turns out, if the system is complex enough, the eyebrows can be programmed.

VOCAL SESSIONS

Evidenced by the abundance of articles written about the topic and the fact that vocal production specialists exist, many people consider vocals difficult to record. Technically, a vocal is simple to capture; use a good quality microphone, mic pre, compressor, and cable, optimize the gain structure, and the less you do, the better the vocal will sound. Capturing a compelling performance is another story. Auto-Tune made it possible to tune any voice, and the power of digital editing can fix timing errors. The greatest vocals on record may mostly be in time and in tune, but good timing and tuning do not define a thrilling vocal. A vocal must demand attention and, ideally, be well recorded with a nicely balanced frequency response and an appropriately managed dynamic range. Audio manipulation can significantly heighten a vocal's impact, but there is art, intuition, and psychology in capturing an emotionally powerful performance.

Of the numerous parameters involved in capturing a commanding vocal, some are quantitative, and others are qualitative and subtle. The song needs to have sufficient intrinsic value. It should also be appropriate for the singer. To take an extreme example: "Trans Europe Express" by Kraftwerk would not be well suited for interpretation by Frank Sinatra. The key must be perfect for the singer—a half step in either direction can undermine the delivery.

It is not a given that an artist will write in the correct key for his or her voice; they often write in one of the two or three keys they are most comfortable playing in. Most vocalists have enough range (the distance from their lowest to highest note) that they can sing a song in several keys, but there is usually one optimal key for a singer and a song. To some extent, the key is quantifiable, as with any instrument—the melody must fit comfortably within the singer's range—but there is always a qualitative consideration. Sometimes the producer has to decide which key emphasizes the singer's most attractive vocal qualities while best complementing the melody and lyrics.

The tempo has to allow for the intended interpretation of the words. No matter how good a groove sounds at a particular tempo, if the singer has to gabble the words, either the words or melody need rewriting, or the song requires recording at a slower tempo. Conversely, if there are uncomfortable gaps, the tempo may be too slow. There is an emotional and interpretive connection with tempo as well: Think about the entirely different weight that "With a Little Help from My Friends" has in Joe Cocker's version compared to the Beatles' original. This is not to imply that tempo is the sole parameter, but Cocker's version expresses a deeper meaning for those words, and the tempo is a factor. The backing track needs to be consistent with and sensitive to the intention of the song and the interpretation, leaving musical space in the orchestration and room in the frequency spectrum for the vocal.

Overly busy arrangements or too-dense mid-range frequencies behind the lead singer's lines will sabotage even the strongest vocal.

The singer's interpretive performance should conform to the lyrical content in the way that an actor's delivery needs to be consonant with the script and the character while avoiding over-emoting. With a singer experienced in recording, this happens intuitively and often without discussion, especially if the singer wrote the song and contributed to the arrangement. With inexperienced recording artists, it is sometimes necessary to discuss motivation, meaning, and attitude in the delivery. If you have to modify the singer's interpretation repeatedly, it can indicate a lack of artistic sensitivity, which can be hard to rectify. Singers in groups that have not recorded much sometimes give a singular and strident style of delivery that they have developed in order to hear themselves on stage. The studio allows a greater interpretative range, and this is where the producer's guidance can be invaluable. Recording is similar to making a film where intimacy is valued, and playing live is like stage acting where projection is perceived to be necessary.

Some producers micromanage vocals, defining every inflection and ornamentation; these are usually the auteurs when they are working with new artists. In order to record great vocals, it is not necessary for a producer to be a singer. Assuming that prior considerations are taken care of (a strong song, the right key and tempo), a well-rehearsed singer should be able to deliver a compelling vocal if you create a conducive atmosphere and comfortable environment for him or her. Session singers can perform under the most adverse circumstances. Conversely, artists have diverse idiosyncrasies, but I have not met any who prefer brightly lit or harsh environments. Low lights, perhaps candles, and a cozy atmosphere tend to be more favorable. This may mean creating a small booth using gobos if the studio is large. Some prefer a setup not in direct view of the control room and others favor a sightline to the producer. Do not forget a music stand for lyrics, should they need them, a chair or stool for in between takes, and somewhere convenient to place a drink.

Making sure that they can hear themselves is vital; this means setting up a headphone mix (foldback) that is both enjoyable and workable. An enjoyable mix may not necessarily be optimal for pitching, timing, interpretation, and volume. A workable foldback allows the singer to immerse him or herself in the atmosphere of the song while still being able to hear him or herself and the necessary rhythmic, melodic, and harmonic elements of the track enough to stay in time and in tune. Often, novice singers will ask for their headphone mix to be set up in a way that sounds good to them but does not support a good performance. When a normally in-tune and rhythmically accurate singer is having problems, an unworkable headphone mix is often the culprit. In addition to affecting intonation, too much of the singer's voice in the headphones encourages them to sing more quietly, and lowering the amount of voice they hear makes them project more. There may be no single more important or individualistic ingredient in capturing a good vocal than providing the singer with the ability to monitor themselves and the track appropriately.

Because the producer's job is to draw the best possible performances out of the artist, making the singer comfortable is sometimes more important than obsessing over a technically perfect recording. In some instances, this can mean recording a vocal with a handheld microphone in the control room or out with the band. Phil Ramone gave Frank Sinatra a handheld wireless mic during the *Duets* sessions at Capital Studios. Although he and engineer Al Schmitt were concerned about the sound quality and unreliability of wireless technology, they determined that Sinatra's comfort level was more important than the technical quality.[24]

A number of producers take this approach with excellent results. It is worth noting that if there is a possibility that dance remixes will be necessary, too much spill on the vocal can compromise the remixer's ability to break the track down or replace parts.

The studio can be an intimidating place for singers. Even the most outgoing and apparently confident stage performers can exhibit insecurities when recording. The producer's job is to create a safe, conducive environment so that singers can give their best performances. Even when specific problems are apparent, such as intonation, timing, or emotional interpretation, directly speaking to those issues is not always the best way to achieve the result that you want. The producer acts as a catalyst in these situations, maintaining an objective and calm demeanor, never appearing judgmental, and psychologically inducing the singer's optimum emotional state to elicit the performance. It is very helpful to know something about vocal technique and the projection of the voice from the body. Even experienced singers need coaching and gentle reminders such as "use a little more diaphragm," "a bit too much from your nose," "it's better when you stand," or "remember not to let your head tip back." However, timing and sensitivity are critical, and this kind of advice, as with intonation and timing comments, can only be given when the singer is completely comfortable with you, the material, and is "in the moment." Building trust is imperative.

The methodology can be very different when the producer is also the writer of the song, particularly if he or she is a good singer. The producer may have sung the demo and, when it comes to making the record, may expect the vocalist to sing the melody note-for-note and inflection-for-inflection, reproducing the demo. With inexperienced singers, this can work. They may deliver vocals that are beyond what they could come up with themselves. However, this may not work so well with artists who have established a style and want to do their own interpretation. Additionally, some singers do not have the technical ability to mimic the inflections of the demo or the producer. Some writer/singer/producers can be dogmatic about each inflection and ornamentation, insisting on stopping and punching in every time there is a deviation. This can be demoralizing for vocalists, destroying the flow of the performance, and may not produce the desired result.

Even the great Jimi Hendrix needed gentle handling in the studio. Eddie Kramer, who engineered many of his classic records, knew what it took to make him comfortable. Kramer said, "From the outset, he had strong reservations about his vocal ability—he never really liked the sound of his own voice." Kramer would partition him off and dim the lights and when the take was done, Hendrix would "poke his head around the screen and ask, 'How was that? Was that OK? Was it all right?'" Kramer said, "[I] would tell him it was fine because, when it came to his singing voice, Jimi needed all the confidence he could get."[25]

Pressure is the enemy of great performances, as Jimmy Jam points out: "Nine times out of ten, the scratch vocals are better than the real thing because the artist doesn't have the pressure—that 'this is it' rolling round in his or her mind." Jam and Lewis used to let the artist take the song home and learn it overnight, but Jam said, "We never do that anymore. You can catch gold while an artist is in the process of learning a song and playing around with addictive new melodies."[26] Jam cites Janet Jackson's lead vocal on "Escapade," one of the biggest singles from the *Rhythm Nation* album, as being a scratch vocal that made it all the way to the actual record.

Speaking from a singer's point of view, Steven Tyler of Aerosmith says,

> When I record my vocal tracks, I don't like to go in and just throw them down. I like to do them at my own pace, which is pretty quick anyway. I prefer to have six or seven tracks and keep singing the same song with different voices and in different ways. I like after hours vocals. It's what I did on *Get a Grip* and it's what I did on *Pump*. I go in there after the band leaves—so it's just me and an engineer. That's when I can have the most fun. No-one's listening and there's no pressure. After hours is when I can get closest to a song and its real meaning. The emotions that come out of me then are always in sync with the song.[27]

Producers recount endless tales of attempts to put singers at ease during a take. Perhaps none is more telling than Beatles engineer Geoff Emerick speaking about George Harrison recording vocals for "Something in the Way She Moves." This was on the *Abbey Road* album, their 12th. Though George was not a primary singer in the band, he had spent many hours in the studio and on stage performing and singing by this time. Emerick relates some of what they did to make Harrison comfortable:

> George was once again very nervous when it came time to do the vocal. No matter what we did to create a vibe—turning the lights down low, lighting incense—he just could not get comfortable. It was a difficult song to sing, but in the end, he did a magnificent job.[28]

Considering these artists had performed on stages in front of tens of thousands of people, the nervousness seems counterintuitive, but this is not limited to Tyler, Hendrix, or Harrison. The studio is a critical listening environment where any flaws are exposed; singers, like all recording musicians, have a sense of finality and a desire to make the performance perfect. Many are uncomfortable singing in front of a control room full of people. Even when you screen-off a vocalist so there is no visual contact with the control room, self-consciousness can negatively affect a performance. The producer's job is to provide a supportive environment. Having sung lead vocals myself, I have experienced how disconcerting it can be to expose yourself emotionally while being aware of your technical deficiencies, only to hear people talking, laughing, or, worse, making negative comments when the talkback button is pressed.

There are those occasions when you are lucky enough to be in the studio with a truly great singer. Producers are invariably great fans of music and wonderful performances, but it is important not to become mesmerized when a vocalist is on the mic. Barry Beckett spoke about how the power of a Joe Cocker performance held him spellbound:

> He broke into a vocal that was just amazingly good on the first take. I was so totally enthralled that I forgot the structure of the song. At one point, he stopped singing and just stood there. The track was going on and I stopped the tape and said, "Is there something that we can help you with?" He said, "No, this is the instrumental part." He couldn't punch in. Dylan was the same way. They are among a few who just can't punch in. They would have to do the vocal all the way from the top, good or bad.[29]

Beckett added,

> I felt stupid as hell. What made matters worse is that I only had one remaining track when I got the tape. . . . I was scared to death that we were going to pass up something else. I could have put it into "input," and done it all the way from the top, but I might have had something else just as good. He ended up being maybe one percent off what I was hoping for, but it was still good.[30]

Beckett touches on an old-time production dilemma—whether to record over a good take in hopes of a better one. Thanks to unlimited virtual tracks on DAW systems, this is no longer a problem.

There is no process as individual as vocal recording and none that requires as much nurturing, sensitivity, and focus on the part of the producer. We can correct so many problems using technology, but despite all the available processing power, the core performance comes from a person. The human voice is the most powerful way of conveying emotion and meaning through music, and there will always be room for great singers, commanding performances, and producers who can draw the best out of them.

Which Method Makes a Better Record—Live, Overdubbed, or Computer?

T-Bone Burnett says that he still prefers using real musicians, and he does not like the overuse of computers in music.

It's good for things to speed up and slow down and be out of tune. Besides being conceptually correct, it's also emotionally true. People even try to program flaws into the music, but it's not the same. Once you program a flaw, it's no longer a flaw; it's a program.

On the other hand, Manfred Mann, who has been recording using a combination of live musicians and computers for decades, is of the opinion that when records ceased to be played live and started to be built up by overdubbing, a lot of the "feel" was lost. He told me,

> If you do live overdubs on a computer track, the musicians are playing to something that is known to be in time. Before computers, if the basic track was not solid, you were layering discrepancy on top of discrepancy.

For better or for worse, certain kinds of music would not have come into existence without computers. I was fortunate enough to be at the forefront of the application of computers to popular music. It was very exciting to realize I could program parts that would otherwise be impossible to play, and I could program all the instruments without having to be able to play them and without having to have my ideas filtered through another musician. Suddenly composers and arrangers were not just the authors of the parts but, for the first time, were fully in control of the performance subtleties. Computers enabled us to separate technical proficiency from creativity. Nonetheless, a bad computer track has little to commend it, even if it is technically proficient.

I think most of us have heard technically proficient musicians "going through the motions," playing without communicating. Music has the capacity to communicate many different emotions and moods, although musicians and instruments vary in their expressive capabilities. The human voice is the most expressive instrument, which is in part because of its immense flexibility: There are no frets or keys or tempering, so all notes, scales, microtones, and inflections are available along with a wide range of timbres. The voice is hardwired to our thoughts and feelings; if someone is stressed, it is easy to hear it in their voice. Additionally, the human voice has access to language. The guitar and its long line of ancestors and relatives have been popular in many cultures for thousands of years, most likely because of their versatility and expressiveness. Other instruments such as the Hammond organ (with an on/off switch keyboard) are inherently less expressive, but talented and sensitive players such as Jimmy Smith learned to manipulate it to generate emotionally charged and exciting music. It seems that a desire to express an inner feeling fuels our drive to make music, and a great musician can articulate emotion using two pieces of wood.

Computers are tools just like the guitar, the Hammond organ, a paintbrush, or a pen, through which musicians, painters, or writers can express themselves. Accomplished musicians and producers have always used the tools available to make great music. But, computers are not simply another performance tool: They blur, and sometimes erase, the line between composer and performer. The recording, in many cases, becomes both the score and the performance, changing the producer's relationship to the composition, performance, and production. This process began decades before DAWs became available but lies at the core of much of the criticism of DAW techniques that involve maximal manipulation.

There will most likely always be some backlash against new technologies. Sometimes, even younger musicians, producers, and engineers who have rediscovered older methodologies and equipment resist new technologies. Many musicians, engineers, and producers who come from the time when everything was necessarily live and analog understand the limitations of that equipment and see new technologies for what they are: new tools.

Miles Davis embraced electronics, computers, drum machines, and synthesizers in the middle of his career, beginning in the '60s. Rudy Van Gelder, jazz recording engineer of the '50s and '60s, was an early convert to digital recording. He said, "I believe today's equipment is fantastic.... I wouldn't want to face a session without the editing capabilities of digital."[31] He also enjoys the fact that digital offers "the ability to record without tape hiss [and] very low distortion if you know how to do it...."[32]

Herbie Hancock has been recording since his first solo album for Blue Note in 1962, after which he played piano with the groundbreaking and virtuosic Miles Davis groups of the '60s. He may be better known for his innovative use of electronics (the album *Future Shock* and instrumental hit "Rock-it") than he is for his acoustic piano artistry. Hancock covers the gamut of possibilities, using live musicians, machines, acoustic instruments, and synthesizers on his records.

"Overall, we record in a very old-fashioned way," says Jimmy Jam of Jam and Lewis. "We just turn on the tape and go for the gold. That's how you make those wonderful mistakes that give your song the unique touch you're looking for." However, Jam and Lewis's sense of the "old-fashioned" embraces the use of programmed drums or beats on their recordings.

Clearly, there is no right or wrong way to make records. There may be, more or less, appropriate tools and processes for any specific session, but producers now have many options. Nonetheless, the methodology that a producer employs has a telling impact on the overall sound and the attitude or emotion conveyed, which, in turn, determines how the record is perceived and received by industry and public alike. There are no hard- and-fast rules, but the aesthetic qualities of a production need to complement the commercial and artistic intentions of the stakeholders. Artists and labels often pick producers by the sound of their previous work or their reputation for a certain style of recording. Understanding your strengths and weaknesses is useful in finding the right projects. As an artist, knowing what end result you want and matching that to the methodology is critical. Some producers define themselves by their sound, which is a product of their methodology and choice of technology. Others embrace a wider range of tools and processes, adapting their approach to the specific needs of the project.

What Are "They" Going to Expect of You?

Bill Cosby once said, "I don't know the key to success, but the key to failure is trying to please everybody." Producers must meet many expectations in making a record, some of which can seem incompatible. Supporting the artist's objectives is important, but there are times when an artist, because of inexperience or other factors, wants to pursue a direction that the producer does not think will meet their stated goals. Labels sometimes push against the artist's desires, and managers occasionally weigh in too, producing tensions that result in delicate political situations for the producer to resolve. These test a producer's mettle, diplomacy, and persuasiveness, and in many ways cut to the essence of the art of record production.

THE ARTIST

The artist wants the album of his or her life. If it reflects their every whim and indulgence, they will be happy on the day it is completed. They may be happy for slightly longer when the A&R person gives it a provisional stamp of approval saying, "Sounds great, let me live with it for a couple of weeks." However, this is A&R speak for "I am going to play it to the marketing and promotion staff, my boss and my kids." If all approve, there may be further guarded endorsements. It is my observation that artists often misinterpret this process and hear highly qualified statements as resounding approbation. Maybe artists are not accustomed to the daily guile of corporate life. Everyone at the label will take full responsibility for the record the moment it is a bona fide hit. Regardless of prior praise, apportionment of blame begins when a record falls short of marketplace expectations. The producer is, with some justification, held responsible. The cautionary note is that there may be a gap between the artist's creative sensibility and what is needed for a successful record. Solving this conundrum is another part of the art of music production.

Alan Moulder believes that bands want to have creative input and want the producer to be their creative ally, supporting and trying their ideas. Albhy Galuten was part of the production team with Karl Richardson and the Bee Gees during their successful Miami period. Richardson, Galuten, and Barry Gibb were in the control room most of the time. Galuten described the roles as Richardson being the engineer, Gibb as the visionary, and himself as the translator. Gibb would play a song to Galuten, who would hire musicians and work out parts and arrangements. Galuten described the process as being collaborative with many talented people, and primarily the three of them "in the studio, all day, every day."[33]

In this case, the group was able to fully realize and extend their creative ideas through a skilled and complementary team. Sometimes bands have disparate influences that they have not managed to pull together into a coherent direction, which is when a producer's perspective can help. The late Michael Hutchence of the Australian band INXS said that they were "scrambling for a style...trying to mix rock and funk" when they met producer Mark Opitz. He was able to "put that into some aural context" for the album *Shahooh Shahooh*. Hutchence said, "We made a giant leap forward. Suddenly it was, 'Ah! We see the light.'"[34]

Although results are the ultimate measure of how a producer did, the pleasure of the process cannot be overlooked. Recording an album often takes months, and artists need to enjoy the journey and feel that the producer is helping them reach beyond what they could have achieved on their own. Even artists who work with auteur producers need to feel included and that they have some control over their destiny. Despite the fact that auteur producers tend to define almost every note and inflection, the best ones demonstrate respect for the artists through conversation, listening, and incorporating the artists' preferences and proclivities into the production.

Supporting an artist does not mean that a producer cannot try to steer them in a different direction. Amidst the anxieties, discussions, and debates that ensue, artists need to feel that the producer has their best interests at heart and that the working atmosphere is affirmative and creative. Hostility, incivility, and uncertainty are not conducive to good performances. It is better to hand over a project to someone else if a producer loses respect for the artist.

When you are dealing with famous artists, things can become bizarre. Jack Douglas was sworn to secrecy when he was hired to produce *Double Fantasy* for John Lennon, who had recorded guitar or piano versions of the songs on a little Panasonic machine. He sent Douglas the tapes, instructed him to hire musicians, and book a studio, indicating that if he told anyone who the artist was, the project would be canceled. Douglas arranged and wrote out the tunes, and hired Tony Levin, Andy Newmark, Earl Slick, Hugh McCracken, and George Small, all musicians around the same age as Lennon. Douglas sang Lennon's parts at rehearsals; the sessions were booked at The Hit Factory in New York, and the musicians did not know whom the artist was until the night before the first session.

As mentioned in chapter 1, functional typology defines the role the producer plays and implicitly sets the artists' expectations. The consultative producer gives guidance and counsel that, ideally, the artist perceives as valuable. An auteur producer makes the record with minimal input from the artist, aside from vocals. The facilitative producer will be in the studio at all times, complementing and supporting the artist. A collaborative producer creates a sense of partnership and creative give-and-take. The enablative producer sets up scenarios in which artists can define themselves.

THE RECORD COMPANY

The producer is the label's representative on the project, although most producers do not characterize themselves this way. The budget is always the producer's responsibility, even though he or she may not have control over the choice of studio or which days the artist shows up. If you are working with successful artists, they might unexpectedly fly to London for a couple of days to film a TV show, to Milan to stock up on clothes, or LA for an awards ceremony. TV film crews sometimes show up, with little notice, to film them recording the new album. These introduce scheduling complications and delays that dwindle the budget and demand strong communications skills. When uncontrollable delays happen, it is important to notify the label and negotiate so that it will not compromise their perception of you or cost you money via the overage clause or all-in budget.

The genre of music affects the expectations that a company has of the producer. Alan Moulder tends to work with (big-selling) indie/alternative-type bands. Speaking of the label's expectations, he said,

> They want a good-sounding record and no problems. They don't really care how you got it. Some are more involved than others; some of them are down there a lot and others stay completely away.

He understands the importance of giving the company "something they can work with" and says that they like to hear a good progression from what the band has been doing, a good change, or at least what they think the band should be doing. He feels fortunate that A&R departments and managers do not get too creatively involved with the kinds of bands with which he works. They give the bands a lot of freedom. He commented to me,

> There is less commercial pressure because the band is known to go its own way and do its own thing. When I've worked on more commercial projects, there have been a lot more problems, a lot more A&R comment, and a lot more pressure.[35]

The cycle constantly turns; the indie/alternative/rock genres, for instance, spawned some of the biggest selling albums of the 1990s. When there is a potential for a big hit on the mainstream charts, there are likely to be outside opinions and pressure to deliver the elusive hit single that will appeal to radio programmers.

Producers working for major labels and most independents are expected to deliver an album that will sell to the labels' projections or beyond. For a small label, this might be 10,000 units or less, but the majors and large indies typically need much bigger sales than that. Niche labels tend to place importance on the appropriateness of the music for their market, knowing that there is an audience of a certain size for a well-produced album of that type. Understanding a label's expectations is a wise move.

THE ARTIST'S MANAGER

Some managers are extremely hands-on, spending a great deal of time with the artist and micromanaging every detail. Others call in every now and then from another continent. Alan Moulder says, "If the manager has a close relationship with the band, then you tend to deal with him and have to deal with him more than if it's someone sitting in an office, miles away." He adds, "They all expect you to make things go as smoothly as possible," but he generally does not feel pressure from the artist's management. Managers want success for their artist and a peaceful life. Management may even be a more difficult job than producing. Managers juggle a great deal of politics, and the support you can expect from the artist's manager can be shallow. Producers are a means to an end. If you keep the artist and the label happy and produce a big-selling album, the manager will be an enthusiastic ally. If relationships become shaky in any direction, the manager hears all voices and balances all concerns. When the next album cycle arrives, he or she may support the idea of another producer. Strong artist management is important for the producer. A manager can influence the label's commitment to promotion and marketing, keep a band signed through tough times, and revive flagging careers. Understandably, artist managers' first priorities are to themselves and their artists.

4

What Are the Timeless Ingredients in a Hit?

Creatively speaking, this list begins with "the song," but a hit is the end product of a complex of processes. Lauren Christy of The Matrix immediately responded, "[T]he label and the right president," citing Arista and its then president L.A. Reid, who "was totally ready to kick ass with" Avril Lavigne. "He heard 'Complicated' and said, 'Oh my goodness, this is amazing.'"[1] Christy is the first producer I spoke with who made this insightful observation. With the major labels continuing to consolidate, the chances of losing the artist's A&R person, label, or entire international music group, mid-production, has increased manyfold. Despite the importance of the right label and personnel, Christy cautioned that it is "a very dangerous guessing game" to try to choose a project because "it's this person at this label." They manage the uncertainty by concentrating on being creative, loving what they do, and putting "100 percent into it." She said she has had her "heart broken before" over failed records and now tries not to be "attached to anything because it's out of your control." She noted that it is in not only the hands of "the label, the president, and the promotion department," but also "whether that artist is going to press the self-destruct button." When she turns on MTV and sees it, she regains enthusiasm, "but most of the time I think, 'I've done my best, there's nothing I can do now.'"[2]

Good managers help their producers avoid volatile corporate situations, but when corporate acquisitions happen, it can be impossible to predict changes that might take place between signing a production contract and the release date of the record. At a time when more artists are retaining rights and releasing their own recordings, a strong creative and business team is necessary for their success. An independent artist with an effective team can offer reassuringly stable support for an outside producer. In any event, producers have to focus on factors they can control, and that brings us back to the song.

The Song (or Material)

The definition of hit material varies widely from one genre to another, but there are consistent factors. Christy described the song as "the right melody, the right lyric that's emotional—to me it has to be an emotional lyric."

Simon Cowell said, "If you've got Max Martin as your writer, you have a better chance of having a worldwide hit than with anyone else."[3] Martin wants to understand the artist he is writing for and before he starts, he talks to them, sees their shows, and finds out what they are listening to. He said, "I want the input because that makes the chemistry of the song." He claims that less than one-third of 1 percent of his ideas are ever turned into demos, saying, "You have to be a mass murderer and kill your darlings." He reputedly keeps reworking parts of songs until he is happy with them.[4]

Dr. Luke told Matt Popkin of *American Songwriter Magazine* that in order to make a hit, he needs to make people go "Wow!" by creating a sense of "urgency" and "musical moments that are 'intrinsic and alarming,' such as a sax player holding a high note and a drummer playing a rapid solo across the kit."[5]

Working in entirely different genres, Rick Rubin is just as emphatic when he says, "I think the most important thing a producer can do is spend time getting the songs into shape before recording. The material is so much more important than the sounds."

L.A. Reid, who subsequently helmed Arista, Island Def Jam, and Epic Records, said that, during his time with the L.A. and Babyface writing and production team, they were "not that into high tech" because they "concentrate on great lyrics and awesome grooves." He thinks they would neglect "the most important aspect of a song"—the melody—if they paid to much "attention to technical tricks." Reid said, "The melody is what we pick up on when we're listening to a song. And isn't that what loving music is all about—being a good listener?"[6]

Ron Fair, ex-chairperson of Geffen Records thinks that "the most absolutely critical production move" is asking, " 'what is the song?' That is the most important thing. Everything else is secondary to me."

In pop music, the song is the primary determinant of a hit. For those who are not fans of the pop charts, this statement can seem antithetical because of the apparent musical and lyrical simplicity of many big hits. However, that deceptive conciseness is a decisive factor in whether a song is a universal hit or not. Katy Perry and singer/songwriter Bonnie McKee wrote "Teenage Dream," which spent more than 300 weeks on various international charts, ascending to number one on several. According to a *Sound On Sound* article by Paul Tingen, they had rewritten the song four times when they played it for Dr Luke, who did not think it was a hit yet and said that it needed to be " 'Benny-proofed' because 'if Benny doesn't get it, America won't get it.' " Benny, as in Benny Blanco, estimates that they rewrote the song seven times:

> You keep cracking away at it, and you know when it is right. You really have to grab people. A song has to be captivating and it has to be relate-able. Nobody wants to listen to a song they can't relate to. A song needs to grab people's attention within the first 10 seconds, otherwise they're going to the next song. And you have to hold their attention for the entire duration of the song.

A song today is like an hour-long DJ set condensed into three minutes. You start, you build things up, you bring them back down, you build them up again. There, continuously, has to be something exciting to the ear, and that has to keep changing throughout the song. The structure of the song: every time it changes—i.e., intro, verse, pre-chorus, chorus—has to be signposted. You can't just flow things, it has to be like "Bam! A new part is coming in!" Even if it's not immediately apparent, on some level the listener has to go: "Oh, wow— that sounds different!"[7]

Many writers have difficulty rewriting and reworking their songs. They would rather write a new one, but the iterative process refines and perfects every aspect so that it works the way it should. As a producer, you can spend much time massaging performances and arrangements, but a fundamental weakness in the song will limit the success of the record. The reasons for recrafting a song vary; pop writers do it for maximum chart impact, and others do it to make the statement they want to make, but in either case, the result is a more appealing song for the target audience. Writers of the stature of Bob Dylan, Joni Mitchell, and Rickie Lee Jones have meticulously rewritten songs to bring them to fruition.[8] Perhaps the most famous of all rewrites is Paul McCartney's two-year struggle with "Yesterday." Allegedly, he tinkered with the chords and for a long time was stuck on the lyric "scrambled eggs" that he had jokingly improvised. It was on a long drive that the words finally poured out of him.[9]

Hip hop and some other genres do not always feature what many people think of as a melody carried by a lead singer. As Phillip Tagg points out, in the *Encyclopedia of Popular Music of the World*, the definition of the term "melody" varies. In some languages, it refers to the whole song with accompaniment. In general, it is a monodic sequence, or series of single notes with rhythmic profile and pitch contour that we perceive as a musical foreground statement separate from the accompaniment and harmony. There are many other parameters associated with melody. The important consideration in this context is that hip hop songs can be considered as such, even if a lack of tonal articulation in the pitch contour does not fit the standard description. Additionally, hit songs are not entirely reliant on a main vocal melody. Underlying harmony affects perception, as can the rhythmic structure or groove, additional rhythmic, melodic, and sonic hooks, and any lyrical content. Examples would be the guitar riff in the Rolling Stones' "Satisfaction," which may be more memorable than the vocal melody and the harmonic progression in "One Note Samba" that sets off the single-note melody line.[10]

A great song can be obscured by poor production. One way this can happen is if the accompaniment or overdubs are allowed to overpower or crowd the vocal melody; Jerry Wexler purportedly referred to this as being "track happy." On extensively overdubbed projects, I always begin by laying a guide vocal. I have also found that having the melody sung is just as important when recording a band live in the studio. Without the melody, some musicians fill the holes they hear, forgetting how their parts are supposed to fit around the vocal. Guide vocals are far from a perfect solution because a great vocal performance can uplift the performance of all the musicians. Occasionally, the guide rises to that level but if not, the presence of the melody and lyrics still provides a focal point and creates a mood for the supporting elements of the song to accommodate.

Lyrics are also important in the success of a song, and the kinds of lyrical content in songs that sell well vary from genre to genre. But are there common-alities in the best-selling songs? In 2011, *American Songwriter* published an article analyzing the 17 number-one songs from *Billboard*'s 2010 Hot 100 chart. They used the Flesch-Kincaid (F-K) readability test, which is embedded in Microsoft Word and used by the military to check the readability of training manuals. The results showed that 16 of the 17 number-one songs were written at a reading level of first grade or below, and the 17th (by Eminem) was around second-grade level. The assessment of readability is based on the average number of words in a sentence, the average number of syllables in a word, word length as measured by letters, and the number of complex words (more than two syllables). All but two songs measured at 100 percent (the highest level of readability), and the two outliers were within 5 percent of the maximum. It should be noted that this test was designed for prose, not songs, and the resulting information does not constitute a repeatable scientific formula (i.e., writing a song that scores 100 percent on the F-K scale will not guar-antee a hit). Nonetheless, the consistency of the results does indicate a statistically strong correlation between the simplicity of a lyric and a song's hit potential.[11]

George Martin has the final word: "The most important person is the songwriter."[12]

The Vocal

George Martin's quote goes on to say: "The second most important person is the artist who performs it."[13] Like Martin, most producers pick the singer as the second most important element in creating a hit. Nonetheless, a great vocal is more diffi-cult to quantify than a hit song. Greatness in a vocal can often have less to do with technical performance or recorded quality and more to do with communicating the intangible emotional content of the song and the unique character of the artist. There are vocals that are regarded as important in the pantheon of recorded music that exhibit pitch issues and audible distortion or other sonic artifacts.

Barry Beckett, of the influential Muscle Shoals rhythm section, produced an award-winning vocal on a Bob Dylan album, which he says they cut live:

> He had been singing those songs over and over to himself, so he had them down backward and forward. He would just get it on the first pass, which blew me away. I did insist on trying to punch him in on one line, but we couldn't match the voice, so we just let it go. He later won the award for Best Vocal on

that song, which was "Slow Train Coming." I went up to him later and said, "I give up." He just laughed.[14]

"I'm looking for voices that are distinctive," said Dr. Luke. "That's the most important thing to me. I mean, obviously they have to be able to sing." Speaking about Britney Spears, he said, "She gets it done, she's pretty focused when she gets in and records, and she sounds good fast, you know? She's a lot busier than I am, so she comes in and gets it done and she's out."[15]

"What I do is only as good as the vocal, particularly when I'm doing a remix," says Danny Saber:

> If there's a good vocal then it's easy. A good vocal is not necessarily something that's sung really well. It's when the lyric goes with the voice that it's coming out of. When the whole thing clicks, then that's special. You can't teach that to anybody, they've either got it or they haven't.[16]

Lauren Christy said that, after the song, "It has to be the right artist, the voice is very important."

Although difficult to quantify, the greatest artists and the ones with longevity, for the most part, have a uniquely identifiable sound and style. Some genres use heavy vocal processing, making the sound more electronic than organic, but the artists that succeed with this sound still manifest a recognizable identity.

The Arrangement

"You nurture every song to make it as good as possible, but a single has to be attractive in a more obvious way," says Steve Lipson. "You don't always need a gimmick. The arrangement has to be exactly right, unquestionably. I learned a lot about that from Trevor [Horn]." Given a strong song and artist, influence over the arrangement is one of the most powerful tools a producer has and can spell the difference between success and failure.

There are two parts to an arrangement, the orchestration and the form or structure. Orchestration is the combination of instrumentation (real and virtual) and the way those instruments work together rhythmically, harmonically, and melodically. The term dates back to the early 19th century, referring to the scoring of parts for an orchestra. The dynamic development or ebb and flow of the track through the addition, subtraction, and changing of parts or voices, including stops and breakdowns, develops the piece. In a recording context, orchestration is often achieved through programming, electronic treatment, and balancing or mixing, rather than by being scored and played. Equalization and the use of reverb, delay, panning, techniques affecting presence, and other effects can be considered part of orchestration. A good orchestrator considers not only the range of the instruments, but also the timbre to maintain clarity and interest. Too many instruments or voices centered in one frequency range can make a mix bottom-heavy, muddy, unclear, harsh, or too bright. Level adjustments, equalization, and other electronic treatment can resolve the problem.

Good orchestration maintains clarity in the mix. It ensures that each element of the track occupies its own space in the audio spectrum and does not compete with other parts. For creating the immediacy needed for a widely popular track, after the song and the vocal performance, the arrangement is paramount. The term "arrangement" denotes a version of a piece of music,[17] and it is possible to register an original arrangement of a public-domain song for which you can receive royalties. Sometimes arrangements are part of the songwriting process, but often melodies, chord sequences, and lyrics are written, and it isn't until the arrangement is finalized that the song has that compelling "play it again" quality.

We do not tend to think about the orchestration of popular music in the same terms as that of a symphony orchestra, but the number of instruments, sounds, and parts on a pop record can match or exceed that of an orchestra. Dr. Luke told ABC's Steven Baker that Katy Perry's song "Teenage Dream" comprised 182 tracks.[18] Even though many of these parts may be nonessential, they contribute to the overall effect and impact of the record and must be blended as any composer, orchestrator, and conductor would.

No matter how beautiful the orchestration, if the structure or form of the song is less than optimum, the track will meander, confusing the listener and thwarting the potential for a hit. The terms "form" and "structure," while being the best we have, are problematic because they have many definitions in music theory. In popular songs, form often refers to the song form, such as blues (often but not always 12 bars with a I, IV, V chord sequence), AABA, ABAB, ABAC (often four eight-bar sections that are then repeated), multi-sectional, or multi-strain, etc. These are usually 12, 16, or 32 measures embodying the basic material that repeats several times in the course of a three- or four- minute version.

Regardless of the underlying song form, recordings usually comprise additional elements: introductions, interludes, breakdowns, instrumentals, outros, etc. that are not part of the song form. They are part of a production and significant in imparting a satisfying flow to the record. The order of these parts along with the repetition of the basic elements of the song is what I am referring to as structure. How these sections flow from one to another is vital to a successful production.

In summation, the structure of a recording is the combination of the underlying song form, additional elements, and the order in which they occur. If you think of a song as being a museum or art gallery full of interesting objects, the structure works like a curated tour. If you wandered around the museum without guidance, you might leave before you found the best part. Good structure gives a recording maximum impact on the first listen, helping the listener learn the song as it unfolds, with some surprises. It must then hold the listener's interest through repeated listens. Balancing immediacy with repeatability is a major challenge of popular music production.

Artists' demos are rarely structured or orchestrated in their best form. The artist or writer who can optimize a piece may not need a producer, and we see this with artist/ producers such as Gotye, David Guetta, and Calvin Harris. Developing bands often write some appealing parts, such as a verse and chorus indicating potential for a hit, but these usually need additional treatment and organization. Producers often have to generate new sections including intros, outros, instrumental sections, stop sections, breakdowns, and sometimes bridges or middle eights (even when they are not eight bars). These parts may be able to be co-opted from elements elsewhere in the song to create a section that contributes to the flow of the recording.

Intros are usually short instrumental setups, using material from the body of the song. Outro is a relatively new term (replacing "coda") for a section that mostly uses elements from the song to create a satisfying conclusion or fadeout to the piece. As in jazz and blues, instrumental sections, stop sections, and breakdowns usually conform to the harmonic structure and, most often, the tempo of one or more of the parts of the song. Bridges, middle eights, releases, B sections, pre-choruses, and channels are terms confusingly used somewhat interchangeably to indicate various parts of a song. The bridge is usually a single, non-repeating section of a song that contrasts with previous material, moves the song forward and, in many cases, introduces new lyrical information. Bridges may be forged from permutations of chords and/or melodic fragments that occur in the song but sometimes modulate to a related harmonic and melodic place, occasionally changing the rhythmic emphasis and/or tempo significantly. Not all songs need a bridge, but a well-constructed one lifts a song to a higher level of experience for the listener.

Producers often have to change the order and/or length of song sections and sometimes the transitions from one to another. Arrangement or structural adjustments of this nature can vastly improve the appeal and commercial impact of a song, and most producers regard this kind of contribution as part of the production. Writing a new bridge or original musical or lyrical material can constitute a co-write by the producer.

Overly long introductions and verses (A sections) are common arrangement problems. A rule of thumb says that the first chorus should begin in under 60 seconds; this is not a strict rule but rather a guideline. Radio program directors receive a plethora of new material, and they tend to stop listening if the intro does not command their attention or if they have to wait too long to hear the main hooks. Exiting the song on a strong hook, even if it is not the main chorus line, leaves listeners wanting to hear more. Thomas Alva Edison is credited with saying, "Genius is 1 percent inspiration, 99 percent perspiration."[19] Strong bridges generally indicate good songwriting skills and a work ethic because they are rarely part of the initial inspiration and demand additional creative effort. Regardless, all sections need to be strong and to flow well from one to another if a hit record is the objective.

It can be difficult to maintain objectivity when assessing a song that has good component parts but exhibits structural problems. In a competitive market, a lukewarm first impression means no second chance. The more often you listen to a song, the more your mind accommodates a convoluted arrangement. For this reason, producers need to act on first impressions. A well-organized structure makes it easy to appreciate a song on the first listen. The intro commands attention, the verse sets the scene and draws you in, a B section or channel lifts you from the verse to the chorus, and the chorus embeds itself in your brain melodically, harmonically, and with the emotional affect the song wants to elicit.

Bridges are often a respite from the reiteration of chorus and verse sequences and may contain a lyrical variation or conclusion. The outro might simply repeat choruses, mix and match content from the body of the song, or be a completely new section that leaves you wanting more. Instrumental sections offer relief from the vocal and can supplant or augment a bridge. When there is one, a lead solo instrument may ad-lib throughout the outro, ratcheting up the intensity to the end.

These rules still apply in formats where the track may not have a conventional melody (such as hip hop) but where there are melodic and rhythmic vocal elements that change and develop from one section to another. Although there are significant differences from one genre to another, a track's dynamics must evolve in a satisfying way to inspire a listener to add the song to their playlist. The producer is really the last resort for a song. If poor structure, uninspired orchestration, unmemorable melodies, or inconsequential harmonic sequences slip through into the mix, that track will be doomed to obscurity.

The Performance

Before the introduction of overdubbing, recordings were simply one simultaneous performance. It may have required many takes to capture the desired qualities and intensity, but what went on the record had to be performed together in the same place and in the same period of time that it would take to play the finished record. Overdubbing split that process apart. When I first became a studio musician, sessions always involved capturing a group of musicians at once and sometimes a whole orchestra—vocals were usually overdubbed. A common syndrome was that most would play their parts well, but someone would make a mistake. This might go on for several takes with different problems that the producer considered unacceptable. Eventually a take would be captured that was considered acceptable, but it might not be any of the musicians' best take—perhaps with no mistakes but not as fresh as the first two. Mistakes were, for the most part, not repairable except by cutting between takes or recording an edit piece for the offending section.

Overdubbing went some way toward solving this problem; each musician optimized his or her performance without being dependent on others. Punching drums in or out was still not possible at that time, so the drum part had to be a complete take. If the first take was good for the drummer but the bass player made a mistake, the take would be kept and the bass mistake corrected by punching in and out. Perfection was easier to achieve, but sessions were not as much fun, and the chemistry between the musicians became a construct rather than a reality. Computer sequencing, drum machines, and eventually digital audio workstations (DAWs) extended this mental and emotional construct making it possible to fix any detail, but removing the interaction between the musicians and also the interaction between a musician and time. Even real-time performances into a computer can be (and are often) adjusted, mitigating the urgency and adrenalin of the performance. However, producers have been creating illusory soundstages and perfecting performances via multiple takes since Edison. They have pieced together faux joint performances from individual overdubs since the late 1940s. With programmed tracks, the producer imagines the performance into existence. This is not to say that a programmed performance needs to emulate a real one, but even if it is clearly ersatz, it must communicate an attitude and energy envisioned by the producer and artist to achieve its goals.

Of course, new methodologies do not completely invalidate or replace the old, and there are still many records made with musicians performing together in the studio. Bruce Fairbairn took the view that "production should always come secondary to capturing a moment." He liked to capture "something great on tape" so that he had a "solid base" to which he could add "the production aspects, mixing in texture and color to the tracks."[20]

Some records need to have a sense of urgency, chemistry between musicians, and some organic imperfection. This entails much more than documenting a performance or performances in tune, in time, and at the right levels. Ideally, producers create an environment in which they incite and inspire the artist's release of imaginative and emotional energy. They use recording technology and techniques to capture and optimize that energy and emotion in order to communicate it to a diverse audience under a wide range of listening conditions.

It is possible to fabricate energy and emotion using studio contrivance, but there is an old studio adage: If you want a great guitar sound—get a great guitar player. Accomplished musicians express emotion through their instruments, and everything they do from choosing the instrument, to how they set it up, and the way they play it is, consciously and subconsciously, working toward communicating what they are feeling. This is true for every instrument, real or virtual, whether the performance is in real time or painstakingly created note by note using a mouse. Irrespective of methodology, these are all creative processes and as such need a sheltered environment where the performer feels empowered to make choices that communicate his or her musical and emotional objective. The producer's job is to allow the performer the space to feel, and to reach for greatness, or as Lauren Christy puts it, "to dare to suck."

Producers have to capture performances, discern the excellent from anything less, and protect the chosen performance through the mix. Even with programmed parts, there is a performance element. No matter how a sound is made, by playing an instrument or by clicking a mouse, we are on a quest for the, sometimes unquantifiable, superior set of musical choices. The differences may be subtle, but when you press play months or years later, you can still identify that one take, track, or version that stands out from the others

Nathan Adan Adam presented a paper at the 2006 Art of Record Production Conference on the impact of digital editing on the last bastion of live rhythm tracks: modern country music.[21] Some country producers still favor the unprocessed performance of the musicians. As Chuck Ainlay said to me, "These are the best musicians in the world."[22] However, others are seeking digital perfection. Although the performances are real, the degree of alignment, time stretching, instrument pocketing, and sound replacement calls into question what is real and what is synthetic. This is an inevitable progression from Edison's idealized performances of more than a century ago. Since that time, the power to perfect a performance has progressively increased to a point where there is debate about whether it is use or abuse of technology. A moral stance on correction is pointless because the market ultimately determines whether the techniques that producers use are worthwhile or not. Moreover, the option to capture a live performance without editing or correction still exists. Regardless of whether a performance is natural or synthetically aligned to a producer's mental image, a production and all its elements must convey a synergistic energy that the audience perceives as an emotionally stimulating performance.

The Engineering

There is probably no concept that is confused and conflated more with production than engineering, because there is no clear demarcation between them. When people speak of a well-produced record, they are often referring to a record that sounds good. Some (but not all) of the reason why a record sounds good can be attributed to the engineering. A track that does not sound good but is a hit (and they do exist) could be called well-produced—if we think, as most labels do, that the producer's job is to generate hits. Additionally, many (perhaps most) producers now engineer at least part of their productions. For much of the 20th century, engineers oversaw all the technical aspects of the recording, while the producer focused on the musical and interpersonal facets. It is easy to forget that the earliest recorders frequently ran the technology, as well as dealing with the performers. The position eventually split into director of recording and technician (or other such titles) but with similar roles to what we now know as producer and engineer. In any case, exemplary engineering alone may not create a hit, although most hits are well engineered. Substandard engineering can detract from the accessibility of a recording. As Les Paul said, "Good quality is terribly important to a hit record ... it's what's in the grooves that sells." Of course, what is "in the grooves" also refers to the song, the arrangement, the performances, and so forth. Bruce Swedien learned from Bill Putnam (engineering innovator of the '50s and Swedien's early mentor) to think musically "more than in technical terms" when it comes to recording instruments.

This reflects the fact that the engineering is a part of the orchestration, and the sonic choices are not, in principle, much different from a 19th-century orchestrator choosing reeds over brass for a particular section. These choices, such as which microphone, what placement, the EQ, compression, expansion, effects, and so on, optimize the recorded quality and make the production interestingly varied, introducing clarity, depth, and dimension or whatever qualities the work needs.

Great songs deserve great sonics. It is glorious listening on a quality system when there are no painful or annoying frequencies, the highs are sweet, the middle is smooth, and the lows are tight and deep. Good engineering best presents the key components of a track in less-than-optimum listening environments, such as the car or the subway (where there is frequency masking from ambient noise) and in public places at low levels.

On a really well-produced track, production, engineering, mix, and arrangement are impossible to parse; they are synergic and seamless. "They are discrete entities and may be done by different people [but] they are incredibly interactive," says Andy Jackson. He gives the example of a Frankie Goes to Hollywood record where "those things all worked together as a package. Not a great song but great records and justifiably big hits."[23]

How Important Is the Mix?

In unamplified live performances, musicians and singers adjust their relative levels by physically varying their loudness to achieve the artistic objectives of the composer, arranger, conductor, and/or performers. Until about 1925, acoustic recordings were balanced in much the same way: by careful placement of the performers around the recording horn, through the musical arrangement, and by the musicians controlling their own dynamics. The recorders also physically moved the vocalist (when not singing) away from the horn in order to allow the band to come through.

It was the adoption of the electric microphone and electric recording technology, in the mid-1920s, that allowed engineers and producers to electronically balance or mix constituent mic channels, albeit still in real time during recording. Some producers and engineers, such as Moses Asch (Folkways Records), continued for decades to record using a single microphone, placing musicians in the most favorable positions around the room and allowing them to dynamically balance themselves as in a live performance. For the first 60 or so years of recorded music history, balancing or mixing was performed live to the recording medium simultaneous with the musical performance. Les Paul's sound-on-sound recordings in the late '40s required live mixing of the overdub with the previously recorded material, but balancing was done in a series of time-separated layers instead of a single pass. His multitrack recording experiments in the '50s introduced mixing as a postproduction function that has now grown to be a considerable part of the production schedule and budget.

The terms "mix" and "remix" are sometimes used interchangeably, but in general, mix refers to the original mix of a track when the instrumentation and vocals are balanced with each other and any needed effects or treatments are added. Remix usually indicates that significant modifications have been made to the first mix and even the original instrumentation and vocal parts. The differences between an original mix and remix versions are usually not subtle. A mix or a remix can make a considerable difference to label, artist, and consumer perceptions and reactions to a track. I once remixed a track that was about to be dropped from an album. We had serious doubts about the basic song, so I took a radical approach but did not change the basic arrangement or instrumentation, just the quality of the sounds. The track became the first single from that album. I was happy that they liked the remix so much, but I expressed concern that the song was melodically weak and, sure enough, the single was not a big hit.

Andy Jackson thinks that "you can screw up a great [song]" with a bad mix but can rarely mix a bad song into a hit.[24] A mix should optimize the song, the vocal, the performances, the arrangement, and the engineering. It should sound good on a wide range of high- and low-end systems, and at any volume. It should be appropriate for the applicable format in a radio or club and hold its own in terms of apparent loudness or excitement with comparable material.

Timeliness

No matter how perfect the song, the vocal, the playing, the sounds, and the mix, if the recording sounds like an outmoded style, it will struggle to achieve widespread success. The most prominent artists in any movement often maintain loyal fans long after that musical sound has ceased to be a trend. Nevertheless, off-trend sales rarely match the artist's peak if their new recordings do not in some way blend with what is current. Revivals do happen, and many producers make a living working with artists who were most successful in the past. It is always important to understand and manage the artists' and labels' expectations, while knowing that subtle changes can shift a passé sound into one that fits into the current commercial soundscape.

It is worth examining artists who have had long careers and mainstream hits in more than one era. Listen to the difference between the sound of Bruce Springsteen's 1975 hit "Born to Run" and his 1985 song "Dancing in the Dark." Both are recognizably him and his style, but the production values shifted to align with the sounds of the era without undermining his musical integrity.

The Heart

Motivation is an important variable in sports success, and psychological research has identified several different types, intrinsic and extrinsic being two broad and extensively studied classifications. Intrinsic motivation is engagement in an activity for the pleasure and satisfaction of participation, whereas someone motivated extrinsically is engaging purely as a means to an end. The research indicates that those who are intrinsically motivated are more likely to realize a good outcome than those who are extrinsically motivated. This is consistent with my observation that believing in an artist, or having your heart in a project, appears more likely to result in success. That may seem like a truism, but experienced producers can do highly professional work when a project is not consistent with their own taste. The question we might ask ourselves before taking on a production is "Below what level of belief or motivation do we lose the necessary edge in a highly competitive marketplace?"

According to the *Encyclopedia of Applied Psychology*, several studies on motivation in sports have unequivocally shown that

> [e]xperimentally inducing intrinsic motivation, as opposed to extrinsic motivation, leads to several positive outcomes, including enhanced creativity, performance, and persistence. In other words, motivation matters.[25]

Most successful producers, and certainly the ones I know, mean what they do, are on a mission, believe in their work, and enjoy it immensely. The music business is challenging, and many voices speak to artists about what they should do if they want success. Sometimes artists want it so badly that they sacrifice what is unique and powerful about themselves. Jim Dickinson said that young bands that compromise "eliminate the very thing that might have gotten them across."[26]

That is a broad generalization, but the right producer for a particular artist can stimulate the artist to uncover his or her deepest objectives.

"I learned from Quincy Jones to trust my instincts," said Bruce Swedien, to "listen to that little voice" and to not "cerebralize the music too much because it has to communicate."[27]

Quincy Jones himself was pressured into producing artists when he knew it would not work. This confirmed for him "that you have to love and adore the sound the artist makes" and "the person too":

> Once that happens, you can treat the artist almost like you're an X-ray machine—to go into them emotionally and musically.... Then you know what gives them goose bumps; the kind of chord sequences, and sonorities, and colors or whatever it is that does it. I love to give singers I work for goose bumps all the time.[28]

This is not to say that producers should pursue their own artistic vision, but to believe in the project, to love the music, and be proud of what you are doing may be essential. It is challenging to make a great production from a cynical viewpoint. Good producers have broad tastes and can be chameleons, which is a fun facet of the job, but ideally you find that confluence where love of the music, respect for the artist, and a sense of satisfaction from doing a great job come together.

Are There Exceptions to These Rules?

There are very few hard-and-fast rules in the music business. Changing demographics, technologies, and social and economic circumstances interact in seemingly capricious ways. Poorly written songs and sonically substandard and badly constructed records with singers who lack attractive and distinctive vocal qualities do, on occasion, become hits. Still, in trying to formulate a theory and methodology that will produce consistent results, it serves no purpose to emulate the exceptions.

The increased dominance of vocal recordings since WWII may be the biggest change in the second half of more than century of recorded music. Through the first half of its history, instrumental records by artists such as Louis Armstrong, Duke Ellington, Count Basie, Benny Goodman, and Glenn Miller were the big sellers. Nowadays, it is rare for an instrumental recording to cross over to the mainstream chart. Nonetheless, even at the height of the swing era with superstar big bands like Benny Goodman's, most bands had singers, and vocal recordings were popular.

The same underlying principles apply today as they did 10, 20, 30, 40, 50, and more years ago, back to the beginnings of the recorded music industry. Regardless of the fact that the sound of recorded music constantly changes, most enduring hits comprise a song with a memorable melody or hook, a relatable lyric, a singer with a distinctive character, and appropriately arranged and orchestrated instrumental parts. This is as broadly true for today's commercially successful rap, country, pop, or rock records as it was for Bing Crosby's "White Christmas."

5

What Can You Expect from a Career as a Producer?

A career in production can range from producing just one track to a lifetime of Grammy awards and platinum albums. As we discuss later, there is a world of interesting and fulfilling production work outside of awards and million-sellers. Manager Katrina Sirdofsky points out that "if you look at music history, many producers have had careers that spanned several decades." Like artists and musicians, the most successful can sustain long careers, but it can be difficult to make and maintain a middle-class living. At any moment, there are a small number of high-earners and a large group at the far end of the socioeconomic spectrum. Even multiplatinum success can vaporize after a few misses or when production styles change. The Arab adage "As the camel falls, the knives that would stab it multiply" and the "next!" proclivity of the industry may explain the rapidity with which work evaporates.

Some producers reach a point where they want to move on. George Martin once commented about having to suffer fools gladly to be a good producer. It is easy to become cynical about how labels treat producers, and the turmoil of mergers, closures, and staff turnover means that there may be nobody with a vested interest in your production by the time you deliver the masters. There are lifestyle issues, the hours can be punishingly long, and there may be lots of travel, which is fun until you have children. There is no financial constancy for freelance producers, and most staff producers do not enjoy long-term security either. Financial stability is based on what you create yourself by careful money management.

Lack of control can be a factor. It is frustrating to make good records and watch them disappear for (what you perceive as) lack of label commitment. A record company's motivation to promote a record can disappear for many reasons: A finished record may not meet its expectations, but the most common reason is personnel changes. Even if the A&R person who signed the act is still at the label (it is often disastrous if they are not), a new president, VP of marketing, or different promotions people can have a negative impact. Staff producers have a better vantage point than freelance producers from which they can read the label's commitment, enabling them to choose prioritized projects. Moreover, an inside producer can influence the future of a project through daily and long-term relationships with key staff.

Some producers start their own labels, which can build value in a catalog but involves more non-creative, administrative, and fiscal responsibilities. As a label owner, you are still subject to the vagaries of promotion, marketing, and distribution, and you have the full responsibility for costs. If the artists you sign become successful, you may sign with a major label to market and distribute your label, and the circle is complete. Nonetheless, a successful label owner generally has more leverage and stability than a freelance producer.

There is a significant attrition rate among producers; the less resilient fall away early, and those who survive the initial flush of success may enjoy a longer run. There are no reliable statistics on producer income and longevity, but my anecdotal observation is that a successful period of more than five years constitutes a "long run." Local and regional producers have proliferated with the DAW revolution. Oversupply depresses prices, and it can be difficult to support even a home or project studio (with capital outlay, maintenance, and upgrades) and make a reasonable hourly wage. Many local producers have multiple sources of income—often working as musicians, live sound engineers, or crew, and some have day jobs as well.

How Is Your Health?

The music business attracts more than its fair share of people who treat their physical beings as if they live by Pete Townshend's credo: "I hope I die before I get old."[1] Despite robust abuse, most face a more down-to-earth reality—if they had known they were going to live as long as they did, they might have taken better care of themselves. Sadly, I have a number of friends, colleagues, and peers who died decades before the average life expectancy because of poor health brought on by alcohol and substance abuse. Of course, these are problems across society, but an unregulated work environment where it is common to tolerate alcohol and drugs (sometimes encouraged by peers) does not help.

Even without this, maintaining good health can be challenging for the hands-on producer. The hours are often long for many reasons. Studio time is expensive and often sold on a daily (24-hour lockout) basis. If you are trying to stay within budget, the inclination is to work long hours; 12-hour days are typical, and 14-to-16-hour days are not uncommon. Depending on the schedule, producers often work six- and sometimes seven-day workweeks. I have done remix sessions that ran for 72 hours with no sleep. The isolation of the few remaining residential studios favors long hours. Because you eat and sleep there, working all day and much of the night is normal. A common residential studio syndrome is the "turned-around day." On the first day, you get to bed around two a.m., the next day three a.m., and so on. Breakfast gets progressively later, until no one is up until the afternoon and you are working through the night. Some people thrive on these hours, but my observation is that undesirable personality traits tend to manifest themselves when everybody is tired around four in the morning. Many of us have been swept through the night on a creative wave and then, after some sleep and a quick listen, scrapped everything, wondering what we were thinking.

Dave Jerden told *Tape Op* magazine that he works a nine-hour day, six days a week starting at noon because of many sessions where "the hours get later and later when you come in" and you "burn yourself out." He pointed out that the artists become exhausted but "they're all excited" and get "burned out without realizing that it is happening."[2] A mutually agreed schedule that accommodates everybody is best. Alan Moulder says:

> On recording, the band sets the length of the day. Different bands have different burnout periods. I have worked with some bands where they'll work almost a strict 12-hour day and at midnight even if they are in the middle of a guitar overdub they'll stop. I've done eight-hour days but some of the bands just don't get going until late at night. If you want to record them, you just have to be around until they are ready. Those days can be very long. I prefer a 12-hour day, and in an ideal world, a 12-hour day and no work on weekends. When you get to the mix, you tend to have more control over the hours and again that is usually a 12-hour day.[3]

If you are in a "hot" phase, the projects come in thick and fast, and it is counterintuitive to turn down opportunities. There may be some wisdom in the adage "make hay while the sun shines," but jumping from one project to another can be physically, mentally, and emotionally debilitating. Starting a new album can be as stressful as starting a new job: The personalities change, you have to familiarize yourself with new material, and your role might be significantly different unless you are an auteur or consultative producer. You may have flown across many time zones to get to the next location. Even with business managers, online bill payment, and web monitoring of your house, things still go wrong at home when you are away for long stretches.

On top of that, there are the difficulties of maintaining relationships and some kind of personal life when you are never in one place for long. Professionally, there is little time to evaluate new projects while you are working long hours, and it is impossible to keep up with what is going on in the outside world of movies, music, and books. This is risky because cultural references are relevant to your work. Physically, it can be hard to find time for exercise, and mental relaxation and stimulation. It is a good idea to take at least a month off between projects to chill out, listen to music just for fun, and reestablish a more normal existence. Taking time off to recuperate and listen to other kinds of music is important to Moulder, and he is in the fortunate position to be able to choose his projects. He still does first or second records for bands that he likes, but "conversely if it's a big band and I don't like it, I won't do it. I try to stick with what I like so I can give an honest day's work."[4] This goes back to the "heart" or belief in a project.

Why Do A&R People Hire You?

IF YOU ARE HOT

The day an A&R person can find your name near the top of the *Billboard, Music Week*, or other national charts, finding work becomes easier. They suggest you to their acts and respond to you or your manager's calls, texts, and e-mails. Part of my motivation for writing the first edition of this book was because producing appears to some as a "black art," reflecting a lack of understanding of its diverse permutations.

The possible combinations of qualities that engender success as a music producer approach infinite and indeterminable complexity. Talent, hard work, experience, education, training, an extensive and well-placed network, prior accomplishments, and goodwill may be precursory but not reliably causative. Perseverance is necessary, and luck is a factor, but I subscribe to the "you make your own luck" and "the harder I work, the luckier I get" school of thought. Nonetheless, I have seen excellent work fail, and the converse too. Any measurable success spells opportunity, and it is essential to consolidate it to improve the quality of artists you can access.

Being arrogant may be survivable in the short term, but the notion that "everyone you kick on the way up will kick you twice on the way back down" is worth pondering. Success is a season of indeterminate length, during which you appear to have the Midas touch and everyone wants you to touch his or her project. When you are in such a period, you can negotiate significantly improved terms, and you should, but doing so with humility can help sustain a career when it begins to flag.

IF YOU ARE NOT QUITE THERE YET

Production careers, like many creative jobs, seem to observe quantum theory, in which energy is emitted or absorbed in indivisible quanta. By this I mean that careers tend to plateau with no signs of advancement despite relentless hard work, and then they abruptly step up to another level. I was very fortunate in that the first record I produced was a hit. Nevertheless, this "break" came after more than a decade as a studio musician and recording artist. I like to think that the opportunity arose because I built a reputation of competence and goodwill in the business. I worked and networked across many circles with the best people I could find, but I cannot identify the final differentiating factors (outside of hard work and serendipity) that led to the success I sought.

You can conserve a lot of energy and time by being strategic, not that I always was. I followed my passions, working for several years in the areas of avant-garde electronic music and free, improvised jazz. I had no illusions that it would lead to a life of opulence in the Hollywood Hills; I did it because it intrigued me. Success came, predictably enough, in commercial music through the major label route.

However, it was those years in noncommercial and avant-garde groups that gave me a fresh perspective in the form of insight into the use of the then-new computer and synthesizer technology that made my work stand apart.

It is fun to work with music you love and useful to be realistic about its potential for success. I found a niche for myself that expanded, in a highly modified form, into the mainstream. A niche area of music can create an advantage, even if it is not unique to you. If fewer people are chasing the same idea, you have a better chance of becoming the acknowledged expert. Niche styles are constantly moving into the mainstream. There are many examples: Punk music was a niche initially, as was new romantic and electronica. Niche genres can take decades to evolve. We printed the letters EDM for "electronic dance music" on our singles in 1980. As it happened, electronic dance music including the various house/techno styles did not significantly penetrate the U.S. pop market for years. At the time of writing, music with a heavy European electronic dance influence dominates the U.S. pop charts. Many of the producers of previous club hits, such as French house music producer and DJ David Guetta (Kelly Rowland, Black Eyed Peas, Nicki Minaj) are now enjoying massive international chart success. Guetta's productions used the Euro four-to-the-bar bass drum groove and were significantly faster than U.S. hits of the time. A number of industry experts told him that he would never have a hit in the United States with that style.[5]

To assess a niche, it is germane to ask yourself why this apparent opportunity exists: "Is it an un-mined vein of gold, or fringe music that may never enter the mainstream?" Trends and movements begin beyond the periphery and are identifiable far in advance. Yesterday's alternative styles are often today's pop vanguard. Hip hop became huge internationally from small beginnings more than 30 years ago. Alternative rock was on the margins in the '80s and became mainstream U.S. pop in the '90s. Even the Beatles were developing in Liverpool and Hamburg for years before they transformed the industry. Nevertheless, some fringe trends never break out. Washington, D.C.'s go-go music has been very popular there since the late 1970s but never expanded into a sustained international movement. Alan Moulder's opportunity came because of his interest in what was at the time a niche market. He says,

> I was very, very lucky that I fell into the alternative market in England at the time when hardly anyone else wanted to do it. Slick records were king at the time, and alternative or indie records were almost like second-rate music. Other engineers thought they sounded awful and trashy. So I didn't have a lot of competition. A lot of the producers that were doing those records were used to working in cheaper studios with assistants, and they came to me because these records are quite difficult to polish up a bit without making them sound slick or smooth. So there weren't a lot of trained engineers who'd come up through the studio system from assistant to house engineer who wanted to make those records. I could co-produce [with bands] and they would only have to pay one

person instead of both an engineer and a producer. Combined with the fact that I was not that expensive in the beginning, which helped since those records weren't selling in huge quantities at the time.[6]

Usually, there are key people at the core of a new movement who have a conceptual grasp of what is happening and, most important, whether there is an audience. This was true with the Beatles, punk, hip hop, new romantic, house, grunge, and electronic dance music. A small, passionate (usually young) fan base can become a large and widespread audience.

IF YOU WERE RECENTLY HOT

This is a difficult position to be in, when it has been some time since your last success. If labels offer you work at all, it may be second division projects that are low priority for them. Labels often deny that they prioritize releases, and they hold that information closely, but majors have too many releases each week to promote them equally well, and it becomes a Darwinian battle for survival. A remarkable production can focus a label's attention, although they do not always assign their marketing and promotion dollars to the best record. Counterintuitive as this is, there are other considerations, such as who signed the act, who the artist's manager and attorney are, and the label's history with the artist. The more productions you have that are under-promoted, the more misses you will accumulate, and the time since your last chart showing will increase. This can damage your morale and diminish offers of work.

Creative management can make a difference. In the absence of a good manager, producers need to be strategic. Changing industry perception by stepping away from your customary genres can broaden possibilities. Producing hip indie artists where sales expectations are lower can increase credibility, especially with unexpected collaborations, which garner industry attention without the focus being solely on units sold. Danny Saber pointed out that critical acceptance can help. This is consistent with manager Andy Kipnes's comment to Peter Collins—that being associated with cool projects can keep you in work.

WHEN THE NIGHT'S CLOSING IN

Most artists, musicians, and producers devote years to consummating their dreams. Having finally stepped into a stream of success, it is natural to assume that you can stay there. However, the ancient Greeks understood that "everything flows, nothing stands still."[7] Furthermore, they said, "You cannot step twice into the same river, for other waters are continually flowing in."[8] Although you achieved your objective, the business, trends, and technologies do not stand still. What most of us do is immerse ourselves in the flood of work that flows from the success. However, in capitalizing on success, it is important to maintain strategic flexibility and continue to be forward-thinking. As the river moves, so must you. When my production career began, I saw excellent 1970s producers, who worked only with live musicians, fall away. Some retired happily. Others would have liked to continue producing, but they had no strategy in place and were unable or unwilling to make the shift to the computerized, synthesized '80s. In the '90s, the pendulum swung back to live bands; this, in turn, left some strictly high-tech producers sidelined.

At the turn of the millennium, digital recording techniques became widely accepted and less expensive. Simultaneously, recording budgets dropped, leaving many big team, big budget producers without a means to compete. It is easier to transmogrify a career before the peak of an industry shift than it is to resurrect one afterward. We unwittingly brand or typecast ourselves with every choice we make. Diversification is not for everyone, but the ideal time to make a change is well before it becomes necessary.

Unlike, say, the sciences or academia—where age, experience, and a long résumé are respected—in the music business, "older" may be (unjustifiably) equated with "out-of-touch." A long discography replete with artists from another era reinforces that notion. There are notable examples of producers, such as Phil Ramone and Arif Mardin, who have sustained lifelong careers. In fact, Mardin is a case in point. He was the victim of a mandatory retirement age limit at Atlantic Records. The mindlessness of this policy was accentuated when he moved to Blue Note and almost immediately produced Norah Jones's diamond-certified debut album *Come Away with Me.*

Most people's expenses increase as they mature and acquire homes, cars, and families. Younger producers can often afford to take more risks, working for less and going for longer periods without income. It is not a career if you cannot cover the costs of raising a family, college tuition, and so forth. However, success can encourage a more lavish lifestyle. Teddy Riley produced big-selling artists such as Bobby Brown, Janet Jackson, Michael Jackson, and Heavy D, but in 2002, he filed for Chapter 11 bankruptcy. Among other penalties, the IRS filed a $1 million lien against him for unpaid taxes. Consequently, he had to sell his house and put his studio up for sale.[9] In chapter 6, I discuss the story of how producer Scott Storch, allegedly, went through $30 million in six months. These may be extreme examples, but once the royalties and big advances slow down, even a slightly excessive overhead rapidly depletes resources and racks up debt. Add another uncontrollable factor or two, such as a serious illness or a divorce, and the proceeds of decades of hard work and success can be obliterated.

When production careers enter a quiet phase, the ability to live as you have become accustomed to will rest on whether you conserved and invested or spent too freely. Experienced producers develop transferable skills, but changing professions is difficult for many after a freewheeling life in music. It is not easy to replace the amount of income a successful producer earns. A cautious approach to personal finances pays dividends by allowing experienced producers time to rest between projects, to strategize, search out new talent, and develop new skills and approaches. Even if you intend to work forever, planning for a forced retirement may be the best hedge against it happening.

WHAT PREVENTS THEM FROM COMING BACK TO YOU?

It can be as simple as habit. You work with a couple of A&R people and they keep coming back to you; some other work comes in from another source, you interrupt the roll, and they find someone else. Once they become comfortable with another producer, it can be years before you work with them again. I did three albums each for two major labels, each album was certified gold, and I had no misses with either label. In each case, there were long periods before those labels offered me work again. Furthermore, in the case of both labels, each request to work with me originated from the artists and/or the artists' managers. There was no resistance from the labels and relationships with the A&R staff were good. Developing relationships with artists and managers is worthwhile.

If you are dealing with major labels, a lack of chart presence will eliminate a great deal of incoming work requests. As long as you are currently successful, even being somewhat difficult to work with or overspending the budget is less likely to create unwanted gaps in your schedule. With independent labels, success is also the primary criterion but, depending on the label, the success is less likely to be tied to the top ten and more likely to a genre chart or lower sales figures.

Please bear with my cynicism for a moment. As I see it, rule number one is most people (including A&R people and some producers) do not really understand how producers do what they do. This is the "black art syndrome," which I define as "this producer has the magic wand this week." That perspective inexorably leads to my rule number two: "Success is the primary measure of your ability as a producer." Exceptions to rule number two might be if you are very young, considered innovative, are inexpensive, if you are managed by the A&R person's management company, or if you have an enthusiastic fan base of artists who request you.

Cynicism aside, success as a primary criterion has legitimacy. Chart positions reflect sales, and labels need revenues. Producers have to understand the labels' objectives, then balance those with the artists' goals and negotiate to deliver records that are capable of achieving both. The music industry is a labyrinthine series of valves, filters, intermediaries, and/or gatekeepers, each of which operates on a knockout basis of pass/no-pass. The final arbiter is the public, but the vast majority of recordings never make it to that court.

When a project of yours fails, analyze what happened—if you cannot measure it, you cannot improve it. Determine the extent of your responsibility and decide how you can avoid the problem in future. Even the most successful producers make records that fail to sell. Rising above failure requires perseverance, an ability to correct personal imperfections, a belief in yourself, and healthy relationships within the industry.

Privately acknowledging your responsibility is constructive. Attributing blame to the label, artist, or manager's failings may be cautionary for future dealings, but it serves no other purpose.

Sometimes good records fail. Producers cannot control many of the myriad parameters that lead to commercial success. They do exercise agency over the quality of the recordings and the interpersonal aspects of the process. This is the empowered producer's ability to choose effectively and transform those choices into achievement. It is the conceit of production and, idealistically, effective choices will guide a project through the industry and media filters giving the consumer the opportunity to choose. The more often you can achieve this goal, the more work will come your way.

WITH OR WITHOUT A&R PEOPLE, WHAT IS THE BEST WAY TO GET WORK?

Until you have produced a successful record, perhaps the only way to get work is by networking. This can be online or in person; it can include label people, managers, and artists, or friends and neighbors, but the wider the network, the more work will come your way. There will probably always be artists who are technophobes, who will need someone else to record their music for them. Depending on the kind of artists they are, you can make a very good-sounding recording with a decent microphone and A-D converter on a laptop with some form of DAW software. Once you have some success, your calling card is each download and CD sold, or track streamed. For this reason, unless you are proud of a work, do not release it to the public under your name. Alan Moulder said he gets his projects from "band requests and previous reputation." At any point in a career, that really is the best way, and it does not only apply to producers who penetrate the *Billboard* charts.

Some producers occupy a niche, such as metal, Americana, world, folk, avant-garde, reggae, etc., and artists in that niche will be familiar with and seek out those producers. This can also work geographically. Local and regional producers are able to make a living working with bands from their area. They make good-sounding records for a reasonable price, and the word spreads. It is worth remembering that Sam Phillips discovered Elvis Presley, Jerry Lee Lewis, Johnny Cash, Howlin' Wolf, Rufus Thomas, and Carl Perkins, among others, by running his local Memphis Recording Service. Phillips recorded everyone who walked through the door and paid for time, in addition to doing location recording for a fee.

Moses Asch focused on recording artists for release on his Folkways Records and Service Corporation label. This was his third, and finally successful, attempt at running a label. Asch built a comprehensive and important collection of world music, spoken word, and children's music, in addition to recording artists like Woody Guthrie, Pete Seeger, Lead Belly, James P. Johnson, Mary Lou Williams, Ella Jenkins, John Cage, and countless others. He released more than an album a week for nearly 40 years, did not restrict himself by genre, and did it all from his tiny New York City studio with very few staff. Even with the limited independent distribution he mustered, his reputation spread. The label became an outlet for ethnographic recordings by other producers and early ethnomusicologists.

When Bob Dylan first moved to New York City, his stated ambition was to record for Folkways. He said, "That was the label that put out all the great records."[10] Instead, he was spotted by John Hammond and signed to Columbia.

Reputation is critical, and building one is a matter of taking advantage of the resources and opportunities you have. The more positive recognition your work receives, the more work will come your way and the more access you may have to major label opportunities, if that is what you want. Major labels gave Danny Saber more work once he had a successful record under his belt. He told me that before that, "I always had to talk them into why they should use me. Once you have a hit record, you have that to stand on." Irrespective of that, "No matter what you did before, it's only going to do them any good if you do good for them."[11]

The need to acknowledge and sustain the symbiotic nature of the relationship between producer and label that Saber refers to is the crux of the matter. Freelance producers function in a free-market economy where each party is defending their own best interests, and it is in your future interest to ensure that the person giving you the work gets what they need.

Branding, Marketing, and Sales

These three words seem to have negative connotations in many circles and especially among musicians. This is understandable when we see the way that large corporations, politicians, and businesspeople knowingly use deceptive techniques to ensnare people with products, services, and concepts that do not deliver what they promise. There is a long history of confidence tricksters and snake-oil sales. Nevertheless, we all brand, market, and sell ourselves every day—mostly unknowingly and often poorly, even negatively. In fact, these are three facets of outreach. Understanding and gaining control over these three techniques can be empowering to any career at any level.

BRANDING

I listed branding first because it should precede marketing and sales. As a producer, your brand is what you and your work represent in the minds of your clients and is your promise to them. Just as a picture of an object is not the object, a brand is not a logo, a slogan, a tagline, or advertising. However, these may represent your brand and should trigger the positive associations people have with you, your company, product, or service. The opposite of a brand is a commodity. A commodity is a product, such as coffee, or a service, like computer repair. Starbucks and Geek Squad both took commodities and branded them. It is disadvantageous to a producer to be viewed as a commodity. Say the names "George Martin" or "Quincy Jones," and a flood of associations and images come to mind. Coffee and computer repair people are generic, but Starbucks and Geek Squad both converted commodities back into brands that consumers demand by name and for which they pay a premium. Commodities compete on price, whereas brands embody powerful associations and benefits that command premium prices and preference. A brand defines (in the target audience's mind) who you are, what you do, how you do it, what you stand for, and how others perceive you. A brand is not simply awareness, which can be positive or negative. It is the goal of marketing to create or increase the positive awareness of the brand.

MARKETING

Marketing encompasses everything you do to move a product or service from concept to customer. What is termed the "marketing mix" has been characterized by the "4Ps" since 1960 when Jerome McCarthy introduced the concepts of product, price, place, and promotion. There are now several competing models, but the 4Ps are the most established.

The 4Ps begin with thinking about your product or service, which is what you offer. It includes, brand, goodwill, reputation, previous success, status, and how it satisfies customers' needs.

Price can be determined in two ways: One is cost-plus (your costs plus a profit margin) and the other is what the market will bear. If a consumer does not perceive sufficient value, they will not buy, forcing you to drop your price or revamp your offering to meet the clients' point of perceived value. Producers' fees are determined by the market and your position within it, neither of which are easy benchmarks to glean in a closed, largely business-to-business (B2B) environment, where other producers are not advertising their pricing. Managers, especially those with large rosters, understand pricing structures and comparative value.

The third P, place refers to the channels through which you sell your services. Production services are mostly sold on a B2B basis, as in your manager contacting A&R people at labels. Regional and local producers who work directly for the artists sell business-to-consumer (B2C). They may be listed or advertised publicly and have no business intermediary such as a record label.

Promotion is the fourth P, which includes any promotional techniques used, such as e-mail newsletters or mailings, a website, a business card on the bulletin board at your local music center or store, and interactive social media including viral means like YouTube, Facebook, or Twitter. These were previously termed below-the-line promotions as opposed to above-the-line activities like radio, TV, and the press. Media advertising is unlikely to be cost-effective for producers because their clients are so specialized.

SALES

If marketing is about finding your target market and persuading them that you have what they need, sales are about closing the deal and signing the contract. A sale often comes down to interpersonal contact, and the producer, manager, or both can be involved at this point. Just as a car dealer wants both the husband and wife present (the decision-makers), the final sales push must include all stakeholders on the buyer's side. If the A&R person is convinced but the band is not included in the process, the deal can fall apart and vice versa. Likewise, all creative parties may want you on the project but, for instance, if your advance or budget exceeds business affairs' financial limits, the deal may not close. There are many potential sticking points toward the end of a deal, and the salesperson's job (that is, you or your manager) is to identify and remove the friction. Knowing who the decision-makers are is cardinal.

The difference between marketing and sales can be confusing, but think of the process as raising energy levels from cold to warm and then to a boil. Marketing identifies prospects and raises some from a low level of interest to a higher level so that the final sales pitch can focus on the warm prospects, bringing them to a boil and closing the deal. Offering a 50 percent or greater discount to people who are not interested in a service is unlikely to result in a sale. When you have an interested prospect, spending time assuaging their concerns and giving concessions (such as a lower fee versus a higher royalty, a cheaper studio, or an earlier start date) may clinch the deal.

Timing in these negotiations and offers is critical. Successful marketing and sales of branded services are not intrinsically tied to price, but rather to perceived value. Clients' requirements vary, hence the necessity for personalized contact and a clear understanding of the decision-makers' wants, needs, concerns, and limits.

THE PRACTICALITIES OF BRANDING, MARKETING, AND SALES

Possibly the most difficult part of this process is differentiating your brand. Why should someone hire you rather than someone else? Spending time evaluating what you are good at, what you like doing, and how you want potential clients to perceive you is helpful in developing personal goals. Those goals and your brand should be consistent, distinct, and differentiated. Companies spend millions trying to figure this out, and it involves some soul-searching and personal adaptation. One way that brands are valued is by assessing the total investment that it took to build them. That includes all the publicity, advertising, and retail marketing the company has done. It may be hard to envisage how this applies to producers, but any interviews, articles, features, and mentions; credits on CDs sold or given away; ads, publicity, and online presence all add up to a significant investment of your time. Understanding this reinforces the importance of prominent and accurate crediting. With each positively associated public (or trade) credit, value accrues to your brand.

A feature in a trade magazine is worth as much as the advertising cost for the same amount of space in that magazine. Producers who work under various pseudonyms split the value of any investment across what are, effectively, multiple brands. Multiple brands make sense in avoiding brand confusion or "extension." If your ultimate aim is to be a leading country music producer, but you are producing metal bands to pay the rent, it is smart to use a pseudonym for the metal bands. On the other hand, if you like working across genres, then using the same name will build that value into your brand.

It is important to understand that everything you do that is visible to your target market contributes (positively or negatively) to the value of your brand, and you must keep your brand current. Credits on millions of albums sold are not worth much in current market value if they are out of date, old school, or stale. Brand value is lost or diminished if you do not receive credit on work done.

Thankfully, the days of physical résumés, discographies, press kits, and show reels are over. Now everything you need can live on the web and, when necessary, you can send it as a link. This is a positive trend for producers who can not only list their entire discography, but also insert links to music clips. The below-the-line promotions via the web and social media are, for the most part, free except for the investment of time and some site fees and hosting. The pressure of having to update multiple outlets can be alleviated by using third-party software, apps, or sites that specialize in integration. Nonetheless, keeping up with new sites and techniques involves a learning curve that consumes time. E-mail lists and newsletters may seem old-fashioned now, but they are still effective and can be a good measure of growth. With any direct marketing, it is axiomatic to avoid annoying clients. Be sure to allow an option for people to unsubscribe. Even with double opt-in subscribers (where they request and confirm), if you blitz them with messages, newsletters, tweets, and so forth, they will block you out mentally, actually block you, or unsubscribe from your lists. It can help, in building a worthwhile list, to disseminate information that is useful to people, along with whatever it is that you wish to communicate. Lists used for different purposes should be separated. Lists of A&R people must be kept apart from lists of artists and friends, and all addresses need to be hidden (by using the blind copy function). If you are actively looking for work, it is imperative to keep sufficient information on all your outlets. Analytical tools such as Google analytics will not necessarily predict how the next person will find you, but they can help focus your efforts on those outlets that are proving to be most productive

My best work came to me by word-of-mouth or personal recommendation. The artist or A&R person heard something of mine they liked or knew someone I had worked with. As Alan Moulder pointed out, that is still the best way; however, it does not always produce enough work. Show reels and websites can give the wrong impression if you are not there to explain the relevance of previous work to the production under consideration. I prefer each of my productions to be different from previous ones. Artists sometimes latch onto the specifics of a previous production (maybe they dislike that band or the voice) rather than understanding what you

contributed. With a market tipped heavily toward the supply side, it favors producers who stamp their productions with similar qualities and sounds. Why would an
A&R person or an artist not make the safest choice? Consequently, it is easy to
become typecast in a genre or style. Building relationships with artists, managers,
and A&R people allows you to establish personal chemistry, possibly turning a miss
into a connection.

"I'm very wary of sending out show reels," says Alan Moulder. "I try to tailor
each show reel to each band. This can be difficult because very often bands come to
you for different reasons than you thought." I have often been surprised when some
productions I have done appeal to artists from completely different genres of music.
A band might have heard something of yours when they were ten years old, and
although they may be strictly hardcore now, they have fond childhood memories of
that pop hit you produced.

Assuming you like his or her music, meeting with the artist as early as possible
is the best way to avoid an accidental disconnect. This is where a good manager
helps. Producer managers need to be in constant contact with labels so they know
what projects are in the works and can connect their producers with projects. The
first meeting might be with the A&R person, the band, or all together. My objective
is to determine compatibilities and any negatives. If there is simpatico, the conversation can be broad-ranging. If asked how you would approach the production,
it is best to speak in general terms. Unless you take a cookie-cutter approach to
production, most projects and artists have their idiosyncrasies. I am more interested
in how they think, what they listen to, what they watch, where they hang out, what
they read, who they are, what makes them happy, and what upsets them. In the case
of a group, it is valuable to figure out how the power structure works: who might be
volatile, who is the peacemaker, who is the natural leader, and how their collective
and individual senses of humor work. Bands often develop their own quirky humor
and language; understanding it can help build rapport. Ideally, there is more work
available for you than you accept. Choosing *not* to produce an artist who does not
fit your strategic objectives helps maintain a strong brand identity.

6

Managers

What Is the Definition of the Term "Manager"?

I use the term "manager" throughout the book, sometimes in reference to the artist's manager and sometimes the producer's. Artist managers are sometimes known as personal managers and are generally referred to as simply the manager, as are producer managers. Both artist and producer managers are typically paid a percentage of revenue generated. Some artist managers represent producers, but often producer managers focus solely on producers. There are producer managers who work on their own, producer management companies with several managers (each usually with their own roster), and some producer managers who are part of a larger management group in which there are other managers who represent other producers and, in some cases, artists.

Several roles include the title of manager. There may be a business manager—usually an accountant or tax attorney—who focuses on the artist's or producer's finances. Business managers may be paid a small percentage of income, although many artists and producers elect to pay them a monthly retainer or an hourly rate.

Artists often have a tour manager or road manager who travels with the band and handles day-to-day logistics and reports to the artist's personal manager. Producers are more likely to have a personal assistant or production coordinator to handle their day-to-day business and production logistics.

What Does a Producer Manager Do?

Producer managers usually find work for their roster and negotiate deals, and some handle the production coordination logistics. They are usually paid a percentage of the advance and future royalties generated by the productions they set up. Nowadays, some encourage their producers to be entrepreneurial in discovering and developing acts, which the manager (and sometimes the producer) will place with a label or release on their own label. In some cases, the producer manager will identify an act and place that act with one of his or her producers for development. The manager may place the resulting production with a label or release it on his or her own or the producer's label.

If you are in the studio on a project, focusing on the work, there is barely time to get your car serviced. It is challenging while producing a project, to identify and negotiate your next project. I have heard many stories of producers spending time in the studio doing business. Artists rarely appreciate it when the producer spends significant amounts of time on the phone, checking e-mail, or texting.

A good management company helps greatly in lining up the next few projects, negotiating the deals, doing the budgets, locating musicians, booking flights and hotels, and summarizing it all in a phone call, e-mail, or text. They keep your name in front of key A&R people. Before you become well known, a manager with credibility can persuade a label or an artist to take a creative leap of faith with you. A&R people have heavy schedules, and there are many producers vying for a small amount of quality work. If a manager has an excellent reputation and a successful roster of producers, A&R people may call them for advice. Ros Earls of 140dB Management said that she recommends producers she respects but does not represent if she has no one suitable. This approach forges strong relationships and builds respect, ultimately resulting in more work for her roster. Linda Perry's manager Katrina Sirdofsky says,

> I believe it is important for most creative people to have someone else being the face of business on their behalf. For most people it's difficult to sell themselves and make their own deals. Most producers are locked away in the studio while the managers are out taking meetings and finding out what's new and in development, thereby hearing things early and having an early shot at projects.[1]

Danny Saber had a manager from very early on in his career:

> Until I had a manager, I didn't have anything. The whole thing with managers is timing. If you have a manager that's too far ahead, they won't have time for you. If you've got someone who's too far behind then they're not going to be able to help you. My manager had all cutting-edge alternative producers in the same vein that I'm in. Shannon O'Shea hooked me up with the Black Grape stuff. They had vision. They were able to put me with the right people and sell me to the A&R people on the backs of their more established producers.[2]

Lauren Christy thinks that "a really great manager is the most important thing a producer can have":

> The three of us were feeling a bit like losers in the music business. Sandy [Roberton] said, "I'm going to make you the most successful writing/production team in America," and we thought "yeah right."[3]

Peter Collins likes "having gurus around." He produced a number of rock acts in the '80s and '90s and could defer to his then-managers Cliff Burnstein and Peter Mensch from Q Prime (managers of Def Leppard and Metallica). "They would give me the skinny as to what they thought of any rock bands I had been offered."[4] Subsequently, Peter moved to Advanced Alternative Media. Talking about the havoc that is wreaked during label mergers and when A&R people move on, he said, "I've relied very heavily on my manager Andy Kipnes, who's clued in to record company politics and has done a very good job of keeping me safe from those traps."

It has never been easy to find a good manager and perhaps less so today than ten years ago. Managing producers is no easy job; the competition for work is fierce, and major and independent labels, as well as artist's managers, openly pit one producer manager against another to push advances, royalties, and terms as low as possible. In a tight market, many unfortunate trends emerge, such as producers working far below their worth in order to sustain some vestige of a career. Labels will ask two or more mixers to work on spec on the same track. They pay for the mix they use, leaving the other mixers out of pocket. Well-known producers are reputed to have made records for no advance, just a royalty. On the other hand, with advances being so severely diminished, in many cases, it is uneconomical to pay a lawyer to write up a contract, and some producers are working with no contract or royalty, just a flat fee payment. In many cases, a flat fee can work out to be more than the producer would make from royalties. Regardless, there is always the risk that the producer will have sacrificed royalty payments worth hundreds of thousands of dollars, and possibly more, should that production result in a substantial hit. The trend in the charts toward producers writing the material may not be only a consequence of inexpensive technology but also economic pressures. Writers receive mechanical copyright royalties (9.1¢/track in the United States at the time of writing) for every track sold (physical and downloaded formats but not streaming) and performance royalties for every radio play. A successful writer or one with a major publishing deal can afford to produce a track for nothing and live on the publishing income. All of this adds up to a very restricted market for producers, and having a proactive manager is more important than ever.

What Does a Manager Cost?

Producer managers' fees generally range from a 10-to-20-percent commission on all sources of revenue that they set up, or as defined in the producer management agreement. Some will work on a flat monthly retainer.

Do They Earn Their Percentage?

When producers are at their busiest and most in-demand stage of their careers, it is easy for a manager to be passive in finding work. In terms of long-range career development, this is when you really need active hands-on management. At the top, the only way to go is down. Every project carries an opportunity cost, and every deal needs deliberation. Make a few bad choices and you find yourself staring down the slippery slope into the black hole of obscurity. During a career high, reacting to inquiries will result in an impressive selection of projects, and a hit is a hit, but sideways movement and more of the same will not necessarily future-proof your career. Successful producers need to be wary of vampire projects, where the other party acquires more benefit from the producer than the producer does from the project. Producers should only donate their hard-won kudos to projects that they passionately believe in, and the deal should reflect the nature of this relationship. Having converted lead into gold, you need to convert that gold into kryptonite.

It is vital that you are comfortable with how your manager represents you. Having a manager who understands your strengths and weaknesses is critical or you can wind up on uncomfortable projects. A broad network with active connections and influence is important for a producer manager. They process many more projects than artists' managers do. Nonetheless, even the best-connected manager who is too busy or not focusing on your advancement is not going to help you progress. A manager with less power and influence (who focuses more time and energy on your career and is more proactive and enthusiastic) may be a better choice. Ros Earls thinks it is important to be in the general information flow, keeping up relationships with A&R people and knowing which artists are looking for producers:

> You're out and about. You present people with the facts, what your guys are up to, and when they're available. If you hear about something that's brilliant, that you're absolutely sure that your guy's right for, then that would be the point that you would pitch for a job. My experience is that the pitching and the pushing isn't as important as the general PR that just trickles along on a daily basis, being in the traffic of people making records and looking for producers.[5]

New producers are developing all the time, but it appears to be getting more difficult to sustain a career. Ros thinks this is because the market for producers and producer managers is very crowded:

> Everybody's up for everything. It's a very busy business now, and a lot of people are settling for second best and not getting the jobs they'd like to get. We have done projects for no advance and higher points. I'd rather not do that because everyone needs to earn a living. I've always thought it was worth getting involved in things that were interesting even if they didn't yield huge dividends immediately.[6]

Sandy Roberton (World's End Management) puts it plainly:

> As producer managers, we always have to come up with new ideas. The days of sitting by the phone waiting for it to ring are over. It's not like the late '70s and early '80s when the labels were making hundreds of records. I visited London this week and two major labels each had only three or four acts.[7]

So is it worth paying a manager 10-to-20 percent of your income? Sometimes, in the music business, it seems like everyone is taking a slice of the financial pie, and there is not enough left for the person who created the value in the first place. It is worth asking yourself where the value does come from. If the answer is that there is a joint effort between the producer and the manager, then 20 percent may be a good deal. Eighty percent of something is better than 100 percent of nothing. Lauren Christy moved to the United States when she was 20 and made two albums, which were not successful. She said, "This is a town [L.A.] that wants fresh meat. I was like, 'Oh no ... Sandy Roberton saved my career.'"[8]

Look for a management situation that makes you comfortable and is a productive business collaboration.

How Do You Make Sure You Receive All the Money Due to You?

In the music industry, there are many ways for hard-earned money to disappear before it reaches you. Major labels do it via largely non-negotiable and draconian contracts. Independent labels sometimes become overextended and either do not pay or fold without paying anyone. The best way to insure against nonpayment by your manager is to have the labels pay you directly. The manager may invoice the record company, but payments should come to the producer. The management company should invoice the producer for their commission, and the contract or agreement needs to reflect these terms. Unfortunately, most managers will not agree to direct payment for the producer. This is understandable, because it increases the manager's risk of not being paid. This becomes even more of a problem if they no longer manage that producer and royalties are still being earned on projects done under their agreements. If a manager insists on receiving the payments, make sure your contract with them is watertight and specific about what is due to you and when.

The production contract with the record label should be in your name or the name of your company, not in your manager's name or the name of his company. Most established managers are aboveboard, but for your peace of mind make sure that you clearly understand your agreement. Do not think that discussions or verbal agreements augment or override your contract. Your contracts with labels and your manager should define everything, as you want it done. You and your independent attorney (not someone who works for your manager) need to read the agreement before you sign it. If you do not handle your own finances, it is preferable to have a separate business manager (who handles and accounts for your money) who is not associated in any way with your personal manager (who solicits and negotiates your work). There have been a number of high-profile cases of business managers embezzling funds from their clients. It is essential to sign your own checks (or make your own payments online). Keeping your money management separate from your career management creates a check and balance. The only sure way to avoid being taken advantage of in any business is to take responsibility and be active in all financial and contractual dealings.

Could You Lose Work to Other Producers on the Manager's Roster?

This can be a difficult problem to identify. I had two situations at the beginning of my career where established producers tried to poach projects from me. Once before the artist had even released anything (prerelease expectations for the group were huge) and the other when I had taken a debut album to gold on the backs of the first three hit singles. I did not lose either project, perhaps because my relationships with the artists and their management were strong, and we were enjoying success together. Had the raiders been part of the same management stable, I may not have known what happened, especially if the other producers carried more influence with (read: made more money for) the manager.

I became aware of this situation because I owned my own producer management company at that time. Our business is competitive, and other producers and their managers will use whatever leverage they have to win a project. When I was well established with many hits to my name, I produced the first track for an unknown artist on spec at the advice of my then-manager. A major label signed the artist because of the track I produced, and it was an international hit, ultimately selling millions of units. I was in Sweden finishing another album when I found out that several other producers in the manager's stable were working on this artist's album. Multi-producer albums were uncommon at that time. I was unhappy not to have the opportunity to finish the album, given my spec work and success with the first single; they would have only had to wait a few weeks. I wound up producing several tracks on the album including all the hit singles, but I shared credits, advances, and album royalties with several other producers who generated no chart success. I dumped the manager immediately.

Once you have considerable success, you often have a choice of projects, leaving some available for other producers. Managers like to retain these for their other producers. One of the biggest producer management companies is World's End run by Sandy Roberton who says:

> If a call comes in for a producer and he doesn't happen to be available, I very rarely let it escape. I try to get somebody else in my stable to get that project. Having a large roster like I do, it's a big magnet. You've got certain producers who are not that keen to work all the time, they want to be very choosy. If they get a call and they don't want to do it, I hang on like a terrier, I don't let go of it.[9]

This may seem fine: You cannot do the project, someone else in the management group can, the label is happy, and the project stays close to home. The label will come back to your manager because he or she solved a problem for them and several producers are working. Any potential downside for you relates to the integrity of your manager. Say you are two months away from finishing your current project when a call comes in to your management company for a band you like. Your manager suggests an up-and-coming stable mate who used to be your engineer/programmer. He knows your style, is a lot cheaper, and has some credits but nothing big yet. Your manager e-mails the link to his bio, discography, and sample tracks (including some tracks he engineered for you without clearly distinguishing them from his productions). The band likes what they hear, they meet, the chemistry seems good, and he does the project.

You could not do it; he is a good second choice. Although the band had never heard of him, he had worked closely with you, costs less, and is available now. Perfect. The band goes on to sell many records. You could not be in two places at once, and whenever you pass on a project, there is always the possibility of missing a big one. However, this could have gone differently. The band called your manager because they wanted you, and the manager should have called and discussed it with you. You might have said that you really like this group, saw their early gigs, and would reduce your price to work with them. Your manager could have asked if the band would wait two months to start. As it happened, the record company's lawyer went on vacation for three weeks, holding up the contract so they didn't actually start recording for nearly six weeks, reducing the time they would have had to wait to a couple of weeks.

There was nothing malicious about what your management company did; they were trying to keep their roster working. Had they bothered to check with you and found out how strongly you felt about the band, they might not have suggested the alternative. You had plenty of good possibilities lined up and would not be out of work, whereas your stable mate was just getting started. It was a surprise to all when what seemed like just another niche group turned into the defining band of the decade.

I am not suggesting that this is a common scenario, but I had the experience of a manager making a critical decision to turn down an album I would have loved to have made, without consulting me. In this case, he did not pass it along to another producer in his stable; it would have been a long project and he wanted me to produce an artist signed to his label. The record I produced for him did extremely well but, given the choice, I would have picked the other artist. Unfortunately, I did not find out about it until it was too late.

The point is not that all managers are devious (some are, and mine was) but it is important to know where your interests and your manager's part ways. You need to be comfortable with this person before you put your professional life in his or her hands. In setting up the relationship, clearly define how you want situations like this to be handled.

In their defense, every producer manager I have spoken to has assured me that they do not siphon off work and that the opportunity rarely comes up. I asked Sandy Roberton how he avoids these kinds of conflicts and allocates work among his 60 or so producers:

> I tend not to have too many producers who are doing the same sort of thing. In the writer/producer category, unfortunately, they're all very much in the same category. But they are writing with the artist so it is slightly different. I don't

have 20 rock producers so that situation has never really arisen. I can't imagine who you give it to if you have that problem. I have quite a varied selection of producers and very rarely has there been a situation where there are two or three people up for the same job and the band has wanted every one of them to do it.[10]

Most artists will have a short list of producers that they are interested in, and often their second and third choices are not with the same management company. Ros Earls had Flood working to capacity with artists such as U2 and Nine Inch Nails. He wanted to be able to work with younger bands also—to reinvent himself—so they brought in Alan Moulder to help out, which, as Earls said, "Is interesting because I don't manage Alan Moulder."[11]

Earls said that she finds it difficult to hand projects down to other producers on her roster. "You end up feeling a bit like a door-to-door salesman." Record companies do call up and ask, in general terms, for someone who would be suitable for a gig. Earls will sometimes recommend a producer she does not manage in order to maintain good relations with the A&R community. If A&R people feel they can trust a manager, they are more likely to call for advice. An essential part of producer management is sales, and good salespeople know that more high-quality points of contact lead to more sales.[12]

I like to control my destiny as much as possible; I want to make my own decisions based on the best information available. If your manager makes you fully aware of the options, and you make a wrong choice (as most of us do at some point), you can at least be philosophical about it.

How Do You Define "Best Manager" for You?

In the simplest terms, the best manager is the one who gets you the productions you need to advance your career when you need them. A good manager can help you define what you need to create and sustain the career you want to have. Other important qualities are an understanding of market needs, a strong network, a well-respected reputation, good ears, a comprehensive understanding of the production process, good negotiating skills, diplomacy, discretion, persuasiveness, creativity, and determination. It is wonderful if you find someone who believes there is nobody who does what you do as well as you, has the ability to convey that to decision-makers, and can close a deal.

As discussed earlier, when you are successful, your manager does not have to do much to keep you working, but that is precisely when they should be strategizing to move you up into the unassailable league. Some producers do not rely on their managers to find work at all; they simply use them to handle the business negotiations. Alan Moulder told me, "My manager doesn't get me work; she just discusses money and the terms of the contract, which I find incredibly difficult. I really like the way she represents me." Like producers, managers come from many backgrounds; there are lawyers, studio managers, artist managers, producers, record company executives, and some street-fighting wheeler-dealers.

How Can You Find Such a Person?

Managers are businesspeople; they need to work with producers who generate enough in commissions to warrant the time spent managing them. Sometimes managers approach producers because the producer's work has come to their attention. The most effective way to find a manager is to elevate your career to such a level that the best management companies notice you. Failing that, researching managers who represent similar producers and shopping around can work, but you need to make a good case beyond "I am an amazing producer." The strongest appeal is a combination of a great set of productions, an established revenue stream, and a pragmatic and specific vision as to how the manager can elevate your career. Your vision may be wrong, but doing good work, making money, and knowing where you want to go demonstrate serious intent.

Managers, like producers, have varied styles, skills, and abilities. What makes the relationship work between a producer and manager can be as much about personal chemistry as ability. If you are comfortable with a manager who has enough skills to be functional, and you have talent, drive, and determination, the relationship can work. If you have a good relationship with any A&R people, because they work closely with producer managers, you should ask them who they like to work with.

How Do You Persuade Them to Take You On?

A producer, who had many multiplatinum albums under his belt but none in the previous eight years, was looking for management. Several companies were interested enough to listen to his work, but they passed on him, in some cases by not even calling him back. He carried on working through his own connections in a low-key way until, inevitably, he had another multiplatinum album, which reignited his career, and suddenly everyone was interested again. Unfortunately, there is a catch-22 where you cannot get representation until you have produced something of note, and it is difficult picking up a worthwhile project until you have representation.

Successful managers are busy, and they want producers who have immediate potential for the kind of work that is available. If you are not coming off a hit record, a solid record of paid work will help. A manager needs to see that you have marketable skills and abilities relevant to the current marketplace. Mostly, some sort of traction is necessary, and it is up to you to create that traction.

Ros Earls used to manage recording studios like Trident and Sarm in London before becoming a producer manager. She tends to specialize in producers from an engineering background. She looks for musical ability, a mature approach to arrangements, humility, and someone who responds to bands well. "An understanding of how to balance personalities in the studio and generally liaise with the record company" is important, and she admits there is an "unquantifiable something." She said, "The best producers don't jeopardize the chemistry by selling themselves too much as a creative person," and, "That kind of mature approach from an early stage would be what turns a manager on."[13]

Managers are in business and need to maximize their return on investment, including their time, contacts, expertise, and overhead. The easier it is to find work for you and the more income you generate, the better for them. The relationship between the manager and the producer is, in effect, a strategic partnership to which you each bring complementary skills. There are many producer management companies with varying specializations. Do the research; look for companies that represent producers, engineers, mixers, or remixers who have skills that approximate yours. Then try to evaluate yourself in the same light that a manager will. Ask yourself hard questions, such as "Am I at a comparable level of ability" (with other producers on their roster) and "Why should this manager invest time and effort in my career?" "Because they will make millions of dollars" is speculative and meaningless unless you are already generating that much revenue.

Visualize yourself from a manager's standpoint, in contrast with their current roster. If you are honest, you may find many shortcomings such as "I have no client base and little income, I am hardly known—even in my area, or I am not proven as a songwriter." In which case, close the gap by setting short-term goals such as increasing your client base, becoming the best-known and most successful local or regional producer, or placing or co-writing a song with a reasonably well-known artist. In other words, create attractive and tangible benefits for the potential manager. Additionally, network as much as you can in local industry circles and wider if possible, so that word spreads about your abilities and accomplishments. Managers do not exist to do the tasks you dislike (although they will do them); they are there to maximize your career and make money for you and themselves.

Looking for a manager too early in your career will most likely not be productive. Development of the first part of your career will be your responsibility. Production has always been competitive and is more so with the new technology and college-level training programs, so be realistic—it's difficult to convince an artist, an A&R person, or a manager to trust you with their project if they haven't heard anything you have done. Relationship-building and polite persistence are more likely to engender results than a single approach. If you are fortunate enough to be able to create a dialogue with an established manager, you could ask them what parameters you would need to demonstrate for them to add you to their roster. It is also worth noting that a manager is not a panacea, and being listed on someone's roster is not a guarantee of work.

Business Managers

As mentioned above, producers may have a business manager, as well as a manager. The business manager deals strictly with financial matters. They are usually qualified accountants (preferably a CPA) or tax attorneys. They file tax returns and handle all incoming and outgoing monies. Producers often travel extensively and knowing that bills are paid is reassuring, although it is easy nowadays to pay everything online, which eliminates the likelihood of wrong charges slipping through. As with any other business relationship, it is important to remember that ultimate responsibility for your finances, bills, and tax payments rests with you. It is tempting to leave these matters to the experts, but the only wise course of action is to keep a close watch on what your representatives are doing for you and your financial situation.

7

The Producer's Relationships

With the Artist

BEST FRIENDS

Bertolt Brecht wrote, "I don't trust him, we're friends."[1] The producer's relationship with the artist needs to be friendly, but some choose to maintain a respectful distance, although for the duration of the project, producer and artist can become close. This is a working relationship, and lifestyles, ambitions, and personality types are often quite different. Once the album is completed, the artist moves into the marketing setup and promotional phase and the producer on to his or her next production. They may not meet again until the next album or when they pickup their Grammy awards.

Depending on where production is taking place and at what stage an artist is in his or her career, there may be a certain amount of socializing just before and during the project. This can help in building rapport and dissipating concerns. Friendly social relations and mutual respect are helpful although, even with successful and ongoing productions, long-term close friendships are not necessarily the outcome. In a rare Robert John "Mutt" Lange interview in which he was both interviewer and interviewee, he amusingly asked himself, "Do you still have contact with music artists you worked with in the past?" He responded:

> No. We have separate lives. Some of them believe I was a merciless tyrant in the studio and obsessed with absolute perfection with each song. Some of those albums took several years to complete. They've seen enough of me for one lifetime.[2]

Vocal producer Kuk Harrell began working with Justin Bieber in 2008 when Bieber was 14. In 2012, Bieber said to the *New York Times* that Harrell has "become kind of an uncle." Harrell expressed concern that that could turn into: "'We're buddies, we hang out,' and I can't press him."[3]

The creative intensity between the producer and the artist becomes a form of closeness, of shared experience and understanding, because the nature of the work demands emotional openness and empathy. As Quincy Jones said, "The personal level comes out of the music anyway."[4] However, he thinks it is advantageous to be closer than that

> because you get a chance to know what's underneath the personality. You can comfort that and soothe it and provoke it. You can make the arrangements a musical metaphor for what their personality is about.[5]

As Jones indicates, a good production reflects the artist's nature. Sometimes the relationship can feel almost psychoanalytical or psychotherapeutic, which may explain the duality of intimacy and distance that producers experience.

Recording with an artist is a deep, shared experience involving needs and concerns generated by aspirations, philosophies, ideologies, and mythologies from both artist and producer. Tensions can arise from the anxiety of unmet needs, real or perceived. It is these moments when the levels of communication and essential quality of the working relationship and friendship are tested and validated.

ABLE TO FIT IN

Whether this is necessary or not really depends on the type of producer you are. The auteur type may not need to fit in. Their artists come in to perform vocals and sometimes co-write but otherwise do not normally spend much time in the studio. Collaborative and assistive producers probably need to fit in the most. A lot of the vibe of the session in this case comes from either being like-minded, complementary, or at least easy-going personality types. Alan Moulder finds that fitting in is important; he likes to hang around with the artist and build a comfortable personal relationship:

> Singing in front of someone can be embarrassing. Many singers aren't as extrovert in the studio as they appear on stage. In fact, they can be quite vulnerable and insecure about singing one to one. It really helps if they can be comfortable with you.[6]

Underscoring the difference between a friendship that is ongoing and one forged for a time and a purpose, he said,

> The relationship does change when you finish the record. On tour, they may be pleased to see you, but it is a different mindset from the one-to-one relationship of recording.[7]

George Martin is one of a very small number of individuals referred to as the fifth Beatle. In his case, it is reverential of his undeniably key creative contributions to their recordings, but it also implies a fitting in with the band. From all accounts, there were commonalities of mutual respect and a shared sense of humor that transcended their generational (Martin is quite a bit older than the band members) and lifestyle differences.

Producers who evolve out of band membership intuitively understand this need to blend in as a contributing member or voice in the creative process, even if they are, functionally, the chairperson or decision-maker with the casting vote.

HANG AFTER HOURS

It depends on your nature and the artist's, but it is not unheard of to find yourself in yet another club at four or five in the morning surrounded by an artist's entourage, listening to another apocryphal tale. When a significant percentage of the sub-teen population heaps its allowance and adulation on someone, personalities and behavior can experience distortion.

Wendy Page, speaking about the film *Laurel Canyon*, said, "In my experience, the drug-taking, excessive drinking, and fraternizing with the artists that the movie depicts is a complete rock and roll myth." Different periods and music styles engender different behaviors, and I agree that the behavior in the movie does not represent the norm—the writers probably rolled together a number of reported or apocryphal tales for dramatic effect. Nonetheless, I have witnessed or been aware of behavior consistent with most of what happens in the movie.

Occasionally a session can descend into unnecessary difficulties created by individuals apparently bent on making what should be an enjoyable, creative experience into a self-destruction zone. The overriding concern for the producer, surrounded by this ethos, is to keep recalcitrant behavior away from the studio so that the production can move forward. It is an individual judgment call as to whether endorsing such behavior after hours risks contaminating the sessions. Fortunately, most artists understand the opportunity they have and are serious and respectful of the production environment. My observation is that most producers lead quite disciplined lives. The demands of the job are not sustainably conducive to constant partying.

PROFESSIONAL OR ALOOF

Aloofness reduces the risk of respect breaking down through over-familiarity, but it increases the difficulty of drawing emotional performances out of the artist. Producer-artist relationships should be professional and respectful, even if there is an apparent friendship or closeness. If the artist wants to maintain a distance, breaching it can evoke a negative response. Speaking about his work with Bob Dylan, Phil Ramone said,

> Bob's a nice guy, but he's not a conversationalist. You don't need that when you're making records: You have camaraderie with someone, and you enjoy them for who they are. Bob's self-imposed isolation wasn't some antisocial posturing; it was clear from his mood and body language that he was vulnerable. My way of working is that you don't break the code of privacy that the artist

sets up, whatever that may be. Dylan shares what he needs to, and nothing more. At one point, we found ourselves in the men's room. I said, "How are you feeling?" He said, "I'm okay." That's Dylan.[8]

Being sensitive to the artist's needs includes allowing them to set up the code of conduct implicitly. This makes them comfortable and is particularly important in working with someone famous. The bigger the celebrity, the more they are likely to reserve, or insist upon, distinct areas of privacy. Some celebrity artists expect to be addressed formally, such as Diana Ross, who famously insisted on being called "Miss Ross."[9]

HOW DO YOU TELL THEM SOMETHING IS NOT WORKING?

It can be mood destroying and counterproductive to tell artists and musicians that they are doing something wrong or that an idea is not working out, particularly when they do not think so. Nevertheless, producers are not paid to settle for less than the best. Tact and diplomacy are essential tools for the producer and so, at times, is a willingness to be direct without being confrontational. The best musicians respond well to encouragement, but occasionally a persistent problem needs to be acknowledged. Benny Blanco says that he "makes a lot of mental notes" meaning that if he detects the artist is attached to something, he lets it go for the moment but gently brings it up later as in "I'm not so sure about that chorus melody."[10]

Good musicians, if their intonation, articulation, or timing is off, respect you for identifying the problem and bringing it to their attention. I have been challenged numerous times by well-known studio musicians when asking them to do another take or punch-in. If they did not hear problem, I identify which notes I am concerned about and let them hear that section. Internal parts such as second and third 16th notes in a run can sound fine on a casual pass, but a detailed listen can reveal them to be rushed, dragged, pitchy, or poorly articulated. Producers usually try to address these issues using positive language and in many instances, this works well. Lead vocal parts are the most delicate to deal with. Vocal producer Kuk Harrell said,

> It's never, "Man, you screwed up." I can tell Jennifer she's not singing it the right way without telling her that she's not singing it the right way: "Give it a sexy vibe like you're singing in the shower," or "Sing it like no one else is in the room."

He is referring to Jennifer Lopez, who said of Harrell that he "can find your strengths, and he can pull those out." She added:

> Everything is always done in an encouraging sort of way. One of his favorite lines—I don't know if he uses it with everybody, but he uses it with me—is: "That's a superstar performance right there! That's it!" And it just makes you feel so great about what you're doing.[11]

Quantifiable problems such as pitch or timing may be delicate, but it is even more difficult to challenge an idea or performance especially when the producer has no alternative that is acceptable to the performer. Ideally, producers establish in the minds of the artists or musicians that they are looking out for their best interests and working as a team to achieve the optimal result. The skill is in attaining the outcome you need without diminishing the performers' confidence. Finally, confrontation and conflict are rarely productive, but avoiding potentially awkward or difficult situations, at any cost, is not either, and it is not a leadership skill. Producers need to be adept and positive leaders.

WHERE DOES YOUR RESPONSIBILITY LIE?

The producer's singular responsibility is to make a successful record in terms defined by the stakeholders. The stakeholders might include one, some, or all of the artist, the label, the management company, and the producer. Depending upon genre, the label, and the career stage of the artist, success may not be defined by multiplatinum sales and a number-one chart position. It is the producer's first responsibility to determine who the stakeholders are and what the measures of success will be. Then it is his or her job to orient every aspect of the project in order to achieve those goals.

To the Artist

It is common for producers to say that their allegiance lies with the artist. It is not always easy to ascertain what represents allegiance to the artist. First, an artist can be a group, and members are rarely in complete accord with regard to their artistic goals. Second, achieving their stated artistic goals could cause a band to be dropped from the label. I produced a highly respected but poor-selling group that was informed by the label that the next album would be the last if it did not make money. The label hired me (with the band's approval) to make the record more commercially viable than the previous ones. The entire process was infused with tension between their well-established work habits and doing what was necessary to achieve the label's commercial objectives. As with many groups, an implicit leader largely defined the creative terms. I respected their artistic intentions; the challenge was not their ideas but their execution through their recording methodologies. They did not like to refine or perfect anything; almost anything they recorded, no matter how imprecise, was good enough for them.

    The album was successful, but if they had made the record the way they wanted, the label would most likely have dropped the group before or immediately after release. Had the leader of the band made it clear upfront how he really felt about what the label wanted, I would not have taken the project. Once I was in the studio with them, I saw the mission as trying to construct an album that fully represented the group's creative ideas but that could also be successful in the label's terms. We achieved the goal, but it was an uncomfortable process because of one dominant member's anarchic ideology, which ran counter to their situation.

The producer's responsibility is to represent the artist in the most favorable light. Ideally, the artist should define or embody their artistic direction while the producer applies musical, technical, and conceptual skills to divine, protect, preserve, and realize the essence of the artist. In practice there can be an intentionality gap between what artists think they want and what they actually need.

Respect for the artist may be essential to the realization of a successful production, but opinions diverge as to how that respect should be manifested. If the nominal producer contributes little beyond recording the artist or group as they present themselves, it can be argued that his or her role is not that of producer. One musician or group may be very particular about their material, sound, timing, pitching, and articulation. Others may be doing the best they can with the knowledge and equipment they have and need the input of a producer to achieve the result they envision. In respecting an artist, perhaps the most important decision is whether to take the gig or not. That initial meeting, conversation, or exchange should focus on understanding and compatibility of objectives. Once committed to the project, the producer's job is to maintain effective 360-degree communication with the musicians and artists. Musicians may initially want things their way but are usually open enough to appreciate the producer's suggestions for improvement.

Masumi Rostad, violist with the Pacifica Quartet, interviewed their producer Judith Sherman for WGBH. Rostad commented that they feel like Sherman coaches them and that the group's performance improves, saying, "After the recording process, we always sound a lot better." Echoing those remarks, Sherman noted that other artists have asked (rhetorically), "Can you come to our rehearsals?" As Edison realized, we have the opportunity to idealize performances, and we produce recordings to be heard many times, which requires attention to detail.

Part of the producer's job is to understand the wider culture in which the music exists in order to achieve the appropriate level of precision for that recording. In most genres, many successful records would not sound at all the way they do if the artists made all the decisions. Diverse producers such as Mutt Lange, George Martin, Quincy Jones, Dr. Luke, Dan Huff, Dr. Dre, and others do not change artists arbitrarily, but they creatively and sonically steer the project as their experience guides them.

In certain instances, producers are working to conceal serious flaws in the artist's musical, technical, or conceptual abilities. An artist may want to be bigger than Lady Gaga, but their vision might be marred by their skills, or lack thereof. Professional songwriters have long been a part of the commercial production process, bolstering up weak material. Before the introduction of drum machines and sequencers, studio musicians would record in place of the musicians in the band (often without credit, for the band's credibility) in order to lay a professional-sounding track. Perhaps the most famous example of this is Andy White's drumming on the Beatles' "Love Me Do," replacing Ringo Starr who had just joined the band (replacing Pete Best at the producer's request). Digital audio workstations with tools such as Auto-Tune, Melodyne, and quantization have made previously undreamt-of levels of control and manipulation available to producers. The producer can now be firmly in control of performance accuracy, although it is my observation that producers often moderate artists, who may "fix" tuning and timing errors and use the power of digital manipulation more than the producer or engineer.

It used to be possible to say that the closer to "live" a record sounds, the more control the artist had, because they performed the music and the producer recorded it well (or not well) but without much postproduction control. Today, unless a recording is very sloppy, it can be difficult to tell what is live and what is manipulated. With heavily processed dance-pop records, it is nearly impossible to determine whether the artist can sing, perform, or write by listening to the record. This does not matter to the record company, and in many cases, not to the artist and probably not to the producer. Seminal Seattle-based grunge producer Jack Endino said of highly manipulated records, "I guess there is some value in that sort of sterile sort of produced music, and there must be a market for it, but it's not the way I work." He thinks, "The most important thing is you gotta let bands be bands."[12]

Of course, this is not the way auteur producers record. There are many parallel conceptions and methodologies under the production umbrella, and there is a cyclical element. In terms of hits, the '90s were perhaps more performance-oriented than the '80s, and there has been a distinct move back to highly manufactured productions in the pop charts. Outside of the pop charts, it seems as though anything goes, producers and artists are using any and every technique of production, and some creative blends of styles are emerging.

Producers can be coaches and advisors when it comes to the creative use of technology and the studio. An artist may not be aware that they are stuck in a rut with their attitude toward studio recording techniques. There are groups who think the only way to record is by overdub because they have worked with producers and engineers who only use that methodology. It may be very liberating for an artist to change their approach to the studio. A producer can have a significant impact on an artist's career by optimizing the recording methodology for that artist and a particular recording.

Alan Moulder pledges allegiance to the artist: "It's their career. The record company and management have other artists. . . . For the artist this is maybe their only crack at it."[13] He will work in cheaper studios to accommodate slower artists, "I do the drums in one studio that's pretty good, then move to a really small, cramped, cheap studio to do the guitars and vocals." If they want to do something he thinks will not work, his approach is, "OK, let's try one," saying, "I've quite often been proved wrong and if I try [the idea] it covers my backside." He allocates a certain amount of time and then points out the pitfalls, but if they still want to proceed, he tries to make it work. He will compromise technical considerations to make the group comfortable and get a good performance out of them.[14] This view-point is largely typology- and genre-related.

On a different level altogether, local and regional producers are not becoming rich from advances or royalties and usually work on hourly or daily rates, work-ing continuously to make a living. Artists operating at this level should carefully examine why they choose a particular producer. They should listen to his or her previous work, talk to other artists he or she worked with, and make sure they and the producer have a clear understanding of their expected result and what it will cost. The producer's responsibility is to make sure the artist fulfills or exceeds their expectations within budget. If their expectations are unrealistic, deliverables should be clarified before a penny is spent. It may be better for the producer to spend the budget producing fewer higher quality tracks than to use the time producing a whole album. However, if the artist needs a ten-track album to sell at shows, three perfect tracks will not serve their purpose. These conversations with the producer must be in writing (e-mail is fine) for reference, should there be later disagreement.

To the Record Company

The producer's responsibility is to understand and ensure that the recording meets the expectations of the label. If it becomes apparent that the recording will diverge signif-icantly from what they anticipate, the producer needs to notify the label to discuss the new direction as soon as a variance becomes apparent. This can avoid later conflict between the label and producer. Every label has different needs. An indie label may be happy with an honest representation of a band that will sell to its fan base; major labels want the record to chart; and everyone wants to recoup costs and make some money. Some labels control the artistic direction, and it is the producer's responsibil-ity to understand what the A&R person expects. An A&R person's directions can be ambiguous, incomprehensible, or at odds with the artist's sensibilities. They can also be out of touch with what their marketing department thinks is a promotable track or album, and that can lead to a complete revision of requirements upon delivery.

The more accurately you can glean the expectations of everyone at the label who is likely to have an impact on the acceptance and success of the record, the more likely you will have a successful experience and work with that label again. Even when you have produced several tracks or albums for a label, attitudes can shift, and it is important to make sure that visions align for each project. Labels hire producers to get it right the first time. Pete Ganbarg, veteran A&R person who's worked on major projects during his various tenures at SBK, Arista, Sony, and Atlantic Records says,

> I've always felt that if I hire a producer, they're working for me and we need to
> have a creative understanding between A&R person and producer. But certain
> guys don't feel that way, they're like, "you're job is to find the band, my job is
> to make the record, leave me alone."

Peter Collins says his loyalties in the studio are

> more to the artist actually; we're making a record for the artist, and if they're happy, chances are the record company will be happy. In most cases though, they [the label] always want the hit single. I always think my job is making the artist's album.[15]

These statements illustrate the somewhat conflicted position that producers are in. In practice, seasoned producers maintain a balance so that both label and artist feel heard and their interests are protected. This requires good communication skills, negotiation, and diplomacy. Because the producer is the label's representative in the studio, playing works in progress for them and discussing any concerns about direction can avoid unpleasant surprises later.

Finally, the producer has a fiscal responsibility to the label that is enforced by an overage clause or an all-in budget. Sometimes contracts define "over" as more than 10 percent above projection. Unless the producer has prior approval in writing, the label subtracts any excess from advances and/or royalties and in some cases requires repayment.

To Yourself

Each project is an opportunity to develop or diminish your career. Your responsibility to yourself is to create the time and the mental, physical, and emotional environment in which you can produce your best work. Every time you embark on a production, a series of processes are set in motion. Before the media passes judgment and the public proclaims a hit or miss, the record company assesses your work. If it does not meet their needs, the record may never be released, or they might terminate the production and complete it with someone else. Both are demoralizing options for you that are damaging to your relationship with the label and artist, and possibly your reputation.

Artists and labels do not necessarily stop using a producer for overspending, especially if the record is subsequently a hit. Nevertheless, the ether is littered with expensive recordings that did not recoup, and unrecouped recordings do not encourage labels to rehire you. Spending your way out of a problem is a risky gambit. Creating a detailed budget and tracking it daily are necessary to stay within budget and deliver the record everyone is expecting.

To the Project

It might be an album, a group of tracks, or just one track, but each project tends to have a life and identity of its own. Even if you work with the same artist on multiple albums, each one has a unique set of circumstances, its own workflow, and sometimes distinct sounds, different personnel, locations, and so forth. Responsibility to the project is in some ways a combination of commitments to the artist, label, and yourself. Yet each project's unique identity has its own demands and engenders its own responsibilities. The producer's obligation to the project is to blend all the input from the artist and label with his or her ideas and whatever else is relevant into a whole that is greater than the sum of the parts.

I want to be proud of every record I make. No one can guarantee that every project will be a hit, but a well-produced record of limited or no success can still be a powerful advertisement for your abilities. Often successful bands are hip in their listening habits, and the obscure group you produced might be what they listen to on the tour bus. Similarly, many A&R people have wide-ranging listening habits. If your work is impressive, it could lead to a work enquiry. Internet searches turn up all your work, including ones you may not be proud of, so make every project count. It is worth remembering that *Pet Sounds* fell short of commercial expectations. Regardless, it inspired *Sgt. Peppers*, and many believe it is one of the greatest albums of the rock-pop era. It marked a shift in the Beach Boys' approach and in how popular music albums were perceived. It achieved integrity as a project.

What about Drugs and Alcohol?

IN THE STUDIO

My observation is that even the most dissolute artists are critical of a producer if they feel that his or her performance is being impaired by indulgences. A producer establishes stability on a session, sets the pace, and ensures the project is progressing on schedule. There are (most likely apocryphal) stories about those who can produce a work of genius in any state of consciousness, but reliable accounts have it that even the great bebop alto saxophonist, Charlie Parker, was less than brilliant when high. Additionally, producing is less about short spurts of inspiration; it demands protracted periods of concentrated focus. I have not seen artists perform better under the influence of drugs or alcohol on a session, and it is hard to survive long-term overindulgence, personally or professionally. Nevertheless, there are producers and artists who do not seem to be able to function, in or out of the studio, without using one drug or another. Andy Jackson thinks this is a wider issue:

> You are dealing with someone's entire life. There is an arguable case that marijuana use can be good for inspiration. There's a very clear case that it's not good for work. There's the rub. Making a record is a combination of the two things. Maybe you can divide the two things. The truth of making a record is the 99-percent perspiration thing. There's a degree of inspiration but really that mostly happens at an earlier stage; the writing, arranging, and rehearsing. Maybe there's the divide. What qualifies as work and what qualifies as creative? It's, arguably, helpful for one and destructive for the other.[16]

He also commented that "you make more mistakes of judgment. You end up redoing things, doing crazy hours, which is very counterproductive."[17]

In the days when rock 'n' roll was less corporate, Al Schmitt's drink was spiked with LSD while working with engineer Allen Zentz on the first Hot Tuna album. Schmitt was ready to start recording in the remote truck. He thought he was drinking apple juice when, "All of a sudden the sides of the truck started to breathe. I looked at Allen and said, 'Buddy, you are on your own tonight.'"[18] Schmitt says he rarely did drugs while working, although "afterwards we all got into it pretty hot and heavy." He noted that "some engineers could smoke joints and keep working, but I couldn't. I didn't drink on the job either."[19]

In a video interview with BBC Radio 1 disk jockey Benji B, Tony Visconti said, "I've been with bands when they're wrecked, and I'm the last person standing because I have to be." He also points out that both marijuana and alcohol use negatively affects your hearing. He said, "I try to keep my bands sober and minimally drug-free."[20]

OUTSIDE OF WORKING HOURS

What producers do in their own time is really nobody's business, but if you do it with the artist, you run the risk of a perception problem. If your habits translate into diminished performances, your career will eventually decline. There is no loyalty in hell. Some of the biggest drug users I have worked with gossip about others' alleged drug use. A producer and artist I know had sniped at each other for years. The artist was a heavy user, but he did not like the producer getting high in the studio. It came to a head and they stopped working together for some time.

An apparently innocuous practice that can trigger the crazy-hours syndrome is going out for after-dinner drinks. Everybody gets back to the studio juiced and ready to roll, but judgment is undermined and it is usually more productive to end for the day.

In the VH1 show "Behind the Music," many artists are portrayed as being brought to a low point in their careers and personal lives through the abuse of drugs and alcohol. Similar stories about producers are rarely publicized, but the same rules apply. MTV.com ran a story in 2009 about producer Scott Storch (Beyoncé, 50 Cent, the Game, T.I., Chris Brown, Christina Aguilera, Dr. Dre, Nas, Snoop Dogg, Pink, and more). Reportedly triggered by cocaine addiction, he spent $30 million in six months. He wound up being "arrested for grand theft auto for allegedly failing to return a Bentley he'd leased in 2006 and had legal problems after falling behind on both his child-support payments and his property taxes." The story states that he kept Janet Jackson waiting in his studio for nearly five hours and others for ten hours or more. His manager, Derek Jackson, said:

> We made a lot of money—I mean a lot of money that year [2006]. And Scott—in all honesty—he was broke by January. It was the quickest [loss] of money that I've ever seen in my entire life.

It was not that he spent all the money on drugs. Storch added,

> The cost of the drug didn't effect [*sic*] my life. It was the poor decisions I made, that were so poor financially, that caused me to go into this situation where I was forced to change my lifestyle... forced to change a lot of things. [I had] 15 to 20 cars at all times. That's not smart. I would take one of 15 half-million-dollar cars I owned and go to the mall and spend that much money. Stupid, stupid stuff. It's like it didn't make a difference. They were ego investments. I would have been great with three or four cars! I didn't need a 117-foot boat.

His manager elaborated on how so much money disappeared so quickly:

> Cars! Private jets are expensive—please leave them alone if you can't afford them. Trips to the Riviera on a private jet is [*sic*] $250,000 one way. I'm talking about, it was a routine [with Scott]. Spending on others—if you can't take care of yourself, how you gonna take care of everybody else? And it got out of control.

This is an extreme example, but it is easy, in the face of sudden money, for people to think they can afford anything and begin living beyond their means. Apart from the expense, drugs and alcohol do not help in making wise decisions. The good news in this case is that Storch went for treatment and began producing again before he completely destroyed his reputation and career.[21]

WHAT IF THE ARTIST DOES AND YOU DO NOT?

If it is his or her sixth album and you are the new producer, if you pontificate, you will probably not last very long on the sessions. If it's their first album and your 51st, you can try giving advice. In one case, I had to call the label and end a project early because the artist did not show up on time or in any kind of condition to perform. Sometimes artists appear to have a Kurt Cobain/Jim Morrison/James Dean/Jimi Hendrix/Janis Joplin/Elvis Presley fixation (usually all at once). Check the posters in their room: If they have three or more of the above, clear the studio of guns, fast cars, baths, alcohol, and drugs and complete the album quickly.

What Do You Do When the Artist Becomes Difficult?

There are many ways artists can be difficult. It can manifest as a constant resistance; showing up late to the studio is so common it is almost not worth mentioning, but it is frustrating and disrespectful of everyone's time. One artist always came one hour late, then went out for breakfast, and when he got back would read the sports pages before he could perform or make decisions. Some days I had things to do and some days it was inconvenient. I suggested we start two hours later so he could eat breakfast and read the sports pages before he arrived at the studio. He agreed and the next day I showed up at the studio two hours later than usual, he turned up an hour after that and said he had to go and get some breakfast; on his return he flipped open the paper and proceeded to read the sports pages. I mentioned this to Mike Clink and he said, "I don't care when they're a couple of hours late, it's when it's days and weeks."[22]

Passive-aggressive behavior becomes wearying. It can be difficult to identify (actions speak louder than words) and to counter because the response is usually some form of denial or avoidance. Responding to passive aggression by "mirroring" the behavior simply fuels and extends the conflict.[23] Addressing the problem directly, calmly, and privately, to try to get the true issue brought out into open discussion, is the best solution.[24]

Disappearing at key moments in the day or for long stretches during a project can also be problematic. I generally try to schedule days so that there is always something to work on even if the agreed plan has to be revised because of unplanned absences. There are several points in a production, however, when you need certain people to be there in order to make progress.

Relationships change between the debut and sophomore album. With success, the artist is now busy and under pressure to deliver a successful follow-up. For the first album, they might have been nice kids who sat quietly in the studio and asked if they could borrow the bus fare home. By the second album, these unassuming kids' proclivities adjust to "Where's the f***ing limo, and why isn't there any Cristal?" and so on. Fortunately, booking limos and ordering champagne are not in the producer's bailiwick, but a sudden philosophical reorientation to the right of self-centered can be disturbing.

This business feeds egos with permutations of adulation, fame, sex, sycophantism, alcohol, drugs, and money, and overstuffed egos can explode. Thankfully, there are artists who remain down to earth and unaffected. It is hard to survive the extremes and excesses of the music industry unchanged, and it usually takes a few career peaks and valleys to gain some perspective. A studio tantrum can be as mild as throwing headphones across the room because the foldback mix is not to someone's liking. In rare cases, these can turn into full-blown verbal attacks. I once wrote out a check for the advance the label had paid me, handed it to the still out-of-control artist, and headed for the hills. I got a call from the label and was back at work with a subdued and more respectful artist within 24 hours. I do not advocate walking out; it should be an absolute last resort in face of uncontrollable disrespect or incivility.

Most producers develop the patience of Job, strong conciliation skills, and restraint in their responses. Daniel Goleman coined the term "amygdala hijack" to describe the explosive rage that is part of the fight-or-flight mechanism and occurs before the analytical part of the brain, the neocortex, can engage a problem. It is an instinctual reaction from the most ancient part of the human brain.[25] Goleman cites Mike Tyson biting Evander Holyfield's ear as an example.[26] The indication that one of these events is occurring is a strong and sudden emotional response that on later reflection can be seen as inappropriate.[27] These amygdalic attacks are survival responses that short-circuit analytical thinking in order to respond instantly to a life-or-death situation. Unfortunately, the amygdala does not differentiate between an ego attack and a tiger attack. When you see a situation that has the hallmarks of an emotional hijack, the best solution is to allow time for the neurochemicals to subside and the rational brain to reengage (about 20 minutes). A break, lunch, change of tack, ending for the day, or a carefully calculated and diversionary joke can be useful devices. Nevertheless, the most effective way to avoid a confrontation is for the producer to read the room and the interpersonal exchanges constantly, to anticipate, divert, and diffuse volatile situations.

What Do You Do When the Record Company Is Unhappy?

In principle, producer and label are pursuing the same objective of a successful record. In practice, egos also run rife on the business side. Inexperience and lack of leadership and management skills exacerbate the problem. Rampaging stars damage themselves, whereas stampeding executive egos can destroy careers.

As a neophyte, I thought the label's objective was to create hits and make money, but there are subplots and hidden agendas. Being aware of them is a matter of self-defense and survival. Executive preferences and incentives can power or destroy careers. With senior executive goodwill, a company will commit to an artist for longer and be more creative in seeking hits. They might set up co-writing situations with notable songwriters, hold top-line outside material for singles, or hire the best producers. They may spend more on promotion and marketing, as well as for artwork and videos. Stars are born at the will of the company, with the cooperation of artist and management. A good artist and album can be lost if label goodwill is lacking. Labels can view artists as uncooperative for standing firm on creative integrity. Once the lines are drawn, positions become entrenched, and it is easy to forget that the label holds the success or failure of the record in its hands. I have seen groups refuse to tour to coincide with the record release or push to incur touring shortfalls when there is no new release to promote. Artists often will not accept that their material is not gaining traction, or that a video concept is too abstract or expensive. Dogmatic, paranoid, or confrontational behavior can lose them the support of the company.

On the other hand, talented artists can have their individuality quashed by uncreative A&R and marketing teams who are thinking only in terms of what is currently happening. Chasing market trends is an established route to success and, for an artist unconcerned with breaking new ground, may pose no moral or creative dilemma. Nonetheless, artist and producer need the cooperation and goodwill of the label. Prevention is better than a cure—by the time the label expresses displeasure, the relationship may be beyond repair. The onus is on the producer to communicate with the company apprising them of what is happening in the studio. The A&R person may have several projects in production along with his or her other company commitments. Often, they don't focus on your project until you deliver finished mixes. By then the budget is spent and if the record is off track, recovery can be costly—financially and in terms of time, diplomacy, and lost kudos.

If the record company is not pleased and you cannot make them happy again, not only is that project at risk but so is future work from them. It can be challenging to be diplomatic when a label expresses doubts about your work, but staying calm is essential. Depending on your restraint, level of influence within the label, and the status of the person who is the source of dissension, carefully considering and complying with their requests may be the only realistic option.

There are established steps that can be taken toward a safe resolution of conflict, which include listening to find areas of agreement and to isolate concerns; eliminating ambiguity (put everything in writing); being flexible; and mutually agreeing upon an action plan and timeframe for the corrective steps.[28]

Specific differences appear smaller and more resolvable than generalized expressions of displeasure. Broad unsubstantiated assertions indicate the disapproving person's lack of analysis. By calmly asking questions, listening carefully to the responses, making concessions, and identifying points of agreement, it is often possible to reach consensus with few changes. For instance, the loudness wars have caused untold problems for producers and mixers who send in unmastered mixes. Best practice is not to over-compress a mix, but if someone at the label or the artist plays your unmastered mix against a mastered recording, there will be a significant level difference and (depending on the listener's sophistication) the mastered mix will appear to be more impactful. This is easily resolved by sending in premastered mixes with added mastering-type compression while holding an uncompressed or lightly compressed version that will go to the mastering engineer. Understanding that this is the problem can require some simple conflict resolution skills.

I have had the experience on delivery where an A&R person has strong initial misgivings about the mix. Upon careful, systematic analysis, it transpired that one or two minor elements such as a reverb on the snare drum and a short delay on the vocals caused the distress. Despite an initial broadly negative reaction, these were two-minute fixes involving no conceptual shift. In expressing opinions about productions, label personnel have widely divergent analytical abilities and production vocabularies that result in generalizations. Ideological or formularized opinions such as "I don't like reverb" are not unheard of (Rick Rubin favors dry mixes). Producers have to accommodate others' preferences—the challenge is in identifying them before any damage occurs.

What Do You Do When the Artist's Manager Is Difficult?

Danny Saber was away from home working with a well-known artist. The manager put him in an apartment with mold growing on the walls. Danny expressed displeasure, and they moved him to a better place. The project went smoothly, and they extended his stay to finish more tracks. He called the artist's management company three times to remind them to renew the apartment lease, which they failed to do. In the middle of recording an album, he had to move to a hotel and waste part of a day doing so. The hotel cost more than the apartment so the artist paid more than necessary. Producers suffer from normal human frailties, and when someone is working 16-hour days, six or seven days a week, a disruption can affect their ability to get the job done on time and on budget.

I was working on four tracks for an artist and as I was lining up my next project, I told the label, the artist, and her manager, several times, that if they wanted me to finish the album, I needed to know by a certain date. The date came and went without response so I booked the next project. Finally, they asked me to continue with the current album, but I could not.

There are many ways managers can be difficult to work with. A common one is by omission—not doing something that is needed, being unresponsive in contract negotiation, not paying bills on time, and so on. Notwithstanding, being an artist manager is no easy job. When anything goes wrong, it falls to the manager who has 360-degree responsibility involving the artist, label, attorneys, publishers, producer, agent, business manager, merchandiser, club owners, and promoters. They oversee that team, each facet requiring different skills and knowledge. Some managers can be heavy-handed at times; this is understandable when you realize the disparate interests, personalities, and politics they have to juggle. It is worth building strong relationships with good managers. They have been known to pluck an album from the brink of obscurity when a label is ready to abandon it.

8

Lawyers

My attorney friends flip immediately to this chapter and are disappointed with their profession's portrayal. Therefore, I want to preface it by saying I do not intend to malign attorneys; they should be the producer's best friend. However, it would be disingenuous not to acknowledge some of the challenges of dealing with the legal profession. Not the least of which is the discrepancy between what most producers are paid (at this time) and the cost of securing a favorable and binding contract.

What Are the Issues?

Since the first edition of this book (1997), with the exception of an ever-shrinking group of top producers, advances have decreased dramatically. Many producers today do not work with labels that can or will pay a substantial advance. In a recent conversation, some top-level producers disclosed that less than 10 percent of their work comes from major labels at this time, whereas little more than a decade ago that figure would have been close to 100 percent. For these producers, it has become uneconomical to pay for the quality of legal advice that they need. Production contracts govern the terms under which the producer will work, deliver, and be paid. In the mid- to long-term, the payment terms are the most important because they define how the producer royalties will be calculated and paid from future sales and use. Royalties are a share of the productivity or long-term value, in part generated by the producer. They represent potential financial security.

Unfortunately, many producers are abandoning contracts. This is in part because the legal costs would deplete or exceed the producer fee, and expectations of future royalties are down due to the past decade's diminished sales. It is a personal choice, but to produce for a fee without a contract sacrifices future potential income to which a producer is legitimately entitled. There are now many more revenue streams for artists and producers, and they are growing. With no contract, producers cannot access these, and they disregard them at their financial peril. We are still transitioning into new models of music delivery. Many producers ignore these income streams because some of these models pay very small amounts per listen or per use of a track. Based on the current user base, these rental systems cannot match past or even present revenues from the ownership or purchase model. However, a fraction of a penny each from a significantly higher percentage of the seven billion people currently on the planet could add up to worthwhile income. Unfortunately, a producer without a contract will not be able to access those monies now or in the future.

WHAT CHANGED TO MAKE HIRING AN ATTORNEY LESS VIABLE?

Nearly a century ago, Will Rogers ambiguously quipped, "Make crime pay. Become a lawyer."

At the confluence of the postmillennial music industry downturn and the democratizing affect of digital audio workstations, the resultant downsizing of recording budgets and producer advances furthered the move toward all-in recording budgets. Additionally, multi-producer albums are on the rise. Producers are not protected by any legislation; they have no statutory rights like the ones songwriters enjoy, so without a contract, producers have no way to be sure they will get paid. A multi-producer album may require a contract for just one track, and that contract may cost as much as a full album agreement, regardless of the fact that the producer advance will be a fraction of that from a full album. Attorneys in large law firms work on billable hours that cover their salary and overhead and generate revenue for the firm. Even given how high lawyer fees are, attorneys often work ten or more hours a day billing every hour possible to meet their firms' targets.[1] Whatever the reasons, legal fees for producer contracts have, for the most part, remained steady or increased, becoming unrealistically large relative to declining producer advances, except in the case of a now smaller number of big budget recordings.

HOW MUCH WILL THEY COST YOU?

Top-level music business attorneys are usually paid an hourly rate or by retainer. Sometimes they work for a percentage of a deal (typically between 5 and 10 percent). This may be relevant if you sign an artist and an attorney helps place the recordings with a label. For regular production contracts, the hourly rate is high, $200 being the low end with the top firms charging $400 and more per hour. Negotiating a production contract can consume several hours, and even a relatively simple agreement can result in a bill of $2,500 or more. Retainers can average out favorably if a producer has a constant flow of work, the premise being that you can receive the advice you need for a regular monthly payment. The concern is that once you are paying the retainer, the firm over-commits its time and responds slowly. Should your business slow down, the retainer becomes uneconomical. Larger companies typically have at least one big-name attorney: a partner who will ostensibly be your attorney. Once you are paying a retainer, a junior lawyer will do most of your contract work and be your primary contact. If you opt to pay by the hour, your attorney will talk to you for as long as you like.

On multi-producer albums, a low- to mid-price producer could pay out 50 to 100 percent or more of the advance in legal fees. This is a producer poverty-trap because working without a formal agreement can potentially result in the loss of significant income.

DO YOU REALLY NEED THEM?

In the United States, you can draw up and sign agreements or contracts without consulting an attorney. If neither party retains a lawyer, the agreement can be simple and still be binding. Verbal or oral agreements are technically binding, but as Sam Goldwyn (some say Mark Twain) pointed out, "Verbal contracts are not worth the paper they are written on." There is usually no way to indisputably establish what the substance of an oral agreement was; therefore, it is preferably to have any deal in writing, signed by all parties. The challenge with any contract is that it will be years before many of the terms are tested. Weaknesses or omissions can cost you royalties and possibly additional legal fees. Attorneys do not guarantee their work; I learned this early on in my career—to my chagrin. Sometimes people talk about renegotiating contracts once a project is successful. A contract is legally binding, and there is no incentive for the other party to renegotiate unless you are able and prepared to concede some terms in order to improve others. Only if you have some form of leverage will the label renegotiate. Some say that you can sue your lawyer if he or she makes a costly mistake. Music business attorneys are a tight-knit community and unless there is an egregious case of malpractice or fraud involving large amounts of money, it would be expensive and difficult to win a case.

Experienced music business lawyers see deals and contracts every day. They know the going rates and standard practices. This translates, in practical terms, to knowing which contractual points are worth fighting for and which are not. Producer contracts rarely transcend the norm or the artist's terms and should be an inexpensive template. Nevertheless, an experienced lawyer can save you money by advising when to stand firm and when to concede. It is almost always a mistake to use a non-music business lawyer to negotiate a producer contract. The music business, like most others, has its idiosyncrasies. Ros Earls said,

> Lawyers are a necessary evil really. I'd rather not use them and for the most part we take the contract as far as we can. There's only so many things that you expect to see on a contract and you could write the whole thing yourself. You do need to involve a lawyer at some stage because most of the contracts aren't binding [in the U.K.] unless you have independent legal advice. You can set up a regular deal so that you ask for the same terms as last time, but they always try to change things so you have to pay through the nose again, although everybody knows, there's only a limited number of things they are going to repair.

Will Rogers's other lawyer gibe, "The minute you read something that you can't understand, you can almost be sure that it was drawn up by a lawyer," illustrates why, expensive as they are, doing business without a reputable attorney is risky. Typically, contracts are written in legalese, not plain English. Certain words, phrases, and terms carry different weight in a contract than they do in conversational language. Additionally, producing today is an international pursuit, and each country's laws vary. Even if you become knowledgeable about the law in your own country, you could miss critical elements in foreign markets.

HOW MUCH SHOULD YOU DEPEND ON THEM?

You are the one who suffers financial damage if an attorney makes a mistake, making it imperative to work with someone you trust. The safest course of action is to learn to understand your own agreements. You should read every agreement and question anything you do not understand before signing. Finding the time to do so is difficult when you are busy. The three most expensive contractual mistakes I suffered all happened during my busiest, most productive period. Not relying entirely on your lawyer means allocating time to read contracts and e-mails referring to, say, clause 13(i), (ii), and (iii). This is boring but so is looking left and right when you cross the road. If you enjoy earning what is rightfully yours, understand your contracts. When you tire of producing or need time off, you will be glad you did.

WHAT HAPPENS WHEN THEY GET IT WRONG?

When lawyers make a mistake, it becomes your problem. If you identify the problem during the project, it may be fixable, but if you do not detect it for several years, you will live with the consequences. You may never know about a mistake unless someone (you or your business manager) checks your statements against your agreements.

In my first production contract, my then-lawyer agreed to a clause that I did not permit in subsequent agreements. About eight years later, the group's greatest hits album went multiplatinum. Their manager alerted me to a substantial payment I would be receiving so I could plan for the tax implications, but when it arrived it was half the amount we expected. Our initial calculations were correct, so I went to the contract and found, hidden away on page 33 or so, the clause reducing my royalties to 50 percent under this specific circumstance. I expressed dismay to the lawyer who negotiated the agreement that he had allowed this clause that experience had taught me could be negotiated out. His response was that I could retain (meaning pay) him to "take a look at the problem." Our only recourse was to sue, and—as discussed—this is a time-consuming and generally not cost-effective option.

Producer manager Sandy Roberton tracks each of his contracts in his computer so that he knows where they are in the negotiations. He uses a "contract guy" who does not rush "around the clubs trying to get bands signed." He said he's "had a lawyer like that before and umpteen contracts didn't get completed."

Roberton highlights another problem that I had later in my career, with another highly regarded law firm of the type he alluded to (one that shops deals to majors for a percentage). They did an agreement that was never fully executed by the label. I signed it and returned it to them, but the attorneys failed to get the label to countersign. I pressed the law firm to use their influence to have it completed, and they promised they would but did not. I did receive royalties but in recent years the lack of a fully executed contract has made it difficult to access new revenue streams. After several sales, mergers, and acquisitions, the new company stopped paying me my royalties. Because I do not have a fully executed agreement, I cannot get them to resume despite the fact that they have a history of paying me and I am credited on all the recordings as producer. Major labels are unforgiving. If they can find a legal loophole, they will not pay, irrespective of the ethics or what is clearly the truth of the situation. These issues are rarely discussed publicly, and if both Sandy Roberton and I have had this problem, it seems unlikely that these are isolated incidents. I read my contracts and understand them. As mentioned, this happened in one of my busiest years and at those times, you become very dependent on your staff and your advisors to do the jobs they have been paid to do.

I have had some very successful professional relationships with lawyers, but then again I lost a lot of money to another one through his consciously deceptive practices. Ideally, find an attorney or law firm that takes a long-term view when it comes to money, one that will not overcharge for the small, early career deals and that will stay with you as your career develops.

WHAT OTHER KINDS OF THINGS CAN GO WRONG?

Carol Crabtree of Solar Management told me, "Music business lawyers are a mine-field. They can cost you a fortune by dreaming up ridiculous things to argue over." She cited a lawyer she caught sending many faxes (charging her for time and materials) over the size of the producer's credits and outside placement on the packaging. This is a legitimate subject to debate; a missing, wrong, or undersized credit on a successful album can cost you future work. What the attorney failed to note, however, was that the record had been out for months, making it a moot point.[2]

Sandy Roberton identified a problem that happens in the United States where the band's attorney negotiates and issues the producer agreement rather than the label. As mentioned, artists often pay lawyers a percentage of the advance for negotiating the deal. If the producer contract is incomplete when the recording agreement is done, the band will have paid their attorneys who then have no incentive to complete the deal. As Roberton said, "You get into a situation where you can't get the producer contract signed." Without a contract, you cannot get the letter of direction (LOD) signed in which the artist gives the label permission to pay you, and without the LOD, a producer cannot get the back end of his or her advance (usually 50 percent). This, again, underscores that it is a caveat emptor (buyer beware) market and you have to systematically check that your attorneys have done their job properly.

WHAT IS A TYPICAL LEGAL PROCESS LEADING UP TO THE
PRODUCTION?

The way negotiations usually proceed is that you, your manager, or your lawyer
will discuss the basic terms such as your advance, royalty percentage (commonly
known as points), number of tracks, and any other deal-breaking parameters with
the A&R person, the business/legal affairs person, or the artist's attorney, depending on where the deal is being done. The negotiating party for the other side may
then send you a deal memo outlining these terms and, subsequently, their standard
producer contract with them incorporated. The agreed terms will be eroded by various terms in the rest of the contract, known as reductions and deductions. From
time to time, I have discovered "mistakes or misunderstandings," which have always
been in the label's favor.

Typically, the headings agreement or deal memo gives you what you want, and
the deductions and reductions take much of it back for the label. Your lawyer then
sends the agreement back to them "marked up" with the modifications and corrections that you and he want. There might be a couple of exchanges, and eventually
there will be a "redline" or marked-up version with the amendments underlined in red
or in "track changes" but somehow visible (which does not mean you shouldn't check
the rest of the terms again). If this version is agreeable, they send signature copies for
the producer to sign. The final contract should be identical to the final markup and
usually is. I recall two instances where there were variances to agreed terms in the final
contract. In both cases, business affairs acknowledged the errors and corrected them.
Nonetheless, had I not noticed them, they would have remained in the contract to my
disadvantage. Others have had the same experience. It may seem unduly cautious to
check signature copies before you sign and return them, but once a contract is signed
and countersigned, those deal terms stand. The next time you might read an agreement
could be years later when you have concerns over royalty payments, rights, or credits.

It is common for producers to begin making the record before they receive the
fully executed contract. This is never to the advantage of the producer. Once you
begin working with the artist, you all but eliminate your leverage on any disputed
points. Ros Earls said she has "never had a situation where the producer would pull
out of the studio because the contract was not in place." Doing so can jeopardize
the creative relationship. Earls tries to "agree things before preproduction starts" so
that "the producer can be the good guy."

Record companies' legal departments are often slow to respond in contract
negotiations, confronting the producer with the difficult decision as to whether to
start recording or not.

What Can Be Done to Protect Producers?

With legal fees outstripping advances, it would help if producers had a guild or
union that could negotiate minimums, or at least set guidelines and supply an

authorized form or template contract for producers to fill in the blanks. No such organization exists, and some are opposed to the idea. The basic terms of producer contracts are quite standard, and it is difficult to understand why each negotiation takes so much time. Nonetheless, the attorneys for the artists or the labels (depending which country you are in) nibble away at the producer's terms, and even when you have done a dozen contracts with the same company and say "same as last time," the legal hours creep up along with the bill.

Fortunately, some attorneys, acknowledging producers' adjusted financial situations, are generating more standardized agreements for lower fees. Some producer managers retain an attorney to negotiate for all their clients, cutting individual costs significantly. As noted, Sandy Roberton has this kind of arrangement, which has two advantages: "I've been able to get him to give us a really good blanket deal for each project so the clients get a really good deal and I don't have to speak to 60 lawyers." The producers still have to pay the fees, but they gain from the economies of scale. Like Ros Earls, Katrina Sirdofsky takes care of the basic terms, which are incorporated in a deal memo: "We do the initial negotiations and the deal memos and let the lawyers handle the long forms" (the full contract).

Producers need to understand contract terms and find a music industry attorney who will work within contemporary financial realities. Some attorneys do take a longer term view. Some producer managers are also lawyers, which can be convenient and economical but strips away a layer of checks and balances increasing the producer's vulnerability. As mentioned, I suffered a serious financial loss due to a corrupt lawyer acting as my manager. You know the saying, "Power corrupts, absolute power corrupts absolutely," and the temptation to steal can be too much for some. It is safer having a manager who is independent from your attorney.

Of the possible solutions, producing without a signed agreement is not a good one. Find a receptive music business contract attorney and negotiate a fixed fee per contract, preferably prorated per track, so you know how much you are going to pay. If you generate many contracts, you may be better off paying a monthly retainer. Regional and local producers should use a short standard agreement to establish their credits, financial terms, and deliverables.

9

Challenges and Controversies

Producers are problem-solvers. Productions begin as concepts that will embody disparate elements, known and unknown. The producer's task is to combine these parts and ideas to make a coherent communicative statement. In his book *Cognition and Thought*, Walter Reitman defined a problem as "when you have been given the description of something but do not yet have anything that satisfies that description." He described a problem-solver as "a person perceiving and accepting a goal without an immediate means of reaching the goal."[1] This is what producers do.

Apart from artist and auteur producers, most do not face the blank page paralysis that confronts creative artists from time to time—sitting in front of a blank page, canvas, or screen with no immediate thought or inspiration for where to begin. Producers function like editors or commercial artists such as graphic designers—they rarely create on a whim. Typically, there are clients, a target audience, an artistic sub-discipline, and a conceptual brief. To be successful the work has to meet the practical requirements while achieving a high level of "aural communication." The term "production," like "graphic design," means both the process and the result.

A primary challenge for producers is meeting the demands of the commissioning entity or entities that will, in turn, satisfy the wants of a substantial audience. Fine artists may choose to starve in order to follow their artistic muse, but it is notable that much of what we consider great art was commissioned, created under patronage, or made for commercial purposes. These artists had to wrestle with the creative challenges of the work and satisfy clients, donors, or a broad audience to survive. A producer has to mollify many interests, while resolving technical, creative, financial, commercial, and interpersonal problems.

Differences of Opinion

Tony Visconti related a difficult time that he experienced with the Boomtown Rats: "It was a nightmare. It was like a Stephen King novel—it starts out in an innocent little village somewhere. Then there's that little touch of evil that starts to grow.... " Speaking about Bob Geldof, Visconti said,

> He's difficult, and he knows it. He's a good performer, a great songwriter, but you have to keep him out of the mixing room. Apparently, he wants everything to sound very sizzly and trebly, so I used to mix a really fizzy top just for him. I used to put this glistening sound on the cymbals, and he loves to hear his sibilance, which was very hard to get on a vinyl record. Then I said, "Bob, there's a limit. We can't put too much of this on tape." His drummer told me, "You think that's bad, he goes home and he takes all the bass off his hi-fi set, and he adds more treble!" It was then I realized I must be dealing with a deaf person![2]

Some artists are hard of hearing from standing in front of live amplification for too many years, and you only hope they have the wisdom to defer to those who can hear. When faced with this problem, I do an A/B session with the artist's favorite records so that they (and I) can get a relative sense of how our work is sounding.

Being at loggerheads with the artist is a concern of Andy Jackson's: "Or worse...members of the band...at loggerheads with each other." He told me he had never seen a situation where the band has completely broken down, but he has seen disagreements where one person gets very upset. "You just have to take the time...to make them feel their concerns are being listened to." Then, "they will back down from their stance."[3]

Bands have complicated interactions. Minor dissent over a part can devolve into a field study of interpersonal relationships and repressed collegial rancor. Relationships in touring groups become familial, veering into dysfunction with regard to communication competence. The producer must assuage the situation and guide the session back to a functional state.

THE ENDLESS ALBUM

Interminable album projects can be mentally, emotionally, and physically exhausting unless your concern is job security and they are paying you by the hour. Endless albums were largely the realm of rich artists who owned their own studios, and there was comfort in knowing the record would eventually draw media attention. Now, many artists own their own studios, budget is hardly a consideration, and there is little pressure to finish. Andy Jackson is a veteran of the endless album: "After six months you think 'I want to go into a studio where they have to pay for it, I want to get this damn thing finished.'"[4] The discipline imposed by having to pay for studio time can be a good thing and a creative stimulus in itself. Unfortunately, those who have the most difficulty making decisions gravitate toward working in their own studios, so the endless album continues.

LACK OF VISION

Andy Jackson spoke of the importance of an overarching vision for a production, asking, "What record are we really trying to make." He mentioned the problem of artists and producers filling up the multitrack and then trying to "make an arrangement in the mix."[5] The producer's calling exists to realize the stakeholders' vision. Difficult as it may be, the producer must understand or define the vision and then exercise control, without dampening creativity, to ensure realization. The caveat being that it is counterproductive to hold creative thought too closely to a predetermined agenda. Producers allow for experimentation, brainstorming, and stream-of-consciousness periods in the budget and the daily work plan. Defining a vision with goals, milestones, and time for creative experimentation creates a measurable strategy that balances flexibility with a high probability of success within budget.

A vision does not include fine details, but neither can it be a broad statement like "This is going to be the best album ever." The vision needs to be aspirational in its end goal. It should draw on the artist's beliefs and be consistent with their values. An album or track should be strategically consistent with the artist's (and other stakeholders') vision of who they are. This becomes a conceptual template by which to judge progress, going beyond the pragmatics of completing guitar overdubs on schedule.

MICRO-VISION

When most people listen to a track, they do not parse the complexities of the arrangement: how parts weave in and out developing the production; they only know that it works. It can be a surprise to first-time recording artists how much detail goes into a three-minute hit. Sometimes, this process triggers a latent obsessive-compulsive nature; endless hours are spent adjusting the length of every third 16th note in the first violin part that happens during the third verse, or the guitarist might want to add eight overdubs on the two-beat acoustic guitar lick leading into the bridge. The wise old studio musicians I grew up around would ask, "Will it help sell anymore records?" We did have the benefit of a limited number of tracks. With unlimited tracks and editing power, producer and artist can stare at the screen for another day adjusting and tweaking. As Andy Jackson said,

> Obsessive artists are very often the problem. You spend hours and hours and hours punching in little bits that won't make any audible difference to the finished track, and probably won't make the mix anyway.[6]

DAWs have exacerbated the problem. Many artists edit with their eyes rather than their ears. Being able to see and correct problems has been transformative, but zooming in on discrepancies can lead to the correction of parts that sounded fine. It wastes time and can eliminate feel, emotion, and even humanity from the music. Some old-school engineers used to tape over the VU meters to ensure that they were using their ears and not their eyes. My rule is that if I do not hear a problem until I see it, I will not fix it. Sometimes I break my own rules. When micro-vision sets in, take a mental step back and listen to the overall track without focusing on details. Attention to detail is an important part of production, but minutiae can become the proverbial "lipstick on the pig" if you do not regularly reference a wider perspective.

THE SINGER IS NOT PERFORMING WELL

If the problem is tuning, although the go-to solution today might be Auto-Tune or its progeny, vocalists can correct many tuning problems organically. A singer who was in tune on the gig but sharp or flat in the studio may be suffering from an unsupportive headphone mix, perhaps lack of harmonic support—chords against which to pitch. Headphone balances can negatively affect timing in the same way if there are insufficient rhythmic elements in the mix. Singers tend to sing louder if their voice is quiet in their mix and vice versa. Seasoned session singers will tell you what they need to hear, but the less experienced often favor a headphone mix that does not support good timing and tuning. Confusingly, what works best for one vocalist may not work well for another. Some singers can work with the track loud and relatively little of their own voice; others need only a little instrumentation with their voice dominating. Some prefer one side of the headphones off their ear and the other on. The singer I worked with who did not like any reverb in the final mix needed Phil Spector-style reverb on his voice (in the headphones) in order to stay on pitch. Some need to emulate the live experience, and you can record them in the control room, without headphones and with the monitors up loud. There will be considerable spillage, but the vocal performance may be better.

In the early '90s, I worked in a residential studio with a singer who could not manage one syllable out of three in tune, and the one that was in tune was out of time. I tried every trick I knew, but recording whole words in tune and in time did not happen. At night, I dreamt of capturing whole lines. Auto-Tune was years in the future. Thankfully, I was beta testing an early prototype random access multitrack, digital-editing system. I was able to compile (out of an average of ten takes on each song) the most in-tune and in-time set of syllables (not words). Then I painstakingly fine-tuned each word. Amusingly, someone suggested singing a harmony part—I said it was better as a single line.

Much antipathy is directed at pitch correction systems, but aside from becoming a recognizable sound in itself, the more subtle uses have expanded our options. Having captured a great performance, some inaudible adjustments can fix intonation errors that may not have been correctible by the singer. Singers no longer have to repeat the same line endlessly, and the producer does not have to choose between pitch and performance. The notion that singers are worse today because of tuning software may not be correct. Producer Frank Farian did not use Milli Vanilli's vocals at all on their album, and studio singers (and other musicians) have ghosted for artists as long as I can recall. Certain styles of music are more forgiving. Alan Moulder takes the view that "with vocals, if the attitude is there, you can stand a certain amount of timing and tuning problems." He is not averse to fixing the tuning but generally tries "to get the best performance I can."

Thankfully, there are still singers who perform in tune and in time, and many legacy records we hear daily on the radio were made with the vocalist performing live in the studio without punching in, and in many cases without headphones.

THE MUSICIANS ARE NOT PERFORMING WELL

As with pitch-correction software, there seems to be a trend toward correcting everything captured—perhaps because we can. A performance is more than a series of in-time and in-tune notes, and it should be more than a set of parts that work together. We can edit dynamics, fix or emulate feel or groove, and comp together the best parts, but there is no substitute for a great performance. I have worked with machine-generated performances since the '70s, and I value them for what they are. Equally, I value what a practiced musician has to offer. Editing a couple of mistakes in an otherwise exemplary performance is maximization. Cutting, pasting, and fixing poorly played parts is exhausting.

Steve Savage presented a paper entitled "'It could have happened'—the evolution of music construction" in which he discusses a performance by guitarist Warren Haynes (Government Mule) on an Elvin Bishop track that Savage produced. Haynes came into the studio late one night, after a gig, and laid down three solos. At that point, he left the studio saying that he thought they had "enough stuff" and that they should assemble the finished solo. Even though Bishop liked the solos as they were being recorded, when Savage and he tried to compile a full 32-bar solo, they found they could not construct a satisfactory final eight bar section. In the end, they had Kim Wilson play blues harmonica for the last eight measures, solving the problem.[7] What is interesting is not that Haynes played badly—he is an excellent musician—but that he was happy to leave the final construction of the solo to the producer and the artist. The performer supplied the raw material and walked away without hearing the finished solo. Had Haynes still been there when they discovered the weakness in the last eight bars, within another take or two, he could have given them what they needed. There is now such familiarity with DAWs' editing power that consummate musicians are treating their parts as raw material rather than a fully crafted piece. This is interesting conceptually, but not if the end result is inferior.

The DAW has been transformative in dealing with lower levels of musical competency. I recall a couple of difficult pre-DAW sessions. One was with a drummer who had replaced the previous drummer with whom the band had made the demos that got them signed. The new drummer could not play in time or with consistent dynamics. I pieced together a three-minute track from many takes using 32 two-inch tape edits. We were under pressure of time. This was the early days of drum machines, and the band did not want that sound. I tried to make it work for the band and the drummer, having seen musicians improve rapidly during debut albums when they realize what is required. In the end, I played drums on the rest of the album until they found a replacement. Fortunately, both the single and subsequent album went gold. I played drums from the outset on an album for another artist. We used early 32-track digital multitrack machines, but rhythm section overdubs (guitar and bass) became painful because the band members could only manage to play about two bars accurately in a row. Inconsistent timbre and dynamics can be as disturbing as timing and tuning issues. The digital tape made punching in fast and clean, and it proved faster to continue punching in rather than copying and pasting. On a DAW, it would have been easy to fix and loop parts.

Some producers will not work with bands or musicians who are less than the best, but for others, virtuosity is not a factor in deciding whom to produce. Creativity can be the basis for respect as much as virtuosity, and using the studio to optimize performances in order to best project the artist's vision is the essence of production. Nevertheless, it is not fun to discover that the artist or the musicians are less capable than anticipated. It is wise to evaluate the musicians' abilities before you get to the studio. With programmed demos, it is difficult to tell what you will be dealing with until you begin recording. Even when you have seen the band live or in rehearsal, it can be hard to assess how they will perform in the studio. This is why film studios do screen tests. An actor may perform well in a live audition, but some blossom in front of the camera while others shrink. Likewise, some musicians rise to the red light while it debilitates others. With recordings being two dimensional, discrepancies are more pronounced than when you are standing in a room with the band.

On the first day in the studio, if the band is not holding steady tempos and you are committed to capturing the band as naturally as possible, it is essential to understand the source of the problem. Were the demos like this? Did they speed up and slow down when you saw them live? When you are recording the whole band or the rhythm section together, are the musicians comfortable in the room? Can they hear their own instruments and see and hear the others well? Isolating instruments to eliminate spill interferes with the group's natural communications. With some players, it may be necessary to trade optimum separation for a better performance. If all else fails, you may have to build the track by overdubbing with a click track. Further timing issues can be straightened out in the DAW, but the less you have to correct, the faster the process and the more natural the recording will sound.

Headphone mixes also affect a musician's ability to perform well. Make sure that you listen to the mix, preferably in the studio on the same type of headphones the band is using. The foldback system feeding the control room can sound very different from the one feeding the studio. Do not forget that when musicians are playing, unless they are DI'd, they are hearing their own instrument in the room, as well as through the headphones. Standing in the studio near each musician will give you a better impression of what he or she is actually hearing. Additionally, each set of headphones can have its own problems. Sending the headphone feed to the control room monitors might give you an idea of the mix, but it will not indicate exactly what the musicians are hearing. Listening on the musician's headphones can be revealing. A problem that an inexperienced player might not identify (even an egregious one) can be immediately obvious to a producer or engineer. When I was a session drummer, players and singers often complained about their headphone mix, and the engineer would adjust the balance without even listening to the feed. When the musician became insistent that there was a problem, it often turned out to be the specific send or set of headphones that was faulty. Producers who take all complaints or comments seriously and are thorough in diagnosing problems minimize frustrations for performers. If necessary, give the performers a five-minute break so you can check the entire signal chain and replace or route around a faulty section. Technical problems happen and can have a damaging affect on performance and morale. Addressing the problem quickly and decisively mitigates everyone's frustration and builds trust.

If you have checked all these things, and the tempo is still not stable, try removing instruments from the drummer's mix and listen to how he or she responds. Sometimes another musician is pushing or pulling the groove. The solution is to identify the culprit and reduce the level of that instrument in everyone else's headphones, or have that musician sit out the initial takes. As a drummer, I used to ask the engineer (discreetly) to take the errant player out of my headphone mix. That way I could hold the tempo steady and the other musicians had to play to me.

This raises the issue of headphone feeds; many engineers and producers try to get away with sending the control room mix to everyone. For a quick overdub, this may work, but for a comprehensive group recording session, it is preferable to set up separate cues for each player. The optimum is individual hardware mixers in the studio under the control of each musician. You send sub-mixes to the system and when the bass player wants more drums, you remind him to turn up that channel on his mixer.

If the track requires a strict tempo, especially if you are making dance mixes, a click track may be essential. Introducing a click track to a drummer for the first time in the studio rarely produces a good result. This is where preproduction time is invaluable. If, during rehearsals, you hear that the drummer's timing is shaky, have him or her practice with a click long before the first day in the studio. This is especially necessary when synchronizing with computer-generated tracks or editing between takes.

With debut artists, studio nerves can cause timing problems. This is "red light fever," perhaps caused by the pressure of the session being a long-awaited opportunity. Making them feel comfortable, letting them know that they can take risks, and that you have enough time to redo a track later helps. It is imperative to record all run-throughs because bands often play better when they think it is a rehearsal. Do not turn on the record light; tell them to "run it down for levels"; hit record and cross your fingers.

Beyond using a click track, it may be necessary to ask musicians to simplify their parts, especially if they speed up or slow down at a difficult section. Laying a simple drum groove with fills overdubbed later makes it easier for a drummer to focus on timing. Likewise with guitarists who have to change sounds from one section to another. Focusing on one sound and overdubbing the other one can alleviate the problem.

If it proves to be impossible for the band to play in time, you will either have to program the drums or quantize (correct the timing of) the recorded audio. Quantization and editing are time-consuming and can sound artificial. Other solutions are to create loops from good sections or edit pieces from another take (or another part of the same take).

It is demoralizing for a band member to be replaced by a studio musician. Many musicians these days are comfortable with sampling, looping, and digital manipulation or even programming their part. Alan Moulder will not replace a drummer with a session player, but he will comp a part if he or she cannot play it well enough. He said, "I might suggest programming the drums, but if they're against it I'll work with what I've got." As he points out, "It may be a time of night or keeping on going back to it":

> Some people like to keep working on it, punching in until they've got it. Very often it's a matter of working on it in frequent short bursts. The hard part is remaining objective. Once you've gone in with the microscope, your perspective is completely lost.

As discussed earlier, micro-vision can quickly become an obsessive spiral in which ever-smaller discrepancies appear to grow in significance. Completing a difficult part, and setting it aside for a day or so allows the wider perspective to return.

Tuning should be less of a problem than it used to be now that every musician has an electronic tuner. I used to record an A440 tone at the beginning of every project so that all the tuners and instruments could be referenced to that tone in any studio or country. Modern electronic tuners have rendered that largely unnecessary. Where it does become vital is if you are tuning to an instrument that is not at A440. Some pianos are tuned to A442 or other frequency, but as long as the instrument is in tune with itself that should not present any problems. Having a reference A-note recorded is a good safety measure.

There are ways to string guitars to minimize tuning drift that young bands often do not know. With a first-time band, it is worth having the guitars and basses set up professionally before recording begins, so that intonation is consistent all the way up the neck. This is less of a problem with experienced bands that have guitar techs, drum techs, and keyboard techs who obsess over the instruments. Always check tuning before every take.

If something is recorded that you later realize is out of tune with the rest of the track, it is now possible to change the pitch of an instrument without changing the speed. Signal quality tradeoff is less than it used to be. Nonetheless, it is better to avoid the problem. With computer-controlled MIDI parts, it is of course easy to retrigger a part by running the program again.

ONE OF THE MUSICIANS IS MESSING UP EVERY TAKE

Tony Brown, founder of Universal Records South in Nashville, and one of the most successful country music producers of all time, said,

> I've seen one person completely start shutting down a tracking session. The artist needs to be creative and shouldn't have to worry about that problem. It's the producer's responsibility, and how he does it is as important as deciding to do it. You can pull the person out of the room, or have him sit in the control room, but you have to give him a reason. If things start getting weird, then I take him outside to talk. Nine times out of ten, depending on his ego control, he will usually say, "Have I got time to run an errand?" That means, "I'm embarrassed. I'm out of here." I find that even great musicians know when they are not cutting it.

It's a delicate situation particularly when the musician is a permanent member of the band. When I was a studio musician, I was hired to replace a number of drummers in bands—there were no drum machines, and it was the only viable option if the drummer could not play the part. Magnanimous as the drummers usually were, it was easy to see that it was upsetting for them. I was aware that had the producers been more sensitive and perhaps given better guidance, they might have coaxed the desired performance out of the band member.

I made very successful debut and sophomore albums with a band that had no experience before the first sessions but improved beyond recognition by the second album. We parted ways, and they later used another producer who told them that the drummer was not good enough and should be replaced. When the band told me this, I realized that the producer had probably intimidated the drummer. The producer was used to recording with studio musicians, who are resilient; band members do not record every day and can be fragile in the studio. Furthermore, one of the last singles (which was a worldwide hit) that I did with this band was a first take, so how bad could the drummer have been? The band dropped the producer and was able to carry on recording as a group.

Producers sometimes have to intervene in ways that could hurt someone's feelings. Empathy is helpful and it is usually better to "confront the beast," meaning to act decisively in addressing the situation calmly, directly, without confrontation, and as sensitively as possible.

WHAT IS DEMO-ITIS OR ROUGH MIX-ITIS?

There are many permutations of demo-itis. The most obvious is when the artist, record company, or management gets so used to listening to an original demo, an early version, or a rough mix of a song that anything you change in the final production or mix will sound wrong to them. Sometimes a demo does have a special quality that needs capturing in the master. As an artist, I worked with several producers who did not bother to see my band live, listen to the live recordings, or seriously reference the demos. At the end of the production, the masters were sonically superior to the demos, but they were lifeless renditions of the songs, missing the optimum tempo and omitting important qualities or parts. The best way to deal with demo-itis is not to ignore original demos (or rough mixes) but to compare to them, reproducing anything of value for the final master. An unfortunate worst-case scenario can result in the band and producer "chasing the demo," an often frustrating experience akin to hunting for unicorns.

Knowing how the stakeholders feel about a demo (or rough) helps to understand which parts, if any, to keep. Sometimes, it is preferable to produce a song with a new tempo, groove, arrangement, orchestration, and attitude. Nevertheless, occasionally a demo has a beautiful feel and atmosphere but cannot be used for technical reasons. Once, I recorded a track from scratch three times. The first two versions failed to capture the feel of the demo, but I could not use parts from it because of its poor recorded quality. I was using the best studio musicians in Los Angeles, but in referencing the demo, there was always something missing. On the third attempt, we bettered the demo by a considerable margin. The track went on to be a substantial hit that launched a multiplatinum album. Success as a producer involves knowing when to change things and when to leave them alone. Today, with digital recording technology, it is possible to use tracks or pieces of a demo in the final master; this helps when there are unique sounds or difficult-to-reproduce performances.

In bad cases of demo-itis, when artists want to reproduce every note and characteristic, projects become difficult. Andy Jackson was involved in an album that came to an early demise:

> The artist had made his demos and as often happens, they fall in love with all these little funny wrong notes. They're so buried in it, they can't see the big picture. In the end [the artist and producer] couldn't communicate in such a way that they could find solutions to the problem. I was asked if we could take a break, and then I saw the producer going home. That was it. That was the last I heard of it. I don't know if the record ever saw the light of day.[8]

Demo-itis was the catalyst, but this was a severe communication breakdown and, irrespective of who was right, the producer should have calmed the situation and addressed the issues. Nonetheless, artists sometimes suffer from the impression that the label loves everything about their demos and that is why they signed them. What they are not considering is that labels sign for potential. Nowadays if the label truly loves the (digitally recorded) demos, they can release them or remix and release them without complete reconstruction, so if they are not suggesting that, they probably think they need considerable improvement.

Another variant of demo-itis is attachment to the rough mixes. Rough mixes are working mixes that the producer or engineer runs off quickly, usually at the end of each day or as recording on each song is completed. Producers make them for their own and the artist's reference and, at certain junctures, for the A&R person. Typically, they are simple balances with little compression or effects. Shortly after completion of the recording sessions, a full mix session takes place. On occasion, the band or A&R person will prefer the roughs. They can be right. The spontaneity and simplicity of a rough mix is sometimes better than an overworked and processed mix. Val Garay said that he could never better the quick monitor mix he did at the end of a recording day for the Kim Carnes hit "Bette Davis Eyes." That rough mix spent nine weeks at number one in *Billboard*.[9]

Monitor mix is just another term for rough mix. They are so called because recording consoles historically had a recording side and a monitoring section. The monitoring section was smaller, with limited facilities for adding effects to the sound. Nowadays most recording and mixing consoles are not split but are built in the inline format where the same channel facilities are available to the signal being recorded and the one being monitored—the input and output. Regardless, when a mix is marked with the terms "rough," "monitor," or "board," it implies that it was done quickly and not highly worked or processed.

Although rough mixes can sometimes have an appealing simplicity, they often have flaws that make them inferior to the final mix. A negative response to final mixes can be reflective of an attachment to the roughs. Repeated listening to rough mixes can cause people to expect and like the idiosyncrasies. The solution is similar to the one for demo-itis; analyze what is good about the rough and try to match it while fixing the problematic parts. If the mixer was also the producer or has access to all the session files, it should be possible to go back to the original rough mix file and build from that again. These situations remind us how important careful labeling, file management, and backup systems are.

The problem with roughs would not occur if producers did not hand them out and for that reason, some producers will not. Of course, for A&R people, rough mixes are essential, and they do not want to wait until the end of the project to get them. Pete Ganbarg explained:

> If you wait 'til the end, you could have problems creatively and financially. I like to get roughs as soon as I can and be able to give educated, intelligent feedback as soon as I can. That way they're finishing up the record in a way that there are no surprises.

Peter Collins told me he tries not to give out roughs:

> I'd rather have them come down to the studio and check it out and if there's anything wrong, we can solo instruments and deal with it on the spot. But I hate rough mixes going out, as I'm sure you do.... When you do roughs and people have them, they get used to them. If they love them, you are sunk when you come to mix the thing.[10]

Roughs can also be damaging in the opposite way. If a rough mix reaches an influential person unaccompanied by explanation, it can cause alarm and interrupt the production. I left the studio late one night and asked the assistant to run off a mix while I was collecting my things. When I listened to it in the car, I realized the saxophone solo was very loud. The next day I brought the mix to the band's manager at his office. Before he played it, I said, "Don't worry about the saxophone solo being too loud, the assistant made a mistake." I left the room for a minute and when I came back, the manager was looking extremely concerned. I asked if everything was OK, and he said, "That saxophone solo is ridiculously loud." People often cannot compensate mentally when listening to incomplete recordings.

In an age of broadband and streaming, it is hard to resist requests for roughs. At the least, I ensure that the filename contains the word "rough" and the date; that way it is possible for all parties to identify which mix they are listening to and for the producer to recall the correct mix should it become necessary.

NEAR THE END OF THE ALBUM, SUDDENLY THE ARTIST IS HAVING DOUBTS

This can be very disturbing. As Tony Visconti expressed it,

> Artists get wacky about 80 percent into the album, or even earlier, and then they go absolutely nuts. They think it's going all the wrong way, and then it hits the fan when they try to take control. They usually don't know how to do certain things, so they'll come up with wild guesses and all that. The two Boomtown Rats albums I did sort of went in that direction. Sonically, I'm not very proud of them, because they sort of slipped out of my control.[11]

I attribute this reaction to "buyer's remorse," otherwise known as "post-purchase dissonance." This is a form of cognitive dissonance and the anxiety that can occur after a (usually large) purchase. Studio burnout exacerbates these feelings. Symptoms include doubts about everything done so far, an inability to acknowledge that the record is complete, and an obsessive need to rerecord parts or remix tracks. In acute cases, the artist will write new songs for the current album during the last days of recording or mixing. Physical and behavioral symptoms can appear in such forms as a loss of voice the day before recording of vocals, severe toothache, migraines, staying up all night partying, disappearing for days, and dramatic relationship breakups.

If any of these situations arise, communication is key. Ask the anxious parties to express any concerns so that you can discuss them and work toward a solution. Logic dictates that if someone liked something for a sustained period, and little changed, then the concern may be unfounded or the fix simple. Often, open willingness to entertain their misgivings alleviates them.

Recording becomes obsessive for some artists, and working long hours for weeks without breaks results in mental, physical, and creative exhaustion, which leads to poor decision-making. When everyone is tired, minor uncertainties become giant fears.

This is the perfect time to take a week off. Afterward, it might be a good idea to bring the A&R person into the debate and take stock by comparing the original vision to what you have recorded. Perhaps improvements are necessary, but these often do not involve big changes.

There is an opposite syndrome of post-purchase dissonance called "post-purchase rationalization," also a form of cognitive dissonance whereby people justify a large purchase. In production, this manifests itself as overconfidence and leaving legitimate issues unaddressed. Sometimes people attribute excessive value to an expensive overdub, a difficult part, or one for which an individual advocated. This is choice-supportive memory that makes "people tend to over-attribute positive features to options they chose." Conversely, they can be negative about other people's choices.[12] These are the situations in which Benny Blanco "makes mental notes," with the intention of addressing the problem later, patience and diplomacy being the best solutions.[13]

THE A&R PERSON DOES NOT LIKE THE RECORD

As mentioned in chapter 2, early in my career, I delivered an album that the artist and A&R person had been involved with throughout. Enthusiasm abounded. Shortly after delivery, the A&R person called to say that she did not like the album. I struggled to understand how she could be so positive and then dislike it less than 24 hours later. I had not yet learned how much A&R people can be influenced by others, and I had not yet dealt with a case of buyer's remorse or post-purchase dissonance. This was a high-profile, big-budget project. She was the champion at the label. I believed in the record so I made my case for it, only making matters worse. Had I been more experienced in such matters, I would have asked for a detailed critique and set up a meeting to plan the fixes. What can seem like major problems in the minds of non-experts (many A&R people, some artists, and everybody else) can often be resolved with minor changes.

I also had not realized that A&R people rarely give an honest reaction (especially a negative one) in the studio. Very few label executives can make final decisions. He or she may be guardedly complimentary and then say, "I want to live with the mixes for a few days," or "I need to hear them on my own system," which indicates that they want other opinions.

Feedback from the marketing department carries a lot of weight. Ros Earls alluded to a problem with a producer who "felt like he'd reached perfection," but the radio promotion guy said, "Can't get it on the radio." Earls said, "It's heartbreaking...something that nobody I have ever met has accepted." Unfortunately, marketing departments are often not involved until after delivery, and a negative opinion from them at that point can be lethal. Andy Jackson worked on records where the company said, "Hmm...no, we'll pass on this," having spent a hundred grand on it. As he points out, this is "a commercial decision. They don't want to spend another $200,000 promoting and marketing a record they don't believe in." As he said, the real reason might be that the original A&R person is no longer at the company and "no one has any personal mileage in promoting the record."[14]

Loss of key personnel is a problem in a period when corporate mergers have become commonplace. When this happens, there is no way to protect against orphaned projects. Some good projects fail because they lost their champion or their label.

WHAT MAKES IT SEEM LIKE HARD WORK?

"To be willing to give of yourself to the project," says Bruce Swedien (producer on Michael Jackson's *Dangerous*), "there are things you have to give up, like free time. But you get out of it what you put into it." The anti-social hours create personal difficulties—it is hard to maintain relationships when you are rarely home. With young children, you tend to be sleeping when they get up and in the studio when they go to bed. Some producers attempt normal working hours, but most artists like to get up late and work into the evening. Six- or seven-day weeks and 12-hour days are common. Auteurs define their own hours, which are often still long and, at times, dependent on the artist's availability. Consultative producers drift in and out as they please. The facilitative producer is tied to the artist's preferred schedule and often works more hours than the artist because of setup time, backing up, cleanup, and general pre- and post-session housekeeping. The collaborative producer can influence the working hours but usually changes his or her pattern to accommodate artists.

The biggest hit singles are often deceptively simple, and as Dr. Luke told ABC Nightline News, "The most difficult thing is to do the most simple thing. Because that means that you've had to weed out every other option." He feels this way about a good pop song: "When it's right, it's perfect."[15]

How Much Loyalty Can You Expect?

FROM THE ARTIST

Most of my work originated from artists. Usually, they had heard one of my records on the radio or in a club, liked it, and wanted to work with me. Once or twice, I knew an artist long before we worked together. Sometimes, recommendations come from a label. Loyalty becomes a factor after the first batch of work. Once there is success, other producers and their managers inundate the artist who may be intrigued by the idea of a different producer. Alternatively, they may think about producing the next record themselves.

Artists rarely use a producer repeatedly out of loyalty. They have a limited period of opportunity to build a career, so they will weigh the hits you created for them and the comfort of the working relationship against whether they think someone else would do better for them.

Tony Visconti engendered loyalty from his artists, producing 13 albums with David Bowie and 13 with Marc Bolan. With regard to the extended partnerships he said, "There's real teamwork going on.... You pick up where you left off, and hopefully it gets better, as long as the artist is making a commitment to improving and going forward."[16]

"When the producer or artist makes a change, the work they did together remains," notes Phil Ramone:

> The tragedy of it is, the record business demands that you have hits almost every time out. And if a producer has a relationship with someone over a number of years, at some point the time will come where someone, be it the artist or the producer, will say, "I think I'd better go make a move somewhere else." Nothing lasts forever. Every time somebody calls me up and says, "I'd like to make another album with you," I'm like, "Oh! Well great!"

"I've done two or three records with bands and then thought I don't think they are going to come back to me again because it's time for them to move on," says Alan Moulder:

> I try never to expect to be asked back and that way I'm not disappointed. Whilst I'm generally tart for hire if you like, it's the band's career and they have to work with who they think can keep it going. You can't really take it personally.

However, he adds, "It can hurt a bit sometimes." For whatever reason, artists will move on to the next producer, and it does stir up emotional discomfort. Ros Earls said, "Everybody feels that way.... You are invested emotionally, not just technically." If it is any consolation, left-behind producers do better financially if the artist continues their success with someone else in the big chair. Large royalty payments soothe bruised egos, and discographies with well-known artists attract more work. The only way to ensure ongoing business relationships with artists is to sign them to your production company or label.

FIRST GIRLFRIEND (OR BOYFRIEND) SYNDROME

Artists who have only worked with one producer may succumb to what I term "first girlfriend (or boyfriend) syndrome." This is when the artist moves on to another producer out of curiosity rather than dissatisfaction. It seems inevitable for producers of successful debut albums. They may produce the sophomore outing, but the artist will change. It may be that long-term production relationships are unsustainable. Ken Scott told Blair Jackson that the most albums he did with an artist was four and, after that, he thinks the relationship becomes repetitive.[17] I have done several first and second albums. Two successful albums establish a solid fan base, sales history, and media platform for an artist; this can cause the third album to sell considerably more than the first two. It can also happen that a new producer fails to consolidate the group's initial success. Mickie Most is reputed to have said, "When you have success, don't change anything, not even the ashtrays."[18]

Producer contracts rarely extend beyond one album, and these days may be track by track. Artists can use a different producer for every album or every track if they wish. The industry is moving further toward multi-producer albums; this raises the issue that the producers who are responsible for the hits generate more revenue than those who produce only album tracks. Depending on their deals, their royalties may be similar, although digital singles and on-demand streaming help rectify this inequity as long as the producers' contracts entitle them to their share of these revenues. Some artists want to self-produce immediately after their first success. In any event, producers' professional relationships with artists are typically temporary. Irrespective of friendship or success, debut album producers should expect to experience first girlfriend/boyfriend syndrome.

FROM THE A&R PERSON

As long you continue to generate hits and are easy to work with (from the A&R person's perspective), they are likely to offer you opportunities. With established, continually successful artists, A&R people rarely decide who produces. Nevertheless, they play an influential role by suggesting names to artists and managers. By considering you for a project that is a creative stretch, an A&R person can help keep you from becoming typecast. With new artists, they may make the final decision if there is debate or a price difference.

Competition is fierce for major label and substantial independent label projects. A&R people are vulnerable: They need hits to remain employed or ascend the corporate ladder. One would expect more loyalty for producers who bring success but, as previously mentioned, even labels for which I produced only hits were slow in offering new work. Record company and A&R loyalty has not been a cornerstone of my career. I asked Ros Earls how much loyalty a producer might expect and she said, "None whatsoever." As she indicated, a lack of new offers "is one thing," but "it's terrible" when A&R people tamper with the producer's work.[19] Even chart positions and substantial sales may not be enough if a key team member thinks they could do better by changing the producer.

Final Word on Loyalty

When times are tough, expecting help from within the music business is unrealistic. As Billie Holiday observed in "God Bless the Child," "Them that's got shall get, Them that's not shall lose."[20] In hard times, the favors you did do not count for much. The goodwill you generate may be the key to the door at the top of the stairs, but you still have to climb them. I asked Pete Ganbarg how important it is for producers to have recent hits. He responded,

> I think that it doesn't hurt. It's more of a smart choice if you've got somebody with a hot hand. I, personally, have been burned by going after the producer who hasn't had a hit in a while, thinking that it's just been the projects, not the producer. I brought a guy out of retirement because I thought the records he made back in the day were so amazing that there was no way we could miss with my artist and this producer. Not only did we miss, but the record never came out because it was so bad.

A production career can slide back to square one very quickly if the work and success momentum slow down. It is the impartial, Darwinian nature of the industry: Adapt or die. Understanding the other point of view helps in avoiding unrealistic expectations. I have long had an ironic motto: "Aim low to avoid disappointment." It may be cynical, but if you do not expect loyalty from the industry, you will not be disappointed, and you may occasionally be pleasantly surprised.

10

Success and Money

How Are Producers Paid?

It is important to understand that producer payments are negotiated and assured only by contract. In the United States, there is neither legislative (statutory) protection nor any default way or amount that producers are paid. Unlike songwriters who have a statutory right defining and protecting their rights and income, producer revenues are negotiated between the parties. Some countries do allow producers access to standard splits of performance royalties. In the United States, even the Digital Millennium Copyright Act (DMCA), which provides legislative protection for labels, artists, singers, and musicians for revenues from digital streams, does not protect producers. They need a signed letter of direction from the artist to access these monies.

Producers without contracts have no reasonable expectation of further income from sales or use of their productions. As quoted earlier and worth saying again, Mark Twain pointed out, "Oral contracts aren't worth the paper they are written on." It is not that verbal agreements are not valid, but they are hard to prove in court; producer agreements should be in writing and signed by all parties.

For the purposes of income, we can divide producers into three categories: staff, entrepreneur, and freelance. A label employs a staff producer who typically receives a salary from that company. Some (by contractual agreement with the company) also receive a royalty against sales or bonuses tied to achievements, the terms of which they must negotiate with the company. Perhaps the best-known example of a staff producer who did not receive a royalty is George Martin during the period when he worked for EMI and produced the Beatles.

Entrepreneur producers embrace risk by financing recordings (along with their overhead), consequently benefiting from a bigger and longer standing share of any success generated. They often find the artists, record them on spec, and license or sell the masters to a label, as Sam Phillips did with Rocket 88 (selling it to Chess Records). These deals might be on a master-by-master basis or through the producer's production company. Alternatively, they might set up their own label, with its attendant risks and responsibilities, the reward being the opportunity to build a catalog and establish a business, both salable assets. Phillips eventually did this by establishing Sun Records

Freelance producers earn money in two ways: payment at the time of the production and/or royalty streams from the sale or use of the produced material. When a royalty agreement is in place, any lump-sum payment at the time of production is typically made as an advance against future royalties. In some cases, producers negotiate payments wholly or partially as a fee not to be deducted from royalties. Most producers working for major labels and well-financed independents operate under a royalty-bearing contract with an advance against that royalty. The label pays the advance according to a contractually defined schedule, usually with a partial payment on commencement of recording and the balance upon satisfactory delivery of masters to the label. Understanding and meeting the definition of "satisfactory delivery" can be critical in receiving the back-end payment. Commonly, the payment schedule is 50 percent upfront and 50 percent at the back end, but it can be negotiable. The producer payment may be separate from the recording fund or as part of an all-in budget out of which the producer must make the recordings and extract income for him or herself.

Some producers make albums for a flat fee with no royalty agreement. Others ask for large-enough advances that the likelihood of recouping and earning royalties is slim. There are scenarios in which a flat fee makes sense, but generally these deals are unwise because, in the event of substantial sales, the producer cannot financially benefit in proportion to the success. There are circumstances in which producers forgo royalty income: when the expense of drawing up a contract exceeds the advance payment, when there is no practical way to assure payment of royalties, and when there is no reasonable expectation that any royalties will be generated. Local and regional producers often opt for a flat fee without royalties for all three reasons. They usually deal directly with artists who have no access to affordable legal advice and who may be justifiably wary of signing an agreement that they do not fully understand.

Nonetheless, finding an attorney who will cost-effectively draw up an agreement protects the producer and ensures income relative to success generated, rather than relative to work done. It is a bad feeling knowing that you were paid a small amount of money when your work generated a large amount that you could have shared in if you had signed an agreement. Additionally, a fully executed contract not only ensures access to royalties should the record sell in quantity, but it also defines both parties' obligations, including deliverables, credits, and so forth. A good contract is unambiguous and reduces misunderstandings.

Sometimes, very successful artists will not offer royalties to a producer. They will most likely still have a written agreement defining terms, but payment will be an agreed amount with no back-end percentage of sales. This is likely to become more common as more established artists decline to re-sign with a major or large independent. Increasing numbers of artists are opting to monetize their brand with some form of self-released materials. These business models can be quite creative, utilizing the pay-what-you-want and "freemium" models—where some product (often digital) is free and increasingly sophisticated permutations are priced progressively higher. Famously used by Nine Inch Nails and Radiohead, these exciting alternatives pose challenges for producers in striking equitable deals that reflect their contribution and that can be monitored and enforced for the life of the contract.

Most producers do not become rich from advances—the real money comes from royalty payments as a percentage of revenues from the sale and use of highly successful recordings. In addition to payment commensurate with success generated, each production is an opportunity to build your brand and career. Every album or track released under your name as the producer becomes a calling card and a passport to future work. It is vital to receive payment and credit for work done. Royalty income helps in strategically planning and pacing a career by allowing needed breaks, time to find new acts, and so forth.

How Much Can a Producer Make?

Successful producers can generate a great deal of income from the sales and use of their productions. Ros Earls said that a good producer can make millions. "Ideally you want to have several albums that go on selling forever."[1] Although this is true, it takes a very big hit or several substantial successes to make millions as a nonwriting producer. No matter how strong your contract and how high your royalty rate (within the range of longstanding major label rates), unless your recordings are consistently selling at gold or platinum levels, royalty income generated for a producer will be modest.

Unknown producers rarely get large advances or high royalty rates. Without hits or an established reputation in a niche, it can be difficult to make a living as a producer. In the '70s, I was a signed to a major label as an artist and working as a studio musician. My first full production was Spandau Ballet's first album. I received a good advance for an unproven producer that amounted to less income per day than I made as a session drummer—until the first royalty payment arrived. The career investment paid off because the album went gold and launched my production career; I still receive royalties from that album.

An extremely rough guide to potential revenue from producer royalties is $75,000 to $100,000 income per 1 percent royalty rate per million sales. Calculating an accurate number is impossible because of the many variables. Nevertheless, this would earn a 3-point (defined below) producer between $225,000 and $300,000 on an album certified gold in the United States. In fact, the calculation is more complex than this, with different rates for digital delivery systems, international sales, licensing, and so forth.

HOW ARE PRODUCER ROYALTIES CALCULATED?

Producers command anything from no royalty to around 3 percent of retail. Successful producers can get 4 percent and a select few make more than that.

There are three bases on which labels calculate royalties: on the suggested retail price (SRP), on the wholesale price (PPD, published price to dealer), and as a percentage of revenues received by the label. Generally, they use a combination of methods, with royalties from sales being calculated as a percentage of SRP or PPD and the producer's share of licensing income as a percentage of the label's receipts. Some smaller labels pay all royalties on a percentage of their receipts. Contracts need to clarify how the label defines receipts. Often referred to as "Hollywood net," corporate accountants can diminish a label's reportable receipts, and even gross receipts can be contractually defined as less than the term implies. Understanding what they will deduct before calculating your share avoids disappointment when royalties arrive.

Additionally, be clear which base price they are using. Royalty percentages, whether of PPD (wholesale) or SRP (retail), and even receipts are often referred to as "points" in verbal and informal written negotiations, but there is a substantial difference between 3 percent (3 points) of PPD, SRP, or receipts (net or gross).

DEDUCTIONS AND REDUCTIONS

Artist's royalties are generally subject to reductions and deductions, and because labels usually calculate producer royalties on the same basis, these diminish payments to producers in the same proportions.

One percent of the retail price of an album that retails for, say, $16.98 amounts to $0.1698. This multiplies out to $169,800 per million units. In fact, $75,000 per 1 percent per million units sold may be closer to what you receive by the time you factor in digital rates, packaging deductions, free goods, reductions on foreign sales, TV advertising, record clubs, and the other creative ways in which labels give with one hand and take away with the other.

In approximate numbers, let us say that the artist is on a 12 percent royalty and the record sells 100,000 units at $16.98 SRP. That means the artist should earn $203,760 (12% x 100,000 x $16.98). In fact, the amount will be much lower because of reductions and deductions. These vary from deal to deal; some include a breakage deduction of 10 percent (from the days of 78s), a packaging deduction that can be 20 percent (higher for special packaging), and there are more. The label simply adds these percentages together and subtracts them from the gross amount that would otherwise be owed.

RECOUPMENT

Labels recoup (recover) costs from the artist's royalty entitlement. Recoupable costs can include all or part of the costs of recording, marketing, sales incentives, promotion, videos, tour support, and more.

Starting with the numbers above and assuming very low total deductions of 20 percent, the amount credited to the artist would be reduced to $163,008.

Wholesale pricing varies slightly from distributor to distributor, but for a $16.98 album, it will be a little more than $10. Let's say $10 for a round number; then the label will receive $1,000,000 in revenues for the 100,000 units sold. Say the label spent $100,000 on recording costs including the producer advance and $100,000 on marketing and promotion. So far, the group is unrecouped (owes the label) $36,992. The label has not yet funded a video or put up money for tour support. The company has other costs, such as manufacturing, that might be in the region of, say, $135,000. They also have to pay mechanical royalties, but they have a 75 percent of statutory rate negotiated for controlled compositions with an 11-track cap, and that amounts to $75,075 that they have to pay out to the writers and publishers. The record company has grossed $1 million for an outlay of $410,075, leaving them with $589,925 to cover overhead and profit.

The producer's royalty of 3 percent has earned $40,752 after the (modest and unrealistic) 20 percent deduction. Depending on his or her contract and despite the fact that the label has made a gross profit of $410,075, the producer will not receive these royalties until the artist recoups, which may never happen. To be clear, the producer's 3 percent royalty comes out of the artist's 12 percent royalty, effectively reducing what they will receive to 9 percent (before their other deductions). For simplicity, these numbers are based on sales of physical goods like CDs, although now much of the revenue comes from digital sales and use. In very general terms, producer royalty payments are calculated in much the same way from digital income, which is discussed below.

PAYMENT FROM RECORD ONE

A primary difference between the producer's and the artist's terms is that the producer royalty will generally be paid from record one (depending on the contract), whereas the label recoups their costs first from the artist's share. Contracts that provide for producer royalties to be paid from the first record sold usually state that no royalties will be paid until the recordings recoup. The label's ledgers can show a positive balance owed to the producer, but he or she cannot receive them until recording costs are recouped. Ideally, recoupment should not encompass costs unrelated to that producer's productions.

Where Can Income Come From?

OVERVIEW

In many countries other than the United States, producers can access performance royalties (payments from airplay and other public performances of tracks they produced). Royalties from digital sales have become important since the launch of iTunes in April 2003, and in the United States, the DMCA or Performing Rights

Act gave artists, labels, and performers access to non-interactive (radio style), online, and satellite streaming royalties. However, U.S.-based producers need an artist-signed letter of direction to receive income from these sources via SoundExchange. Interactive or on-demand streaming services (where users control their choice of tracks) also pay royalties for sound recordings played. These rates are negotiated between the labels and the streaming services. Some of these amount to fractions of pennies per play, but they can add up to meaningful amounts. Producers forfeit these without contractual agreements.

DIGITAL DOWNLOAD ROYALTIES

Digital download royalties are now a substantial part of music industry revenues. Once again, the producer's share of digital download income will depend on a contractual agreement with the artist. New producer contracts include this provision, and older ones may be interpreted to include digital downloads as an income stream along with regular sales and licenses. The labels treat downloads as a sale (not a license) paying the artist some permutation of their normal royalty against retail or wholesale price (in the case of iTunes retail is $0.99 and wholesale $0.70). If downloads should ever be deemed to be a license (as was found in the Eminem case), then the artist would be paid under that contractual provision, which is often defined in artists' contracts as a 50/50 split of receipts. This would be better for artists and producers but worse for labels. Several other similar lawsuits are allegedly working their way through the court system. The labels will reword new contracts to make sure they are not at risk of having to pay out 50 percent of download revenues

SOUND RECORDING PERFORMANCE ROYALTIES

With the financial restructuring of the music industry over the past ten years, many labels are signing artists to 360 deals. Some producers and their managers negotiate shares of artists' other income streams. The labels' rationale for 360 deals is that they build the artists brand and should participate in all revenues. Some producers are applying the same logic.

In countries such as the United Kingdom, France, Canada, Japan, Mexico, and Poland, radio stations pay a performance royalty to the artist and copyright owner (usually the label) of the sound recording every time they play a track on air. This is in addition to and separate from payments for use of the musical composition. This royalty does not exist in the United States for over-the-air broadcasting (terrestrial radio). Notably, the countries besides the United States that do not pay this royalty are China, Iran, Rwanda, and North Korea. In the United Kingdom, the performing rights organization PPL collects this performance royalty. Fifty percent goes to the label or copyright owner and 50 percent goes to the performers. The money comes from a negotiated per-play payment from noncommercial stations like the BBC and from a portion of advertising revenue on commercial stations. The performers divide their 50 percent between featured and non-featured performers. Featured artists receive 65 percent, and non-featured performers, such as studio musicians, receive 35 percent. Thus, a featured performer such as Kylie Minogue would get 65 percent of this performance money, and the remaining 35 percent would be split between the musicians and singers who performed on the track.

This gets more complicated with regard to producers who can only receive a share of the 35 percent if they made a musical contribution to the track (usually interpreted as playing an instrument). Until recently, PPL did not consider producers to have made a musical contribution unless they played an instrument on the recording. Tell that to George Martin! Thankfully, there has been a successful lobbying effort to treat producers' musical contributions similarly to those of orchestral conductors. There are further improvements underway. Even then, producers are only entitled to this money if they either recorded in the United Kingdom or are a citizen or resident. Other territories have their own agreements and collection agencies with reciprocal agreements, but U.S. producers (and performers and labels) are excluded because of the lack of a U.S. terrestrial right. For example, when a U.S. terrestrial radio station plays Aretha Franklin's version of "Respect," a payment is made to Otis Redding (the songwriter), but Franklin who sang it and Steve Cropper who produced it are not paid.[2] This creates inequity between songwriters, performers, and producers. It also denies performers, producers, labels, and the U.S. Treasury revenues from territories that collect these royalties. There was a recent move by Clear Channel, the largest single owner of radio stations in the United States, to establish a deal to pay sound recording performance royalties to the Big Machine Label Group.[3] However, the only equitable solution for non-writing performers and producers will most likely be through legislation. This would also release billions of dollars of reciprocal royalties owed to U.S. performers from overseas airplay and other performances.

Commercial radio stations with music formats earn revenues by attracting advertisers interested in selling to the station's audience. They play songs from their chosen format that market research shows will attract listeners of a certain demographic. The number of listeners the station accumulates (known as the "cume") determines the station's ratings. Stations use that rating to put a price tag on the airtime they sell to commercial advertisers. The radio station owners make the argument that airplay is promotion that helps sell records, thus making the artist and producer money. It may be that airplay promotes sales on new releases (as opposed to legacy, catalog, or "oldies" recordings), but it also promotes advertising sales for the station. Stations do not play music to help artists, musicians, and producers—they use it to sell advertising. Lowry Mays—founder of Clear Channel—said to *Fortune* magazine in 2003, "We're not in the business of providing well-researched music. We're simply in the business of selling our customers products."[4]

Oldies or classic stations play older music to target a certain type of listener in order to attract advertisers who want to sell to this demographic. The advertising money that the station earns is directly due to the music they are playing, and yet the producer and performers of that music receive nothing from the airplay unless they wrote the song. The "promotion value" argument is not supported by the facts because performers and producers receive very little from sales of deep catalog material. This material is not on "heavy rotation" (for airplay) like new releases and is often not widely available to buy because of the costs associated with distributing deep catalog. Simply put—performers and producers in other parts of the world receive payment for the use of their work, and it should also be so in the United States.

The DMCA ensures that a performance royalty is paid on digital broadcasts in the United States. However, this legislation does not cover FM and AM airplay (or HD radio); it applies to all non-interactive digital performances such as cable music services, satellite radio, and Internet radio stations. Non-interactive refers to the listener's ability to choose the channel, not the song. This royalty is split 50/50 between the copyright holder (usually the label) and the performers. The nonprofit organization SoundExchange administers the performer's share of the royalty. The performer's 50 percent is split once more, with 45 percent going to the featured artist and 5 percent going to non-featured performers such as background singers and musicians; this is paid equally (2.5 percent each) to the unions, AFTRA and AFM, that distribute them to the performers. If you play or sing on a record, you can receive a portion of the 5 percent from AFTRA or AFM.

Currently, the only way that producers receive digital performance royalties is by contractual agreement with the artist. SoundExchange supplies a boilerplate letter of direction (LOD) that, when signed by the artist, instructs the PRO to pay the agreed percentage of digital performance royalties directly to the producer. Producers should ideally have their attorney include an LOD when they prepare the producer agreement. The artist is not obligated to sign an LOD, and there have been notable examples of major artists refusing to do so. Failing to negotiate an LOD at the time of drawing up the producer contract drastically reduces the producer's chances of accessing this important source of income.

PRODUCERS WHO ALSO WRITE THE SONGS

Certain genres of music such as hip hop, R&B, and pop are more likely to use multiple producers on one album, although other genres are beginning to adopt the technique. In these genres, the producer is also often the songwriter or part of the songwriting team. Not only can you receive a portion of sales revenue from the use of the sound recording copyright, but you also receive the mechanical royalty for the underlying musical composition on every record and download sold. Additionally, you receive a performance royalty every time your song is played on the radio. The mechanical royalty currently amounts to $0.091 per track in the United States. In the United Kingdom, distributed labels pay writers 8.5 percent of the dealer price (the wholesale price that dealers pay or PPD), and non-distributed labels pay 6.5 percent of the retail price (excluding VAT). It is worth noting that U.S. writers are paid this money via Harry Fox, and U.K. writers are paid via MCPS. MCPS does not collect for non-members, so if you wrote a song on an album, you need to register it with a mechanical copyright collection agency such as MCPS or Harry Fox, as well as a performing rights organization such as PRS (U.K.) or ASCAP, BMI, or SESAC (U.S.). The major collection societies have reciprocal agreements with each other, and they collect from the other agencies all over the world. Composers should join the societies in the country where they live. They do not have to join societies in every territory.

We have talked about reductions and deductions that diminish the artist and producer royalty and, as indicated in the recoupment section, labels want to reduce what they pay for use of the musical composition. As the producer, if you write even part of a song you are producing, U.S. labels term it a controlled composition, for which they pay a reduced amount, typically 75 percent of the statutory mechanical copyright royalty. This is odd because a statute is a law, but instead of producer/composers earning $0.091 per track, they get $0.06825. This may not sound like a big difference, but if you wrote one song on a million-selling album, instead of $91,000 (assuming ten tracks on the album), you would receive $68,250 forfeiting $22,750 to the label. Additionally, your contract will most likely cap the number of tracks to 10 or 11 that the label will pay mechanicals on, thus further reducing royalties. If there are non-controlled compositions on the album, they will be paid at "full stat" (100 percent of statutory rate or 9.1¢/track) and that further erodes the royalties paid to the composers of the controlled compositions.

SUMMATION CAP

Royalties used to be simple: A record sold and a producer received a percentage. Now the subject could fill a book, especially considering new technologies and international entitlements. The proliferation of income streams and the systems and laws that govern how and to whom they are paid have become Byzantine. The billions of mobile users in the world open up the likelihood of previously undreamt-of amounts of tiny payments for the use of music. It suffices to say that producers must be aware of the various income streams. Accessing most of these monies requires a contract and action on the part of the producer. All the collection agencies are online and are helpful to varying degrees. Make sure your contract covers all known and future non-statutory income streams.

How Many Producers Make Millions?

Neilsen Soundscan reported 76,875 new album releases registered with them in 2011 as selling one or more copies—up slightly from the previous year and more than 25 percent up from 2005. There is no accurate measure, but there were many more titles released by artists and small independents in the United States unreported by Soundscan. The nearly 77,000 new releases accounted for sales of approximately 113 million units in the United States, and 88.5 percent of those sales (about 100 million) came from only 1,500 releases—less than 2 percent of the total number of releases. The producers who worked on these 1,500 releases have the opportunity to make a considerable amount of money. Nonetheless, one major hit single for a non-writing producer will not generate enough income for that producer to retire comfortably. Neither does it guarantee a career that will provide a middle-class lifestyle. Depending on personal needs, long-term financial security for producers usually requires multiple hit productions made under enforceable contracts over a period of years. As previously mentioned, producers who write broaden their revenue streams.

Most of the producers of the other (more than 75,000) releases did not make a great deal of money. Many of the 98 percent of new releases sold only one copy, and the average number of units sold out of the nearly 13 million remaining works out at less than 200 copies per title. Using approximated numbers, if an album sells 10,000 units at $16.98 SRP, a three-point producer (of the whole album) will make less than $5,000, and at 1000 units, less than $500 in royalties from sales. The business model behind single-digit producer points was predicated on mass sales. However, in 2011, there were only 11 albums that sold a million or more copies and 35 that sold between half a million and a million.[5] Assuming a relatively high SRP of $16.98, and four-point producers making whole albums, the gross potential is $679,200 each for the 11 albums that sold a million copies. With reductions and deductions, that could be less than $500,000—a good income but not retirement money or long-term financial security.

If sales remain lower or spread thinly over a greater number of releases, more producers will gravitate toward alternative business models such as production deals, label ownership, and 360 deals. We are already seeing more emphasis on upfront money and favorable all-in budgets and, as outlined in chapter 1, producers who write dominate the pop charts. Interestingly, the writer of just one album track would make $91,000 (without a controlled composition clause) from mechanical copyright royalties with the (U.S.) sale of one million albums. This does not include single sales (downloads) or streams or performance royalties from airplay (which are hard to calculate).

The Terms

As discussed, producer royalties are taken out of the artist's royalty. In the United States, the contractual agreement is between the producer and the artist, although producers want direct payment and thus need an LOD from the artist instructing the label. As unfavorable as major label deals are, you will most likely be able to find the major record label in some form in 20 years' time. This may not be true for an artist, manager, or production company. The label wants to approve the choice of producer, budget for recording costs, and producer advance. They will want approval of the masters. Technical approval is fine, but they usually want commercial approval, which is difficult to quantify and could result in a producer not being paid the second half of his or her advance.

It is less of a financial burden for a solo artist to pay between a quarter and a third (and sometimes more) of their royalty to a record producer. When there are five members in the band sharing, say, a royalty of 14 percent, if the producer commands a 4 percent royalty, that leaves each band member with only 2 percent. The songwriters in the group will earn performance and mechanical copyright income, but there are often non-writing members in groups. Bands can also make money from sponsorships, touring, and merchandise sales. Nevertheless, a producer royalty can seem oppressive to a non-writing band member.

Do Producers Earn Their Percentage?

Unfortunately, producers' advances and royalties are recoupable from artists' accounts. As discussed, the vast majority of major-label artists never break even on their deals and do not make any money beyond advances. In part, this high fiscal rate of failure is due to the inequitable contractual relationship between the label and the artist. The label assumes risk and for that, they retain more than 55 percent of the suggested retail price, as well as the copyrights, and the artist will repay most of their costs. Signing with a major label (and most indies are no different) is a long-odds, winner-takes-all game. The entire generative group, the artist, producer, manager, attorney, and business manager have to survive financially on (often considerably less than) 25 percent or so of revenues earned from sales and use of recordings. Until this situation changes, the hope is that, through the recordings, the artist might build a brand that will feed the other four financial pillars—touring, publishing, merchandising, and sponsorships. Majors recently diminished this possibility by introducing 360 deals.

Producers need to make a living like everyone else, and they are hired to make a positive difference. It can be difficult to parse the various contributions to a production, but there is no lack of competition for production work and by that measure, producers who continue to have success are most likely making a measurable difference. As mentioned, very successful artists, when sales are a foregone conclusion, often elect to pay their producers a fee with no royalty. An artist who does not need the creative input should pay a flat fee to an engineer, rather than a royalty. Steve Albini said,

> Paying points to a producer is a standard industry practice, and it's one of the reasons why bands go broke. They have to give a lion's share of their income to other people in the music industry, and everybody ends up making money off them, except them. I think it's criminal for a producer to take a royalty on a record that he produces—especially before the band itself has recouped.[6]

Albini conflates several issues here: Should producers receive a royalty? If so, should it come from the artist's share? And should producer royalties be paid from record one? In my view, producers and artists should not be viewed in opposition; they should stand together in creating a more equitable system for the generative group. If there is a lion's share, it is the more than 55 percent of suggested retail price that the labels retain. They have costs and risks, but as my previous rough numbers indicate, neither are high enough to justify such an inequitable split. Labels say they need those margins for research and development, but they spend a great deal of money on expensive buildings, executive salaries, inflated promotion costs, and perks. Publishers split their revenues 50/50 with their writers, and in many cases, they strike even more favorable deals. Labels cite greater costs and risks, but publishers pay advances and have costs and risks as well. Publishers insisted on a performance royalty, the majors decided that airplay is promotional, and then they started paying the stations to play their records. Additionally, if producers really are the label's representatives in the studio, why are they are paid out of artist royalties? These historical anomalies may exist in part because the publishing industry is much older than the recording industry.

It is difficult to defend the label position of recouping all costs from the artist's share, especially when the label owns all rights in perpetuity. Precedents exist for labels picking up producer costs when they occasionally pay the extra 1 or so percent to get a four- or five-point producer they deem worthwhile. Good producers help establish careers, and by the time a producer receives the first royalty payment, the artist will be well on the way to an established career with improved income prospects from touring, merchandising, licensing, and sponsorships. With regard to producers receiving royalties before the band has recouped, most contracts do not pay out royalties until they exceed the producer advance and recording costs for the tracks. Albini goes on to say,

> Royalties are for producers who say people are buying this album because I worked on it, it has my signature sound on it, and so I deserve a cut from every record that's sold. With the points system, the producer has a personal financial stake in making sure the record is commercially successful. The money he makes for himself and his family is more important than the band sounding like itself.[7]

There is much philosophical and ideological complexity embedded in this statement. The auteur by definition stamps the artist with his or her sound. Other typologies do so less, but any collaboration, even with musicians or engineers, will likely color the final recording. The argument for producers minimally influencing the sound of an artist points to the facilitative typology or simply using an engineer (who would typically not be paid royalties). Some would argue that Albini's recordings embody a recognizable quality. On the other hand, if a producer does not make a creative contribution to the artist's sound, then maybe he or she is not producing at all and should be paid on a fee basis.

There is a stylistic gulf between producers making a creative contribution and those stamping an artist with their signature sound. If an artist wants creative control, they should not sign with a major label or many independents unless they have a contractual guarantee of artistic freedom. Major labels sign artists because they see sales potential, and they hire producers to realize that potential by creating hit singles and albums that they hope will sell in large quantities. This requires skill and experience, and oftentimes involves modification or optimization of an act's sound. Artists who regularly appear in the top ten rarely complain about this. This is not meant to endorse the egregious destruction done to many artists whom major labels sign, change, and then drop when they fail. Nonetheless, success is paramount to many artists and groups. Maroon 5 and Train have embraced producers who drastically modified their original sounds in order to maintain chart success. When the label really wants an artist to remain unchanged, they either release prerecorded material or allow the act to self-produce. This is atypical of the majors, but some independents habitually use this approach.

So the decision to pay a producer to modify an act's sound depends on the artist's and the label's priorities. If an artist is confident of their direction and sound, and has the ability to go into the studio and record the album they want without help, they should do it themselves or pay a fee to an engineer and avoid producer points. The real reason why signed artists struggle financially is the more than 55 percent of SRP (after deductions and reductions) of revenues that go to the label, combined with inflated marketing and video costs and lack of ownership or control of copyrights. Furthermore, 360 deals reduce the chances of artists sustaining themselves financially. Not to be overly dramatic, but most record deals are a Faustian pact. Artists need to be clear about how much long-term sustainability and creative control they are prepared to sacrifice in return for a perceived short-term opportunity when they sign a record deal. If an artist needs help in creatively shaping their record, then the person who helps shape it needs to be paid for their time, and his or her expertise should be rewarded if the record sells. Many acts are not capable of making the record they envisage without production help. Part of the vision for many aspiring artists is to sign with a major label and work with a well-known producer to make a record that far exceeds what they could achieve on their own. These decisions are part of the pros and cons of signing with a major or large independent label.

Signing a major label type of deal is analogous to buying a lottery ticket; you could win, but most likely you will not, and the losers go home empty-handed. The major label winners have careers and comfortable lives, and the others have to seek different options. Very few artists sustain a long-term, middle-class income on a major label. Major labels do not exist for that purpose. They have quarterly profit and growth targets, corporate and shareholder accountability, a blockbuster business model and, to stay in business, they need big hits on a regular basis. Their success rate with signings is low (numbers are not disclosed but guesstimated to be less than 5 percent).

With their expensive methodologies and high fail rates, deals are set up so that the few successful artists cover costs for those who fail (that's what the labels call A&R). Individual artist development beyond the first album is rare; new artists, for the most part, only move to a second single if the first is successful. Even with a so-called guaranteed two-album deal, without a hit, an artist is unlikely to make their second album for that label. This is why producers who regularly deliver hits are highly valued.

Independent label deals are typically no more favorable than the major label's, but they usually spend less money on recording, as well as promotion and marketing, allowing their acts to develop more organically with lower levels of debt. Consequently, indie artists tend to have greater freedom in the production process and earn royalties at lower sales thresholds. Success develops incrementally.

Pop artists who break at a very young age, such as Britney Spears or Christina Aguilera, often have five or more years of hard work and development behind them, much of it done by the artist themselves and/or parents and management. Once a major label becomes involved, producers and writers are key elements in the development of the artist's brand. Producers (and particularly auteur producers) work with the artist, writing, choosing, adapting, and refining material to fit the artist's identity.

Producing one hit that makes money is a feat not achieved by many. It is a much smaller group of people who continue to produce hits and who can sustain a living by doing so at any given time. Producers who provably increase artists' and labels' chances of success are generating many times their cost in revenues. They are launching careers and building back catalogs that will underwrite the label and other acts for years.

A thriving commercial record producer understands the process and consistently generates recordings that are successful with the target audience, often with multiple artists. Many people have an opinion, a small number can reliably predict hits, but few can consistently fashion them.

Some producers earn their percentage through organizational and project management skills. Artists who produce themselves have been known to spend years and millions of dollars attempting to materialize their dreams. A well-chosen producer can counsel the confused, placate the warring, and galvanize the unmotivated. Pragmatic organization of the sessions and musicians can save the label and ultimately the artist a great deal of time and money—offsetting part, if not all, of the producer's advance and royalty.

The world of freelance record production functions according to free market principles of supply and demand. If producers do not generate a positive return on investment (ROI), the label will not hire them again. Producer advances and royalties can amount to a significant slice of the artist's income from music sales. Nonetheless, even if they produce the record that establishes the artist's brand, producers have not historically participated in other streams of revenue from merchandising, touring, publishing, and sponsorships. Nor do they earn royalties from future albums that they do not produce. The producer's work may be a key component in elevating an act to a point where they can capitalize on these other sources of income. Consequently, some producers now participate in multiple revenue streams. If an artist can create the same result or better without a producer, then they should. Gotye's hit "Somebody I Used to Know" is an example, as is Calvin Harris's solo work and, of course, Prince, who has long represented the artist producer typology.

Labels and managers typically have multi-year, multi-album contracts that continue to reward them for helping to build success for the artist. In contrast, producer contracts are typically for one album or one track. During periods that are more about creating artists than just developing them, the producer's role comes to the forefront. Producer/manager Katrina Sirdofsky said,

> As producers have once again become the driving force of the music business, the deals have gotten better. Lately it seems most producers are infinitely more talented than a lot of the artists they are creating careers for, so it has certainly tipped the scales.

In summation, the generative team—the artist, manager, and producer—largely encapsulate the expertise required in the creative development of an artist's recorded identity. However, the artists ultimately pay all the costs of production, most of the marketing costs, and mortgage their rights forever. This entire team is rewarded with less than 25 percent of revenues generated. In return for more than half of the pie, the label provides seed money and expertise, but the equation is unbalanced. Neither producers nor artists are paid their fair share of revenues generated, especially given that they completely lose control over their joint creative work. Rather than the creative entities fighting over scraps, we should be seeking to make the splits between the funding entity (the label) and the generative group (those who create the recorded work) more equitable.

Major versus Independent Labels

"Overnight success" is usually a five-to-ten-year process, and an independent artist might even take longer. Many indie labels are content with lower levels of sales, and their artists tend to have more control over their careers and music than major-label baby bands. Astute, hardworking independent artists can sustain mid-level careers for decades, especially if they have a strong touring base. Consequently, producers who specialize in these acts are not paid big advances and rarely receive large royalty payments. In compensation, they are not under the same commercial pressures as those producing top ten singles.

The majors often pay better and spend more on marketing priority recordings but, as discussed, the statistical probability of achieving a hit is low. Industry revenues dropped by more than 50 percent in the first decade of this millennium, and the majors consolidated from six in 1998 to three at the time of writing. The short-term consequence of these mergers has been many dropped acts, reduced signings, cutbacks on new releases, and thousands of lost jobs. Draconian as the deals are, it is harder to get an act signed to a major label today than it was ten or 20 years ago. This means less major label work for producers. Meanwhile, independent labels in the United States now have a larger market share (more than 30 percent) than any major. Many artists have started labels and become free agents in the industry.

How Will Producers Make Money in the Future?

The Hollywood movie-studio system collapsed in the late 1940s after the Supreme Court verdict that ended their control of the movie theaters and thus distribution. Actors became free agents, directors became auteurs, and TV affected the movie industry the way that radio in the 1920s had impinged on the music business. Movie ticket sales fell from more than 50 million in 1950 to 20 million in 1960. The industry reshaped itself; freeing stars and directors from their long-term contracts, making films on a one-off basis, and embracing new technology—initially TV, then videotapes, DVDs, and now the Internet.

Technology, including the Internet and specifically Napster, disrupted major label control of music distribution. Some artists, such as Nine Inch Nails and Radiohead, successfully achieved free-agent status. At the time of writing, the top ten of the *Billboard* Hot 100 is filled with tracks produced by auteur producers—for major labels and others. The Hollywood movie studios are still with us but performing different roles than they did before 1950. Music producers embody skills fundamental to the industry, the ability to identify and cultivate raw talent. The major labels were vertically integrated, controlling content, manufacturing, distribution, and, for a time, the hardware and firmware. They were the venture capitalists: supplying the money, taking the risk, and controlling the marketing and promotional channels as well. They did this using their oligopolistic control of distribution and economic influence on the media. Distribution, marketing, promotion, and manufacturing—each increasingly supplanted by digital means—are no longer tightly controlled by the oligopoly. Entrepreneurial producers have the opportunity to acquire and develop assets independently in much the way the independent film sector has. Producers can build value in their own catalogs.

Can You Increase Your Chances of Success?

Andy Jackson attributes continued success to ability: "You can be lucky for an album or two, but I don't think you can stay lucky."[8]

Find mentors and role models. Study and become an expert. Identify your strengths and weaknesses and what kind of producer you can become.

Just as it is now impossible to do office work without computer skills, a thorough knowledge of a digital audio workstation system is now essential. This is the "music business," so study both music and business. Know your music history; understand how the music you like evolved. The great composers built on the past, as did the biggest artists of the past 60 or so years such as the Beatles, the Rolling Stones, Led Zeppelin, Michael Jackson, Miles Davis, Bob Dylan, and so on. Become an expert in your chosen field.

The adage "the good is the enemy of the great" is useful, because being merely good is insufficient. The public jury in a competitive marketplace assesses our work. To achieve success, our creations must stand above those of our peers, in their originality and excellence, and through innovative marketing or in some other way. Everyone needs a lucky break, but that cannot happen unless people hear your work. The time and effort spent developing production skills needs to be matched with outreach and networking, marketing your work and yourself. If you cannot do it, find someone who will. Whatever you are missing, concentrate on acquiring those skills, or form a team with someone who has them. Patience and persistence, problem-solving and peacemaking, enthusiasm and energy are all essential qualities. Develop the ability to hone details while keeping the overall objective in view.

Almost any story of success in the music business highlights the necessity for perseverance. Brian Epstein's refusal to accept the Beatles' rejection by every label led him back to a company that had turned them down. What if he had accepted that first rejection from Ron White at EMI and not pursued a meeting with George Martin?

There is a psychological concept known as "learned helplessness." It is a model of depression initially developed by Martin Seligman from a series of experiments beginning in the '60s. Animals were repeatedly subjected to mild pain. Initially, they attempted to escape, but they were restrained and after a time they gave up. The restraints were then removed, the pain stimulus was applied again, but the animals no longer tried to escape, even though they could. They had "learned helplessness."[9]

In the music industry, the roads to success are named "rejection and failure." Acceptance appears suddenly and inexplicably. Epstein was the same person, with the same story about the same group, yet only after exhausting all possibilities did he find acceptance. Pete Waterman wanted to place Kylie Minogue's single "I Should Be So Lucky" with a label. Meeting with rejection and incurring great financial risk, he released and promoted it himself. It became the biggest selling single of the year and set up Waterman's PWL label for a remarkable run of hits.[10] It is essential not to "learn helplessness." Each attempt is new, and you can never know when the restraints may not be there.

Credits

Credits actuate future work and income by establishing your brand. Brand aware-ness for producers may be primarily internal to the industry because many consum-ers do not notice who produces what. Pete Ganbarg talked about how he goes about choosing a producer:

> It's a very fun process for an A&R person because all A&R people should be music junkies. This is an opportunity to go through their music collection and say, "OK, this act that I've just signed really owes a lot to these types of songs or these types of artists." Usually there are two or three names that keep pop-ping that you feel are kindred spirits to the artist you signed. You start making a wish list, [which] is five names, ten names, 15 names. You have the band do one as well, and you cross-reference the lists. You come up with a final wish list of maybe half a dozen names.[11]

Clearly, ensuring your credits are correct is imperative. Here is a clarification of a common selection of production-related credits.

EXECUTIVE PRODUCER

The executive producer is usually someone in a position of power who has some responsibility for the project. It may be the artist's manager (Peter Grant was cred-ited as executive producer on Led Zeppelin albums), the A&R person (Jeff Fenster on the *Fast and Furious* soundtrack), or the president of the record company (Clive Davis on Whitney Houston albums).

A record may have several executive producers, each of whom earned their credit differently. Roles that typically earn an executive producer credit include cre-ating the concept for the project, financing or sourcing the funds, championing the project at the label, assembling the creative and business team, and being a close advisor to the artist. Executive producers in music perform a role somewhere between that of the producer and the executive producer in film.

Day-to-day involvement ranges from nonexistent to active monitoring of the project. It is generally non-technical and credits those who perform a significant role in bringing a recording into existence. It is not Grammy-eligible.

ALBUM PRODUCER

This is a relatively recent title, appearing mainly on multi-producer albums and substituting for or in addition to the executive producer credit or A&R direction. Guiding a multi-producer album is a significant task usually handled by the A&R person, artist's manager, or with high-profile artists, the head of the label. It is not Grammy-eligible.

PRODUCER OR PRODUCED BY

This is the primary producer credit, which should be reserved for the person controlling the overall creative and technical aspects of the project who is present during recording working directly with the artist and engineer. This is a Grammy eligible role.[12]

CO-PRODUCER OR CO-PRODUCED BY

This usually indicates an ad hoc team, possibly with the artist or songwriter. There may be a hierarchy with a producer and a co-producer. Formal teams are typically credited in this fashion: Produced by The Matrix, Produced by Jimmy Jam and Terry Lewis, and so on. Co-producer is a Grammy eligible role.

ASSOCIATE (OR ASSISTANT) PRODUCER

This signifies the delegation of responsibility to someone reporting to the producer and is not Grammy eligible.

ADDITIONAL PRODUCTION BY

Mixers or remixers sometimes claim this credit for overdubs and additions to the track. Unless producers specifically exclude it in their contract, additional production credits can appear without their prior knowledge. It is less than gratifying to pick up an album that you worked on for months to see an additional production credit given to someone who spent less than a day on a mix. It is not Grammy eligible.

VOCAL PRODUCTION OR VOCALS PRODUCED BY

This person has overall creative and technical control of the vocal recording, working directly with the vocalist(s) and engineer to realize both the artist's and the label's goals in the creation of the vocals. This role is Grammy eligible.

COMPILATION SOUNDTRACK ALBUM PRODUCER

This person works together with a film's director and/or music supervisor and is responsible for selecting previously produced material and may oversee restoration work, liner notes, mastering, and the budget. It is eligible in the "Compilation Soundtrack Album" category only.

STRINGS (OR ANY OTHER INSTRUMENT) PRODUCED BY

This defines a person who works with individual instruments/elements of the recording, and it is not a Grammy eligible role.[13]

The Recording Academy defines eligibility for Grammys but does not pre-approve assignment or placement of credits. Sadly, at the time of writing, digital distributors and stores (apart from Rhapsody) have still not acknowledged the importance of the production team (or musicians, arrangers, conductors, background singers, and the like) by allocating space for their credits in their player interfaces. This has resulted in these important contributors being difficult to trace in the digital domain. There are third-party sites such as allmusic.com, albumcredits.com, discogs.com, musicbrainz.org, and, of course, Wikipedia, all of which are valuable but also incomplete and inaccurate. Producers, musicians, and other contributors have been prominently credited (often by contractual agreement) on or in physical packaging for decades. Recordings are a rare instance where the digital domain offers less information than on the physical product.

In 2012, the Recording Academy (U.S.) launched their "Give Fans the Credit" campaign, and the Music Producers Guild (U.K.) debuted their "Credit Where Credit Is Due" program.

What Is the Secret to Longevity?

Arif Mardin may have had one of the longest continuously successful production careers. In the '60s and '70s, he was working with such artists as Aretha Franklin, the Young Rascals, and the Bee Gees; he produced hits for Chaka Khan and Bette Midler through the '80s and '90s, and in his 70s, he helmed Norah Jones's diamond-certified debut album *Come Away with Me*. He had begun on a different path, earning an economics degree from Istanbul University and studying at the London School of Economics. At the same time, he developed his musical talent, winning the first Quincy Jones scholarship to the Berklee College of Music in the '50s. After graduation, he worked for Atlantic Records for more than 30 years. Although the level of his musicianship was high before Berklee, he "learned to formalize it" there, acquiring new techniques and opening up "new horizons."[14]

Mardin was a gracious person with highly developed people skills and a deep love and understanding of many kinds of music. He had an open mind to new ideas and appreciated the emotional connection that the right combination of lyrics and music can make. Three of the most successful and enduring producers, Mardin, Quincy Jones, and George Martin, had formal musical training, arranging and orchestration skills, and label experience in common. Those were the skills and development processes of the time, but those abilities would be as valuable today.

Russ Titelman's career also spans from the '60s to the present. He started in a group with Phil Spector while in high school and wrote songs with Barry Mann and Cynthia Weil, and Carole King and Gerry Goffin. He played guitar on the internationally successful '60s TV show "Shindig!" and worked with Randy Newman, James Taylor, Paul Simon, Chaka Khan, Steve Winwood, and Eric Clapton. Titelman was part of the A&R department alongside Mo Ostin and Lenny Waronker at Warner Bros. during its creative heyday. On his run of successes, he commented, "Being in the right place at the right time is part of it." In Titelman's case, he used his musicianship to enter the inner sanctum of the business:

> We played behind Jerry Lee Lewis, Jackie Wilson, on and on. I got to see everybody and play music behind these great artists. . . . I used to hang out at Metric Music with Lenny Waronker [later of Warner Bros. and then DreamWorks], go over to Screen Gems where Brian Wilson would be working. I started taking sitar lessons at the Ravi Shankar School of Music [where] I met Lowell George [Little Feat].[15]

This is the music business education that you cannot get in school. To be able to observe, work, and network with the most talented people of the time is inspiring and instructional.

Ros Earls thinks that the secret to longevity is to restrict your work to projects that you have your heart in. "That's my personal golden rule," she says, "If you look to the money all the time, something's bound to go wrong."

Add Entrepreneur to Your Portfolio

Business is an integral part of music production. Producers who combine creative and technical skills with business acumen and the ability to find the right artists can build substantial companies.

Production companies act as A&R sources to sign and develop artists. The company may contract with a larger label to release and distribute the material, but the artists sign to the production company and not directly to the distributing label. Alternatively, using the Web and contractors in a modular approach, production companies and small labels can assemble a flexible marketing, sales, and distribution team. Some artists treat production companies as a last resort after approaching the majors and the larger independents, but increasingly they are becoming a first option as majors further withdraw from artist development. The master recordings remain the property of the production company, potentially creating long-term value for it. Established production companies often have an ongoing partnership with at least one major label. As Sandy Roberton pointed out, "Urban producers were in control of acts long before rock producers . . . signing acts, making deals, and writing songs." He thinks that more acts will be signing to production companies to make their albums, citing The Matrix who had just formed a label and signed their first act. "They're going to make a finished album, and I will make a distribution deal for the label." Roberton favors their proactive approach in "creating a brand name" rather than being "just producers for hire." He said that their deals are "very fair," better than 50/50 splits between the artist and production company. This requires "some investment from the producers, but it's mainly a spec situation." To protect their investment, production companies need to sign the artist for as many albums as any subsequent major label deal might require. Roberton pointed out that it is possible to adjust the deal later if there is a disparity in terms. If the major label wants the act but only as a direct signing, he will strike the deal so the label "either hires the producer for the second record or [the producer] gets an override." If the label wants to remake the album with another producer, Roberton negotiates a kill fee for his producer, so that "if the record scores," they are compensated.

Production deals and labels make it possible for producers to build an identifiable and valuable brand, and to cross-market within the label. Hip hop has been particularly effective in using the piggyback marketing strategy, featuring new signings as guests on the label's most successful artist's tracks or vice versa.

Sometimes the production company positions itself as a label and there is not always a clear distinction, but if it is acting as an A&R source and producing the music but depending on the major or independent to handle marketing and distribution, it is, effectively, a production deal.

Production companies go in and out of favor. At the time of writing, they are in vogue, filling a need for artist development. Sometimes production companies are accused of taking advantage of the artist's naïveté and desire to succeed. With success, artists learn more about the business, and rebel. This was the case with Bruce Springsteen and his first manager/producer Mike Appel. Springsteen had signed to Appel's company, Laurel Canyon Ltd., and Appel signed Laurel Canyon to CBS Records. After two and a half albums, Springsteen and Appel fell out over money and production methods. When the case went to court, Springsteen was eventually set free to go with his succeeding manager/producer, Jon Landau, but not without conceding a substantial payout to Appel who successfully argued that he had discovered Springsteen, nurtured him, and supported him before the big time beckoned.

The group TLC initially signed a production deal with the singer Pebbles, who then signed them to LaFace Records through her production company Pebbitone. Pebbles's then-husband, L.A. Reid, and his production partner, Kenneth "Babyface" Edmonds, owned LaFace. L.A. and Babyface were one of the most prolific and successful auteur-style production teams of the '80s and '90s. LaFace was a joint venture with Arista Records, which was distributed internationally by the RCA/Jive Label Group. TLC sold millions of albums worldwide, but four years into their career they declared bankruptcy, citing debts of $3.5 million. Personal issues likely factored in to the bankruptcy, but it was alleged that their production deal was unfavorable. The more entities in the revenue chain, the less cash can filter through to the artist.

Perhaps the biggest jackpot of all went to American producer Shel Talmy, who in the early '60s was in London producing several bands that followed in the wake of the Beatles. One of them was The Who. Talmy signed them to a six-year production deal in 1964, giving them a 2.5 percent royalty. He took their records to American

Decca, which released them in the United Kingdom on the Brunswick label, and doubtless gave Talmy a royalty in excess of 2.5 percent. The Who's management soon realized how little they were earning and persuaded Talmy to increase their royalty to 4 percent, but this was most likely still far less than Talmy was receiving.

After three singles and one album, The Who wanted out. They thought they could make better records and more money without Talmy, but he would not budge. To force Talmy's hand, The Who's manager, Kit Lambert, took the group's next single, "Substitute," to Robert Stigwood, who put it out on his Reaction label (distributed through Polydor). Talmy sued, and in an out-of-court settlement was granted a 5 percent royalty on all of The Who's records and singles for the next six years, up to and including *Who's Next* in 1971. This covered the period of much of their best-selling work. Talmy earned more in royalties from The Who's record sales than the individual members of the band, and he still collects royalties from every track that The Who recorded during that period.[16]

Many artists find themselves entangled in similar situations. This does not mean that production deals are intrinsically unfair. Once success happens, much money is at stake, perspectives change, and disagreements ensue. Artists understandably resent earning less than they could in a direct signing with the distributing company and often try to get out of the deal, sometimes encouraged by the distributing company. The producer or company owner who took the initial risk, investing time, money, and expertise in breaking the act, feels justified in continuing to benefit because he or she launched the artist's career. Even though they add value to artists' careers, some of these deals are exploitatively long and unfavorable.

Production companies often run into difficulties if their accounting practices are not rigorous and transparent. *The Guardian* recently reported two lawsuits with Bangladesh (aka Shondrae Crawford), producer of Lil Wayne's hit "A Milli," and Jim Jonsin, who produced the song "Lollipop." Each claimed half a million dollars in unpaid royalties from Wayne's label, Cash Money. The production team Play-n-Skillz also claimed lack of payment. Bangladesh told Sean Michaels that Wayne's label

> don't [*sic*] pay royalties—all the money from album sales goes to Cash Money. I get checks from Sony for [work with] Beyoncé, checks from different labels for different artists; it just comes to you. You don't have to call them, sue them and all that junk. This is what you're owed.... [But] you have to sue these guys so that they pay up.[17]

Bangladesh attributed the problem to the CEO of Cash Money, Bryan "Baby" Williams. He told *Vibe Magazine*,

> Wayne is not getting money [either]. He is GIVEN money, he's not getting money. If Baby gets a million dollars, he'll buy Wayne a Phantom [car], but that's in Cash Money's name. That 14-bedroom mansion isn't Wayne s**t.... All those Young Money artists don't even know that they not getting [*sic*] royalty money.[18]

In my career, I signed three deals with production companies/labels. One worked out fine, and one was the best deal I ever made with the most reliable and transparent payments that continue more than 30 years later. Unfortunately, the third company and its owner assiduously avoided paying me any royalties and did the same to a number of other well-known artists and producers. In some cases, these companies get into trouble because the owners are not experienced or fastidious in business management and accounting. In other instances, the failure can be attributed to greed and dishonesty. The latter companies invariably attract lawsuits, and the owners often become personae non gratae in the music business.

Production deals are not for every producer. They involve running a multifaceted business with the costs of additional time, expertise, and money invested. Signing artists increases the amount of nonmusical work. On the positive side, creating a business increases the return on investment for those with an aptitude for finding artists with sales potential. It puts more artistic control in the hands of the producer and moves him or her from contract employee to a business owner who can build convertible value in a catalog.

11

Why Are There So Few Women Producers?

Even people familiar with the field struggle to name more than a handful of women producers. I have been writing on this topic since the first edition of this book in the mid-'90s. Katia Isakoff and I are the joint editors-in-chief of the *Journal on the Art of Record Production* and, witnessing no appreciable increase in the number of women in music production over many decades, we presented a paper and a panel on the topic at the 2011 Art of Record Production Conference in San Francisco. The most recent information here is adapted from the research that Isakoff and I did for the paper.

What We Know

There is little data available, but the rosters of producer/engineer management companies and the staff listings for commercial studios show very few women producers or engineers. A membership search of MPG (Music Producers Guild) and APRS (Association of Professional Recording Services) in the United Kingdom shows only five female members. In the United States, the Recording Academy's Producer and Engineer Wing with more than 6,500 members and a successful woman engineer as its senior executive director reveals a female membership of less than 13 percent. In compiling a list of gender-identifiable producers from multiple international sources, we found 837, of which 42 are women, 5.02 percent. This is a longstanding situation. Even in 1980 when the industry was robust, Pamela W. Paterson presented a paper at the 66th Audio Engineering Society (AES) Convention postulating the primary reason for the lack of women in audio production as "[a] historical separation from the practice and theory of technology combined with a gruesome lack of entry-level positions." In 1995, the AES formed a women's audio subcommittee, which launched the Women in Audio Project: 2000 to focus on researching "the disproportionate number of women in the field of audio engineering." In 2000, Cosette Collier of Middle Tennessee State University and chair of the AES's Women in Audio Committee announced its dissolution, saying,

> Our research showed that the average number of women in recording or audio
> engineering programs was about 10 percent. The problem did not seem to be

within the industry, but actually something more related to society and early education; the AES didn't feel that this was something a technical standards organization could effectively address.

In 2003, Terri Winston started a nonprofit organization called Women's Audio Mission (WAM), dedicated to the advancement of women in music production and the recording arts. In the 31 years since Paterson's paper, there has been a technological revolution that made personal studios cost-effective. There are now many more music technology, engineering, and production courses, and it would seem likely that we should have seen greater numbers of women entering the profession. WAM's website cites 5 percent as the representation of women in production and the recording arts; this is consistent with the numbers uncovered by Isakoff and myself. WAM's Winston later guesstimated average enrollment around 10–15 percent and stated that "City College of San Francisco was in the 40–50 percent range" when she was there.

Beginning in May of 2011, we contacted 233 U.S.-based schools regarding their female enrollment levels and by December that year, only nine schools had provided statistics or anecdotal information, and 27 more promised to send data, but more than a year later, despite multiple follow-up e-mails and calls, the data have not arrived. Four other schools responded but were unable or unwilling to share any relevant statistical data. Despite a 17 percent response rate, only 3.86 percent of schools contacted supplied any useful data, with just two showing how many women and men entered programs versus how many graduated. These statistics showed that, in one case, women made up 19 percent of students beginning the program and 43 percent of those graduating. In the other, 24 percent of the entering class was women and they accounted for 26 percent of the graduating students. Two schools is an insufficient sample size to draw any meaningful conclusions. This dearth of accurate data presents a significant challenge in identifying and addressing causative factors that may underlie the statistical under-representation of women working professionally and as educators in the field of music production.

If, as an industry, a profession, and an academic discipline, we consider lack of gender diversity to be indicative of real or perceived barriers for women, capturing and disseminating accurate statistics would be a valuable step toward identifying and rectifying precursory factors.[1]

The Higher Education Statistics Agency in the United Kingdom supplied figures showing an average of 9.15 percent female enrollment in courses with some form of music technology content (2004 through 2010). Some individual university statistics were obtained through ASARP (Association for the Study of the Art of Record Production) and JAMES (Joint Audio Media Education Support). These showed an increase in female enrollments to an average peak of 11.28 percent (2005 through 2011). Encouraging as any growth is, these percentages hardly indicate significant progress toward equity. The lack of collected and shared data on the topic might indicate entrenched attitudes toward the situation. This is particularly difficult to understand in the field of higher education. Women clearly represent a large untapped pool of potential students who could expand these programs.

Marcella Araica was a 2002 Full Sail graduate who became a sought-after engineer/mix engineer working with Usher, Timberland, Missy Elliot, and Britney Spears, to name a few. She was one of only five female students in her cohort of 165. Her break came when she had been an intern for only two months at the Hit Factory. The studio manager asked her to assist on a Missy Elliott session. Araica, a "super fan" of Elliott's, was understandably excited and nervous. She said,

> We ended up working very well together and we would talk from time to time. She definitely loved the fact I was a woman trying to break into the business and [she thought] that it would be a challenge but that I had it in me to make it. I believe strong women can recognize other strong women.[2]

In a February 2008 *Sound On Sound* interview, Araica spoke about the early part of her career at the Hit Factory when she started mixing: "It was a challenge to get people to believe in me. As a female, I had more to prove." She said that when men were "thrown in," people tried "to make them feel comfortable," but with "a woman, it's like 'Hold on, this is different!'" Araica confirmed to Isakoff that she encountered this response from both men and women recording artists. She thinks more should be done to promote audio engineering and production as a career option to young female students:

> I have students reach out to me all the time that are in grade school or high school, letting me know that they want to follow in my footsteps. I'm always surprised but happy because whether it's a school or a trade magazine that they have read, they are now "in the know."

She went on to describe her schools as being "very closed-minded," sharing limited study and career opportunity information. As role models, Araica cites Jimmy Douglass (whom she studied under, eventually becoming his mix engineer) and Linda Perry:

> Because of her fearlessness in this industry and being so confident as a female producer. To be honest, when times got tough for me in the studio, I would ask myself WWLD (what would Linda do?).

Over the years, I have worked with women engineers and assistants, each one of them a pleasure to work with. None that I know of rose up through the industry. This is in stark contrast to the considerable number of men assistants and engineers I worked with who became well-known producers. Based on anecdotal evidence and the incomplete data that Isakoff and I have been able to assemble, a small number of women enter the profession, and many of them drop out.

During the '70s and early '80s, Michelle Zarin managed the Record Plant in both Los Angeles and San Francisco and, subsequently, the Automatt in San Francisco. Zarin only recalls one woman engineer (Deni King) at the Record

Plant, and said that she never received résumés from women. On moving to the Automatt in San Francisco, she inherited three women, including Leslie Ann Jones (now director of music and scoring at Skywalker Sound) and Maureen Droney (now senior executive director of the Recording Academy's Producer and Engineer Wing). Zarin describes both as wonderful and thinks they could have survived at the Record Plant. Droney and Jones were the only two women that Zarin worked with over many years. Three of the studio managers and, at one point, 50 percent of the engineers at the Automatt were women. Producer David Rubinson owned the studio and apparently took an egalitarian approach to hiring.

Gender discrimination is irrational. A woman studio manager said, "I was never really into hiring women and not many applied; it's just like on the tour bus— when you have a woman on the bus, it causes problems." She went on to say that she felt women were too emotional and that, although men can be very emotional, it is manifested very differently.[3] A male producer claimed that "for a lot of guys to have a woman around in the studio is inhibiting." He thought it might be because men curse a lot. My observation is that many women can match men in the cursing department. Nonetheless, he said a woman in the studio can "make it uncomfortable for at least one person in the band." Although uncommon, I have encountered at least one male band member who was opposed to working with a woman.

Surveys by TechNet and *EQ Magazine* in the early '90s indicated that few women actually produced music or engineered audio, but mainly held administrative and support positions. The survey reported less than 20 percent of all technical positions held by women and less than 2 percent of those in "first" or "lead" positions. Evaluating a list of factors that have led to this scarcity of women in audio production, women cited an absence of prominent role models and lack of encouragement by primary and secondary educators.[4]

Some women producers and engineers think that many women find the hours too socially debilitating, especially in the early years when you have little control over your schedule. As Lauren Christy of The Matrix said, "Sitting around the studio until two in the morning, for women, is probably not the best career to have." Wendy Page thinks that "the ridiculous hours don't attract women." She said that being in a recording studio "until dawn does not appeal to many of my female friends! They see behind the glamour of working in the music business." She went on to say that she does "not have a normal home life" and that writing and producing an album "is mentally and emotionally exhausting." She added, "Relationships can suffer too with the antisocial hours and shoptalk" and that "it does not leave much time for having babies."

Some Women Producers in History

They may be few in number, but women producers date back to the early years of the recording industry. Frances Densmore visited and recorded American Indian communities as early as 1907. Helen Oakley Dance (1913–2001) produced jazz recordings for the OKeh label in the mid-'30s and continued working as a freelance producer for many great jazz artists.[5] Producer and manager Helen Keane said, "This business requires total commitment. I believe that's why I've succeeded." Keane won seven Grammys and many more nominations for her productions of Bill Evans's albums. Her break into production came when she was Evans's manager. Creed Taylor, Evans's producer at the time, "opened the door for Keane to produce Evans for MGM/Verve," leading to her long production career and jazz discography.[6]

Joan Deary joined RCA in 1954 as secretary to Elvis Presley's producer Steve Sholes. Sholes died unexpectedly in 1968, and Deary moved into the position of assistant to VP Harry Jenkins (who handled Presley's material). Deary became an acknowledged expert on Presley's recordings, producing many albums for RCA. She recorded *Aloha from Hawaii* sitting on boxes in a room the size of a closet with no sightlines to Presley.[7]

Women Producers Today

The higher incidence of female artists and musicians in the charts may stimulate change. In this week of writing, six of the top ten slots on the *Billboard* Hot 100 feature women artists. The corresponding week in 1980 showed only two.

Lauren Christy began at 18 while working for a publishing company. She wanted her songs heard and thought, "I guess I'm going to have to be an artist." She began making demos at home on a four-track. "In those days, you thought you were going to get a male producer who would make you sound amazing and that's it." She got a deal and "started to work with lots of male producers who were all wonderful in their own way and I'm sure I drove most of them crazy being so involved." That "involvement" led to a production credit on the second album. Then she "had a rude awakening" about how hard it is "to be successful in this business." She said, "The stars don't always align for you and I was 27 years old. I wasn't an ingénue any more." She met Sandy Roberton, who tried to get her a new record deal, and then she "realized I was too old for this." This was the turning point when she realized that she "wanted to be behind the scenes." Her husband Graham was in a similar situation, as was Scott Spock who had been doing remixes. The three decided to form a production company. "We had no money. It was all about desperation." They found "two gorgeous actresses who could sing a little bit, and we realized we could make a superb sound." They worked all hours "making this big production" to compensate "for their weak vocals." Then they were asked to write something for Christina Aguilera's record. Recognizing the opportunity, they "stayed up all one weekend, knocked out a song, and that was our big break. We co-produced 'The Fear.'" I asked Christy for her advice to young women interested in becoming producers, and she said, "Listen to music. Analyze what you like about it. Try to study writing." Also, "Find a good manager. Find a mentor." She did not come through the engineering route. "For me, sharing the success and finding partnerships is the key to being a good producer." She thinks she would not have become a producer without her partners, although she has produced so much now that with "a great song and an engineer... I could probably do it, but it wouldn't be as much fun. You can't do everything."

Wendy Page who produces with Jim Marr thinks that "there ought to be more" women producers. She thinks that production "was a man's world" before "computers and home studios" and although many "female artists have co-produced," solo women producers have not been prevalent. Page attributes this to the historically male-dominated record labels that have been "mistrustful of giving a woman the reins of an immense, creative project like making a record." However hard it is for "women to break into this field" she thinks, "If you are determined, patient, obscenely hard-working, and have a talent in music, you can break through." Despite the difficulties, Page says, "I love music, I love my job. I consider myself blessed to be able to do this, and I cannot imagine living my life without singing and songs." On the positive side, she said,

> The difficulties are usually very short-lived. Once people realize that you can do your job, sexism tends to lower its ugly head. I tend to create a happy studio "family" where everyone is glad to be there, especially the artist. Good communication and diplomacy usually sort any little problems out.[8]

As to whether there are advantages in having a female producer, she thinks that, with a woman producer, "the studio experience is less intimidating for female artists, particularly if they are very young." She added this caveat: "If I accept that this is an advantage, then I am conceding to a stereotype of female producers being more sympathetic and sensitive." She thinks it is most important that the artist trusts you with their music and that "gender should become irrelevant." For young women wanting to produce, she recommends learning as much as possible about music, including playing an instrument "well enough to write with." She added, "See as many gigs as you can, get a home computer setup, GarageBand is fantastic..., and develop a thick skin.... Remember, you cannot fail, you can only quit."[9]

Linda Perry was the lead singer and main songwriter in the group 4 Non Blondes, which had a hit with "What's Up" in 1993. After the band broke up and she did a stint as a solo artist, she moved into production through two songs she wrote and produced for Christine Aguilera—"Beautiful" and "Cruz." She is perplexed as to why there are few female producers:

> If this question was asked in the late 1800s, I might have had a good reply. But being in 2004, well, I'm a little stumped. I would assume it's the same reason there are few females running major record labels, networks, and [in] most executive positions.[10]

Perry has produced a number of female artists such as Pink, Christina Aguilera, Courtney Love, and Gwen Stefani. I asked her if this was something she consciously preferred to do. She said,

Pink and Courtney found me, Christina and Gwen, I went after. All four of these women are incredibly talented in so many ways, how they turned up in my life doesn't even come into question, I just know I'm lucky that they did.[11]

I asked if she thinks a female producer brings a different quality to a project than a male producer, or if the differences are individualistic and gender-neutral. She replied,

As an artist, I have worked with many male producers, three of them completely free of ego, open to my suggestion, very creative, and we collaborated well, which made for a wonderful experience because it was equal. Four of them—completely full of themselves, made me feel less than, never heard a word I said, [were] not open to suggestion, and very disrespectful. Basically intimidated and threatened by my presence—obviously not a healthy creative environment. I have come to realize that the reason why I had a good experience with the three is that our characters made a connection. The four others . . . we had no connection, which caused friction. As a female producer, I feel I bring in all qualities mentioned, but ultimately it comes down to the connection with the artist.[12]

Children's and traditional music producer Cathy Fink points out that in the children's music and folk world, "there are certainly women artists that get involved in producing their stuff. But there is a big disparity." She thinks that being engineers has helped her and her collaborator Marcy Marxer. They say they are not "the best engineers out there," but it helps them know how to tell an engineer what they want. There are "some really fine women producers," but not that many "doing it on a major level." Like Page and Perry, they think that it is "harder for women" in the record production world for the same reasons it is harder for women in "other places in the work world."[13]

Missy Elliott launched her career at a time when there were not many women hip hop artists, but she could also produce, as she proved with her many productions and co-productions, including her collaborations with Timbaland. She said in a *Remix* interview, "Once you're confident, you make everybody else around you believe that you got some hot s**t."[14]

In addition to those mentioned previously, women engineers and producers have amassed considerable credits. Maureen Droney engineered recordings for George Benson, Whitney Houston, John Hiatt, Tower of Power, and Santana. Leslie Ann Jones is the director of music and scoring at Skywalker Sound. Susan Rogers started in the business as a field service technician for MCI and became famous for her work with Prince. Trina Shoemaker engineered for Sheryl Crow among many others. Sylvia Massy also worked with Prince. She went on to engineer and produce alternative groups such as Tool, Sevendust, Powerman 5000, and Skunk Anansie. Female artists Beyoncé, Madonna, and Kate Bush have co-produced or produced themselves for many years.

Inconclusive Conclusion

Computers and home studios may not remove all the barriers from the workplace, but they can offer women a more conducive environment for music production. A positive sign of progress for women in the audio production world would be increasing enrollment in the available educational programs. Unfortunately, according to my research, there appears to be little interest in the United States in tracking this indicator of equal opportunity.

12

Frequently Asked Questions

How Much Is Learned; How Much Is Natural Ability?

Even though we learn to question our first inclinations, they often seem to hold true. In the studio, so much of what we do seems intuitive, almost instinctive, but this ease with the process is the product of years of honing. Instinct is inborn and natural to a species, and it is possible that there are interpersonal skills used in the studio that are innate or learned at an early age. Nonetheless, most of what happens in the production process is the result of years of deliberate practice. Cognitive psychologist Gary Klein has extensively researched the decision-making process, and he says,

> We used to think that experts carefully deliberate the merits of each course of action, whereas novices impulsively jump at the first option. [When actually] it's the novices who must compare different approaches to solving a problem. Experts come up with a plan and then rapidly assess whether it will work. They move fast because they do less.[1]

Klein had a conversation with a flight instructor pilot that really stuck with him:

> When he first started flying, he was terribly frightened. If he made a mistake, he'd die. He had to follow all of these rules and checklists in order to fly the plane correctly, and it was an extremely nerve-wracking time. But at some point in his development, he underwent a profound change. Suddenly, it felt as if he wasn't flying the plane—it felt as if he was flying. He had internalized all of the procedures for flying until the plane had felt as if it was a part of him. He no longer needed any rules.[2]

You are unlikely to die because of a poor decision made in the studio. Nonetheless, it is a fast-moving and multifaceted environment. Procedures become internalized, and an intuitive confidence in decision-making develops through conscious, practiced immersion with the music, musicians, technology, and necessary business aspects. *Harvard Business Review* published a paper entitled "The Making of an Expert" in 2007, which said,

Intuition can lead you down the garden path.... While it may be true that intuition is valuable in routine or familiar situations, informed intuition is the result of deliberate practice. You cannot consistently improve your ability to make decisions (or your intuition) without considerable practice, reflection, and analysis.[3]

The authors K. Anders Ericsson, Michael J. Prietula, and Edward T. Cokely in their research on complex cognitive practices say that

[e]ven the most gifted performers need a minimum of ten years (or 10,000 hours) of intense training before they win international competitions. In some fields, the apprenticeship is longer: It now takes most elite musicians 15 to 25 years of steady practice, on average, before they succeed at the international level.... One notable exception, Bobby Fischer, did manage to become a chess grand master in just nine years, but it is likely that he did so by spending more time practicing each year.[4]

As we have previously identified, there are six broad types or categories of producer, each requiring different skills and relationships with the artists, musicians, technology, and business of recording. There are many permutations of these styles, but regardless of an individual's approach, good producers acquired their skills through assiduous practice. DJs with little or no musical or studio engineering knowledge often become excellent producers. They play a great number of records and experience firsthand how people respond to them. They are effectively testing many parameters and programming themselves to be able to reproduce this excitement in their own tracks, and they intuitively recognize when it is present and when it is not. Les Paul purposefully used this analytical process:

After we discovered that the sound on sound was working, that night we went to work at the Blue Note. And after a couple of weeks there, I told Mary, "There's something bothering me. If you listen when we play 'How High the Moon' on Monday, the crowd just goes crazy. Tuesday is almost as good as Monday, but by Wednesday we've got a problem. By Thursday and Friday it's worse, and by Saturday it's almost forget it. Then Sunday is pretty good, and again Monday is a great one. The reaction should be the same no matter what night it is, so we're playing 'How High the Moon' wrong. We're playing it for professional people who are off on Monday; bartenders, maître d's, musicians, and they want to hear it the way we play it. But on Wednesday, Thursday, Friday and Saturday we've got people who want to get away from the kids; blue-collar guys who are far removed from musicians and professionals." So, when we next moved on to places like Rockford, Illinois, and Omaha, Nebraska, we kept trying "How High the Moon" each night in three different ways until I was pretty sure that I'd found the arrangement that went down great every night of the week. It was very unusual to do this, but when the guys over at Capitol asked, "What in the world makes you think that this record is going to make it?" I said, "Because I've put it to the test, and my jury says this is the way it should be." And after we made it, the jury bought it right away. This was what we did with all our hit records—I would make sure that there was a jury of people who could tell me if something was good or not. However, I never told them they were part of a jury or that I'd like their opinions. I'd just watch their reactions.[5]

The adage "There is no such thing as a bad audience" can be interpreted in several ways, but I take it to mean that the responsibility lies with the performer, or in this case the producer, to communicate with the audience. An unresponsive audience indicates a lack of connection, and that is what Paul identified and improved.

Missy Elliott likes to test her tracks in clubs in major markets such as Miami and New York. She said to Kylee Swensen,

If it don't [sic] have the drive that the record before mine had, then it's a problem. I see how the crowd reacts to it, and if they semi danced, then I'll feel, "Okay, maybe there needs to be some other stuff to go on in this record." So I'll pretty much let a club crowd determine whether something's missing or not. If they ain't moving to it, then it's back to the lab, because you're on the wrong page.[6]

Beyond direct testing of material, DJing and learning successful material in your chosen genre can help hone your intuitive understanding of what comprises a hit. I played in top 40 bands when I was young even though I preferred to play original material. When I started to write and produce, I realized that playing all those hits imbued me with an inherent sense of what works; I did not have to think about how to construct a hit, I just knew. Lauren Christy's partner in life and production, Graham Edwards, played with his father's band in Scotland. She said, "He knows every genre of music inside out. He can write a song in two minutes." This intuitive sense of what works becomes ingrained and is manifested as a natural ease in the studio. As the research demonstrates, we acquire "natural ability" over a long period of time, through a deliberate and assiduous process.

How Do You Pick the Right Project?

As we have discussed, if good is the enemy of great, accepting what is good can prevent us from achieving the great. Projects that are not suitable or not good enough are easy to identify. Sifting potentially excellent artists (or songs) from the good and very good ones is not so simple. There always seems to be plenty of good acts (and songs), but the great ones are rare. If great productions begin with great material and artists, then the smart strategy is to structure your life so that you can afford the time to seek out the right artists, material, and projects. Highly successful producers can afford to take the time to research and listen until they find the next great artist.

Less financially independent producers have to consider how to pay their bills, and producing filler projects carries an opportunity cost by taking away time that might otherwise be used in tracking down a truly great act. Even the most organized and proactive approach produces a higher percentage of good than great. It is important not to settle, and this requires a combination of persistence and patience.

Mickie Most was arguably one of the most successful independent British producers from the '60s through the '80s. He was entrepreneurial from the start, discovering the Animals and then financing and producing their first album. He had long runs of hits with such diverse artists as Herman's Hermits, Donovan, Jeff Beck, the Yardbirds, Hot Chocolate, and more, reportedly selling hundreds of millions of records. For five years during the '60s, Most would alternate a week in New York or Los Angeles, listening to new material at publishers' offices, with a week in London, recording what he had found. Interestingly, his early hits, "The House of the Rising Sun," "I'm Into Something Good," and "Tobacco Road," were all turned down by American labels, saying that they were not right for the market; yet within six months, his productions of each had hit the U.S. number-one slot. In the '80s, he felt he was losing his feel for the market, so he sold his label, "because music was turning in a way that I didn't understand."[7]

Taking on productions primarily for the money is not a good idea. It is easy for a producer with broad tastes and a solid musical grounding to understand how to make a project better. Producing a hit or a recording that stands out in its genre is several orders of magnitude beyond making something better and can be surprisingly difficult when the "heart" ingredient is missing. Sandy Roberton said,

> It's the right projects. It's so easy to get tempted to take a project just because you need the money. But it might be the wrong project. It's important to be very selective. It's hard because producers panic if they're not working. I think they should really consider doing something else, like actors. The ones who are selective about what they do—their career goes on.[8]

If you are not convinced about a project, there are two reasons to avoid taking it. One is because any inferior work you do will diminish your reputation and damage your brand. The other is opportunity cost, a term originated by Friedrich von Wieser (1851–1926) that refers to the value of the alternative use of the resource. In this case, the resource is your time. Making money producing an artist, even if he or she is less than the best, may seem like a reasonable use of time. Nevertheless, producers need time out of the studio, not focusing on a specific project, to think, strategize, and find artists and material with the potential that best moves them toward their career objectives.[9]

Should You Share in Songwriting Royalties?

It may be that you are producing an act because you wrote the song. This is common in genres such as R&B, hip hop, dance, and pop. However, there can be a fine line between producing and writing. When producers feel they have contributed to the writing, asking for a credit can be delicate. It is the producer's job to make the best possible recording for the artist, and because the material is central, it is irresponsible not to optimize it. It is important to differentiate between personal preference and improvement. Some producers contribute and demand a writing credit; others waive writing credits and royalties regarding their contribution as part of the production. "Songwriting is not my job," said Bruce Fairbairn. He wanted to "help a band create the album they wanted to make." He was not "rewriting choruses"; he was more involved in "structuring and arranging the song." He did not want the band to feel "threatened that they're going to lose 10 percent of a song" every time he brought up an idea.[10]

Restructuring, arranging, or orchestrating material the artist wrote is part of a producer's job, but writing or rewriting choruses, bridges, or substantial parts of a lyric deserves credit and a royalty share. There is also the ethical consideration of the power gradient between an experienced producer and a new artist.

If modifications to someone else's composition seem unavoidable, it is crucial to minimize friction with the writer(s). It may be possible to point out the weakness as you see it and encourage the writer(s) to come up with a solution or alternative ideas. Sometimes they will be open to the suggestion and write something much stronger. It becomes a challenge for the producer if the writer does not agree, or if he or she offers weak alternatives. At that point, you or someone else has to make a tangible musical or lyric suggestion that can be used or that stimulates an acceptable solution from the writer. When there is a substantive change to the music or lyrics, the sensitive issue of writing credits must be considered. In a flurry of brainstorming, history can be rewritten in a matter of seconds, and there can be diametrically opposing views of who came up with what. The producer has to consider the well-being of the production in these situations.

New versus Established Artists?

Established artists have an existing sales base so productions for them are more likely to result in sales and royalties. However, there are disadvantages. You will be working within some constraints of their existing recorded identity, and they may be unused to honest critique. They usually define the schedule and the location. If the album you produce sells less than their prior album or is poorly received by the media, it can damage industry perceptions of your abilities. Established artists can become set in their ways and less receptive to new ideas. They tend to change producers when they need a shift in approach, but if the motivation for change is not theirs, the recording process can become a struggle.

New artists are usually open to the producer's ideas, but with no sales and media base, the onus is on your production to excite the label enough to invest marketing dollars that engage the media. It is exciting to introduce a new artist to the possibilities of the studio and success, but the statistical chances of a miss with a new act are in the high 90th percentile. The producer's relationship with the artist is different on a debut album than on subsequent records, and even experienced producers working with a musical legend can be intimidated. Barry Beckett produced Bob Dylan's *Slow Train Coming* album:

> It took Bob three or four days, while we were cutting, to even trust me. When he finally did, he let me know with a very slight smile, or something like that, to say I was OK. I was pretty nervous when we started.[11]

Most producers begin their careers producing new artists. With success, working with established acts becomes an option that will fatten your résumé and most likely your bank account. An established artist has a professional business team in place, a fan base, and receptive media, and labels are more likely to commit marketing dollars to them.

What Is Involved in Being an Independent or Freelance Producer?

No matter your field of endeavor, working for yourself is both a liberating experience and an immense responsibility. Paul Getty purportedly said, "Going to work for a large company is like getting on a train. Are you going 60 miles an hour or is the train going 60 miles an hour and you're just sitting still?" When you work for yourself or run your own company, you are never a passenger. You not only drive the train, you also have to build it, maintain it, and find the fuel to run it. I realized early in my career that I have two basic needs in life, autonomy and creativity (perhaps they are wants, but they feel like needs). I found I could survive adverse conditions if those two qualities were present. Stress does not easily grow in a field of autonomy, and boredom melts in the fire of creativity. Of course, no job offers complete autonomy or creativity, and some people value security more.

In order to sustain a freelance production career, you have to be independent, self-sufficient, confident in your abilities, and sure of your opinions. Patience, negotiating skills, and some understanding of human psychology will help. Diplomacy can extend a career. Even freelance producers are beholden to someone or something. It may be the artist, the label, or simply his or her own monthly expenses. Company politics definitely affect independent producers. Nonetheless, not depending on a single employer creates some sense of personal sovereignty. There is no regular paycheck, but independent producers are not by nature company people.

Quincy Jones became an A&R person at Mercury Records in 1961 and rose to become the first black VP of a major label by 1964. Despite his success, he did not like some aspects of the job, saying,

> I was behind a desk every day. Awful! I had to be in there at nine o'clock, and you had to wear these Italian suits. You had to fill out expense reports and all that kind of stuff. That really made my skin crawl.[12]

George Martin began in the industry in 1950, before the term record producer was consistently used and before independent producers were prevalent. He produced the Beatles while a salaried staffer at EMI, and the company paid him no royalties or bonuses for the unprecedented success he brought them. Embittered by the inequity of the financial deal, he left EMI and set up Associated Independent Recording. AIR started as a semi-communal or cooperative independent production house with Martin, Ron Richards, and John Burgess from EMI, and Peter Sullivan, who had recently move from EMI to Decca. The four men produced many of the major acts of the time including the Beatles, Cilla Black, Gerry and the Pacemakers, Billy J. Kramer, the Fourmost, Adam Faith, Manfred Mann, Peter and Gordon, P. J. Proby, the Hollies, and many more. The individual and collective magnitude of the acts for which the four producers were responsible somewhat forced the hands of the major labels to hire them as independents. Eventually they went on to build the famed AIR studios and organization, all the while developing a remarkable discography of independent productions.[13] Martin, speaking about the role of producer to Mel Lambert said,

> The role was something that evolved....Producers come in all shapes and sizes....A good producer has got to really have an understanding of music, and a catholic love for it. Unless you're very specialized, I think that you have to have a very universal approach to music, to have the temperament to like a lot of music. Which, fortunately or unfortunately, I do! If you're very narrow in your outlook, you're not going to make a good record producer, because you have to be pretty tolerant, too. But in terms of music, it is very important to have an understanding of how music works, although I don't think it's absolutely a prerequisite that you have a musical education.[14]

What he did not talk about here was the entrepreneurial risk that the four of them took in setting up AIR. They had no guarantee of work and no history of a royalty deal with the majors. They did not even have the capital to start the business. They leveraged their considerable accomplishments as producers to raise the startup capital and established a very meager royalty deal through a first-option agreement with EMI.[15]

What About Being a Staff Producer?

Many of the earliest producers, such as Fred Gaisberg, were staff producers, and although freelance producers have long been a part of the recording industry (almost since the beginning), many labels still have producers on staff. Much of Columbia's success in the '50s was due to their in-house producers like John Hammond, Mitch Miller, Teo Macero, and George Avakian. Warner Bros. had a substantial run of success in the '70s and '80s with their team of staff producers including Ted Templeman, Lenny Waronker, and Russ Titelman. In the United Kingdom, through the late '50s and '60s, EMI records had Norrie Paramor (who produced many hits for Cliff Richard and the Shadows, among others), John Burgess, Ron Richards, and of course George Martin. Arif Mardin was on staff for decades at Atlantic and after they forced his retirement due to a corporate age limit, he went to work for Manhattan Records. Bruce Lundvall, president of EMI Jazz and Classics, asked Mardin to "step in on a project with young singer Norah Jones, whose initial sessions hadn't captured the intimate quality that had prompted Lundvall to sign her."[16] The subsequent debut album was certified more than ten times platinum in the United States. Even without actually producing hits in-house for a label, having strong recording, mixing, budgeting, and troubleshooting abilities on staff can be worthwhile for a record company.

Unfortunately, with the wave of consolidation and downsizing that swept through major labels in the new millennium, there are fewer positions available. There are advantages to being a staff producer at a major label. Apart from the regular paycheck and benefits, staff producers often have the first look at the acts being signed, and they know the label's priorities. They may be able to define their own role within the company and function more freely than other employees. Arif Mardin liked being on staff at Atlantic for most of his career:

> I think it was maybe security. I had a financial arrangement. Also, it's a legendary company and Ahmet Ertegun is still there and I love to be with him, you just feel attached. I'm not too much of a freelance person, where I would have to hustle. They come to me.[17]

Mardin had studied business and enjoyed the various other duties he had as one of Atlantic Records' officers. Ron Fair was for a long time a staff producer and A&R person before becoming president of A&M and then chairman of Geffen. He pointed out some advantages of being in-house:

> I oversee all of the areas of delivering the record and how they're handled in the various departments: promotion, advertising, publicity, marketing, distribution. I maintain very close relationships with everybody in the chain, so that I can watch over my records. Independent producers have very little input or even ability to get knowledge of what is going on.[18]

This is no small advantage for a producer. If there is a standout frustration for freelance producers, it is their loss of control over a project once they deliver the masters to the label.

What Are the Best Moments?

Coaxing a transformative performance out of a singer, instrumentalist, or group is exciting and especially gratifying when the performers recognize that they have stretched themselves. "Great playing, great musicians" was Andy Jackson's first response to this question:

> When something fabulous happens, something that moves you. That thing that made us all do this in the first place, that got so fouled and embittered with the years. We stopped listening to music for fun many years ago. Occasionally, you get that spark that you remember, "This was like when I was 14." It just occasionally happens.[19]

It is exhilarating when a perfect part falls into place that shifts a track from good to extraordinary.

Can You Successfully Genre-Hop?

I suspect that very few people enjoy only one genre of music. Producers are no exception, but it is easy to become typecast in one style of music. I genre-hopped in my career and there is a cost. Veteran A&R person Muff Winwood said, "Artists are very often looking for someone whose last four albums sound exactly the way they want their next album to sound."[20] It is reassuring for some artists to know how their record will sound, but it is unlikely to create a work of originality. Prior to the Beatles, George Martin produced a range of comedy acts, traditional musicians, and actors. Had he been a freelance producer, a label would have been unlikely to choose him to produce the Beatles. As it turned out, his classical training, appreciation for humor, and perhaps his lack of a sense of limits in producing pop were all valuably manifested in the Beatles' recordings.

Artists and A&R people are sometimes limited in their musical breadth. If you are a multi-genre producer, they may only know one sector of your discography, which diminishes the impressiveness of your body of work. If your name comes up for a rock artist, your R&B or country hits may mean nothing to them or be perceived negatively. For non-producers, mentally translating production techniques from one genre to another is not easy. If you can successfully produce in several genres, the decision-makers may assume that you can produce anything. Overcoming the circular, catch-22-like logic that you will not be able to do something until you have already done it can be challenging.

The fundamentals of production contain genre-free commonalities. Details change, but a producer skilled in the rudiments can function above stylistic details. Nonetheless, producers do become genre-bound. Auteur producers may most easily be typecast because they are responsible for so much of the detail that comprises the character of a record.

One of the last producers you might expect this to happen to was Phil Ramone. His career was long and diverse. It would seem his versatility should have been a given, but he was thwarted at one point when he tried to branch into country. "You're typecast from day one as a rock producer," he said. "I was a big fan of Lyle

[Lovett]; we were about to make a record, and then the country people got scared that I would take him somewhere else."

SOME EXAMPLES OF GENRE-HOPPING PRODUCERS

My background was jazz, blues, and rock, but my first production was computer-generated pop. I went through the pop/alternative of Spandau Ballet and King. Colonel Abrams is categorized as dance music, and success with urban/R&B projects came in the form of New Edition, Melba Moore, and Five Star, followed by a hit with the blue-eyed soul group Living in a Box. I moved back to alternative/modern rock with Shriekback and XCNN. Along the way were pop, dance, ambient productions, and club remixes, as well as TV and film music. I look for artists I like and interesting opportunities. I try to avoid clone artists—those who want me to emulate something I did for someone else, and I turned down a lot of work because of that. I do shy away from artists and genres outside of my taste or understanding.

Peter Collins successfully produced artists as diverse as Rush, Philip Bailey and Phil Collins, Bon Jovi, Musical Youth, Tracy Ullman, the Indigo Girls, Elton John and Leann Rimes, Alice Cooper, and Blancmange. When genre-hopping is systematically pursued, as Rick Rubin has done, you can jump from hip hop (Beastie Boys, Run DMC, Public Enemy) to alternative (Red Hot Chili Peppers) to rock (Tom Petty) to nu-metal (Slipknot) to Johnny Cash and then Neil Diamond. George Martin, who has demonstrated great versatility in his career, said,

> I've always made different records from rock to spoken word, and it's all music and it makes life interesting doing more than one thing. I would be bored stiff if I made records in only one format.[21]

Measured by sales, Robert John "Mutt" Lange may be the most successful example of a genre-hopping producer (and perhaps overall). After leaving South Africa for the United Kingdom, he produced Graham Parker in the '70s, moved to Australian hard rock with AC/DC, arena rock with Foreigner, R&B pop with Billy Ocean, American new wave with the Cars, pop-metal with Def Leppard, pop-country with Shania Twain, and pop-dance with Maroon Five. AC/DC, Def Leppard, and two Shania Twain albums have been RIAA-certified diamond (ten million albums sold in the United States). He also worked with Michael Bolton, Celine Dion, Britney Spears, the Backstreet Boys, and the Corrs. The common factors in Lange's productions are hit songs that have a radio-friendly production.

How Stable Is a Producer's Career?

The stability of a production career depends, to some extent, upon expectations. Regional and local producers can work steadily for a very long time, but the trajectory of a hit producer tends to be ballistic rather than linear or exponential. Other music business behind-the-scenes people, such as attorneys or business managers, build reputations, clients, and businesses over a lifetime. Producers build reputation, but it is often associated with a period or style. They develop clients, but the clients are artists, A&R people, and sometimes managers, none of whom tend to be long-term reliable sources of work. They move on to the next wave of producers or their own careers fade.

Successful producers tend to experience one busy, highly paid period, and only a few sustain themselves at that level for decades. Most experience slower periods that may not support their peak lifestyle. For those who invested wisely or who made recordings that continue to generate substantial royalties, this is not necessarily a bad thing. However, if the successes were not big enough or the royalties slowed to a trickle, a change of lifestyle may be necessary. Despite undeniably transferable skills, it can be difficult for successful producers to replace the levels of income they are accustomed to with other work, in or out of the business.

Most freelance producers are one-person service businesses. Apart from investments and some equipment, the only value built is in goodwill, your reputation, and your brand, none of which are convertible business assets. Skills and knowledge that were valuable one year may be considered obsolete the next. In a competitive market, impressions may be enough to cause work to dry up. Should you become famous enough, your celebrity may have transferable value, but producers rarely become household names except through A&R-based music shows like "American Idol."

Staff producers may enjoy more short-term security, but the number of long-standing staff producers at labels has diminished in recent years. Those who survive often move further into the corporate world and take on more executive tasks. Local and regional producers who own their own studios tend to be less vulnerable and may be able to sell their businesses and assets. However, if work has slowed enough to force a sale, any value may be limited to the physical assets.

It is counterintuitive to prepare for a successful production career to be short even though the dearth of producer names that carry over, from one decade's charts to another, is instructive. However, producers can continue to carve out a decent living without constant hits. Achieving this may mean occupying a niche that provides enough paying work while carefully managing business and personal finances.

How Does a Production Career End?

My observation is that production careers often end quite gradually. There are some difficult-to-discern indicators. Projects coming in may be not as exciting as they had been. A&R people are slower in returning calls. Early conversations and meetings lead to work less often. The faces at the labels change and develop a new circle of trusted producers.

When royalties slow from a torrent to a trickle and the latest productions do not generate any income, without conscious adjustment, money going out can quickly exceed money coming in. Sometimes, this can be on an extravagant level, as in the earlier examples of Scott Storch and Teddy Riley, but it is commonly a more subtle occurrence where monthly expenses are building debt and/or depleting investments. At this point, career alternatives become a consideration.

Making Plans and When?

Overall industry revenues were down more than 50 percent in the first decade of the millennium. Major labels have merged, putting tens of thousands of lifelong music industry employees out of work. The large corporations dropped untold numbers of acts, resulting in less production work. Even successful producers need to plan strategically and understand their goals. Being prepared to stretch into areas that are unfamiliar and figuring out how your skills can transfer may be necessary. There are very successful artists and labels in the independent sector, although producer advances and recording budgets are likely to be smaller than those of the majors.

Boring as it may be, sensible financial management can be a decisive factor for a long career. It is easy to make the mistake of allowing your lifestyle to meet peak levels of income. The sustainable approach is to live below your means during the good times, investing for leaner periods. Being entrepreneurial in signing artists, as well as building and maintaining relationships within the industry, can be effective hedges against involuntary retirement.

Successful producers should begin financially future-proofing from the first point of significant income. When work slows or stops, recovery can be impossible. Producing is a business, and stable long-term businesses are forward-looking. SWOT analysis—examining your strengths, weaknesses, opportunities, and threats—is a useful planning tool. You may be one of the leading producers in a genre (strength), but the genre could wane or competitors might take market share (threats). Weaknesses might be a limited source of projects or an inflated cost structure. Opportunity might lie in a related genre that is in a growth phase. Most production techniques are adaptable from an older style to a new one. Alan Moulder trained in the '80s but became a frontrunner with the indie sound while the slicker '80s production styles were still predominant. These shifts can be an opportunity if you identify the new market early—before it becomes highly competitive. There is the world as you would like it to be and the world as it is; regularly adjusting to reality is a hedge against obsolescence.

Strategic plans need to be in writing, and it helps to keep updated lists of short-, medium-, and long-term goals along with action items. Lists help mentally materialize actions that will achieve your objectives. When opportunities arise that align with a list item, you notice and can act on them more readily. One technique is to make lists using a stream-of-consciousness approach; you then whittle and prioritize the lists by preference and practicality. Write them down without judgment and edit later, separating and balancing the left- and right-brain approaches. An unsystematic approach to a career may work, but it is undependable. Don Gehman said,

> Everybody's career has its ups and downs. I had four or five records with John Cougar Mellencamp that were all pretty successful. Then we got to a place where we had basically worked together for ten years and enough was enough. I moved on to other things. I had *Life's Rich Pageant* (R.E.M.) and enough other things that people were looking at me as a record producer. It was no problem getting work, but getting hit records is difficult. You don't have multi-platinum artists every day.[22]

Shortly after making this comment, Gehman produced the multiplatinum and award- winning debut album for Hootie and the Blowfish. Nevertheless, his comment regarding the difficult of consistently producing big-selling hits remains true in every era. Producing hits is not unlike winning gold in the Olympics. In music production, competition, the state of the media, trends, corporate politics, and other factors affect results.

What Do Producers Do When Work Starts to Slow Down?

Because the mainstream industry is so success-oriented (hits = quality), a career dip when both the quality and quantity of projects drops can be scary. Do you take less appealing projects to keep working, or do you wait? Sandy Roberton thinks it is important to be selective, if necessary picking up other work, as actors do, between jobs. Other producer managers agree. It is tough to hold out when money is tight, but it is better for your career to be proud of every production.

If work does not recover, the perfect scenario is that you invested well and can consider your options calmly. Nonetheless, many producers are relatively young when their production work slows, and they have no desire to retire. Becoming a manager can be an option; few have more contacts or understand the intricacies of the business better than an ex-producer. As his production career was winding down, Sandy Roberton launched his management business by getting a gig for the engineer he was working with. Studio ownership was for a time popular with producers, especially those who built their own facilities during their very active years. Unless you have a business model that differentiates your studio in the market, this is a less viable option today. In fact, the real estate may be worth more than a working studio. After selling Elvis Presley's contract to RCA, although he still had a viable business in Sun Records, Sam Phillips invested early and wisely in the Holiday Inn chain.[23] Some producers simply go along with the slowdown and retire altogether or produce something here and there, as opportunities present themselves. Some pursue their fascination with technology, make solo albums, move into music for film and television, or utilize their business skills and devote their time to new ventures. Producers do develop transferable skills and although formal qualifications may not be necessary for record production, if a music career ends early, a college degree can help with a backup plan. Teaching at the university level often begins with occasional lectures or an adjunct position that may eventually become a full-time and, for many, very fulfilling profession. Many universities want professors with terminal degrees, so lifelong educators rather than experienced professionals may be preferred for any open positions. Some producers go back to school to complete their doctorates.

Producers, like managers, often rise to senior positions in the music industry. The skills that producers develop are at the core of what makes the industry profitable—finding talent and material, and then working with a team to optimize both. Doug Morris, chairman/CEO of Sony Music Entertainment—one of the two largest record companies in the world—wrote the Chiffons' hit "Sweet Talkin' Guy" in 1966 and produced Brownsville Station's 1973 hit "Smokin' in the Boys' Room."[24] Andy Slater had management experience and production credits with artists such as Macy Gray, Fiona Apple, and the Wallflowers and became president/CEO of Capitol Records during the early 2000s. Matt Serletic emerged as the producer of Matchbox Twenty, Carlos Santana's *Smooth*, Aerosmith, and Celine Dion and became chairman of Virgin Records. L.A. Reid—previously president and CEO of Arista, chairman/CEO of Island Def Jam, and now chairman/CEO of Epic Records—wrote and produced 33 number-one singles as half of the L.A. and Babyface production team. Jimmy Iovine is the chairman and co-founder of Interscope Records. In 2011, Blue Note installed producer Don Was as chief creative officer and later president, and the list goes on. There is an optimum time to move into an executive position in a corporation, and that is close to your peak of production success. This may seem counterintuitive because many producers consciously sacrificed a salary to maintain independence. Knowledge of industry precedents, foresight, and strategic thinking pay dividends in the long term.

Why Do People Want to Produce Records?

Even before my first experience in a recording studio, I had fallen in love with everything about the recording process. When I began work as a studio musician, the process was less painstaking and time-consuming than it later became. Then, we often recorded and mixed an album in a day. Performing live is an evanescent experience; no matter how great the gig, unless you record the show, it lives only in the memories of the performers and the audience. Production creates, captures, and perfects special moments. As a composer and arranger, it is appealing to be able to preserve the nuances of a composition and arrangement that written music cannot capture. It would be fascinating to hear recordings of Bach, Beethoven, or Mozart produced by them, the way they imagined their compositions sounding. Beyond the composition and the arrangement, being able to paint a sonic picture using technology to scrutinize and optimize each instrument or sound adds another artistic dimension of auricular creative interpretation.

For more than a decade, I worked as a studio musician, and I thought the producer's job seemed tedious. I would play on the basic tracks, and weeks later, they would call me back to overdub percussion. I would walk into the studio and see the producer and engineer in the same place they had been sitting weeks ago. Spending all those hours in windowless rooms repeatedly listening to the same tracks did not appeal to me. However, I began to notice that certain producers, using a similar pool of musicians, were achieving superior results. This intrigued me. I noticed that the producers getting the best results were the ones who created a more conducive atmosphere that motivated musicians to deliver special performances. These producers quickly and accurately identified good takes. They knew when something was amiss and how to fix it. Conversely, less capable producers missed great performances or pushed the musicians beyond their best, failing to identify problems or solutions. Additionally, it was all too common to lay a strong rhythm track, only to hear it later, weakened by out-of-time, inappropriate, or too many overdubs.

In many ways, it was the less talented producers who inspired me to produce. It was evident what they were doing wrong. What was not so clear was how the producers I admired achieved their results. They appeared effortless and intuitive in the studio. Eventually, what committed me to long days in sunless, soundproofed rooms was the annoyance I felt as a signed artist working with producers who were more interested in their artistic vision than mine. I wanted to emulate those effortless, intuitive producers and capture the creative essence of the artist, even if the artists did not fully understand it themselves. The subjugation of my own musical personality was already a part of my professional life as a studio musician. I enjoy this form of role-playing, and that made me gravitate toward the collaborative typology.

Jim Dickinson, producer of Ry Cooder, the Rolling Stones, Big Star, the Replacements, and G. Love & Special Sauce, explained that he thought the drive to record is because, "The unretainable nature of the present creates in Man a desire to capture the moment."[25] This is the documentation of ephemeral nuances, the energy, and the intent. Once this involved capturing an entire event, and now it is more likely a collage of events. Before multitracking, it was all about "the decisive moment," that special take containing the magic. Now production is a series of decisive moments that are stacked, manipulated, and rearranged according to the producer's (and hopefully the artist's) musical vision. The producer is the author and/or the editor of the recording, in control of the many nuances—sonic and musical—and the creative work exists on a scale from complete aural fiction to a nonfiction snapshot in time.

Do You Know When You Have Produced a Hit?

There are many factors involved in creating a hit record that fall outside of the producer's control. The potential of a track may be identifiable, but there are other determinants that can cause it to remain unrealized. A record that goes multiplatinum embodies a virality that is not always obvious beforehand. Arif Mardin told me that when he was working with the Bee Gees on their *Main Course* album,

> We didn't realize that we had hits. We were just working and having a great time, very energetic, electrifying sessions, and when the Bee Gees' managers and Ahmet Ertegun came to listen to it they said "Oh wow, you've got massive hits." We said, "Really?" We didn't know [laughs]. This is a good surprise.[26]

Tom Lord-Alge, co-producer of the predictively entitled *Back in the High Life* by Steve Winwood, said,

> I had no idea that it would take off like it did. When we were finished and all the mixes were done, I realized the caliber of the record but had no idea that it would go through the roof.[27]

When asked if he ever thinks "this is a hit" early in the recording, Ron Fair said, "The funny thing is the ones when I said that, weren't hits and the ones where I said, 'I don't know what the hell this is,' were."[28] The parameters of a big hit are not completely obscure—as discussed before, catchy melodies, great vocal, relatable lyrics, and so forth—but even with all of these in place and a really well-produced track, there are many more obstacles to overcome before the money can be banked.

How Do Producers Feel about Mixers and Remixers?

It is important to distinguish between mixes and remixes. Generally, for the primary album mix and possibly the single, an outside mixer will use most of what the producer recorded. Recently, there has been a trend toward mixers adding material to the original production and the producer leaving more choices for the mixer. These might include such things as multiple tracks of background vocals that need to be compiled or percussion parts that are continuous throughout the track but need to be arranged.[29] The result will be termed a "mix" with a credit that will read "mixed by." "Remix" usually refers to a radical remake of the track, mostly for clubs but sometimes for singles and cross-genre promotion, where very little of the original production is used. The dance scene has become so fragmented and specialized that most producers do not have the expertise or the inclination to generate dance remixes. Some producers resent having their productions mixed by others for the album or singles, especially when the label does it without consultation. Producers build tracks around their aural impression of the desired result, and an outside mixer may not capture that vision. Other producers do not enjoy mixing or don't regard it as one of their strengths. If a mixer or remixer is mandatory for the label (and they usually have that contractual option), most producers prefer to choose the mixer and discuss their ideas with them. Many want to participate in the mix sessions, although some mixers do not allow that. Successful mixers and remixers generally receive a fee and a small royalty. Peter Collins does not mind having his work mixed by someone else, but prefers to be present. Linda Perry said,

> I am a horrible mixer. Mixing is another art form, a very important one. I oversee the mixes. Dave Pensado is my mixer. He is incredible, he understands what I'm trying to accomplish in the production, then drives it home on the mix. Dave experiments a lot with the mixes. He knows I don't want the same old tricks. We work really well together.[30]

Lauren Christy said that The Matrix covers both options:

> We mix most of [our records]. We always present our mix. We also kind of like to get someone else's point of view on it. Bob Clearmountain has been doing a lot of our stuff, just because he is so amazing.[31]

Sometimes the label will choose the mixer's version over the producer's, even when the producer does not think it is as good. Christy puts that into perspective:

> Yeah, that happens, but then sometimes our mix gets used like on "Complicated." Our mix got used on the radio and they put our mix, as well, as a hidden track on the record. To be honest, you can't get too attached to it. A mix is important and sometimes you hear it and you're like, "That's f***ed up, that blows," but it's still a hit.[32]

Wendy Page is generally positive about outside mixes of her work, saying that a fresh set of ears can be a really good thing. What concerns her is when "the original vision...is right" and is "lost in the mix." She said, "The trick is to make the monitor mix as close to perfect as possible."[33]

Sandy Roberton said that because bands generally pick the producer, the A&R people can be worried that they are "not going to have much to do with the project." So they generally get their way when they suggest someone to mix.[34]

A&R people can become quite invested in their choice, and it can be hard to convince them the remix is inferior no matter how obvious the problems are. This is the choice-supportive memory discussed earlier, when "people over-attribute positive features to options they chose."[35] It is nerve-wracking when a label mixes tracks without your input, and a big relief when they turn out reasonably well.

As discussed, mixes fall into two general categories, the straight mix and the radical remix, but completely straight mixes are becoming less common. Most rock, alternative, and even pop mixes stay closer to the original production concept, mostly using the material recorded by the producer. Club or dance remixes, based on any genre of music, may not use much original material. The more removed the original genre is from the current sound of dance music, the less source material will be used

As specialized as it has become, mixing is not easily divorced from the production process. Producers mostly mixed their own records prior to the mid-1980s. Tony Visconti said this about who makes the decision to have a project remixed:

> Sometimes it's the artist. They want the benefit of all possible worlds. They keep remixing with people; they might even edit your mix into someone else's

mix. Or some A&R person might think it's cool to have someone else mix the album. A lot of times, it's not the best decision to get someone on the outside to remix the album. They don't know why you put a certain track in a certain place; they don't know what level it should be at; and the whole original concept is being placed in the hands of a third party who doesn't know what went into that concept.[36]

It is frustrating to spend weeks incorporating the tweaks and idiosyncrasies the artist wanted, only to lose them at the remix stage. Often the artist is not present, and the remixer does not have to consider the producer's or the artist's preferences. "They're bypassing the months of blood, sweat, and tears that went into making those sounds, and that's what music is about—not technical tricks," says Visconti:

> The musicians and the producer, make the music. In the '70s, the vision of the producers and artists was always respected—you would never tamper with a Led Zeppelin album or an Elton John album or a Queen album. You'd get your balls cut off. The manager would have your guts for garters if you went near it. Now there's no protection from it. If someone told me they got their six-year-old son to remix someone's album, I'd believe them. It's lawless.[37]

Richard Gottehrer (Blondie, the Go-Gos, Joan Armatrading) said that they used to describe the mix as "Seeing God: The End."[38]

Historically, the splitting of the mixer and remixer roles from that of the producer was simply another inevitable step in the continuing fragmentation of the production process. Engineers and producers used to have to mix and master a recording directly to disc during the performance. Magnetic tape (and wire before it) separated out the mastering process, and multitrack tape introduced the concept of a postproduction mix. The fragmentation of charts into many genres creates an incentive for remixes, and club DJs need specialized mixes. Mixing and remixing by separate entities is here to stay, and the right marriage of market timing, track, and remix sometimes works together to create phenomenally successful results.

What's the Mixer's Viewpoint?

The Lord-Alge brothers Chris and Tom have built indomitable reputations as remixers. Chris, talking about what they find when the multitracks arrive for them to mix, said, "Sometimes you have to be 'Audio Maid.'" Tom added,

> I get tapes that are recorded well, and I get tapes that aren't. The ones that I find challenging are the ones that are butchered. There are great engineers out there, but unfortunately, there are too many bad ones. There are a lot of guys who cannot record live drums. What I've found in the tapes that I mix is that often the drums sound dull. On vocals, you find a lot of guys who aren't careful enough with the vocal comping and the vocal punching, breaths, words, bad punches all the time.[39]

Chris interjected,

> The worst thing about mixing, aside from bad-sounding recordings, is getting track sheets that make no sense. They're not notated properly, there are no tempos written down. You'll have four or five vocals, and it's not written what happened or how they did it, no notes. You feel like the engineer didn't care who got the tape next. You have to get their mix to figure out what the hell was done with the vocal.[40]

Bob Clearmountain was one of the first specialist mixers. Having produced records as well as mixed them, he thinks that it's harder for a producer to be objective,

> because you know every note and every nuance. I find that when you remember what it was like to get the guitar player to play that solo, and the singer to give that vocal performance, you tend to feature things with that in mind. When I mix something I've never heard before, it's a clean slate, because I have no prior connection to it.[41]

Clearmountain said he enjoys the producer's or artist's input, but in one case,

> Roland Orzabal from Tears for Fears…listened to what I'd done and said…"That's absolutely nothing like what I had in mind!" So I just had to say, "OK, point me in the right direction." He gave me some clues and I worked on it for another couple of hours and then he said…"No!"—so we moved on to another song![42]

With DAWs, it is easy for mix engineers to add, replace, or move parts around and make structural changes to the song. Jack Joseph Puig said to Paul Tingen in a *Sound On Sound* interview,

> We can do almost anything at the push of a button, and it's all non-destructive. The day and age when we threw up the faders and thought "I wish I had this or that" are over. It's massively acceptable now, and even expected, that we add things.[43]

Echoing the Lord-Alges' comments, Puig has his assistant prep the Pro Tools session because they sometimes arrive in a "massively disorganized" state. He prefers the artist and the producer to be there for the mix, and he will listen to the original producer's rough, but only when his mix is where he "wants to have it." He said that if he hears something "fantastic in [the rough] that I didn't think of, I'll incorporate it in my mix."[44]

The "additional production and remix" credit became common in the early '80s, when the vocal was one of few parts retained from the production. Sometimes remixers made producers unhappy by claiming the "additional production" credit when they added only inconsequential overdubs. Today it is more common to see "remix produced by…" for dance mixes, and this has been a Grammy award-qualifying category since 1998, acknowledging the specialist contribution.

HOW IMPORTANT IS AN OUTSIDE MIX TO AN A&R PERSON?

I asked Pete Ganbarg if he prefers the producer to mix his or her own tracks, or if he prefers to bring in somebody.

> It depends on the producer and their track record. How good they are as an engineer. With some guys it's not up for debate, if they produce, they mix, if you say "no, you can't mix," then they don't do the record. If you let them know upfront that you don't want them to mix, then there are no surprises.[45]

If a producer insists on mixing, it will be in his or her contract. Ganbarg elaborates: "It can say that you are hiring so-and-so to produce and mix the record." It comes down to "how badly you want that producer. The label doesn't want to give up control." They want to reserve the right "to finish the record with the best people."[46] Very few producers at any one time command that level of contractual control. I was curious about how much difference Ganbarg thinks an outside mixer makes:

> It depends on the outside mixer. If all they do is mix and you listen to their records, you know why it's worth giving up a point and the fees and taking it out of a producer/engineer's hands. They are the best there is. If you know that this is the guy for the job because of his track record, then it brings a lot to the project. There are only six to ten mixers in that league. There's so few A&R people out there that the majority of veteran, seasoned professionals have worked with these people. So there are no surprises. So if you are working with a band, it's like, "Is it Tom Lord-Alge, Chris Lord-Alge, Jack Joseph Puig, Alan Moulder, or Andy Wallace?" The names are not mysterious names; they have great track records and reputations based on their work, not with smoke and mirrors but because they are great at what they do.[47]

I've worked with all of these mixers with the exception of Andy Wallace, and they are not only good, but fast. Tom Lord-Alge regularly mixes two tracks a day. I wondered whether Ganbarg considered speed as a factor.

> Most of these guys are quick. Most of them we hire regardless of whether they spend five minutes on a mix (which one of these guys who shall remain nameless is known to do) or a day on a mix, it's going to sound good. I don't care how much time they spend on a mix as long as it sounds good. The majority of these guys are getting a flat fee, and they've done so many records that singles budget is X, album budget is Y, the fee is the same, the studio time is the same, there are no surprises.[48]

Labels do not like surprises. They do not tolerate budget overages or mixes that they do not like. It is hard to break into the inner circle of A-list producers and mixers, because they are consistent, reliable, and proven.

What Is the "Sophomore Slump"?

The so-called sophomore slump is the second album that sells significantly less than the first. Second singles that fail to connect spell trouble, but failed second albums can be the downfall of a promising career. Artists often spend years writing material for their first album. If it sells well enough for them to make a second, they may have only months or weeks to write. Usually, the act has been on the road promoting the first album. Some artists cannot write in hotel rooms or while on the move, so they have from the end of the first album's promotional cycle until they start recording the second to create the material. There is legitimate urgency to keep the career momentum going by quickly releasing a strong second album.

On the first album, the objective was to make a great record. With success, there is pressure to repeat the formula, sometimes from the label or management but often from the band itself. Songs written under those conditions can tend to be inbred reproductions rather than inspired originals. The opposite, and possibly more dangerous, syndrome is when artists significantly change musical direction for their second release. Occasionally this works; more often it alienates fans. The label guides artists carefully on the first release but with success, the act has some creative freedom. The producer can become complicit in this shift of direction. It will fall to him or her to assess whether the fans, media, and label will perceive the new direction as artistic growth or find it puzzling. Motown thrived on the formula spelled out by their Four Tops hit "The Same Old Song." That may not have been what the lyric meant, but second releases on the Motown label usually emulated the first.

There was an artist whose sales slumped from more than seven million units on the debut to below 200,000 by the third album. The label continued to support the act for a while. Big-selling artists pay for costs out of their pipeline royalties, but when idiosyncratic offerings continue, labels drop them. Nowadays, major labels might drop a multiplatinum act when the follow-up sells less than gold, particularly if they do not like the demos for the proposed third album.

Muff Winwood, ex-producer and longtime CBS/Sony A&R person, said that second albums are problematic because artists become less open to advice and harder for labels to guide. He indicated that sometimes the best commercial decision a company can make is to drop the artist if he or she is in decline after the second album.[49] They can become very demanding once they experience success, wanting to fly to gigs, staying in first-class hotels, and so on, even if their current sales do not warrant it. Company support, even if it is the artist's pipeline royalties from the prior hit paying the expenses, creates the illusion in artists' minds that they are still in favor. A paucity of material combined with bountiful confidence can make second albums challenging for producers.

Digital versus Analog?

This section relates to high-quality digital audio versus professional analog formats. MP3s, AAC files, and other semiprofessional or consumer formats are convenient but substandard with respect to audio quality.

A small number of artists and producers still prefer to record to analog tape. There are many theories about why it is preferable to use analog tape and several preferred methodologies. Some like to record and mix entirely in the analog domain. Others will record to analog tape and then bump it over to a DAW for mixing and storage. The latter method saves two-inch tape, which is now expensive and difficult to find. Some producers record digitally but prefer not to mix "in the box," instead breaking out the individual digital tracks through an analog console and outboard equipment for the final mix-down.

This book is not a technical work, and many others have written authoritatively on this topic, so I will give only a very brief overview of the debate. The qualitative comparisons of analog and digital recordings hinge on scientific, subjective, and emotional premises. One position against digital relates to the brick-wall digital filter cutoff frequency, which is (as Nyquist defined) at half the sampling rate. The sampling rate for a CD was set at 44.1kHz, giving a highest possible reproducible frequency of 22.05kHz. This is above the range of human hearing (20Hz to 20kHz), but analog tape captures frequencies much higher than that. It is possible that these very high harmonics interact to produce an audible difference and a fuller richer sound, or that we detect these frequencies by other means. We do know that many instruments produce frequencies well above human hearing and even above 100kHz.[50] Other arguments against digital revolve around phase deviation, aliasing, quantization noise, dither, and digital overload characteristics.

On the other hand, a well-recorded 44.1kHz/16-bit digital file has a greater dynamic range (~96dB) than any known analog system (~80dB). Noise reduction technology can increase the dynamic range of analog, but it introduces distortion. A higher digital bit rate (such as 24-bit words) produces a dynamic range of about 144dB. The human ear from the lowest threshold of hearing to the threshold of pain encompasses approximately 130dB.[51] For perspective, an orchestra produces a dynamic range of about 110dB. A 192kHz/24-bit recording will reproduce frequencies up to 96kHz—nearly five times higher than our ears can detect—and sounds so quiet and so loud that they reach both below and above the range of human hearing.

Regardless of the science, some producers still prefer the sound and/or the process of recording to analog tape. Sonic preference may be due to the familiar and pleasant distortion that occurs with tape compression, often characterized as warm by aficionados, who describe digital recordings as cold or harsh. Fans of digital hear its sound as less colored, unmediated by the storage medium and more like the original input signal. The analog tape recording process is linear (not random access), offering less editing and manipulative capabilities and thus forcing greater focus on performance, which some consider advantageous to the artistry. Although it does not supply the alleged "warmth" of analog, many believe that a 192kHz/24-bit digital recording achieves a more "natural sound" with its extended frequency response and dynamic range. Using analog tube and class-A solid-state microphones, EQs, compressors, and so forth—in the analog part of the signal chain prior to digital conversion—can compensate for digital's supposed lack of warmth. Analog emulators available as plug-ins meet with mixed reactions.

Most music on the charts today would sound very different if it had been recorded using analog tape, primarily because the ability to edit and correct timing, pitch, and parts is limited when using a linear format. The manipulative power of digital has undoubtedly diminished emphasis on performance and the capturing of the moment. Nonetheless, DAWs do not inherently force manipulation. Producers edit and correct because they need to or because they cannot resist doing so.

13

Working outside the Mainstream

For much of this book, I have referenced hit records and the charts although, in many cases, I used the term "successful" rather than "hit." Most people who corresponded with me regarding the first three editions of the book have been interested in producing mainstream popular music. These are productions aimed at the *Billboard* Hot 100 and other such charts. The ability of records to cross over from precursory genre charts to the pop charts changes over time, usually in accordance with shifting radio formats. Nonetheless, the top-selling music is typically from genres such as pop (although any Hot 100 hit could be classified as pop), rock, country, hip hop, R&B, or dance music. In 2012, the global breakdown of sales was approximately 31 percent pop, 25 percent rock, 6 percent country, 5 percent classical, 5 percent dance, 5 percent rap/hip hop, and 2.5 percent jazz, and everything else added up to around 13 percent.[1] "Everything else" includes folk/traditional, children's, world, gospel, Latin, and so forth. Producers, artists, and labels carve out careers making records that may never grace any of these charts. Throughout the book, I have referenced local and regional producers. Their records may succeed in their geographic area, but they do not, by definition, scale national or international charts.

Many producers began this way; Sam Phillips's Memphis Recording Service was a walk-in studio where anyone could record for a fee. This small, local, and viable business became an A&R source that changed the music industry and Phillips's life on the day when a teenager named Elvis Presley walked through the door. Many local and regional producers build solid businesses recording artists who have not risen to national attention and most of whom never will. Similarly, the vast majority of records produced for major labels will also reside in obscurity, the difference being that a small single-digit percentage of them will reach hundreds of thousands and perhaps millions or tens of millions of people. The odds are longer, but this can also happen for local producers. As further described below, John Kurzweg produced the first ten-million-selling Creed album out of his home studio in Tallahassee. Collectively, local producers work across all genres, some specializing and others recording a wide range of styles, but their recordings are often of artists from their own geographic areas.

There are other non-mainstream producers making records that rarely sell quickly or in quantities enough to penetrate the main *Billboard* charts. They specialize in niche genres—those that, when combined, account for low single-digit or fractional percentages of overall music sales. What distinguishes these producers from regional producers is that they may have national and international sales. *Billboard* expanded its chart offerings to include many genres. Nevertheless, there is a largely untold story below the bottom slots of those charts, where artists and producers enjoy careers known only to fans of those artists and genres.

Classical

It is hard to think of classical music as a niche or non-mainstream genre because it is the primary music taught in conservatories and schools around the world. But, in terms of sales, classical music amounts to only about 5 percent of the global recorded music market.

The objective of the classical producer, like all producers, is to showcase the artist in the best possible light, but unlike in pop recording, classical producers are usually striving to capture someone else's musical interpretation and to make the sound as natural as possible. The conductor and/or performers typically interpret a written composition while the producer acts as the intermediary between the conductor, artists, engineers, and technical crew. Classical producers are less likely than in other genres to be running the equipment or communicating in technical terms. In discussing the sound, they will more than likely do so in musical terms, and depending on the piece they are recording, they help the engineer navigate through the score, advising of upcoming tutti, where the sound levels might jump dramatically. Classical recording is often done on location and—especially in the case of large ensembles—occurs where the musicians are based.

Co-founder, senior producer (and, until 2009, president of Telarc), Robert Woods won 11 of Telarc's 40 Grammy awards and as of 2012 had won seven in the "producer, classical" category. Woods said,

> There is craftsmanship in what Telarc does. If it were only a result of the equipment we use, anybody could make recordings like ours.... We're not out to make hyped-up recordings.

Woods credits Telarc engineer and other co-founder of the label, Jack Renner, along with engineer Michael Bishop, with crafting the Telarc sound "into an art form." Woods's objective as producer is to capture the sound as heard by the conductor "standing on the podium." The team achieves their award-winning results, according to Renner, by optimizing every step in the process, choosing venues with superlative "natural sound," and using optimum components for the signal chain, "including microphones, cables, recording and playback electronics, speakers, and even control room acoustical materials." Over the years this has included developing customized, proprietary, and cutting-edge digital equipment in collaboration with Tom Stockham, who is often referred to as "the father of digital recording." Both Woods and Renner are classically trained musicians.[2]

Andrew Cornall is a multiple Grammy nominee and winner in the "producer, classical" category. He began at the Decca Record Company as a producer in 1977, working his way up to senior executive producer and general manager of the revamped classical label Argo. He has won many awards and worked with numerous artists, including the conductors Vladimir Ashkenazy, Bernard Haitink, and Michael Tilson Thomas; the singers Joan Sutherland, Cecilia Bartoli, Luciano Pavarotti, Angela Georghiu, and Andrea Bocelli; and the instrumentalists Joshua Bell, Viktoria Mullova, Jean Yves Thibaudet, and Mitsuko Uchida. Most classical producers have extensive conservatory training, and Cornall's was in composition and oboe at the University of Manchester and the Royal Northern College of Music, and then electronic music and recording techniques at the University of East Anglia. Composer and orchestrator Michael Torke (termed the "Ravel of his generation" by the *New York Times*) said this of his long working relationship with Cornall:

> It's a great fortune to have someone anticipate my needs before I am aware of them. His ears bring about the best aural advantage for my music. It's nice to know someone can read my mind.[3]

Steven Epstein has won seven Grammys for his classical production work (the most any classical producer has won—placing him on a par with Robert Woods). Additionally, he produces recordings of jazz and Broadway musicals. He developed his love of classical music when he was a toddler. Later he became intrigued by hi-fi equipment and decided to pursue record production while in high school. "My ears had been opened to what was considered state-of-the-art sound when I started exploring records like *The Fabulous Philadelphia Sound* on my neighbor's new Magnavox stereo." Epstein said,

> I read the liner notes by Tom Frost about his responsibilities as a producer. So I wrote to ask him what qualifications were needed to enter the field. In those days, there were no programs in sound technology, so he suggested that I major in music to get overall experience.[4]

Epstein graduated with a degree in music education from Hofstra University and, during his time there, programmed classical music for the campus radio station. Epstein again contacted Frost, who brought him onboard at Columbia Masterworks as a music editor. Epstein rose to the level of senior executive producer at Columbia. As is common in other genres, he was expected to "learn by doing," he said. "On my very first day of work, I was asked to edit an album of Rudolf Serkin playing Beethoven sonatas." Regarding his production role, he told Thomas May,

> I used to be reluctant to offer interpretive points unless it had to do with drawing attention to wrong notes. As I've gained experience, I find, more and more,

that artists will ask for my opinion on certain matters. Even so, you're not making a record of what the producer wants but of the artist's interpretation. You learn to respect the temperament of each artist.[5]

Because he also produces jazz and Broadway recordings, he understands the different challenges. He explained, "You're not adhering to a written musical score in jazz. These artists are composing from their heart, playing solos on the spot." Broadway cast recordings are different again in capturing "the dramatic aspect of the show" for the production. Epstein indicated there are similarities across genres:

The most important thing—for any genre—is to offer an honest overview. You're not just looking for mistakes but for an awareness of whether the artist is delivering a successful overall performance.

He added, "That's why it's so important for a producer to have a solid musical background." Summing up what he sees as the classical producer's role, he said, "Creating the most fertile environment possible for an artist is one of my main responsibilities," and "to make sure the sound is balanced."

Thomas Edison realized that recordings should be an optimized version of a performance, and Epstein's philosophy is similar:

To create a concert hall experience in an idealized acoustic setting—without all the distractions that come with live performance. As soon as an audience comes in, it affects the quality of sound. I like to recreate the sense that I'm in the concert hall, with music emerging from velvety background abstractness.

Classical recordings rarely use complex multi-microphone setups or close mic-ing. Telarc favors minimal mic-ing and so does Epstein: "I've made many symphonic and chamber music recordings with just two mics, since that allows for a greater sense of depth and more accurate imaging." He also emphasized the importance of the venue, which "becomes part of the instrument," the goal being to create a recorded perception of "a natural concert hall sound." Epstein thinks that musicians tend to play more aggressively to reach the back of the auditorium when there is an audience, so he favors recording without them.[6]

Jazz

Jazz accounts for around 2.5 percent of the global music market. Usually the musicians play together in the studio using a high degree of improvisation. The environment needs to be conducive to good inter-musician communication. Since the 1960s, jazz has diversified, and production techniques now cover the gamut from live, through layered overdubs, to computer-programmed parts.

Teo Macero was probably most famous for his work with Miles Davis. He studied at Juilliard, was friends with electronic music pioneer Edgar Varese, played saxophone himself, and recorded with Charlie Mingus. As a producer, he worked with Count Basie, Tony Bennett, Duke Ellington, Ella Fitzgerald, Lionel Hampton, Johnny Mathis, Glenn Miller, Thelonious Monk, and many more. Macero pioneered new techniques in jazz production, with his editing and reworking of Miles Davis's groundbreaking '60s fusion albums. He treated the studio as his laboratory, using modified equipment and editing techniques as an integral part of the recording process. He edited recorded improvisations into compositional structures. Far from being a purist, Macero favored new ideas, techniques, and equipment. He kept tape rolling during the recording sessions for the breakthrough album *In a Silent Way*, capturing all the pieces that the musicians improvised. Maccro was not averse to adding effects and electronic treatments later. He edited the album down to its final LP length from as many as 20 reels of tape using razor blade edits. He thought of himself as being like the editor of a book; Miles supplied the material and Macero edited it into its final shape.

Legendary producer Orrin Keepnews has more than 500 releases to his name, preferring live recording for jazz. He started three labels, Riverside, Milestone, and Landmark. He told Heather Johnson in a *Performing Songwriter* interview how they could make a jazz album in the '50s for under $500, recording live in the studio to mono. On the move to multitrack and overdubbing, he said, "…all I seem to recall is a bass player telling me he wants to punch in some right notes.… It's got to be about the interaction between people."[7] He explained to Johnson that one of the differences between producing jazz and other genres is that jazz is "more artistically oriented," which is why it makes less money. He said that commercial artists try to duplicate the sound and success of previously successful recordings, whereas the jazz artist may pursue a new musical direction that is interesting to his or her audience. Making recordings inexpensively made it possible for his label and other jazz labels to survive without massive sales.

> …[I]t's partly a matter of economic realities and partly a matter of the essential nature of the product that leads you to have this drastically different approach in the studio.[8]

He indicated that the economic and artistic needs complemented each other:

> …[I]f jazz recordings had ever been rehearsed and constructed to the degree that's just about automatic in the pop world, chances are all of the juice and creativity would have been sucked out of them in the preparation, and you would have gotten something very formularized.[9]

Of course, approaches to recording jazz have diversified considerably since the '50s, and jazz producers now range from purists who capture the music as played, to studio alchemists who manipulate the sound and music during and after the session. Jazz producers come from many backgrounds, which may include being an audio engineer with experience in recording groups of acoustic and electric musicians, an experienced jazz musician, or a jazz aficionado/entrepreneur. Recording improvised multiplayer music requires a good deal of studio technique and a recording environment where the musicians can hear and preferably see each other comfortably. As always, the relationship with the artist is vital. In some cases, the producer puts together the musical elements including the material, musicians, and arrangers. A jazz producer needs to understand the idiom intuitively. A number of jazz producers, such as Creed Taylor (CTI), Manfred Eicher (ECM), Alfred Lion (Blue Note), and Bob Weinstock (Prestige), have run their own labels and developed distinctive production styles. Much jazz is performance-based, so producers frequently record albums in hours or days, rather than weeks or months.

Country

Country music is the biggest of the single-digit genres, at more than 6 percent internationally, and the genre is stronger in the United States than in many other parts of the world. Country music producers are often on staff at the record label, although this has begun to change. The top producers sometimes run the Nashville branch of a major label, yet remain active in the studio. Because they frequently come up through the ranks of the musicians, they may play on their productions. Country recordings are strongly associated with Nashville, and that is where the majority of country music producers live. The studios and equipment rental facilities are state-of-the-art, and the musicians are among the best in the business.

Tony Brown's run of success from the early '90s included Vince Gill, Reba McEntire, George Strait, Steve Earle, Kelly Willis, Lyle Lovett, and Nanci Griffith, among others. He played piano for Elvis Presley in the 1970s and moved to Nashville in 1980, eventually becoming president of MCA Nashville at a time when it dominated country radio. In 2001, he launched Universal South with Tim DuBois, founder of Arista Nashville. Then in 2007, Brown stepped down as an executive at Universal to return to his first love, producing.[10]

Country music superstar Tim McGraw says that he loves producing and that he tries to bring an artist and fan perspective to the studio. He went on to say, "But I really rely on [co-producer] Byron Gallimore. He and James Stroud have been my teachers in the studio. Any success I have had as a producer, I owe to them."[11]

James Stroud has been vice president of A&R for Giant Records Nashville and label head of DreamWorks Records Nashville, as well as running his own labels Stroudavarious and R&J Records. He has produced many number-one records,[12] beginning as a studio drummer alongside Tony Brown, Paul Worley, Keith Stegall, and others making gospel records. He remembered that "Paul and Tony and me had a hard time getting productions" in the beginning. At the time, 150,000 units was a big seller for Nashville, which was considered "a branch town in the music industry." Eddie Rabbitt went platinum and "it sort of blew the top off. We learned to make country records with a pop edge."[13] Stroud built his production experience on R&B records in Los Angeles and Muscle Shoals and was well positioned for the new style of production. His productions included the Bellamy Brothers, Eddie Rabbitt, and Dorothy Moore's "Misty Blue," which sold three million units and was nominated for five Grammy awards, making Stroud a force to be reckoned with in Nashville.

Jimmy Bowen spoke about getting started in Nashville:

> If you have to start by custodial engineering and producing a shine on the floors of the studio, then do it. Then, finally, you'll get that first chance to sit down and work at the board, and everybody will see if you've got what it takes, or not. It's very much a trial by fire, but that's how it works.

Bowen is complimentary about the colleges that teach engineering, having taken students in as trainees and hired graduates. He said, "Project studios are great." When he was in college, they "recorded their band at night in the college studio for a few hours, going straight to disk." He thinks that anything you learn about recording music properly "can only help you later on."[14]

Bowen was influential in bringing country music production techniques up to date, flying studio musicians in from Los Angeles when he needed them and moving to digital recording early. When he first arrived in Nashville, budgets were so low that artists had to cut three or four tracks in every three-hour session. Bowen spent a day or two on each song, bringing in recording techniques and sounds from New York and Los Angeles and thus reaching a wider audience than previously thought possible for country music. Because of his innovation and success, he was the president, at one time or another, of most of the major labels in Nashville.

Traditional, Folk, Roots, and World Music

We can listen to centuries' old Western European classical music in close approximation to its original form because of written documentation. But tradition-based musics are mostly handed down orally, and prior to recording technology, there was little information about how the music sounded. Oral traditions change or die, and with no manuscript or recording to reference, we have only interpretations by heirs of the tradition, if there are any. Recording technology enabled there to be snapshots in time of vernacular musics. Ironically, the very technology that could preserve these traditions combined with radio to homogenize and, in some cases, obliterate cultural differences. Communities and cultures constantly change, but mass communications along with social forces (such as colonization and slavery) hastened cultural shifts.

John and Alan Lomax spent much of the first half of the 20th century documenting vernacular American musical culture against the tide of radio, records, and the recording industry. Alan Lomax said,

> We now have cultural machines so powerful that one singer can reach everybody in the world and make all the other singers feel inferior because they're not like him. Once that gets started, he gets backed by so much cash and so

much power that he becomes a monstrous invader from outer space, crushing the life out of all the other human possibilities. My life has been devoted to opposing that tendency.

Daniel Sheehy is the director of the Center for Folklife and Cultural Heritage, home to Smithsonian Folkways Recordings—the record label of the National Museum of the United States. Smithsonian Folkways' mission is to document, preserve, and disseminate spoken word, sounds, and tradition-based music styles representing world cultures. Releases feature extensive notes with background information on the music, the tradition, and the artists. Focusing on Latino culture, Sheehy has produced many albums, some of which have won or been nominated for Grammys and Latin Grammys. Sheehy holds a Ph.D. in ethnomusicology and performs Mariachi music. He produces music (in exotic places) returning home clutching digital masters of some of the best music you have never heard. Producing for Sheehy involves "a lot of cultural brokering." He bases decisions about whom and what to record on the label's mission to document and release underrepresented musics. When he was studying music at UCLA, he wondered why he had not been taught about James Brown or Kwasi Badu (master drummer from Ghana), or Jarocho music from Veracruz. He "got mad" because of the unjustness of major educational institutions channeling people "toward a very limited view of what's valuable in music."[15]

He learned about what some call the Alan Lomax school of folklore and ethnomusicology, and production of grassroots music. He worked with Lomax's sister, Bess Lomax Hawes. His primary tool is fieldwork—getting to know the people, community networks, music repertoire, and social and cultural dynamics within the tradition. In order to proceed with confidence, he likes to "hear it firsthand from individuals who live the life." He looks for "artists who have a story to tell" and a broader overview from a specialist who might be a scholar.[16] He tries to focus attention where it can have a positive effect on society and the represented community. Mariachi Los Camperos's founder Nati Cano recontextualized Mariachi music, breaking it out of its social origins as cantina music. The group had never released a record, and the National Museum's label is influential. For Smithsonian Folkways, contextual liner notes are vital, and none of the other contemporaneous Mariachi recordings detailed the stories behind the music.[17]

Musica Llanera or Joropo is an exciting national music of Venezuela, mainly found today in a "watered-down form." Also played in Colombia but not valued in the same way, the Smithsonian Folkways Recordings album *Si Soy Llanero* was Grammy-nominated, attracting international attention to the music and the performers, and increasing the sense of its value in the home territory of Colombia. In authenticating traditional talent in other countries and cultures, it is vital to identify key figures and Sheehy was introduced to Carlos Rojas, a leader of the Llanero music. Rojas worked for the Ministry of Culture, understood the larger perspective, and was training people to teach in cultural centers throughout Eastern Colombia.

Like Sheehy, Rojas was "totally frustrated" by "commercial pressures on traditional music," feeling that it takes the excitement and energy out of it and relegates it "to the whims of a star singer" who is using it purely for profit and personal success. The two had a common vision that Sheehy described as a "magic moment."[18] The artists wanted to record the music the way it is played at parties in cattle country on the plains, and in the studio, "it just clicked."

I was curious to find out if these situations ever go wrong. Sheehy gave an example of another group from a musical tradition he did not know so well and with whose leader he did not have a strong personal connection. They discussed deal points and the traditional form, which did not include the "bells and whistles that appealed to the new age audience," before the session. Things fell apart in the studio between Sheehy and the leader/co-producer who demanded more money (for himself, not for the musicians) and wanted to add nontraditional rainsticks. The leader was steering the music toward the "popular audience," which was "outside of the mission" and the understanding Sheehy thought they had reached. Sheehy felt they did not know each other well enough and lacked the collaborative sense of a shared mission. Grassroots artists often do not understand the potential for the traditional forms of their music in the global marketplace.[19]

Commercial producers also encounter this problem of believing they and the artists have common goals until the communications break down. It is easy to underestimate cultural differences and the difficulties of bridging them, as Sheehy said, in cultures, "where people don't really depend on the written word very much," but rather "on human relationships," networks of people or communities knowing somebody, "where there are all these ties that are inbuilt controls of trust."[20]

Even in a commercial environment, when relationships break down, you may get paid because of a contract, but the project may be unsalvageable.

Cultural context is essential to ethnomusicologists, and academic training is advantageous. Sheehy brings academic rigor, finance, and an infrastructure to "get this music out and around" to people who may not know about it. Recording traditional music in this way is not about making an appealing record that will sell or demonstrate virtuosity. Sheehy says he is "looking for something beyond just the sound," and talks about a heartfelt sound with "a sense of strength that a people have given it over time" that comes across to outside audiences.[21]

Paying artists is important to Smithsonian Folkways Recordings, but this presents challenges with artists from hard-to-reach places, who sometimes have different understandings about intellectual property. The responsibility to arrange a payment system that is acceptable to the artists falls to the producer. Ethnomusicologists recording music "two miles high in the Andean Mountains"[22] can find it hard to get money back to these artists and communities without documentation, legal agreements, and a prearranged system.

Most freelance producers do not have to think about rights because the label has the artist under contract for the sound recording rights, and statutory rights protect compositions. Field recordings should not be released without permissions from the artists, composers, and—sometimes, in the case of traditional music—the community, no matter how remote the location. Some producers are tempted to offer cash buyouts. Artists may agree, but the world of intangible cultural heritage considers the practice unethical if not illegal. Some cultures do not consider performances or compositions to be rightfully theirs as individuals. In such instances, Smithsonian Folkways has made royalty payments to community funds that have paid for college for their children, a new canoe, and such.

Although folklorists have a passion for the music and people and want to do right by them, goodwill is no longer sufficient. Signed contracts are important to protect the artists and the label. Complications ensue if contracts are not signed at the time of recording. Sheehy did a CD to accompany a textbook 10 or 15 years after the recording sessions. He sent a form to Chile, and the folklorist took it "to this pea farmer about an hour away from the nearest town." He got it signed and "we got them an honorarium."[23]

These recordings rarely produce significant revenues, but small royalties can make a difference in another culture. Moses Asch, the founder of Folkways Records, focused on disseminating underrepresented people's voices and music. He evolved a long-tail business model, selling a small number of copies of many recordings to fund the label so he could achieve his social and cultural mission. Smithsonian Folkways has more than 45,000 tracks and without a considerable body of work, income may be insufficient to support even a modest lifestyle. Sheehy "can't think of any person who has made a living producing traditional music" outside of an institution like the French government, the Smithsonian, a nonprofit such as the World Music Institute, or by starting their own business.[24] Chris Strachowitz founded and for many years has run the traditional music label Arhoolie Records. As Sheehy says, running an independent label for this music genre or working somewhere like the Smithsonian involves more administrative and bureaucratic obligations than are usually considered part of the producer's job.

Children's Music

When my children were very young, I wanted to introduce them to quality music as early as possible, but I had difficulty finding children's music that they would find interesting and that I could bear to hear repeatedly. I was looking for what I called "music that wouldn't make me want to jump out of the minivan." Cathy Fink and Marcy Marxer achieve this balance. They do not dumb down their music; they make sophisticated and varied productions featuring high standards of musicianship. They are multiple Grammy nominees, winning the children's music category in 2004 and 2005. I was fortunate enough to work with them on one of those winners, *cELLAbration*—a Smithsonian Folkways tribute album to Ella Jenkins, also known as the "First Lady of Children's Music." A Grammy Lifetime Achievement Award recipient, Jenkins is one of the most influential children's artists of all time.

Marcy Marxer described her beginnings as a producer: "I volunteered to work on people's albums in exchange for them working on my albums."[25]

They now encourage other artists to contribute with the aim of getting them to produce themselves. Marxer explained that Fink is better at "paperwork and contracts." Marxer will write the arrangement charts if she is "playing a bunch of instruments."[26] They plan budgets carefully "because nobody has huge budgets," keeping a couple of contingency days for end-of-project fixes. She makes "a huge chart" for the studio wall so they know what "there is left to do."[27] Fink adds, "We are incredibly flexible" and indicates that the direction of each project dictates how they operate. Fink and Marxer were empowered as producers by the recording technology revolution. Marxer "wanted to get into producing, but the equipment was cost-prohibitive."[28] As equipment prices fell, they were fortunate to be mentored by Greg Lukens from Washington Professional Systems. With rapidly changing technology, a network of advisors or mentors is helpful. Their background was decidedly non-technological. Marxer started out in an old-time string band in Michigan:

> My grandma was a barrelhouse blues honky-tonk piano player and also dabbled in hammer dulcimer. My mother and her two sisters used to sing jazz songs. But I had some family members who played traditional music. I grew up playing music with everybody.[29]

She played for children at summer camp groups when she was 12 and did whatever other gigs were available. She likes the fact that you can find traditional music in every corner, pub, and old folks' home. Alongside the old time string band, they played "school assemblies, concerts, and festivals."[30] They say that they try to produce children's music like any other album, but with more musical and stylistic freedom. Most albums have to fit a genre or style so that retail outlets know where to put it in the store (physical or virtual). But Marxer says, "We're bringing the world to kids"; they try to make it "a complete picture," both educational and fun. She sees it like "a plate of food," so kids can sample different styles, and "the glue that holds it together is that it's for kids."[31] The biggest difference with children's music production that Marxer identifies is "that kids judge how much fun they are having by what they are doing and not by what I'm doing." They consider children's voices (because it is inspiring to other kids) and activity songs to be crucial.[32]

Like other producers, they regard choice of material as the most important factor in a successful kids' album. The music has to inspire them or it is "not going to inspire kids to take up music," and they at least want them to hear the differences between the instruments, so they mix their solo parts "up front" in their own space, saying, "if you can't hear it clearly, then take it out."

Marxer says they feel like "kids deserve the best."[33] She remembers thinking that some children's albums "were pretty bland" compared to "playing a honky-tonk tune with my grandmother." She loves traditional music and thinks it's great for kids because they need a "personal connection," which is difficult to have "with a computer…as great as they are."[34]

Fink and Marxer immerse themselves in the material and the project goals, matching them with a budget and outlining the possibilities to help the artist achieve his or her dream. They have less pressure to create a hit than in the commercial pop world—airplay is rare for children's music. They think their "30 years of experience in this field" as performers and producers puts them "in a good position to give sound advice to an artist." They critique the songs, advise on direction, and discuss whether they think audiences will connect with the music. Fink said they don't take a project "unless we feel like everybody's on the same page."[35] She is emphatic about defining deliverables (something all producers should do) and creating an agreement that says what the budget covers and defines any changes that will alter the numbers.[36]

Neither Marxer nor Fink thinks that it would be easy to make a living exclusively producing children's music. Fink's advice is to "have a couple of other things you like to do." She said that being musicians feeds into the producing and vice versa.[37] They are adamant about using real musicians. Many artists build synthesizer tracks to save money, but Fink said, "When we have a Dixieland band, we want kids to hear a real horn section and a real drummer." Whatever the style of music, they "want them to hear the real thing."[38]

With small budgets, they use fewer musicians rather than MIDI. Fink likes to see artists live and understand how the songs work with kids. "After 30 years, [we] have a pretty good idea of whether a song is going to fly." Even with "a great artist like Tom Paxton," they will "go to a local elementary school" to find out "if kids are going to connect with this stuff." Artists will tell them that their own kids love the songs, and Fink's response is that their kids will "love anything you do." She said that the great children's artists are out working to hone and tweak their material before recording it.[39] This is what Les Paul did with his "jury." There is no substitute for testing material before the session. Finding out that music does not connect with the audience after time and money are spent is a waste.

Producing is part of a whole "life of music" package for Cathy Fink and Marcy Marxer. They love what they do and believe it is "good for the world." They don't make an album unless they "think it is really important" and "know that there is nothing like it" in the market. They see emotional, intellectual, and cultural value in their music for kids.[40] Fink echoes Marxer's sentiments, saying, "Even if it doesn't make you wealthy, it makes you rich in every other way."[41]

Some children's artists own their own labels and sell much of their music at shows, as well as through distribution channels. This creates more non-music work but gives the producer more control and access to that 55 or so percent of the retail price that would otherwise go to a label.

Local and Regional Producers

Affordable professional and semi-professional equipment has allowed many musicians, producers, and engineers to set up their own studios. Some musicians and artists put together studios initially for their own artistic output and then start producing and engineering for other local and regional artists. Production can be a source of ancillary income for working musicians, and some morph into full-time producers, engineers, and studio operators. Frequently, the owner is the studio manager, producer, engineer, and assistant with time billed as "all-in." More established studios might have a small team of people with a menu of options and charges. In any case, the rates are usually reasonable—sometimes as low as $20 to $50 an hour, which can include amps, drums, and guitars from the owner's personal collection along with the recording equipment. At those kinds of rates, these producers are not getting rich, and they are often working without any kind of agreement that guarantees them royalties or credit on releases. Many of their productions will not sell enough to justify the legal expense of a contract, but not having one exposes them to financial loss and the potential for bitter feelings toward the artist on the off chance of a big seller. Often, all that separates these producers from international success is the lack of the right artist and/or material, or a label to promote the recordings.

John Kurzweg had been regionally successful as a musician in Florida. By 1997, he was known around Tallahassee as being capable of producing professional-sounding tracks at a reasonable price in his home studio, which he called "The Kitchen." Kurzweg was approached by the manager of a then-unknown local band called Creed. The story goes that he was somewhat reluctant to take on the project, but their manager and his own gut feeling convinced him. Working at night after finishing their day jobs, the band functioned on little sleep. Emotions ran high at times. Kurzweg sifted through all their material and with equipment sprawling around his house for weeks, he produced and engineered *My Own Prison* for $6,000. After signing with Windup Records and a Ron St. Germain remix, the album went multiplatinum. Kurzweg's second production for the band was certified diamond.[42]

John Alagia had been performing live and producing his own music, along with other local and regional bands. He had transitioned from four-track TEAC to eight-track TASCAM, learning by trial and error, with a seminar at Omega Studios, a semester of music theory at Berklee, and advice from experienced engineers at Bias Studios. He met such then-unknown artists as Ben Folds and Dave Matthews during his own live touring work as a musician. One night in Washington, D.C., he saw the Dave Matthews Band (DMB) play in a bar and by coincidence received a call the next day from the band's agent regarding production. Alagia had been recommended to DMB's agent by Ardent studios, where the producer had been working with another D.C.-area group. He initially recorded DMB live, and over an extended period built a relationship with Matthews who invited him to help produce the first DMB album.[43] Consequently, John Mayer, who was a big Dave Matthews fan, sought out Alagia through a contact at ASCAP, which resulted in more hits and a well-established career for Alagia.[44]

Not every regional producer owns his or her own studio; some set up a relationship with a professional studio or several studios in their area. Working out of your own room is financially advantageous if you keep the overhead low, because you can charge a single hourly, daily, or even per track/per album rate. Of course, there is the capital outlay of setting up the facility and the ongoing maintenance and upkeep costs. If the studio is in the producer's house, there is the inconvenience of artists going in and out, but the balancing factors are low costs and no commute.

Producing and engineering local and regional artists, who are often unsigned, can be a way to establish or revive a production career. It is a chance to experiment with various styles of music, which can open up possibilities that you may not otherwise have considered. Typically, budgets are tiny, so you develop speed in setting up sounds, recording, and mixing. Frequent short projects offer practice in dealing with diverse personalities. If the artist is shopping for a deal, your productions may gain exposure with A&R people at major and independent labels. Sometimes producers have the opportunity to produce the major or indie record after doing the artist-financed recordings. A&R people and managers notice impressive production even if the artist does not get signed. Local and regional producers assess new talent early because developing artists need to record demos to shop or sell. Producers with a network of industry contacts and good negotiating skills can help place new artists with a label. Entrepreneurs have the chance to identify and sign artists early in their careers, and the opportunity to build relationships with up-and-coming artists can result in highly visible work if those artists become successful. Labels often require that artists work with more established producers for their first outings, but as success matures, artists gain more control and can choose people with whom they enjoy working.

14

Where Are We? How Did We Get Here? Where Are We Going?

Will Mobile Modify the Internet that Crippled Cable but Vivified Video, which Killed the Radio Star?

The digital audio workstation (DAW) revolution combined with the proliferation of information has affected producers in much the same way as the Gutenberg press affected the monastic profession. Before Gutenberg, monks were not only the primary readers in the community, but they also controlled the reproduction of books, copying them laboriously by hand. Prior to DAWs, gaining access to recording equipment and the expertise to make professional-sounding recordings was available to only a few. With a DAW, some personal application, and modest resources, many more people have learned to produce music. This has generated more recordings than ever, although most of these new producers do not earn meaningful amounts of money from their endeavors. Regardless, the most disruptive shifts are the unexpectedly oblique ones from an outside source that are not incremental to existing technologies or paradigms. Buckminster Fuller said, "You never change things by fighting the existing reality. To change something, build a new model that makes the existing model obsolete." Digital production, promotion, and distribution move inexorably toward the obsolescence of old industry models.

Our industry, born of Edison's technology, was threatened by radio, a depression, strikes, materials shortages, and recessions. Corporate consolidations negatively affect creators, and independent expansion introduces new musical movements. However, no change was as disruptive as the evolution of the digital supply chain, which was transformative from conception to consumer.

Demographics affect our industry, as does the wealth of nations. There are approximately seven billion increasingly older people on the planet.[1] Despite disparities of wealth and continuing poverty, in many sections of societies around the world, there is an aspirational and actual trend toward upward mobility.[2] Production, storage, and distribution for music have close to zero manufacturing, distribution, and inventory costs per unit in the digital domain, and the number of mobile devices now exceeds the world's population.[3] Epic released Michael

Jackson's *Thriller* at the height of MTV's music video era, an active time for FM radio and coincident with the launch of compact disc technology. *Thriller* developed into a promotional "perfect storm," selling an estimated 65 to 110 million units worldwide.[4] The subsequent mass-media fragmentation and free access to music stalled music blockbusters for the past decade. However, if sufficient cross-cultural commonalities can be conflated (think PSY's "Gangnam Style" as a precursor), engaging the viral potential of the mobile Web, Jackson's numbers could be dwarfed. Blockbuster models aside, electronic networks allow long-tail businesses to aggregate the likeminded in sustainably sized global villages.[5]

How Did We Get Here?

Although this book does not discuss specific engineering techniques, the history of music production and the changing roles of music producers are functions of technological development. Computers changed the way we record, process, distribute, promote, and listen to music. As Fred Gaisberg began, so music production has become again: a one-person operation. Sandy Roberton thinks that producers who cannot operate technology "are over." Computers not only changed how we capture music but the music itself. Making records with the Roland MC-8 MicroComposer in the '70s, I realized I was constructing performances not capturing them. DAWs continue this shift toward a performance construct that began when the earliest recording machines allowed artists to perfect their performances by recording another take. The desire to eradicate mistakes and interpretive weaknesses is at the core of production (as opposed to documentation), but for more than half of music production history, making a recording required a simultaneous and complete performance. Magnetic tape made editing practical and subsequently multitracking enabled an incremental time- and space-shifted, layered approach to arrangement, orchestration, and idealization.

Analog sequencers date back to the 1940s but were not popularized until the '60s and '70s with the advent of machines like the Buchla, Moog, and ARPs. Drum machines date back to the 1930s with broadening use from the late '50s and '60s. These machines electronically automated performance for musicians within strict limits on length and expression. The MC-8 was the first commercially produced music computer that allowed unlimited sequence length (>5,000 steps but synchronizable) and individual note-duration control—improving expression. Making music this way is a direct act by the composer, arranger, and/or orchestrator, unmediated by a performer. This was not a conceptual breakthrough; mechanical instruments such as barrel organs and music boxes were programmed in non-real time, and automatic instruments date back thousands of years if you consider wind chimes and the like. Perhaps most notably, Raymond Scott, who composed music for Looney Tunes and Merrie Melodies cartoons,[6] created a massive electromechanical sequencer in the 1940s.[7] Nonetheless, the wave of music computers that quickly followed the MC-8 made unprecedented creative and corrective capabilities widely available.

Computers relieved many pressures that characterized studio life as recently as the '70s. Musicians no longer have to record a complete performance without mistakes. In the '70s, you could punch in drums on some 24-track machines, but punching out was unreliable. We mostly recorded drum tracks in their entirety. I played on the Buggles' *Age of Plastic* album. This was prior to the introduction of realistic-sounding drum machines such as the LM1 or LinnDrum. Disco required drummers to play with near- perfect timing and precision dynamics. Rhythm tracks were beginning to sound like the machine tracks that would characterize the early '80s. Trevor Horn and Geoff Downes wanted machine-like accuracy. I had played with click tracks on sessions for years, but this was another magnitude of precision: not just precision in time but with perfectly even dynamics and tone across the drum set. Horn had occasion to listen to the multitracks recently and he recalled that,

> Richard Burgess was pale! He was so worn out because we insisted that it sound perfect and that he played it perfectly. And the funny thing is that when you listen to it, it sounds like a drum machine.[8]

When I did the first programmed drum sessions (with the MC-8 driving the SDSV prototype drum module[9]), it was exciting to be able to control the timing, dynamics, durations, and tone of every note in non-real time without retakes. Programming was painstakingly time-consuming, but progress was incremental, and it was a clear harbinger of future control and editing power.

Until 16- and 24-track machines became standard, manual mixing was manageable. Beyond eight tracks and before computer control, the process often entailed many hands on the console, moving faders, pan pots, effect sends, and equalization knobs from one grease pencil mark to another, precisely on cue. Band members frequently favored their own instrument, and the moves had to be rehearsed, memorized, and accurately performed in one session. If you did not finish that night, it could take hours to get everyone working together smoothly the following day. Only when you committed the mix to two-track could you really evaluate. Invariably, there would be questionable parts. Long days focusing on details play perceptual tricks on the mind. Once you reset the console, if tweaks were necessary, it was laborious to recreate a mix. You would solve one problem and create another. Paul C. Burrs's Allison automation reduced reliance on performance and allowed us to hear the moves with the mix still in a malleable state. Then SSL's 1981 introduction of the total recall console[10] made it possible to reset a mix in a couple of hours with final adjustments by ear.

Now, DAW recall is instantaneous for "in the box" mixes, but physical outboard gear still requires careful note-taking. There are many advantages to being able to take a break from a mix: You are tired, dinner is ready, you are not feeling creative, or you want to work on another song. When you come back to a mix, solutions are often more obvious. Even with total recall, if another overdub was required during mixing, it disrupted the flow, requiring a certain amount of dismantling of the mix setup. In a DAW, last-minute additions or changes are simple.

Scientist and writer C. P. Snow said, "Technology is a queer thing. It brings you great gifts with one hand and stabs you in the back with the other." Endless refinement is now possible. Clear objectives are necessary to avoid becoming lost in minutiae. It is possible to spend days fiddling with computer parts, when musicians could play them to better effect more cost-effectively. Because random access permits us to construct performance does not mean that we must. As described in chapter 8, musicians will "throw down a few ideas" and leave it to the producer to piece together a "performance." This is now a standard working practice, but whether it is preferable to a coherent, contiguous performance is questionable in many cases. Bill Gates is widely quoted as saying,

> The first rule of any technology used in a business is that automation applied to an efficient operation will magnify the efficiency. The second is that automation applied to an inefficient operation will magnify the inefficiency.[11]

The entire range of performance from live to a construct is available to us, and we should select the appropriate tool or combinations of tools for the task, controlling the technology to most efficiently and effectively reach the desired objective.

The Revolution Continues

Movies did not replace newspapers and books. TV did not supplant movies or radio. The Internet has not yet displaced TV and may not. History shows that new technologies take market share from the old but rarely entirely replace them in the short-to-medium term. Nonetheless, the demand for older production methods continues to diminish. As new technology penetrates deeper into society and the music business, there are fewer opportunities for producers needing big budgets to manage teams in luxurious studios with large-format consoles.

Some may think of that period as a golden era in the music industry. Sales were robust, and listening to music on demand necessitated buying it on a physical format. The major labels controlled marketing and distribution. Money accrued to the few, and most could not gain access. Producers who operate in this environment still exist, but versatile, self-contained, and often entrepreneurial types are replacing them. These producers may be artists who produce, such as Gotye, David Guetta, Calvin Harris, Skrillex, J. Cole, or the archetype himself, Prince (and of course there was Les Paul).

For the creatively ambitious who are musically challenged, there are many tools available, including samples, prerecorded MIDI files, and a plethora of music software. They range in cost from free to a few thousand dollars and include not only computer software but impressive smart-phone and tablet applications.

Music is intrinsically mathematical. Various pieces of algorithmic compositional software exist, but at the time of writing, there is no widely accepted methodology for algorithmic music creation in the field of commercial popular music. I experimented with Hybrid Arts' algorithmic compositional tool "Ludwig" in the '80s, and Eno worked with SSEYO's "Koan Pro" algorithmic generator in the mid-'90s.[12] If, as Eno said, "Artists are people who specialize in judgment rather than skill," then the artistry is in defining parameters and selecting ideas to use in the final composition from possibilities offered up by the software.

Likewise, entirely computer-generated lyrics that evoke an emotional response in humans seem remote. Nevertheless, influenced by William Burroughs and Brion Gysin, David Bowie has been using cut-up techniques since the 1970s. In the mid-'90s, he talked about using a computer-based cut-and-paste lyric generation and organization method for his album *Outside*, on which he collaborated with Eno:

> I work about 40 percent of the time with the William Burroughs-Brion Gysin cut-up method....I feed into it the fodder, and it spews out reams of paper with these arbitrary combinations of words and phrases.[13]

Many writers including Tristan Tzara in the 1920s and later, Burroughs, Gysin, Kurt Cobain,[14] and Thom Yorke, have used paper cut-ups of words and phrases.[15]

Sampling and waveform-emulation techniques were in use[16] for many years before the first commercial sampler, the Australian Fairlight CMI, became available. When I heard about the Fairlight, I flew from London to Sydney to visit the Fairlight offices, taking charge of one of the first two machines in 1979; Peter Gabriel had the other. John L. Walters and I demonstrated it to many U.K.-based musicians and on the BBC's "Tomorrow's World" program. We used it on Kate Bush's album *Never Forever*, sampling and playing breaking-glass sounds on "Babooshka" and the sound of rifles cocking on "Army Dreamers," among others. We kept sample lengths short because of the limited frequency response of the early eight-bit samples. One of Walters's and my crewmembers, J. J. Jeczalik, familiarized himself with our Fairlight and in 1983 went to work for Trevor Horn on Yes's *90125* album. Horn had purchased his own Fairlight and, by that time, the sample rate was higher, improving the quality and opening up the possibility for longer samples. Jeczalik did some innovative programming with longer samples on "Owner of a Lonely Heart" and continued working with that production team as a member of the Art of Noise.

The Fairlight was expensive, which limited early market penetration. It was the first sampler to market by several years but, like the MC-8 MicroComposer, despite its significance and influence, only a few hundred units were sold. Mass proliferation of sampling technology came later via cheaper machines such as the Emulator, the Ensoniq, and the Akai S900, which became cornerstone technologies for evolving production styles in hip hop and electronic dance music. Hip hop was built around the use of samples, albeit analog ones, spun in from vinyl discs, so the adoption of digital sampling was natural. Beat matching and aligning samples live from a vinyl disc requires considerable control of the turntables, and once again technology trumped the necessity for real-time performance.

Mass proliferation is how many define the success of a new technology. Philo Farnsworth did not invent television to deliver soap operas, game shows, and reality TV.[17] Corporate economics and popular taste steered it in that direction. The uptake of digital recording was slow, in part because early commercial digital recording systems (on tape) such as the 3M and Mitsubishi X800 were expensive, and extensive manipulation of music was still difficult. In 1988, I remixed some tracks for Thomas Dolby's *Aliens Ate My Buick* album, involving synchronization using manually calculated SMPTE offsets to copy sections from one digital 32-track machine to another. What would now involve a few key strokes took many hours.

Alesis's ADAT system brought digital recording within everybody's reach, albeit still linear. Substantial manipulation required two or more machines, but they were affordable and synchronization was relatively reliable. Nevertheless, the digital revolution did not flourish in the mainstream until there was wider access to hard disk and solid-state recorders. Random-access digitized music brought the multifaceted manipulation of music within the economic grasp of anyone who could afford a computer, expanding the user base to near ubiquity and increasing creative application of the technology exponentially.

In a 1970s interview, I said that the exciting thing about making music on a computer is that you can separate an idea from the technique required to execute it. This democratizes the process; if someone has a musical thought, a computer can play it without spending ten years practicing, studying, or trying to raise the funds to have someone play it. With effort, well-proven recording and production techniques, and a few thousand dollars of equipment, it is possible to make, market, and distribute music. Artists are creating works of art or commerce at home or on the move—even collaborating with other musicians virtually—and then delivering them electronically to a label, consumers, or stores.

Labels, managers, and producers find new artists and monitor their progress using the Web. Artists who are committed to their careers build and maintain a strong electronic presence via their websites and all the social networking outlets. They make sure their material is available on all the download and streaming sites and often allow free streams of their music from their primary site and others. YouTube and other outlets have made it possible for news about new artists to spread virally. Producers can do the same.

Justin Bieber may be the most famous artist, up to the time of writing, to have launched a career online. Scooter Braun, who later became his manager, discovered him on YouTube after Bieber's mother posted his videos so friends and family could see him perform. Bieber subsequently appeared on "The Today Show," "The Ellen DeGeneres Show," and "Good Morning America"; he even performed for President Obama at the White House. He is the first solo artist to have four singles enter the Top 40 before the release of his platinum-certified debut album.[18] Labels now use data and online research extensively to discover and vet potential signings.

It is possible to detect manipulated numbers such as purchased YouTube views and Facebook likes, so build your online story and statistics organically.[19]

Online discovery and overnight success are not assured, but everyone needs a robust Web presence. If nothing else, it will put more people in that club after a long day in the van. Virtual activity offers equal opportunity, with bands from out-of-the-way places having the same chance of visibility as those based in major music centers. The Web is not only a promotional outlet but also a potential performance platform for those who do not play live.

Low-cost technology, a populace that is increasingly comfortable with complex software combined with intuitive systems, and a plethora of training information reduce the need for years of experience and training in expensive facilities. This is not to say that training and experience are unnecessary; just that obstacles (such as the expense of a college education and a limited number of opportunities in major studios) are surmountable. In keeping with the societal trend, computers allow those willing to learn to do more independently. As Thomas Whisler, professor of business at the University of Chicago said in 1964:

> Men are going to have to learn to be managers in a world where the organization will come close to consisting of all chiefs and one Indian. The Indian, of course, is the computer.[20]

Maybe one day the computer will be the chief.

What Does This Mean to the Professional Music Producer?

Artists who develop technical and musical skills may be able to produce themselves, and that is happening. Outside producers are necessary only if the artist lacks the skills or objectivity to bring a project to successful fruition.

Some jobs disappear. The apprenticeship system has all but ceased to exist for reasons such as smaller budgets, the closing of major studio complexes, and a reduced need for labor-intensive tasks like the alignment and running of tape machines, large studio setups, and complex patch bay plugging. Only the most commercially successful producers use heavily staffed studios, and many successful producers do not choose to spend their budgets on such rooms at all.

The charts paint a telling picture. As shown in chapter 1, producers who were writers or co-writers of the song they produced almost exclusively held the top ten positions on *Billboard*'s Hot 100 (one sample week in 2011). For the corresponding week in 1980, that figure for songwriting producers was 50 percent. In that same week in 1960, none of the top ten producers had any writing involvement with the songs they produced. This phenomenon is not preexisting non-writing producers adapting to the environment; rather it is an evolving species of producer that is being selected for the new ecosystem. Clearly, the *Billboard* Hot 100 does not represent the entire production panorama, but the dramatic shift over five decades is instructive.

Looking at *Billboard* charts other than the Hot 100, there is more evidence that supports this trend. The Black Keys' "Lonely Boy" was a *Billboard* number-one rock song. It is from their seventh album, co-produced by the band and Danger Mouse (aka Brian Burton). Danger Mouse is credited as a songwriter along with the two group members, Dan Auerbach and Patrick Carney. Likewise, the rock band Train began working with writer/producers on their comeback album, including the Norwegian songwriting and production duo Espionage (Espen Lind and Amund Bjorklund) who co-wrote the hits "Hey, Soul Sister" and "Drive By."

Adele made a clean sweep at the 2012 Grammys with her 2011 release *21*. She charts in the categories of Adult Contemporary, Adult Top 40, Mainstream Top 40, Rock Songs, and Digital Songs–Rock, in addition to the Hot 100. Adele co-wrote all 11 songs on the album. Either her co-writer or Adele and the co-writer produced five of the 11 tracks (including the biggest hit singles). The only non-writing producers on the album are Columbia Records co-presidents Rick Rubin and Jim Abbiss.

Clearly, writer/producers dominate the dance genre. Furthermore, at the time of writing, permutations of electronic dance music are the primary influence in the pop charts. Such writers, who mostly became auteur producers, include David Guetta, Shellback, Benny Blanco, Dr. Luke, and Skrillex. This trend can be traced back at least as far as hit makers like Holland, Dozier, and Holland, and Gamble and Huff, who monopolized the R&B/pop genre of their time.

In the big-selling commercial genres, this leaves country music as the last bastion of the non-writing producer. Material is so critical in country music that even artists who are proven hit writers perform outside songs, and the majority of charting singles are still not written by the producer (at the time of writing). Nevertheless, there are signs of change; Jon Randall and Brett Beavers both produce and write for Dierks Bentley. Jeremy Stover wrote and produced for Justin Moore, and Dave Brainard writes for and produces Jerrod Niemann. Rodney Clawson, who co-wrote hits for George Strait and others, has also charted as a producer for James Wesley.[21]

A part of my early session work in London involved playing on songwriters' demos. Writers used to have to hire a studio, engineer, musicians, and singers to make demos. Likewise, bands needed a facility and help recording their demos. Now, those recordings are mostly made at home without need for musicians, producer, or engineer. These productions are, as they were 40 years ago, a training ground for new producers, and in circulating demos to labels, they act as a marketing tool for the writer's production skills.

As I write in 2012, auteur producers abound in the charts. There are teams such as The Matrix, the Neptunes, Shellback, Rock Mafia, and the Smeezingtons, as well as solo producers such as Red One, Dr. Luke, DJ White Shadow, Afrojack, David Guetta, Deadmau5, Skrillex, Jim Jonsin, Bangladesh, Benny Blanco, and more. These producers interweave technology, writing, and production. Collaborative producers who co-write or can song-doctor the artist's ideas will also find work with the majors and large indies. Consultative producers can operate in a home or project studio, as well as in a castle or five-star studio. Some bands have a strong idea of what they want musically and do not need outside material or co-writes but still need some mediation. A facilitative or collaborative producer may be a good fit.

None of these styles of producing necessarily requires an expensive commercial facility, although some artists want to work in the best and most comfortable environment. Large groups of musicians are not easy to accommodate in a home or project environment. Sought-after vintage analog equipment has become ever more expensive, and some studios increased their appeal by accumulating specialized collections. However, analog tape machines are now cheap to buy, if not to maintain. Most analog equipment can be rented, and there are reasonably priced hardware reproductions of many key pieces.

Daily alignment of analog tape machines is necessary, as is frequent maintenance; both are time-consuming and can be expensive. Nonetheless, the Foo Fighters recorded their multiple Grammy-winning seventh album *Wasting Light* completely in the analog domain in Dave Grohl's two-car garage studio. Reunited with producer Butch Vig (from Nirvana's *Nevermind*), Grohl wanted to capture the performance element as they used to, with no computer manipulation. Alan Moulder mixed the album manually on the same API console they used for tracking.[22]

Happily, analog is still a choice for those who want it, but it is the digital revolution that is generating many of the new names in production and the increasing number of artists who are producing themselves. Tony Visconti, seeing this trend some time ago, commented that we may see an end to the professional producer role altogether:

> ...[I]t's no longer a great mystery of how to make a record. There are zillions of books on the subject, whereas when I started 25 years ago, there were none whatsoever. Now, the information is available to anyone.[23]

Having said that, after more than 45 years as a producer, Visconti's latest production of David Bowie's 27th studio album (in this week of writing) entered the *Billboard* Top 200 at number two and hit the number-one slot in the U.K., becoming the fastest selling album of 2013. There undoubtedly has been a proliferation of information, but information alone did not build a career like Visconti's. There was hard work and time invested in his development as a musician and writer combined with learning how to get the best out of people, including the difficult ones. Visconti was the first producer I worked with who could seamlessly manipulate the console and outboard gear, write out parts for musicians, make ad hoc creative suggestions, and maintain a sharp ear for great performances. Increased availability of information and equipment only presents opportunity. Individuals have to put in the hours and persevere—as previous generations did. The path that leads to success may be open to all who aspire, but the final doorway into the hallowed halls still opens for only the dedicated few.

Where Are We Going?

Paul Saffo (director and Roy Amara Fellow at the Institute for the Future) identified a tendency toward "forecasting double vision," in which mass excitement over
a coming technology—or for that matter, mass fear—leads people to overestimate
its short-term impact. They tend to forget that technology diffuses slowly, and when
cold reality fails to conform to overheated expectations, that disappointment leads
us to underestimate impact over the long term. Personal computers are a good case
study. Saffo says, "In 1980 everybody said that, by 1983, everybody would have one.
It didn't happen. So by 1985–86, people said homes would never have them." When
digital recorders first became available in the early '80s, there were predictions that
analog would disappear within five to ten years. In fact, analog was the format of
choice until the early 2000s. Vinyl continues to grow within low single-digit percentages of the recorded music market and finds new generations of consumers.
Cassettes have also made a modest comeback. Through the '90s, rock and alterna-
tive/indie artists tended to prefer analog recording. During that time, lower-end studios embraced digital recording (usually the eight-track modular machines) because
of the cost-to-quality ratio. These and DAW technology led to many major studio
closures. Inevitably, there is a time lag between innovation and the uptake or prac-
ticability of new technology. Saffo notes, "You've got to look beyond the common
wisdom. The expected future always arrives late and in utterly unexpected ways."

Likewise with social trends; in the '80s, an increase in home studios caused
major Los Angeles studios to panic. They lobbied to ban home-based studios, citing residential zoning laws. Two decades later, many of the commercial studios
involved no longer exist. Recording began in improvised spaces, formalizing into
label-owned and independent commercial studios. They have been decentralizing
again for several decades.

Enabled by communications technology, society appears to be returning to
a cottage-industry state, the difference being that the workplace now travels with
the connected individual. Only a couple of decades ago, internationally successful producers clustered in major music centers like London, New York, Los
Angeles, and Nashville. Facilities were a major factor. Excellent records required
elite studios. Now, many producers achieve international acclaim from outside previously acknowledged music centers. Red One is Moroccan but bases himself in
Sweden; the Neptunes (Virginia Beach, Virginia), Shellback (Karlshamn, Sweden),
David Guetta (France), Stargate (Trondheim, Norway), Afrojack (Spijkenisse,
Netherlands), Max Martin (Stockholm, Sweden), to name a few.

Being connected increases our potential for productivity. It would severely
limit me if I could not operate from anywhere. I am writing this sentence in transit,
and I wrote much of the first edition of this book on a laptop, sitting in a London
park, watching my kids play, on planes between London and New York, and on
trains en route from Washington, D.C. to New York. Laptops and mobile devices
negate the necessity for place, and significant parts of the production process can

now be done on portable/mobile devices.[24] Fully functional access can be liberating for the self-determined. Lack of personal downtime can become an issue, but technology has an on/off switch.

Unlicensed peer-to-peer networks may have diminished a myopic industry, but they introduced us to the concept of any music, anytime, anywhere. International Federation of the Phonographic Industry (IFPI) numbers from 2009 showed that "95 percent of music downloads are unauthorized, with no payment to artists and producers."[25] This means that many more people are listening to music than at any other time in history. Adjusted for inflation, recorded music is also significantly cheaper now than it was in the '60s, and there are many different ways to access it.[26]

Unfortunately, neither the generative group, including the artist, writers, producer, and manager, nor the label that invested in the creation are directly benefiting from the increased access to music. In addition to major labels wicking away the bulk of revenues, now tech companies that contributed nothing to create the work, build value in their businesses by using others' creative content and returning nothing to the creators or owners. The many creators who unwittingly collaborated in building the value of YouTube did not share in the $1.65 billion that Google paid for it.[27]

Until we learn to dematerialize and rematerialize atoms, we will still move physical things by truck, train, ship or plane. As I write, CD sales have declined steadily for more than a decade, although in 2011, they still accounted for more than 50 percent of the dollar value of the U.S. market.[28] The CD is now three decades old. It will eventually diminish to a small market share and may disappear. Various forms of digital delivery will replace it. Thirty-four years after its introduction, the displacement of vinyl as a primary format began when Sony and Philips launched the compact disc. CDs improved upon vinyl's dynamic range, frequency response, portability, and robustness. Philips compact cassette tapes had earlier taken market share from LPs because of their portability, but they lacked vinyl's quality. Prerecorded tapes, including the eight-track, had opened up the in-car market for personalized music.

It was blank cassette tapes and the ability for anyone to copy an album that changed consumer expectations. The transistor radio coinciding with the music-buying phase of the baby boomers had an impact on record sales and growth in new music acts. For the first time, people could have music wherever they went, via car radios and pocket-sized portables, albeit with music chosen by someone else. Pre-recorded cassette tapes increased personal choice while on the move, and recordable cassettes enabled fully personalizable portable music. Twenty or so years after recorded music had saved radio from the onslaught of television,[29] AM radio with its limited choices had serious competition again. The radio industry responded with the spread of the almost counterculture FM stations,[30] which targeted boomers and eventually fragmented music into advertiser-friendly formats. As the '70s came to a close, the Sony Walkman launched the next phase in the mobile revolution, eschewing the shared experience of radio in the home, at work, or on the beach. The

Walkman, especially when combined with the recordable cassette, provided the first anywhere, personalized, and isolationist music experience. Now we have the familiar specter of people everywhere wearing ear-buds or headphones listening to their own music collections, streaming non-interactive or on-demand music.

CDs have defied the shift to digital delivery for longer than many expected, and although sales have declined significantly, they remained above 50 percent of sales in 2012. Despite the massive capacity of the iPod and other players, digital downloads are being challenged by streaming services. These services (Rhapsody, Spotify, Rdio, Mog and others) offer interactive access to bigger selections of recorded music than ever before. Access can be on- or offline from many devices, and the hope is that all recorded music will be available instantly in this way. Pricing ranges from free to about $10 per month. The premium service currently provides better quality sound, mobile access, and no ads. Streaming services introduce another level of spontaneity into the listening experience. On a whim, a listener can jump from comedy to avant-garde music or whatever appeals at that moment. The only premeditation necessary is to save playlists for offline listening when mobile access is not available.

What is significant for producers and artists is that payment shifts from purchase to use, or from ownership to rent. Additionally, subscription (or the ad-supported free service) removes the cost barrier to experimentation for subscribers. It costs nothing extra to listen to a new or obscure recording, and the service makes a small payment to that label, artist, and producer every time a track is played. This model, combined with mobile's access to billions of users, offers potential for the expansion of the music industry.

Lossy-compressed digital music codecs such as MP3, WMA, or AAC, where part of the sound is discarded according to psychoacoustic principles of perceptual redundancy, do not sound as good as CD audio or uncompressed WAV files, and they especially fall short when compared to high-resolution audio files (192k/24 bit). Some compression algorithms are better than others, and improvements have been made such as "mastered for iTunes." Lossless compression algorithms, such as FLAC and Apple Lossless are viable for downloads. Video content is delivered online, and the bandwidth required to download or stream movies is such that downloading a three- or four-minute FLAC or uncompressed WAV file is relatively insignificant. Once it becomes standard practice to package high-resolution digital downloads or streams with substantial metadata—including artwork, images, video, and extensive notes—it is hard to imagine why anyone would want to buy a CD.

Since the introduction of the CD in 1982, digital audio quality to consumers has been pegged at 44.1kHz/16-bit quality giving a top frequency of 22.05kHz and a dynamic range of ~96dB. Bandwidth and storage kept most engineers recording either at 44.1kHz/24-bit or 48kHz/24-bit, both of which gave an expanded dynamic range of ~144dB and the latter a top frequency of 24kHz. As George Massenburg points out, Moore's law has brought us to the point where neither storage nor bandwidth remain considerations in moving to 96kHz/24-bit or even 192kHz/24-bit recording or delivery. Again, compared to video, streaming or downloading music in high-resolution formats is trivial.[31] Services like HDtracks are already delivering millions of dollars of high-resolution music to consumers annually.[32]

Producers should be future-proofing their catalogs by recording at high resolutions well before consumer formats catch up so there is a body of high-resolution work ready for release. It is just a matter of time before consumers consider current digital masters outdated. Columbia anticipated the microgroove LP by recording many classical pieces on longer format discs so they would have uninterrupted masters for the new consumer format. George Massenburg speculates that a variable streaming format could deliver very high resolution to consumer devices when bandwidth is available and would automatically adjust to a lower resolution when bandwidth is limited.[33] This would minimize access failures while ensuring optimum quality audio when there is a strong signal. He speculates that high-quality audio creates opportunities for new business models and renewed willingness to pay for music. For producers and engineers who have compared the sound of a master recording with its sadly diminished MP3 or AAC version, this is a point that resonates.

Revenue Streams Are Multiplying

At the turn of the century, there were two basic sources of revenue from sound recordings: retail distribution to stores through a wholesale distributor and licensing to television, movies, games, and so forth. Today there are nine commonly accessed sources of revenue: retail distribution to stores, licensing, direct sales of physical goods to consumers (from your own site or at gigs), retail digital downloads (from stores like iTunes), direct downloads (from your own sites), subscription downloads (from services like eMusic), statutory non-interactive streaming (from Web and satellite radio paid through SoundExchange), subscription interactive streaming (like Rhapsody), and ad-supported interactive streaming (such as Spotify and YouTube).

The obstacles of physical distribution no longer exist. Producers can eliminate manufacturing and physical distribution, uploading from anywhere to all the online stores and services. Albums and album cycles have become irrelevant for thinking artists. They can make tracks available regularly and retain the ability to modify music, text, or visuals after release. A consumer accessing the work could hear and see different versions over time, which can have a significant marketing benefit and create an ongoing, interactive relationship with the audience. Ownership of a hard copy of music or video is becoming unnecessary, which means that artists and producers who can generate more use of their music will make more money. Pay-per-use reduces the impact of marketing dollars, which motivated the consumer toward a front-loaded, single act of purchase. Marketing is still essential and the advantage remains with well-financed organizations, but in a streaming world, the music has to be "sticky" for the consumer, because every play generates revenue, not a single purchase. In a socially networked world, users have to want to identify with your music in order for it to "go viral."

If rights owners and creators are fairly remunerated, this model is preferable to the system we had, where the majority of label music holdings are deleted and become inaccessible. Unfortunately, the major labels and many indies still function under the Pareto principle or the 80/20 rule, where they delete slow-moving product from their catalogs.[34] The basis of this outmoded model is the economics of physical manufacturing, storage, and distribution. Virtual shelf space for both distributor and retailer is close to free (per individual title), but access to everything ever released has significant appeal to consumers. Music is part of our cultural heritage, and all of it should be available for anyone to discover and enjoy, irrespective of its sales history. It is damaging to the artist (financially and creatively) and to the free flow of information within society for a commercial entity to enclose an artist's work, using contractual rights to keep it unavailable. For the well-being of artists and society, copyright owners should forfeit their rights to a work if at any time they fail to exploit it or make it available (use it or lose it). It is impossible to envisage a situation in the United States where this is likely to happen without legislation, although artists and production companies with leverage can negotiate these kinds of terms into their contracts. Producers with royalty deals may need contract wording that would accommodate changing ownership and royalty status of the artist in order to continue receiving their share of revenues. The terms "out of print" or "deleted from the catalog" are unnecessary in today's technological environment.

Apple iTunes' $0.99 digital download model has been the most popular, with billions of downloads. Much to the industry's chagrin, it has diminished the value of the album and reintroduced consumers to the pleasure of being able to buy only the tracks they want.

The manufacturing cost of a 120mm CD single was identical to that for a CD album, although mechanical and artist royalty costs were lower, because labels pay on a per-track basis and often contractually reduce those entitlements. Companies experimented with cheaper 80mm mini-CDs, but they were incompatible with slot-loading CD players (as in Macs and many cars). The little discs became stuck inside if inserted without an adapter. Eliminating singles boosted major label profits significantly by forcing consumers to buy the album when they only wanted the track they had heard on the radio. Results follow rewards, and albums were produced (for which no single could be purchased) that contained one or two strong tracks (the ones aimed at radio airplay) with the rest being substandard filler. This became so common that a Google search for "filler tracks" produces pages of returns.

Other digital business models are eMusic's monthly download subscription, Rhapsody's subscription streaming, and Spotify's "freemium" model, which produces revenues from advertising to the free users and the subscription fee for the premium service. Spotify lost $59.3 million in 2011 on revenues of $249.1 million. Both their losses and revenues have increased dramatically every year during the five years they have been operational.[35] Royalties per play are fractions of a cent, requiring many plays to generate a meaningful amount of money for artists and producers. Nonetheless, an A&R person from Warner Music Group, Sweden told me in early 2012 that Spotify generates 40 percent of their revenues.[36] Even so, some significant artists and labels have not licensed their material to the service, and gaps in the catalog diminish its value to consumers.

Consumers like to listen before they buy, which is why radio play is so sought after and why labels pay for in-store listening station placement. To that end, music download sites offer free promotional clips ranging from 30 to 90 seconds of the track, making it easier to discover music not played on radio. Streaming services allow consumers to listen, on demand, to any track on the service for no additional charge, eliminating the cost barrier to discovery for the consumer. Unfortunately, no service (at the time of writing) allows searches (or browsing) by producer, engineer, non-featured musicians or vocalists, genre, instrument, or a plethora of other useful ways that people find the music they want to hear. This diminishes the consumer's ability to discover music toward the end of the long tail. Artists or recordings still have to rise to prominence through other media for a listener to discover them in the millions of tracks on offer. Nevertheless, being able to audition any recording at no extra cost obviates the problem of buying an album only to be disappointed. Measuring and paying for usage shifts success and revenue to music that people repeatedly listen to, rather than marketing-driven one-time purchases.

Labels treat downloads as a sale for the purpose of royalty payments. Legal claims that they are a license would entitle many artists with pre-digital-era contracts to a 50 percent share of revenue. Eminem prevailed in his suit against Universal, although the label stated that the case did not create legal precedence.[37] Contractually defining digital download royalties at the lower rate closes that loophole for labels. These decisions and percentages affect producers insofar as producer royalties are calculated on the same basis as the artist's. Business models are changing rapidly, and producers' contracts need to cover all eventualities so they can receive their fair share of income generated by the recordings they produce.

Jukeboxes have been digital for some time, and the largest service, TouchTunes®, delivers music over the internet to tens of thousands of commercial venues. These machines contain hundreds of thousands of songs that refresh daily with new release and catalog updates from TouchTunes' central library of millions. Consumers at a venue access music by song title, artist, album, or playlists, and the system automatically logs every request, increasing the ease and accuracy of usage statistics.

XM and Sirius satellite radio stations are now one company. They deliver over 70 channels of commercial-free music to more than 20 million subscribers coast-to-coast in the United States. Under the Digital Millennium Copyright Act (DMCA), every play generates performance royalties for artists and those producers who have filed a letter of direction (LOD) from the artist with SoundExchange. Shamefully, performance royalties still do not exist for artists, musicians, and producers on terrestrial radio (FM, AM, and associated HD stations) in the United States. John Smith, president of the International Federation of Musicians (FIM) commented,

> There is just no logical explanation why musicians can earn radio royalties in virtually every market of the world and yet not in the country with the world's largest commercial radio sector.[38]

By international and ethical standards, those who create value should benefit from it, but the radio industry has thus far out-lobbied the music industry in Washington, D.C.

Previously nonexistent ring tone revenues expanded rapidly in the early 2000s, and in 2011 accounted for $2.1 billion dollars worldwide. Worldwide sales of digital downloads the same year were $3.6 billion dollars.

History shows that the introduction of new technologies and formats tends to result in a reduction (and sometimes—as in the case of terrestrial radio—elimination) of artist and producer royalties. Labels reduced royalties for CDs far beyond the time when additional costs were a factor. Likewise, they introduced the 360 deal to compensate for monies lost from piracy. As legitimate digital business establishes itself and profits exceed those of physical sales, they will want to continue with 360 deals. These deals do not align labels' and producers' interests, just as "record clubs" like Columbia House did not. Artists and producers generally did not receive royalties from these sales, but they were profitable for the labels. Similarly, the major labels have taken ownership positions in some of the new digital services. Artists and producers do not benefit, despite it being their content that labels are leveraging in order to become stakeholders. Ideally, producers and artists would earn income from any source related to the direct or indirect use of their work. Few artists or producers have that kind of leverage. Some producers are realigning their interests with the labels' by insisting on a 360 component in their deals with artists, meaning that they share in other artist revenue streams for a contractually defined period.

With more artists dropping out of or never partaking in the label system, producers must ensure that their contracts cover these circumstances. Producer royalties around 3 or 4 percent of SRP were predicated on hundreds of thousands or millions of units being sold. Artists are figuring out that they can make more money with fewer sales if they own and distribute their own recordings. An artist could make as much as ten times the money from a self-released recording than from a label deal with its reductions and deductions.

To sell 25,000 CDs over a period of months is not difficult for a touring band that has a couple of hundred fans in multiple markets. At $15 per unit, that produces $375,000 revenue. With less than $35,000 in manufacturing costs and a recording budget of, say, $40,000, the band could make a gross profit of $300,000 in less than a year (not including digital revenues). However, a producer with three points of retail (SRP) would only realize $11,250 from those sales. With high-margin sales where the expectation of total units sold is lower, a split-profits deal would be fairer for the producer. This needs to be addressed with unsigned artists and when an artist might opt out of their deal and move your production to their own label or other high-margin/low-sales situation.

Will We Even Need Labels in the Future?

The major labels used to control radio promotion and distribution, which meant that they controlled the means of marketing and selling recordings. Radio promoted the records and distribution shipped them to stores. Placement on the airwaves or in stores required significant investment. Synchronization of distribution and promotion was critical. If stock ran out while the record was in heavy rotation, sales dropped, and radio interpreted falling sales as lack of consumer interest and pulled the record off the air. If the record did not get the expected "adds" or "spins," sales would be low in those markets; inventory in stores would not sell, causing those stores to stop ordering and to return surplus stock to the label. Market timing and psychology were delicate and critical. Manufacturing and shipping physical goods is not an instantaneous process. Because a gap between radio spins and stock in stores can destroy a record's chances, manufacturing large quantities ahead of the airplay, while risky, was often undertaken. Marketers considered other factors, such as press and touring, television if the artist was successful enough, and, for a time, MTV. Nonetheless, without a successful radio campaign and perfectly timed distribution, a record would not usually make it into the top ten.

In order to achieve a top-ten hit on *Billboard*'s Hot 100, a record still needs heavy rotation on many top 40 stations or another powerful precursory format. However, digital delivery offers an instantaneous distribution system with low costs for inventory, shipping, and storage, and no delays. Timing is still critical: Recordings must be available on all digital services before the airplay and the tour cycle. If the public tries to buy and cannot, those sales are lost, and radio again reads that as a lack of public interest. Nonetheless, accurate manufacturing estimates and placing product in the right place at the right time become less critical as digital sales replace physical ones. However, charts still rank sales on a weekly basis, making chart placement a function of both quantity and speed.

An artist, producer, or small label can now upload their music to the various digital music stores and services, choose a release date, and launch their product through every digital outlet, just as the majors and large indie labels do. The advantage that the majors and large indies still have is marketing money. If the record is radio-worthy, they can afford the promotional dollars and the expertise and connections to service the appropriate stations. As with the sales charts, timing is critical to radio campaigns; losing one station as you gain another is ineffective and damages the release's credibility with stations adding and spinning the track.

It is hard for indies to compete in physical distribution. Once a title gains traction, better-resourced companies can afford end-caps at Best Buy, Target, and other major retailers that carry limited selections of fast-moving titles. The music business is no different from any other in this respect. A new brand of corn chips pays for favorable placement on supermarket shelves and for a presence in the weekly flyer. Large stores vet and approve every product they carry. To an increasing extent, this model is extending to online stores. Label resources, in the form of promotional expertise, time, and/or hard cash, pay for music prominently positioned on the home pages of large commercial online stores. "If you liked that, you might like this" kinds of promotions are charged as a marketing cost, sometimes in the form of discounts to the retailer. At a minimum, there is a human resource cost to a label for any marketing effort. These "soft costs" cannot be ignored in calculating the investment in marketing campaigns. In a free-market economy, successful organizations use their financial power to influence the market in their favor. This is a function of supply and demand; end-cap space is scarce; price increases until spaces available match those prepared to pay that price, the same with radio promotion and online campaigns. Marketing resources, including hard and soft costs along with expertise, are the primary reason why well-financed corporations will continue to dominate the upper tier of a digital distribution environment.

Increasingly sophisticated browse and search functionality, search engine optimization (SEO), niche or specialist websites, and social networks and bloggers help small labels and artists reach their audiences. Otherwise, the sheer quantity of new (and existing) music makes it difficult for consumers to find a label or artist. The mainstream media, overwhelmed with requests for reviews, needs standout stories of prior development before they will feature artists. That development could be in the form of a large social network, good live show attendances, and impressive music sales numbers. Signing to a credible or influential label, tidbits such as who the artist toured with, and which agent or manager is interested in the act can attract attention and are commonly known as "the story."

Despite the financial advantages, many artists comment at panels and seminars that they do not want to run their own labels; they want to be artists. I felt the same way when I was an artist, and as a producer, I preferred simply to create the recordings. In a perfect world, artists would be artists, producers would produce, businesspeople would run labels, and revenues would be shared equitably. Unfortunately, as previously indicated, something like 55 percent of the SRP goes to the label, about 35% to the retailer, and less than 10 percent (after deductions and reductions) to what I call the generative group (i.e., the artist, producer, and management team). Out of that 10 percent royalty credited to the artist, the label deducts all the recording and many of the marketing and promotional costs. Major label artists' albums can be certified gold or platinum without recouping costs. Until recoupment, artists do not receive royalties. Sheryl Crow went on record at a May 2000 House Judiciary Committee hearing, saying that she did not receive royalties from A&M Records until she had sold three or four million units. For perspective, Ann Chaitovitz, then director of sound recordings for the American Federation of Television and Radio Artists (AFTRA) in her prepared statement to the same committee pointed out that in the prior year,

> Nearly 39,000 recordings were released, but only three singles and 135 albums—0.35 percent—were certified as selling three million units, and notably, many of these records had been selling over a number of years before finally reaching the three million unit sales mark in 1999.[39]

Labels also customarily retain the copyright in perpetuity (forever) to everything recorded under the contract. They have no obligation to make the material available in any form, and if they choose not to, there is very little the creator can do about it. Most major label contracts are now 360 deals, where the label shares in all revenue streams. This encompasses all five financial pillars of an artist's career: merchandising, publishing, touring, and sponsorship income, the fifth being revenues from the sale or use of recordings. These deals make it very difficult for all but the most successful acts to make a living from music.

There seems to be growing doubt in some quarters of the artist community whether it is possible to reach the highest levels of the industry without major or well-established indie label help, even if it is simply distribution or early career help in brand development. Artists such as Radiohead, Nine Inch Nails, Jill Sobule, and Aimee Mann have enjoyed success as independent artists, but each established their brand using major label resources. However, some artists are making a good living without the assistance of a major or indie label. Early examples are Fugazi (which owned Dischord) and Ani DiFranco, who founded and has successfully run Righteous Babe. More recently, Corey Smith generated millions of dollars per year[40] completely independently, as did Jonathan Coulton, about whom NPR said,

> In 2010, Coulton's music brought in about $500,000 in revenue. And since his overhead costs are very low, most of that money went straight to him.[41]

In Australia, the John Butler Trio released five studio albums and three live albums on their own label, Jarrah Records. All were produced or co-produced by Butler and amassed five Australian Recording Industry Association (ARIA) awards and 16 nominations, along with four Australian Performing Rights Association (APRA) wins and seven nominations. The group played many large festivals and concerts in the United States and charted on the *Billboard* 200, Digital, Independent Albums, and Top Rock Albums charts.

In 2009, CNet reported "unsigned hip hop artist" Drake as selling "300,000 singles through TuneCore in 14 days; the *New York Times* listed him as having the No. three download in the U.S." They pointed out that he probably "earned around $150,000 in two weeks" and that this was not an "advance that needs to be earned back." Shortly after, Drake "signed a deal with the world's largest record label, Universal."[42]

As discussed earlier, moderate success as a free agent can generate more money for an artist than millions of units sold on a major or independent label. Retention of copyrights maintains the potential for future income. However, not all artists value their artistic freedom. Some are prepared to assign their rights in perpetuity and the majority of future revenues in exchange for help, an advance, and production and marketing dollars. It takes more than musical ability and a desire for success to set up a studio, produce, engineer, and master an album, as well as manage marketing, promotion, and distribution.

The ease of building a large fan base through social networking may have been overstated but "big things begin in small places." The early '60s British blues movement that revived interest in American blues and spawned many "British Invasion" groups traces back to a few enthusiasts like Alexis Korner and Cyril Davies. The Beatles developed out of the Star Club in Hamburg and the Cavern in Liverpool; "punk" came from CBGBs in New York and the Roxy in Covent Garden, London. The '80s "new romantic" movement coalesced at the Blitz Club in Covent Garden, and much of '90s alternative rock was shaped by Seattle's "grunge" movement.

In his book *The Tipping Point*, Malcolm Gladwell talks about the "Law of the Few"—the people he calls connectors (who have large social networks), mavens (who love to share information by word-of-mouth), and salesmen (who are highly persuasive, stimulating trends and societal change). Gladwell is describing the basis of viral marketing and an underlying factor in how the movements of British blues, punk, new romantic, and grunge became identifiable worldwide phenomena without marketing or corporate dollars that directly promoted these movements or their titles. I am credited with coining the term "new romantic" in a comment with reference to the first band I produced, Spandau Ballet. Once the media picked up the term, its use proliferated to near ubiquity within weeks in reference to the entire subculture that became a sonic and visual movement.

The matter of whether artists should sign with a major (or independent) label is moot if they cannot get a deal. With major labels being reluctant to develop careers until a certain stage, artists and sometimes producers or managers are putting in the hard work of moving the act's career from nothing to something. As discussed earlier, producers are well positioned to sign and develop artists via their own labels or production companies. Doing it yourself can be daunting, but as a business you can build a staff using your own resources, loans, passive investors, or active business partners. Ownership means more control and more responsibility but also greater freedom.

Charts

Charts are marketing tools, a feedback loop for the industry that reinforces or diminishes confidence in a release. Labels manipulate chart positions as best they can, using promotion and marketing techniques. Positive chart movement engenders label confidence, encouraging more marketing investment and vice versa.

Chart action not only affects optimism and investment at the label, but also radio play, television exposure, and press (physical and digital). As previously discussed, if stations are spinning a track and it does not chart high enough or early enough, they drop it. Strong upward chart movements influence stations to add songs they have resisted. Promoters and agents watch charts carefully; this affects touring schedules and fees. The music business is metrics-driven, and charts reflect and drive sales.

Major label marketing money is still the dominant influence on the *Billboard* Hot 100, 200, and airplay charts. Nielsen SoundScan compiles these charts from the online services and major retail outlets, as well as more than 2,000 radio, satellite radio, and music video channels across North America. They do not gather sales from an artist's site unless it is registered as a SoundScan reporter. Similarly, they will not count venue sales unless you report them directly to Neilsen. In order to report venue sales, you must register with SoundScan as a label, have been in business for two years, and pay a $500 annual fee.[43] Many artists and small labels do not report their sites or venue sales; no harm is done if sales are low, but artists who sell significant amounts through their sites and at shows do not gain the advantage of the chart feedback loop on the industry ecosystem.

If you are looking for a major label deal, substantial and verifiable statistics attract attention. Jay Harren, A&R manager at Columbia Records said,

> When searching for bands for my label, sales history is one of the first things I look at. Anyone can say they've sold "X" amount of records, but SoundScan is pure proof, and we tend to rely on that as a resource. I would highly encourage any band not reporting live venue sales to Soundscan to do so, and IndieHitmaker is the way to do it simply.[44]

Substantial sales or airplay, even in limited markets, can lead to slots on festival stages or tours and interest from substantial agencies. Booking agent Jordan Burger at the Agency Group said,

> First thing every Wednesday morning I check out the Soundscan charts, who did well, who didn't, who are all the artists on the New Artist charts selling, which are smart tour packages or possible support slots, which are new bands I haven't heard of, how my clients did, etc. I also study my clients' charts for market research.[45]

Independent rock band State of Man charted their single "Swallow Your Fears" for eight consecutive weeks on *Billboard*'s single sales charts, peaking at the number ten slot.[46] Thomas Panza, guitarist and writer for the group, later said,

> Venue sales reporting was a component. . . . Had we not been able to report to SoundScan this would never have happened.[47]

The number of sales that it takes to chart in any week is achievable by an unsigned or independent artist who has a good-sized following. David Claassen, associate director at BMI Atlanta points out that

> it only takes 1,000 sales and sometimes less to make the weekly New Artist charts. A CD release show if done well can lead to almost half of those sales. Add pre-release orders to that and you're on the charts!...Why? It's the only way for industry to know when and where an artist is doing well. Those that utilize a blended strategy focused around regional touring, good promoting and smart thinking can leverage SoundScan to create success.[48]

Charting in *Billboard* will not necessarily turn an artist or producer into a superstar or guarantee a long and successful career. Careers require perseverance and continued successes. There are several interpretations for the aphorism "a journey of a thousand miles begins with a single step," but taking action is essential for any achievement. It is easy to forget, however, that after that first step, there are approximately two million more required to complete the thousand miles. Similarly, there are many steps needed to chart in *Billboard*, with many possible routes, and a chart position in *Billboard* is not the destination; it is a flare that informs the industry you exist and are making progress on your journey. Chart positions attract the help of industry intermediaries, making the journey easier and faster.

Notwithstanding, some artists, productions, or labels cannot sell units quickly enough to chart, even though their sales objectives may be met over a longer timespan. Many musicians, artists, and producers have satisfying careers without ever appearing on the *Billboard* charts. Labels can sustain themselves without charting consistently. For instance, Smithsonian Folkways Recordings supports a staff of 17 from revenues without ever appearing on the Hot 100 or Top 200 and with rare appearances on niche genre charts.

Marketing

There must be some form of marketing to attract attention to a release. Absent airplay and press attention, this can simply be playing live shows, online efforts, or a combination, but coordinating outreach with the release is essential. Online marketing has the potential to reach many more people than a local show, but there is more competition online. There are services such as Topspin, CD Baby, Bandcamp, and more that have built-in marketing tools, many of which are free or low-cost. It is essential to maintain contact with your fans and to cross-market between your shows, website, social media outlets, blogs, and any traditional media such as local press, magazines, fanzines, and television or radio that you can muster.

Guerrilla campaigns in a local market that go viral via a live fan base are an effective way to build a mailing list and boost gig revenues. A good marketing campaign creates a whole that is greater than the sum of the parts. This depends upon synchronizing the publicity with the events. Posting video clips and free music shortly before a gig can bring more people out to the show, enabling bigger merchandise and music sales. Reporting the music sales back to SoundScan makes a developing career visible to the industry.

Of course, even with effort and money spent on marketing, the music itself eventually has to resonate with an audience. There is a commonly held opinion that enough marketing dollars can sell "ice to the Eskimos." If that were true, major corporations would not spend fortunes on failed products. Marketing dollars prime the pump, but eventually the water has to flow on its own.

How does this affect a producer? With more music recorded regionally than ever before, fledgling producers have more opportunities to gain experience. As discussed, it is possible to make a living producing music for local and regional artists, building a reputation while being in a prime position to assess the talent pool. There is the chance, albeit slim, of selling millions of albums as John Kurzweg did when he produced Creed's debut—before they were signed to Wind-up Records. A well-promoted group is more likely to build a local fan base that is sufficient to attract wider attention. Similarly, producers must market themselves, if only within the industry. This can include e-mail newsletters, a blog, Facebook entries, tweets, soliciting reviews and interviews, submitting for local awards nominations, and so forth. Contributing to the marketing of productions and ensuring that credits are always present and visible, help in raising your profile as a producer.

Will Music Producers Survive the Revolution?

Jazz recordings still sell, although they represent a smaller market share than in the '30s and '40s. Recorded music requires production; even if the producer is the artist or an uncredited person, someone will mediate the technical and creative elements. It is most likely that current and past styles of production will coexist with new methodologies. A broad skill base is advisable for improved chances of survival; in the future, using the "blank tile in the Scrabble game" analogy, producers may have to supply more than engineering, arranging, and people skills. Video, graphics, words, and music travel through the same digital pipeline, and the boundaries between disciplines may disappear.

Early recordings captured optimized sonic impressions of events that took place at a time and in a place. Les Paul's sound-on-sound productions synthesized events across time and space with performance, arrangement, and composition coalescing. Many artists, engineers, and producers subsequently furthered this development, including Brian Wilson, George Martin, and numerous others. To compose, arrange, and perform most of the elements that comprise a recording in addition to controlling the production, performing live, and creating videos in the way that Prince, for example, has, was unimaginable in the '50s. At the time of writing, there are several artist/producers (such as Gotye and Calvin Harris) in the charts. As with all human endeavors, the next generation stands on the shoulders of the previous one, viewing earlier peak achievements as their baseline.

Hollywood movies co-opt the emotional connection between audiences and tracks. MTV and other video music channels have melded music and visuals together in the minds of viewers. Avid, the creator of the Oscar-winning professional non-linear video-editing system, also owns Digidesign—the company that makes Pro Tools. Most DAWs can manipulate audio and video together. Simple, inexpensive tools and constant connectivity means that creators can capture, edit, publish, and share their work. Audio-visual artists are producing multimedia works using consumer technology and smart phones. Video has been important in the marketing and development of artists since before MTV, and YouTube increased the need for video exponentially, providing an outlet for every artist, signed or not. Although rare, clips that garner massive numbers of views can launch an artist. It seems inevitable that some producers will add visual skills to their arsenals.

Producers are artists who paint sonic images using people, music, words, and technology as their tools, shifting constantly from the analytical/logical to the intuitive state (left to right brain thinking). Adding visuals is not a huge stretch.

Godley and Creme left the group 10cc to succeed as a duo, directing the video for their hit "An Englishman in New York," which established them as video directors for artists like Sting, the Police, Herbie Hancock, Peter Gabriel, Duran Duran, George Harrison, and more. Most early stage artists now build an online presence that includes images and video, for which fans have a voracious appetite.

Production evolved in response to technology, and some producers will likely respond to multimedia demand for cross-disciplinary productions.

15

Conclusion

WHAT IF?

New recording artists have a brief window of opportunity, especially with major labels. Without success, the company moves on to the next artist. Correct matching of a producer to an artist can trigger commitment from the label and elicit positive responses from media and audiences.

A historiographic counterfactual is a "what if" question that asks, "If A had not happened, what might have been the different consequences?" It is interesting to perform a thought experiment in checking the relevance of producer typology (outlined in chapter 1) in the outcome and cultural influence of a recording. This involves suppositionally substituting one producer for another in a preexisting recording and positing the outcome. The effect of inappropriate typology choices often becomes apparent.

Buddy Holly's Nashville recordings for Decca are examples of a typology misfit. The Nashville producers, including legendary country music innovator Owen Bradley, changed Holly's sound by using their musicians and arrangements, which is typical of an auteur-style producer. Lacking success and unhappy with the results, Holly returned to Clovis Studios in New Mexico—where he had made his demos with the Crickets—and recorded the tracks for which he became renowned. Norman Petty, who eventually became Holly's manager, was the owner/engineer and seemingly acted as an enablative or assistive producer, allowing Holly and the musicians to define their sound. Petty listed himself as co-writer, but this is widely considered a claimed credit rather than an actual contribution.

Bradley's auteur style, which resulted in success for so many other artists, did not work for Holly. The Decca recordings (among them a version of "That'll Be the Day") received favorable reviews, but sales were poor. Clearly, the failing was not substandard material or inadequate marketing; the productions simply did not connect with the public. The change to Petty's more artist-centered production style reverberated well beyond the commercial success of those records to influence many artists, including the Beatles. This is no judgment on Bradley or the auteur style; he was clearly one of the great country producers. Holly was lucky and probably excited to work with someone of Bradley's stature, but it was a mismatch.

Would Holly's music have resounded the way it did if he had not returned to Clovis? Sadly, the success he enjoyed resulted in him being on tour with Ritchie Valens and the Big Bopper on February 3, 1959, when all three of them died in a plane crash.

Like Owen Bradley, John Hammond's success as a producer is unassailable. So is Aretha Franklin's as an artist, yet Franklin's first three albums that Hammond produced for Columbia failed to define her direction. They garnered jazz awards and modest sales. Franklin made many albums for Columbia, bouncing from one producer to another, but she didn't blossom until she moved to Atlantic Records. Hammond's production style was reputedly laissez faire. His talent was in discovering transformative artists and then allowing them to define their identity in the studio, positioning him as an enablative producer. His colleague Teo Macero said of him: "He never really had control of the artist. It was the artist who was really controlling things." According to Macero, Hammond let the artist pick the takes, a task that the producer usually performs.[1] Conversely, Jerry Wexler (who produced Franklin's breakthrough album for Atlantic) tightly controlled her artistic direction, a characteristic of the auteur role. Wexler took Franklin back to her gospel roots, but in a secular setting, something he had done with Ray Charles more than a decade before. Franklin's first Atlantic album and single, both entitled "I Never Loved a Man (the Way that I Love You)," produced by Wexler at Muscle Shoals with the studio's legendary rhythm section, established her as the indisputable "Queen of Soul."

Of course, there are caveats galore. If a particular typology of producer has success with an artist, can you substitute any successful producer from the same typology (and genre) and achieve similar results?

Counterfactual thinking uses, as an analogy, chaos theory, which embraces concepts such as the butterfly effect, complexity, recursivity, criticality, and more. The butterfly effect is the notion that small events can cause large changes. Complexity deals with multiple variables having unquantifiable beginnings, which recursive processes exaggerate. Criticality is the tipping point at which prior equilibrium ceases to exist. All these intricate, integral, and interrelated parameters are active in the pairing of producer with artist. Perhaps one day they will be calculable, but for now, they fall into the realm of the artistic blending of intuition, rationality, and experience—surely the essence of the art of music production.[2] Although typologies alone do not guarantee a perfect match, they can assist in the consideration process.

It is fascinating to ponder what might have happened if Elvis Presley had not walked into the Memphis Recording Service in 1953. What if he had but Sam Phillips had not persevered until they came up with their famous take of "That's Alright, Mama"? How different would Presley's career have been? What if he had gone with a major label in Nashville, or what if Mitch Miller had signed him to Columbia and recorded him in New York in 1953 before Phillips had divined and defined his sound? With any producer other than Phillips, it seems unlikely that the influential, raw rockabilly edge would have come out. It is hard to imagine that Presley's later recordings at RCA (ostensibly produced by Steve Sholes) would have sounded the way they do without Phillips's prior work. It is impossible to know the result of any counterfactual change, but given the far-reaching impact of Presley's, recordings with Phillips, it is possible that any other pairing could have changed the future of rock 'n' roll.

There was an unquantifiable complexity combined with seemingly random chance that led to the success of the Presley-Phillips working relationship. The Sun recordings represented the first formula in a recursive sequence that defined RCA's starting parameters for Presley's next phase. If one element had been changed, his influence on pop culture and the music industry might have been very different or perhaps even nonexistent.

I have seen less-than-ideal pairings of a producer with an artist that, in my opinion, limited, changed, or eliminated success for the artist. Aretha Franklin's talent shone when Atlantic matched her with Wexler. The producer credit is Wexler's, but he would be the first to acknowledge his team, including Arif Mardin, who was also involved in these sessions. Nuclear physicist Tom Dowd was at the controls (how appropriate given the ensuing "chain" reaction). Franklin contributed to the popularization of soul music and became an American icon, but not every artist gets so many opportunities. My hope is that these speculations underscore the importance of favorable pairings between artists' needs and producers' typologies.

The Final Cut

As said before, it is impossible to identify a small number of producers as the best or most influential. "Best-of" lists are rarely comprehensive over time; they tend to slant toward fame and recent success. Career longevity is a rare accomplishment that deserves respect. Pragmatically, it is difficult to compare, say, Ralph Peer's work with "Mutt" Lange's. When producers sit around and talk about other producers, certain names do emerge as sources of inspiration. A very partial list, from one important and transitional generation in the field, includes George Martin, Quincy Jones, Phil Ramone, Jerry Wexler, Arif Mardin, and Phil Spector. Spector's production career was short, but he helped establish independent record producers in the public mind. His sonic stamp was so distinctive that people tend to refer to his hits as "Phil Spector records," rather than by the artists' names. This is a remarkable achievement given the brevity of his production career, his youth at the time, and the anonymity under which producers typically labor.

Quincy Jones has enjoyed a long creative career encompassing successes in many roles with some of the greatest artists from each decade. He commented,

> Our whole life is about the blank page: "What are we going to do, because right now we have nothing!" Ideas are the sustenance of creative life. What's always amazed me is how one person will take the first idea that comes or the second surge of inspiration and say, "Fine." Another person will say, "That's

not it yet." They get to the 27th layer before they say, "That's it." How do you know that?...I'm the 27th through the 40th. I don't know how, but somehow you know, you just say, "That's it." But that's a very important decision in creativity....I guess the trick is to dream real big. But if you do that, you have to get off of your ass and execute real big! That's the killer. I think our higher power likes our dreams to be very specific. Don't just say, "Oh God, I wish I was happy." Give me a break, man! It doesn't have to be like a machine, but I think when you start dreaming and visualizing, you've got to be very specific or it won't happen.[3]

Music producers share certain qualities, yet each brings a unique combination of skill and experience to the recording session. If successful producers have a trait in common, it might be that they do what is needed and do it well—no trivial feat. Freelance producers are as secure as their next successful project. Staff producers are only slightly better off. The complexity of the work requires extensive experience and knowledge, both of which are hard-won and frequently undervalued. Recent success is the most respected qualification, and a comprehensive network of connections is essential—there are no want ads or job sites for record producers. I have never met a producer who does not love his or her job. There is always something to learn—if you stagnate, the world turns without you; the only constant is change.

Richard James Burgess
Washington, D.C., October 2012

NOTES

Introduction

1. Oxford Dictionary, http://oxforddictionaries.com/definition/art, accessed 3-22-12.
2. http://www.artofrecordproduction.com/.
3. arpjournal.com.

Chapter One

1. *Encyclopedia of Archaeology: History and Discoveries*, s.v. "Classification," http://ezproxy.aacc.edu/login?url=http://www.credoreference.com.ezproxy.aacc.edu/entry/abcarch/classification, accessed 3-24-12.
2. Mark Lewisohn, *The Beatles Recording Sessions: The Official Abbey Road Studio Session Notes 1962–1970* (New York: Harmony, 1988), 6.
3. Pascal Kamina, *Film Copyright in the European Union* (Cambridge, UK: Cambridge University Press, 2002), 156.
4. Ibid.
5. Lauren Christy interview by the author, 6-14-04.
6. Dale Kawashima, *Legendary Trio Holland-Dozier-Holland Talk about Their Motown Hits, and Their New Projects*, Songwriter Universe, http://www.songwriteruniverse.com/hdh.htm, accessed 5-26-12.
7. Ibid.
8. Ibid.
9. Ibid.
10. Dale Kawashima, *Classic Songwriter Story: How Walter Afanasieff Wrote the Classic Hit, "Hero," with Mariah Carey*, Songwriter Universe, http://www.songwriteruniverse.com/hero.htm, accessed 8-12-12.
11. Brad Leigh Benjamin, ed. Barbara Schultz, *Walter Afanasieff*, Music Producers: Conversations with Today's Top Hit Makers (Emeryville, CA: Intertec, 2000), 61.
12. Geoff Boucher, *Practicing the Fine Art of Production*, Cyptron Industries, http://www.maxmartinfansite.com/CyptronLATimes.htm, accessed 6-8-12.
13. Conversation with the author, 11-10-12.
14. Anthony Savona, *Swinging Lessons: Teddy Riley Takes the Birthright of New Jack Swing and Heads toward "The Future,"* Console Confessions: The Great Music Producers in Their Own Words (San Francisco: Backbeat, 2005), 88.
15. Jimmy Jam, "Dynamic Duo," *EQ Magazine*, Feb. 1993.
16. Andy Jackson interview by the author, 1994.

17. Artistshouse Music, *Teo Macero on Working with John Hammond and on "The Graduate" Soundtrack*, http://www.artistshousemusic.org/videos/teo+macero+on+workin g+with+john+hammond+and+on+the+graduate+soundtrack, accessed 12-17-11.

18. Jazz and radical politics, posted to www.marxmail.org on 11-30-05, http://www. columbia.edu/~lnp3/mydocs/culture/jazz_left.htm, accessed 8-27-12.

19. Dunstan Prial, *The Producer: John Hammond and the Soul of American Music* (New York: Farrar, Straus and Giraud, 2006), 203.

20. Jake Brown, *Rick Rubin: In the Studio* (Toronto: ECW, 2009), 4.

21. Leadership quotes, http://www.tennessee.gov/dohr/learning/pdf/CoachesCorner/ LeadershipQuotes.pdf, accessed 8-27-12.

22. Jake Brown, *Rick Rubin: In the Studio* (Toronto: ECW, 2009), 171.

23. Ibid., 91.

24. Johnny Firecloud, "Corey Taylor Calls Producer Rick Rubin 'Overrated, Overpaid,'" *Crave Online*, 11-22-11, from a Q&A session with the audience at a concert on 11-18-11, Dallas, TX, http://www.craveonline.com/music/articles/178639-corey-taylor-calls-producer-rick-rubin-overrated-overpaid, accessed 6-10-12.

25. 93.3 WMAR Rocks, "Slipknot/Stone Sour Frontman Blasts Rick Rubin," last updated 11-23-11, http://beta.wmmr.com/music/news/story.aspx?ID=1576293, accessed 12-12-11.

26. Ros Earls interview by the author, 1994.

27. Brian Eno and Peter Schmidt, *The Oblique Strategies*, edition 1 (1975), http:// www.rtqe.net/ObliqueStrategies/Ed1.html, accessed 8-12-12.

28. Phil Ward, *Brian Eno Interviews & Articles: Ambient Reflections* (originally sourced from Studio Sound), Oct. 1995, http://www.moredarkthanshark.org/eno_int_studiosound-oct95.html, accessed 8-12-12.

29. Camran Afsari, "Brian Eno: Mixing the Ingredients of Pop in Culture's Cauldron," *Mix*, July 1993, 147.

30. Adam Beyda, ed. Barbara Schultz, *Flood Rising, Music Producers: Conversations with Today's Top Hit Makers* (originally sourced from a 1995 *Mix* article) (Emeryville, CA: Intertec, 2000), 7.

31. Arif Mardin interview by the author, 7-28-04.

32. Greg Kot, "Bruce Iglauer interview: 40 years of Alligator Records," *Chicago Tribune*, 2-16-11, http://leisureblogs.chicagotribune.com/turn_it_up/2011/02/bruce-iglauer-interview-40-years-of-alligator-records.html#more, accessed 6-10-12 (additional material from interview with the author, June 2012).

33. Peter G. Northouse, *Leadership: Theory and Practice*, fifth edition (Los Angeles: Sage, 2010), 3.

34. Daniel Goleman, "Leadership that Gets Results," *Harvard Business Review*, March–April 2000, 82–83, sourced from http://infopeople.org/sites/all/files/past/2006/ exploring/cg_EI_leadership_styles1.pdf, accessed 6-22-12.

35. Alan Murray, "Which of These Six Leadership Styles Works Best?" *Wall Street Journal*, http://online.wsj.com/article/SB10001424052748704041504575045163417674970.html, accessed 6-22-12, adapted from Alan Murray, *The Wall Street Journal Essential Guide to Management: Lasting Lessons from the Best Leadership Minds of Our Time* (New York: HarperBusiness, 2010).

36. Ibid.

Chapter Two

1. Malcolm Gladwell, *Outliers: The Story of Success* (New York: Little, Brown, 2008), 39–40.

2. Mr. Bonzai, "Lunching with the Lords: The Lord-Alge Brothers," *Mix*, Sept. 1993, 42.

3. Conversation between Benny Blanco and the author, 11-10-12, and Jeff Chu, "Top of the Pops," *Time Magazine*, March 9, 2001, vol. 157, no. 11.

4. Wendy Page interview by author, 7-26-04.

5. Helienne Lindvall, *David Guetta: The Man Taking Dance Music into the U.S. Charts*, http://www.guardian.co.uk/music/2010/jun/01/david-guetta-dance-music, accessed 9-23-11.

6. John Philip Sousa, "The Menace of Mechanical Music," *Appleton's Magazine*, vol. 8, 1906, http://explorepahistory.com/odocument.php?docId=1-4-1A1, accessed 4-6-12.

7. Mark Katz, *Capturing Sound: How Technology Has Changed Music* (London: University of California Press, 2010), 214.

8. Nona Lyons, *Handbook of Reflection and Reflective Inquiry: Mapping a Way of Knowing for Professional Reflective Inquiry* (New York, Springer, 2010), 87.

9. David R. Henderson, *Opportunity Cost*, Library of Economics and Liberty, http://www.econlib.org/library/Enc/OpportunityCost.html, accessed 6-16-12.

10. K. Anders Ericsson, Michael J. Prietula, and Edward T. Cokely, "The Making of an Expert: New research shows that outstanding performance is the product of years of deliberate practice and coaching, not of any innate talent or skill," *Harvard Business Review*, 4, http://hbr.org/2007/07/the-making-of-an-expert/ar/1, accessed 8-27-12.

11. Alison Bonaguro, *Producer Dann Huff: The Man Behind the Hits*, April 22, 2009, http://blog.cmt.com/2009-04-22/producer-dann-huff-the-man-behind-the-hits/, accessed 6-16-12.

12. Bill Appleberry, *Producer/Mixer/Engineer/Songwriter/Musician*, http://www.blog.music180.com/pros/3490, accessed 6-16-12.

13. Ros Earls interview by author, 1994.

14. Ibid.

15. Panel on "Women in Producing" that both Araica and the author participated in at San Francisco University for the 7th Art of Record Production Conference, 12/3/11.

16. Andy Jackson interview by author, 1994.

17. Ibid.

18. Ibid.

19. Alan Moulder interview by author, 1994.

20. Ros Earls interview by author, 1994.

21. The Who scrapped the material from these sessions, rerecording the tracks for *Who's Next* at Olympic Studios in London, with Glyn Johns producing. Told to the author by Chris Charlesworth, The Who's biographer.

22. Aerosmith and Stephen Davis, *Walk This Way: The Autobiography of Aerosmith* (New York: Dogeared, 1997), 209.

23. Paul Tingen, "Benny Blanco: Songwriter & Producer," *Sound On Sound*, June 2012, http://www.soundonsound.com/sos/jun12/articles/benny-blanco.htm, accessed 6-16-12.

24. Helienne Lindvall, *David Guetta: The Man Taking Dance Music into the U.S. Charts*, June 1, 2010, http://www.guardian.co.uk/music/2010/jun/01/david-guetta-dance-music, accessed 9-23-11.

25. Anthony Savona, *Console Confessions: The Great Music Producers in Their Own Words* (San Francisco: Backbeat, 2005), 97.

26. Daniel House, *Jack Endino*, http://www.rocknrolldating.com/interview.php/5, accessed 6-17-12.

27. Camran Afsari, "Jack Endino: The Godfather of Grunge," *Mix*, Dec. 1993, 92.

28. Blair Jackson, "Tucker Martine: Sonic Experiments in the Great Northwest," *Mix*, June 2012, 52–54, 75.

29. Mr. Bonzai, "Russ Titelman: Warner Bro'," *Mix*, Sept. 1994, 119.

30. A single, "And the Sun Will Shine," b/w "The Dog Presides," featuring Jeff Beck on guitar, released by Columbia in 1968.

31. Willie Dixon and Don Snowden, *I Am The Blues: The Willie Dixon Story* (Cambridge, MA: Da Capo, 1989), 78–79.

32. Steven Baker, "ABC Nightline News," Meet Dr. Luke, Pop Music's Maestro, Feb. 17, 2011, http://abcnews.go.com/Entertainment/lukasz-dr-luke-gottwald-produced-songs-britney-spears/story?id=12943564#.UAaozO6iG5J, accessed 7-18-12.

33. Mr. Bonzai, "Lunching with Bonzai: Albhy Galuten," *Mix*, vol. 19, issues 7–12, 1995, 100.

34. Mr. Bonzai, "Tony Visconti: A Brilliant Career," *Mix*, Oct. 1993, 102–107.

35. Matt Schudel, *Mitch Miller, record executive and 'Sing Along' host, dies at 99,* posted Aug. 3, 2010, http://www.washingtonpost.com/wp-dyn/content/article/2010/08/02/AR2010080202954.html, accessed 12-17-11.

36. Gary Marmorstein, *The Label: The Story of Columbia Records* (New York: Thunder's Mouth, 2007), 324.

37. Mr. Bonzai, "Lunching with the Lords: The Lord-Alge Brothers," *Mix*, Sept. 1993, 42.

38. Ibid

39. Personal observation by author.

40. Andy Jackson interview by author, 1994.

41. Quincy Jones and Bill Gibson, *Q On Producing*, (Milwaukee, WI: Hal Leonard, 2010), 25, 28.

42. Mr. Bonzai, "Lunching with the Lords: The Lord-Alge Brothers," *Mix*, Sept. 1993, 42.

43. The Banff Centre, *Judith Sherman Biography,* www.banffcentre.ca/faculty/faculty-member/3541/judith-sherman/, accessed 8-13-12.

44. Masumi podcast, *Producer Judy Sherman,* WGBH, undated, http://www.wgbh.org/programs/Inner-Voice-1821/episodes/Producer-Judy-Sherman-37086, accessed 8-13-12.

45. Marc Prensky, *Digital Natives, Digital Immigrants* (Bingley, UK: MCB University Press), http://www.marcprensky.com/writing/prensky-percent20--percent20digital-percent20natives,-percent20digital-percent20immigrants-percent20--percent20part1.pdf, accessed 8-15-12.

46. Alexander Gilmour, "Masterclass: Joe Boyd," *Financial Times*, Aug. 22, 2012, arts section, 9.

47. Mr. Bonzai, "Lunching with Bonzai: Albhy Galuten," *Mix*, vol. 19, issues 7–12, 1995, 100.

48. Arif Mardin interview by author, 7-28-04.

49. Alexander Gilmour, "Masterclass: Joe Boyd," *Financial Times*, Aug. 22, 2012, arts section, 9.

50. Jeff Chu, "Top of the Pops," *Time Magazine*, March 9, 2001, vol. 157, no. 11.

51. Gail Matthews, "Study Backs up Strategies for Achieving Goals," Dominican University, http://www.dominican.edu/dominicannews/study-backs-up-strategies-for-achieving-goals, accessed 8-27-12.

52. David Nathan, "Quincy Jones: The Producer," *Billboard*, Dec. 16, 1995, 28.

Chapter Three

1. From author's conversation with Padgham's manager Dennis Muirhead, June 21, 2012, New York; confirmed by Richard Buskin, *Sheryl Crow: No Fool to This Game* (New York: Billboard Books, 2003), 68.

2. These overage costs are usually subtracted from the back end (final payment) of the advance or, in some cases, future royalties. Advances are usually paid in stages—often two payments: a front-end payment on signing the contract or beginning the project and a back-end payment on delivery of acceptable masters.

3. Ann Chaitovitz, *Music on the Internet*, Hearing Before the Subcommittee on Courts, the Internet, and Intellectual Property of the Committee on the Judiciary House of Representatives 107th Congress First Session, May 17, 2001, 90 (attended by author).

4. David H. Rosenthal, *Hard Bop: Jazz and Black Music 1955–1965* (New York: Oxford University Press, 1992), 120.

5. Mr. Bonzai, "Barry Beckett: From Muscle Shoals to Nashville," *Mix*, July 1994, 130.

6. Paul Tingen, "Benny Blanco, Songwriter & Producer," *Sound On Sound*, www.soundonsound.com/sos/jun12/articles/benny-blanco.htm, accessed 6-16-12.

7. From Garay's keynote presentation at the Art of Record Production Conference, San Francisco State University, Dec. 3, 2011.

8. Jerry Wexler, "Remembering Ray," *Rolling Stone*, July 8–22, 2004, http://www.rollingstone.com/news/story?id=6214207&rnd=1088673620142&has-player=u\nknown (posted June 16, 2004), accessed 8-27-12.

9. Phil Ward, "Brian Eno Interviews & Articles: Ambient Reflections," *Studio Sound*, Oct. 1995, http://www.moredarkthanshark.org/eno_int_studiosound-oct95.html, accessed 8-12-12.

10. Ibid.

11. Ibid.

12. Andy Jackson interview by author, 1994.

13. Ibid.

14. Anthony Savona, *Console Confessions: The Great Music Producers in Their Own Words* (San Francisco: Backbeat, 2005), 32.

15. Frank Houston and Sir George Martin, http://www.salon.com/2000/07/25/martin_6/, accessed 8-27-12 (quoted from an interview on the promotional site for *In My Life,* Martin's all-star Beatles tribute album).

16. Anthony Savona and Joe Perry, *Console Confessions: The Great Music Producers in Their Own Words* (San Francisco: Backbeat, 2005), 111–112.

17. Anthony Savona and Steven Tyler, *Console Confessions: The Great Music Producers in Their Own Words* (San Francisco: Backbeat, 2005), 117–118.

18. *706 Union Avenue Sessions,* http://www.706unionavenue.nl/64258514, accessed 8-20-12.

19. Rick Clark, "Jim Dickinson: Memphis Maverick," *Mix,* Oct. 1992, 186–187.

20. Andy Jackson interview by author, 1994.

21. Paul Tingen and Kevin 'Caveman' Shirley, "Mixing Led Zeppelin's Live DVD & Recording Iron Maiden," *Sound On Sound,* Nov. 2003, http://www.soundonsound.com/sos/nov03/articles/kevinshirley.htm, accessed 8-16-12.

22. Bruce Swedien and Quincy Jones, *Make Mine Music* (New York: Hal Leonard, 2003), 71–72.

23. Roger Nichols, "Walter Becker," *EQ Magazine,* Dec. 1994, http://www.steelydan.com/eq.html, accessed 8-13-12.

24. Phil Ramone and Charles Granata, *Making Records: The Scenes Behind the Music* (New York: Hyperion, 2007), 8.

25. Eddie Kramer, "My Hendrix Experience," *EQ Magazine,* Nov. 1992.

26. Jimmy Jam, "Dynamic Duo," *EQ Magazine,* Feb. 1993.

27. Steven Tyler, "Not the Same Old Song and Dance," part 2, *EQ Magazine,* March 1993.

28. http://www.the-beatles-history.com/abbey-road.html, accessed 5-26-12.

29. Mr. Bonzai, "Barry Beckett: From Muscle Shoals to Nashville," *Mix,* July 1994, 125.

30. Ibid.

31. David Taylor and Rudy Van Gelder, *Jazz Listener's Guide,* http://dave369.wordpress.com/2009/07/27/rudy-van-gelder/, accessed 12-26-11.

32. Andy Karp, *In Conversation with Rudy Van Gelder,* http://www.jazz.com/features-and-interviews/2009/4/11/in-conversation-with-rudy-van-gelder, accessed 8-17-12.

33. Mr. Bonzai, "Lunching with Bonzai: Albhy Galuten," *Mix,* vol. 19, issues 7–12, 1995, 105.

34. Mr. Bonzai, *Global INXS,* Jan. 1994, 156–158.

35. Alan Moulder interview by author, 1994.

Chapter Four

1. Lauren Christy interview by the author, June 14, 2004.

2. Ibid.

3. Jeff Chu, "Top of the Pops," *TIME,* http://www.time.com/time/magazine/article/0,9171,102126,00.html#ixzz23eOjy5Ig, accessed 8-15-12.

4. Ibid.

5. Matt Popkin, "Dr. Luke: A Pop Star's Best Friend," *American Songwriter,* May 2, 2011, amwww.americansongwriter.com/2011/05/dr-luke-a-pop-stars-best-friend/, accessed 8-15-12.

6. L.A. Reid, "Tag Team: How L.A. Reid and Babyface, another dynamic duo, work it out," *EQ Magazine,* Feb. 1993.

7. Paul Tingen, "Benny Blanco, Songwriter & Producer," *Sound On Sound*, www.soundonsound.com/sos/jun12/articles/benny-blanco.htm, accessed 6-16-12.

8. Paul Zollo, *Songwriters on Songwriting* (Cambridge, MA: Da Capo, 2003), 85, 376, 483.

9. Bob Spitz, *The Beatles: The Biography* (New York: Little, Brown, 2005), 559–561.

10. Philip Tagg, "*Melody and Accompaniment*," *Continuum Encyclopedia of Popular Music of the World*, vol. 2 (London: Continuum, 2003), http://www.tagg.org/articles/xpdfs/melodaccU.S.pdf, accessed 7-4-12.

11. Bud Tower, "Seven-Word Lines and Four-Letter Words: The Science of Songwriting," *American Songwriter*, Sept. 15, 2011, americansongwriter.com/2011/09/seven-word-lines-and-four-letter-words-the-science-of-songwriting/, accessed 8-17-12.

12. Steve Zuckerman, "Beatles Producer George Martin on Record Production: Know What You are Doing Before You Enter the Studio," *MusicDish*, http://www.musicdish.com/mag/index.php3?id=5242, accessed 3-2-12.

13. Ibid.

14. Mr. Bonzai, "Barry Beckett: From Muscle Shoals to Nashville," *Mix*, July 1994, 125.

15. Steven Baker, "Meet Dr. Luke, Pop Music's Maestro," ABC Nightline News, Feb. 17, 2011, http://abcnews.go.com/Entertainment/lukasz-dr-luke-gottwald-produced-songs-britney-spears/story?id=12943564#.UAaozO6iG5J, accessed 7-18-12.

16. Danny Saber interview by author, 1995.

17. "Performance and Production" (s.v. "Arrangement"), *Continuum Encyclopedia of Popular Music of the World* (London: Continuum, 2003), http://ezproxy.aacc.edu/login?url=http://www.credoreference.com.czproxy.aacc.edu/entry/contpmwpp/arrangement, accessed 2-19-12.

18. Steven Baker, "Meet Dr. Luke, Pop Music's Maestro," ABC Nightline News, Feb. 17, 2011, http://abcnews.go.com/Entertainment/lukasz-dr-luke-gottwald-produced-songs-britney-spears/story?id=12943564#.UAaozO6iG5J, accessed 7-18-12.

19. Thomas Alva Edison, "Genius is one percent inspiration, ninety-nine percent perspiration," *Harper's Monthly*, Sept. 1932, http://www.phrases.org.uk/meanings/genius-is-one-percent-perspiration-ninety-nine-percent-perspiration.html, accessed 8-27-12.

20. Nick Armington and Lars Lofas, ed. Barbara Schultz, "Bruce Fairbairn: Vancouver's Sonic Crusader," *Music Producers: Conversations with Today's Top Hit Makers* (Emeryville, CA: Intertec, 2000), 46–47.

21. Nathan Adan Adam, "The Times They Are a Changin': The Impact of Digital Editing Techniques on modern Country Music," Art of Record Production 2006 Conference, Edinburgh University, which the author attended.

22. Chuck Ainlay in conversation with the author, Sept. 29, 2012, New York City.

23. Andy Jackson interview by author, 1994.

24. Ibid.

25. *Encyclopedia of Applied Psychology*, s.v. "Intrinsic and Extrinsic Motivation in Sport," http://ezproxy.aacc.edu/login?url=http://www.credoreference.com.ezproxy.aacc.edu/entry/estappliedpsyc/intrinsic_and_extrinsic_motivation_in_sport, accessed 2-24-12.

26. Rick Clark, "Jim Dickinson: Memphis Maverick," *Mix*, Oct. 1992, 186–187.

27. Marc Salama and James Cote, "Bruce Swedien Interview," http://www.absy.com/ABSMMI/ITV/SWEDIEN/ukitvbsw.html, accessed 8-9-12.

28. Davin Seay, "Quincy Jones: Breaking the Soundtrack Barrier," *Billboard*, Dec 16, 1995, 48.

Chapter Five

1. Pete Townsend, *My Generation* (London: Decca, 1965).

2. Jonathan Saxon, "Dave Jerden," *Tape Op*, issue 86, 2011, http://www.tapeop.com/articles/86/dave-jerden/, accessed 8-11-12.

3. Alan Moulder interview by author, 1994.

4. Ibid.

5. David Guetta in conversation with Gilles Babinet at MIDEM 2011 (author present).

6. Alan Moulder interview by author, 1995.

7. Heraclitus, quoted from Heikki Hyötyniemi, "Emformation Theory: Theory of Emergent (In)Formation," Presentation for Natural Philosophers, Helsinki University of Technology, Nov. 1, 2011. http://neocybernetics.com/publications/pdf/natphi2011.pdf, accessed 12-29-11.

8. http://faculty.evansville.edu/tb2/courses/phil211/burnet/ch3.htm, quote from Heraclitus, accessed 12-29-11.

9. Marc Davis, "Hit music producer's studio for sale in Virginia Beach," *Virginian-Pilot*, Feb. 2, 2008, http://hamptonroads.com/2008/02/hit-music-producers-studio-sale-virginia-beach, accessed 7-6-12.

10. Bob Dylan, *Chronicles: Volume One* (New York: Simon & Schuster, 2004), 15.

11. Danny Saber interview by author, 1994.

Chapter Six

1. Katrina Sirdofsky interview by author, 7-13-04.

2. Danny Saber interview by author, 1994.

3. Lauren Christy interview by author, 6-14-04.

4. Peter Collins interview by author, 6-16-04.

5. Ros Earls interview by author, 1994.

6. Ibid.

7. Sandy Roberton interview by author, 6-2-04.

8. Lauren Christy interview by author, 6-14-04.

9. Sandy Roberton interview by author, 6-2-04.

10. Ibid.

11. Ros Earls interview by author, 1994.

12. Frank Lee, *Sales Is A Numbers Game*, Sales Academy Inc., http://www.irmi.com/expert/articles/2001/lee08.aspx, accessed 12-31-11.

13. Ros Earls interview by author, 1994.

Chapter Seven

1. Bertolt Brecht, English version by Eric Bentley, *Mother Courage and Her Children*, (New York: Grove, 1996), scene 3, 43.

2. Mutt Lange, *Robert John Mutt Lange Interviews*, http://www.muttlange.com/robert_john_mutt_lange_interview_exclusive_interviews/mutt_lange.html, accessed 3-2-12.

3. Jon Caramanica, "Pitched to Perfection: Pop Star's Silent Partner," *New York Times*, June 29, 2012, http://www.nytimes.com/2012/06/30/arts/music/kuk-harrell-justin-biebers-vocal-producer.html?pagewanted=all.

4. Davin Seay, "Quincy Jones: The Billboard Interview," *Billboard*, Dec. 16, 1995, 48.

5. Ibid., 50.

6. Alan Moulder interview by author, 1994.

7. Ibid.

8. Phil Ramone and Charles L. Granata, *Making Records: The Scenes Behind the Music* (New York: Hyperion, 2007), 155.

9. J. Randy Taraborrelli, *Call Her Miss Ross: The Unauthorized Biography of Diana Ross* (Secaucus, NJ: Carol, 1989).

10. Benny Blanco conversation with the author, 11-10-12.

11. Jon Caramanica, "Pitched to Perfection: Pop Star's Silent Partner," *New York Times*, June 29, 2012, http://www.nytimes.com/2012/06/30/arts/music/kuk-harrell-justin-biebers-vocal-producer.html?pagewanted=all, accessed 8-21-12.

12. Camran Afsari, "Jack Endino: The Godfather of Grunge," *Mix*, Dec. 1993, 91.

13. Alan Moulder interview by author, 1994.

14. Ibid.

15. Peter Collins interview by author, 4-16-04.

16. Andy Jackson interview by author, 1994.

17. Ibid.

18. Mr. Bonzai, "Al Schmitt: The Unforgettable Touch," *Mix*, Oct. 1993, 298.

19. Ibid.

20. Benji B, "Tony Visconti: Be sure he knows what he's talking about–Part 2," Red Bull Music Academy, http://www.redbullmusicacademy.com/lectures/tony-visconti-2, accessed 4-14-12.

21. Shaheem Reid, *How Scott Storch's Cocaine Addiction Made Him Spend $30 Million in Six Months—Miami hit producer is back after almost losing everything to drug addiction*, posted June 11, 2009, http://www.mtv.com/news/articles/1613761/scott-storchs-rise-fall-return.jhtml, accessed 2-09-12.

22. Mike Clink conversation with the author, 9-29-12, New York City.

23. Signe Whitson, "Passive Aggressive Diaries: Understanding passive aggressive behavior in families, schools, and workplaces," PsychologyToday.com, http://www.psychologytoday.com/blog/passive-aggressive-diaries/201003/revenge-counter-passive-aggression-in-families-schools, updated March 25, 2010, accessed 9-14-12.

24. Jake Lawson, "Eliminating Passive Aggressiveness," LiveStrong.com, http://www.livestrong.com/article/14713-eliminating-passive-aggressiveness/#ixzz26STSeXxO, updated Aug. 11, 2011, accessed 9-14-12.

25. Daniel Goleman, *Emotional Intelligence: Why It Can Matter More than IQ* (New York: Bantam, 1995), 14, 25.

26. Daniel Goleman, *Working with Emotional Intelligence* (New York: Bantam, 2000), 74.

27. Shel Horowitz, "Emotional Intelligence—Stop Amygdala Hijackings," UMass Family Business Center, http://www.umass.edu/fambiz/articles/values_culture/primal_leadership.html, accessed 7-13-12.

28. *Conflict Resolution,* Office of Human Resource Development, University of Wisconsin, http://www.ohrd.wisc.edu/onlinetraining/resolution/index.asp, accessed 9-14-12.

Chapter Eight

1. "The Truth about the Billable Hour," http://www.law.yale.edu/documents/pdf/CDO_Public/cdo-billable_hour.pdf, accessed 9-14-12.

2. Carol Crabtree conversation with the author, 1995.

Chapter Nine

1. Walter R. Reitman, *Cognition and Thought* (New York: Wiley, 1965), quoting from James W. Wilson, Maria L. Fernandez, and Nelda Hadaway, *Mathematical Problem Solving*, University of Georgia, http://jwilson.coe.uga.edu/emt725/PSsyn/Pssyn.html, accessed 7-15-12.

2. Mr. Bonzai, "Tony Visconti: A Brilliant Career," *Mix*, Oct. 1993, 301.

3. Andy Jackson interview by author, 1994.

4. Ibid.

5. Ibid.

6. Ibid.

7. Steven Savage, "'It could have happened'—the evolution of music construction," originally presented at the 2008 Art of Record Production Conference, University of Massachusetts, Lowell, MA, Nov. 14–16, 2008, http://www.artofrecordproduction.com/content/view/175/109/, accessed 7-15-12.

8. Andy Jackson interview by author, 1994.

9. Val Garay statement during plenary presentation at the Art of Record Production Conference, 2011, San Francisco State University, 12-3-11.

10. Peter Collins interview with the author, 4-16-04.

11. Mr. Bonzai, "Tony Visconti: A Brilliant Career," *Mix*, Oct. 1993, 301.

12. Mara Mather, Eldar Shafir, and Marcia K. Johnson, "Remembering chosen and assigned options," *Memory & Cognition*, 2003, 31 (3), 422–433, http://memlab0.eng.yale.edu/PDFs/2003_Mather_Shafir_Johnson_MemCog.pdf, accessed 7-16-12.

13. Benny Blanco conversation with the author, 11-10-12.

14. Andy Jackson interview by author, 1994.

15. Steven Baker, "Meet Dr. Luke, Pop Music's Maestro," ABC Nightline News, posted Feb. 17, 2011, http://abcnews.go.com/Entertainment/lukasz-dr-luke-gottwald-produced-songs-britney-spears/story?id=12943564#.UAaozO6iG5J, accessed 7-18-12.

16. Mr. Bonzai, "Tony Visconti: A Brilliant Career," *Mix*, Oct. 1993, 130.

17. Blair Jackson, "Ken Scott: New Memoir Sheds Light on an Exceptional Career," *Mix*, vol. 36, no.7, July 2012, 45.

18. Mickie Most, possibly urban legend but heard through the London studio-musician network in the '70s.

19. Ros Earls, interview by author.

20. Billie Holiday and Arthur Herzog Jr., *"God Bless the Child"* (New York: Carlin America, 1939).

Chapter Ten

1. Ros Earls interview by author, 1994.

2. The Performance Rights Act, http://www.grammy.org/recording-academy/producers-and-engineers/advocacy, accessed 2-12-12.

3. Ed Christman, "Exclusive: Clear Channel, Big Machine Strike Deal to Pay Sound-Recording Performance Royalties to Label, Artists," *Billboard*, June 5, 2012, http://www.billboard.biz/bbbiz/industry/legal-and-management/exclusive-clear-channel-big-machine-strike-1007226762.story, accessed 7-20-12.

4. Christine Y. Chen, "The Bad Boys of Radio, Lowry Mays and sons, made enemies building Clear Channel into an empire. Now they want to tell the world they're not...," *Fortune*, March 3, 2003, http://money.cnn.com/magazines/fortune/fortune_archive/2003/03/03/338343/index.htm, accessed 2-12-12.

5. "The Nielsen Company & *Billboard*'s 2011 Music Industry Report," *Business Wire*, Jan. 5, 2012, http://www.businesswire.com/news/home/20120105005547/en/Nielsen-Company-Billboard-percentE2-percent80-percent99s-2011-Music-Industry-Report, accessed 9-16-12.

6. Camran Afsari, "Steve Albini: Nemesis of Corporate Rock," *Mix*, March 1994, 110.

7. Ibid.

8. Andy Jackson interview by author, 1994.

9. Martin E. P. Seligman and Steven F. Maier, "Failure to escape traumatic shock," *Journal of Experimental Psychology* 74 (1967), 1–9.

10. Story told in keynote speech by Pete Waterman at the Art of Record Production Conference, University of Glamorgan, UK, 2009 (author present).

11. Pete Ganbarg interview by author, 4-16-04.

12. Producer Grammy® Award Eligibility, Crediting Definitions (approved May 2008), http://www.grammy.org/files/pages/Producer_Definitions.pdf, accessed 2-27-12.

13. Ibid.

14. Arif Mardin interview by author, 2004.

15. Mr. Bonzai, "Russ Titelman: Warner Bro'," *Mix*, Sept. 1994, 116.

16. Paragraph contributed by Who biographer Chris Charlesworth (editor of the first three editions of this book).

17. Sean Michaels, "Lil Wayne sued for half A Milli, Incarcerated rapper facing another lawsuit for unpaid royalties, with producer Bangladesh claiming he is owed $500,000," *Guardian*, May 6, 2010, www.guardian.co.uk/music/2010/may/06/lil-wayne-sued-producer, accessed 7-22-12.

18. Ibid.

Chapter Eleven

1. Containing material adapted from a paper by Katia Isakoff and Richard James Burgess, "Women in Music Production: Education, Representation and Practice," presented at the Art of Record Production Conference, San Francisco, 12-3-11.

2. Katia Isakoff, e-mail interview with Marcella Araica, Oct. 2011.

3. Adapted from a paper by Katia Isakoff and Richard James Burgess, "Women in Music Production: Education, Representation and Practice," presented at the Art of Record Production Conference, San Francisco, 12-3-11.

4. Jennifer M. Brown, "*De-gendering the electronic soundscape: Women, power and technology in contemporary music*," Southern Cross University, Lismore, NSW, AU (masters thesis), (1996), citing S. D. Potts (1994), "Women in Audio: The TechNet Survey," *EQ Magazine* (May 1993), 57.

5. Francis J. Dance, "Helen Oakley Dance: Writer, producer, publicist," Jazzhouse. org, updated 2001, http://www.jazzhouse.org/gone/lastpost2.php3?edit=991165404, accessed 7-23-12.

6. "Helen Keane: Biography," Jan. 1992. http://www.pitt.edu/~pittjazz/individual_htmls/helen_keane.html.

7. "Joan Deary and Elvis Presley," Elvis Australia website, www.elvis.com.au, updated April 18, 2012, http://www.elvis.com.au/presley/joan_deary_and_elvis_presley. shtml, accessed 5-4-12.

8. Wendy Page interview by author, 7-6-04.

9. Ibid.

10. Linda Perry interview by the author, 7-31-04.

11. Ibid.

12. Ibid.

13. Cathy Fink interview with the author.

14. Kylee Swenson, "Wide-Open Spaces," *Remix*, vol. 5, no. 12, Dec. 2003, 41.

Chapter Twelve

1. Bill Breen, "What's Your Intuition?" *Fast Company*, posted Aug. 31, 2000, http:// www.fastcompany.com/magazine/38/klein.html?page=0-percent2C1, accessed 2-25-12.

2. Ibid.

3. K. Anders Ericsson, Michael J. Prietula, and Edward T. Cokely, "The Making of an Expert: New research shows that outstanding performance is the product of years of deliberate practice and coaching, not of any innate talent or skill," *Harvard Business Review* 6, http://hbr.org/2007/07/the-making-of-an-expert/ar/1, accessed 8-27-12.

4. Ibid., 4.

5. Richard Buskin, "Classic Tracks: Les Paul & Mary Ford 'How High The Moon,'" *Sound On Sound*, posted Jan. 2007, http://www.soundonsound.com/sos/jan07/articles/classictracks_0107.htm, accessed 2-24-12.

6. Kylee Swenson, "Wide-Open Spaces," *Remix*, vol. 5, no. 12, Dec. 2003, 39.

7. Richard Buskin, "Racking Up the Hits," *Studio Sound*, Aug. 1998, 45.

8. Sandy Roberton interview by author, 6-24-04.

9. Sourced from McGraw-Hill Online Learning Center. Original source: Friedrich von Wieser, *Social Economics*, trans. A. Ford Hinrichs (New York: Adelphi, 1927 [1914]), 99–100, http://highered.mcgraw-hill.com/sites/0070886695/student_view0/chapter2/origin_of_the_idea.html, accessed 7-22-12.

10. Nick Armington and Lars Lofas, ed. Barbara Schultz, "Bruce Fairbairn," *Music Producers: Conversations with Today's Top Hit Makers* (Emeryville, CA: Intertec, 2000), 46–47.

11. Mr. Bonzai, "Barry Beckett: From Muscle Shoals to Nashville," *Mix*, July 1994, 125.

12. Davin Seay, "Quincy Jones: Record Making Executive," *Billboard*, Dec. 16, 1995, 38.

13. George Martin with Jeremy Hornsby, *All You Need Is Ears: The Inside Personal Story of the Genius Who Created the Beatles* (New York: St. Martin's, 1979), 183–184.

14. Mel Lambert, "George Martin," *Electronic Musician*, posted Jan. 7, 2009, http:// www.emusician.com/news/0766/george-martin/134697, accessed 7-30-12.

15. George Martin with Jeremy Hornsby, *All You Need Is Ears: The Inside Personal Story of the Genius Who Created the Beatles* (New York: St. Martin's, 1979), 184–186.

16. Richard Cromelin, "Arif Mardin, 74; Record Producer and Arranger Had Hits over 4 Decades," *Los Angeles Times*, obituaries, June 27, 2006.

17. Interview by author, 7-28-04.

18. Doug Minnick, "Ron Fair, Senior VP of A&R, West Coast, RCA Records," undated, http://www.taxi.com/music-business-faq/ar/fair.html, accessed 3-3-12.

19. Arif Mardin interview by author, 1994.

20. As told by Muff Winwood in conversation with the author, 1993.

21. Steve Zuckerman, "Beatles Producer George Martin on Record Production: Know What You Are Doing Before You Enter the Studio…," *MusicDish*, posted Feb. 7, 2002, http://www.musicdish.com/mag/index.php3?id=5242, accessed 3-2-12.

22. Rick Clark, "Gehman's New Budget Multiplatinums," *Billboard*, July 15, 1995, 76.

23. Calvin Gilbert, "Sun Records Founder Sam Phillips Dies," *CMT News*, July 31, 2003, http://www.cmt.com/news/country-music/1475109/sun-records-founder-sam-phillips-dies.jhtml, accessed 7-30-12.

24. "Doug Morris: Record company executive, songwriter, and producer," *Encyclopedia of World Biography*, http://www.notablebiographies.com/newsmakers2/2005-La-Pr/Morris-Doug.html#ixzz227Zc8oxF, accessed 7-30-12.

25. Jim Dickinson, Zebra Ranch: Production Manifesto, http://zebraranch.com/manifesto.htm, accessed 5-17-13.

26. Arif Mardin interview by author, 7-28-04.

27. Mr. Bonzai, "Lunching with the Lords: The Lord-Alge Brothers," *Mix*, Sept. 1993, 39.

28. Doug Minnick, "Ron Fair, Senior VP of A&R, West Coast, RCA Records," undated, http://www.taxi.com/music-business-faq/ar/fair.html, accessed 3-3-12.

29. Conversation with Tim Palmer, 3-15-13.

30. Linda Perry interview by author, 4-16-04.

31. Lauren Christy interview by author, 6-14-04.

32. Ibid.

33. Wendy Page interview by author, 7-6-04.

34. Sandy Roberton interview by author, 6-2-04.

35. Mara Mather, Eldar Shafir, and Marcia K. Johnson, "Remembering chosen and assigned options," *Memory & Cognition* 31(3), 2003, 422–433. http://memlab0.eng.yale.edu/PDFs/2003_Mather_Shafir_Johnson_MemCog.pdf, accessed 7-16-12.

36. Mr. Bonzai, "Tony Visconti: A Brilliant Career," *Mix*, Oct. 1993, 131.

37. Ibid.

38. Said on a panel with the author at SXSW, 3-15-13

39. Mr. Bonzai, "Lunching with the Lords: The Lord-Alge Brothers," *Mix*, Sept. 1993, 41.

40. Ibid., 42.

41. Dave Lockwood, "Bob Clearmountain: Master Mixer," *Sound On Sound*, June 1999, http://www.soundonsound.com/sos/jun99/articles/bobclear.htm, accessed 8-12-12.

42. Ibid.

43. Paul Tingen, "Secrets of the Mix Engineers: Jack Joseph Puig," *Sound On Sound*, Nov. 2007, http://www.soundonsound.com/sos/nov07/articles/insidetrack_1107.htm, accessed 8-12-12.

44. Ibid.

45. Pete Ganbarg interview by author, 4-16-04.

46. Ibid.

47. Ibid.

48. Ibid.

49. Conversation between Muff Winwood and the author circa 1993.

50. James Boyk, "There's Life Above 20 Kilohertz! A Survey of Musical Instrument Spectra to 102.4 KHz," 1992, http://www.cco.caltech.edu/~boyk/spectra/spectra.htm, accessed 7-30-12.

51. "Dynamic Range of Hearing," http://hyperphysics.phy-astr.gsu.edu/Hbase/sound/earsens.html, accessed 7-30-12.

Chapter Thirteen

1. "Pop to the rescue of the music industry," Music & Copyright's Blog, posted June 13, 2012, http://musicandcopyright.wordpress.com/2012/06/13/pop-to-the-rescue-of-the-music-industry/#more-804, accessed 8-6-12.

2. "About Telarc: Telarc and the Dawn of Digital," http://www.telarc.com/about/Digital.aspx, accessed 8-13-12.

3. Michelle Ryang, "Michael Torke: An Interview," http://www.classical.net/music/comp.lst/articles/torke/interview.php, accessed 3-4-12.

4. Thomas May, "The Producer: Legendary producer Steven Epstein on the art and science of making records sound right," *Listen Music Magazine*, http://www.listenmusic-mag.com/music-in-my-life/the-producer.php.

5. Ibid.

6. Ibid.

7. Heather Johnson, "Orrin Keepnews," *Performing Songwriter*, issue 73, Nov. 2003, http://performingsongwriter.com/orrin-keepnews/, accessed 8-10-12.

8. Ibid.

9. Ibid.

10. "Famed producer now operates his own office," *Nashville City Paper*, Sept. 23, 2007, http://nashvillecitypaper.com/content/city-business/famed-producer-now-operates-his-own-office, accessed 8-6-12.

11. "Tim McGraw biography," http://www.curb.com/artists/tm/tmbio2.html.

12. "About R&J Records," http://www.randjrecords.com/index.cfm?id=3, accessed 8-6-12.

13. Dan Daley, ed. Barbara Schultz, "James Stroud," *Music Producers: Conversations with Today's Top Hit Makers* (Emeryville, CA: Intertec, 2000), 162 (originally sourced from *Mix*, June 1993).

14. Jimmy Bowen, "Nashville Here They Come," *EQ Magazine*, April 1992.

15. Dan Sheehy interview by author, 2003.

16. Ibid.

17. Ibid.

18. Ibid.

19. Ibid.

20. Ibid.

21. Ibid.

22. Ibid.

23. Ibid.

24. Ibid.

25. Marcy Marxer and Cathy Fink interview by author, 2004.

26. Ibid.

27. Ibid.

28. Ibid.

29. Ibid.

30. Ibid.

31. Ibid.

32. Ibid.

33. Ibid.

34. Ibid.

35. Ibid.

36. Ibid.

37. Ibid.

38. Ibid.

39. Ibid.

40. Ibid.

41. Ibid.

42. Marc Shapiro, *Creed: From Zero to Platinum* (New York: St. Martin's, 2000), 56–60.

43. Mr. Bonzai, "Producer's Desk John Alagia," *Mix*, updated Aug. 1, 2005, mixonline.com/mag/audio_john_alagia/, accessed 3-8-12.

44. Chris McKay, "John Mayer Full-Length Interview," recorded Jan. 25, 2002, http://concertshots.com/john_mayer_full-percent20interview-percent2012502.htm, accessed 3-8-12.

Chapter Fourteen

1. Public data, http://www.google.com/publicdata/explore?ds=d5bncppjof8f9_&met_y=sp_pop_totl&tdim=true&dl=en&hl=en&q=current+world+population, accessed 8-2-12.

2. Martin Walker, "The World's New Numbers," *Wilson Quarterly*, Spring 2009, http://www.wilsonquarterly.com/article.cfm?aid=1408, accessed 8-2-12.

3. Sarah Perez, "The Number of Mobile Devices Will Exceed World's Population by 2012 (& Other Shocking Figures)," http://techcrunch.com/2012/02/14/the-number-of-mobile-devices-will-exceed-worlds-population-by-2012-other-shocking-figures/, accessed 7-2-12.

4. Martin Gitlin, *The Baby Boomer Encyclopedia* (Santa Barbara, CA: ABC-CLIO), 2011, 96; Kyle Anderson, "Michael Jackson's *Thriller* Set to Become Top-Selling Album of All Time, RIAA says Jackson classic is poised to surpass Eagles' greatest-hits collection in U.S. sales," www.mtv.com/news/articles/1616537/thriller-set-overtake-eagles-top-selling, July 20, 2009.

5. Eric McLuhan, "McLuhan Studies: Issue 2, The source of the term 'Global Village,'" http://projects.chass.utoronto.ca/mcluhan-studies/v1_iss2/1_2art2.htm, accessed 8-2-12.

6. William Grimes, "Obituaries: Raymond Scott, 85, a Composer for Cartoons and the Stage, Dies," *New York Times*, posted Feb. 9, 1994, http://www.nytimes.com/1994/02/09/obituaries/raymond-scott-85-a-composer-for-cartoons-and-the-stage-dies.html, accessed 3-9-12.

7. "The 'Wall of Sound,' an electro-mechanical sequencer designed & built by Raymond Scott, 1950s," http://oldsite.raymondscott.com/1946.htm, accessed 3-9-12.

8. Ian Peel, "Trevor Horn: 25 Years of Hits," *Sound On Sound*, March 2005, http://www.soundonsound.com/sos/mar05/articles/trevorhorn.htm, accessed 3-9-12.

9. This was prior to the release of Roger Linn's LM1 machine.

10. *SSL 4000G Console Operator's Manual 1-2*, belmont-studios.org/index.php?.../SSL.../SSLConsoleChap1.pdf, accessed 3-9-12.

11. Christian Hudspeth, "50 Quotes from the Wealthiest Man in America," *Investing Answers*, posted July 14, 2011, http://www.investinganswers.com/education/famous-investors/50-quotes-wealthiest-man-america-3088, accessed 8-11-12.

12. Robert Mills, "My Ever Changing Moogs," *Q Magazine*, issue 118, July 1996, http://www.eno-web.co.uk/interviews/qmag96b.html, accessed 3-10-12.

13. Rick Moody, "Returning to the Sound of Those Golden Years," *New York Times*, Sept. 10, 1995, http://www.nytimes.com/books/97/04/27/reviews/moody-bowie.html.

14. "Kurt Cobain Bio," http://www.moono.com/html/kurt-cobain/kurt-cobain-biography.cfm, accessed 3-10-12.

15. Alexander Tudor, "Radiohead re-issues: new editions of Kid A, Amnesiac and Hail to the Thief assessed," *Drowned in Sound*, updated August 27, 2009, http://drownedinsound.com/in_depth/4137663-radiohead-re-issues—new-editions-of-kid-a-amnesiac-and-hail-to-the-thief-assessed, accessed 8-27-12.

16. At IRCAM in Paris and Stanford University in California, among others.

17. "There's nothing on it worthwhile, and we're not going to watch it in this household, and I don't want it in your intellectual diet," quote from Kent Farnsworth, son of the inventor of television, Philo T. Farnsworth, in summation of his father's view of what television had become, http://www.byhigh.org/History/Farnsworth/PhiloT1924.html, accessed 3-10-12.

18. "Justin Bieber biography," A&E Television Networks, posted 2012, http://www.biography.com/people/justin-bieber-522504, accessed 3-10-12.

19. Big Data: The New Oil or the New Snake Oil?, panel at SXSW 2013, 3-16-13.

20. Thomas Whisler, *Christian Science Monitor*, April 21, 1964, 61, quoted from *The Big Book of Business Quotations: More Than 5,000 Indispensable Observations on Commerce, Work, Finance and Management* (Cambridge, UK: Bloomsbury, 2003), 61.

21. Tom Roland, "Nashville's New Wave," *Billboard*, Dec. 10, 2011, 10–11.

22. Tom Doyle, "Foo Fighters: Recording *Wasting Light*," *Sound On Sound*, June 2011, http://www.soundonsound.com/sos/jun11/articles/foo-fighters.htm, accessed 8-3-12.

23. Mr. Bonzai, "Tony Visconti: A Brilliant Career," *Mix*, Oct. 1993, 301.

24. Conversation with the National Steering Committee of the Producer and Engineer Wing of the Recording Academy, 3-21-13 (of which the author is a member).

25. "IFPI publishes Digital Music Report 2009," posted Jan. 16, 2009, http://www.ifpi.org/content/section_resources/dmr2009.html, accessed 3-16-12.

26. http://www.measuringworth.com/uscompare/relativevalue.php, accessed 3-16-12; http://www.courierpress.com/news/2008/mar/05/looking-back-at-cost-of-living-in-the-sixties/,

accessed 8-3-12; "Money and Inflation 1960s," http://www.thepeoplehistory.com/1960s. html#cost_of_living, accessed 8-3-12.

27. Matt Marshall, "They did it! YouTube bought by Google for $1.65B in less than two years," *Venture Beat News*, posted Oct. 9, 2006, http://venturebeat.com/2006/10/09/they-did-it-youtube-gets-bought-by-gooogle-for-165b-in-less-than-two-years/, accessed 8-3-12.

28. 2011 Year-End Shipment Statistics, RIAA, http://76.74.24.142/FA8A2072-6BF8-D44D-B9C8-CE5F55BBC050.pdf, accessed 8-3-12.

29. Dave McQuown, "Radio, The Chicago School of Media Theory, 2012," citing Jim Cox, *Music Radio: The Great Performers and Programs or the 1920s through Early 1960s* (Jefferson, NC: McFarland, 2005), 145.

30. "FM Radio & the Counterculture," *Revolutions in Radio*, http://www.revolution-sinradio.com/fm.html, accessed 8-3-12, citing Susan J. Douglas, *Listening In: Radio and the American Imagination, From Amos 'n' Andy and Edward R. Murrow to Wolfman Jack and Howard Stern* (New York: Times Books, 1999), 263.

31. Author's conversation with George Massenburg, July 12, 2012.

32. Conversation between the author and major label senior executive, Sept. 28, 2012.

33. Author's conversation with George Massenburg, July 12, 2012.

34. Arthur Hafner, *Pareto's Principle: The 80-20 Rule* ("Pareto's rule states that a small number of causes is responsible for a large percentage of the effect, in a ratio of about 20:80. Expressed in a management context, 20 percent of a person's effort generates 80 percent of the person's results. The corollary to this is that 20 percent of one's results absorb 80 percent of one's resources or efforts"), Ball State University, updated March 31, 2001, http://www.bsu.edu/libraries/ahafner/awh-th-math-pareto.html, accessed 3-16-12.

35. Paul Resnikoff, "Spotify CEO: Profitability Is Absolutely Not a Priority...," April 13, 2012, http://www.digitalmusicnews.com/permalink/2012/120413spotify, accessed 8-4-12.

36. Conversation with the author at MIDEM, Cannes, France, Jan. 2012.

37. Ben Sisario, "Eminem Lawsuit May Raise Pay for Older Artists," March 27, 2011, *New York Times*, http://www.nytimes.com/2011/03/28/business/media/28eminem. html?pagewanted=all, accessed 3-16-12

38. "Digital music report 2009—quotes," http://www.ifpi.org/content/library/ DMR2009-quotes.pdf, accessed 3-25-12.

39. Ann Chaitovitz, Music on the Internet, Hearing Before the Subcommittee on Courts, the Internet, and Intellectual Property of the Committee on the Judiciary House of Representatives 107th Congress First Session, May 17, 2001, 90.

40. "Indie Artist Makes $4.2 Million in 2008," *New Rockstar Philosophy*, Dec. 22, 2008, NewRockstarPhilosophy, accessed 3-17-12.

41. Alex Blumberg, "An Internet Rock Star Tells All," *Planet Money*, May 13, 2011, http://www.npr.org/blogs/money/2011/05/14/136279162/an-internet-rock-star-tells-all, accessed 3-17-12.

42. Matt Rosoff, "TuneCore ties up with world's largest record label: A new deal between TuneCore and Universal Music Group Distribution could spell more opportunity for independent musicians," CNet News, July 9, 2009, http://news.cnet.com/8301-13526_3-10283224-27.html?tag=mncol;txt, accessed 3-19-12.

43. Nielsen SoundScan U.S. Venue Sales Procedure, http://nielsen.com/content/dam/ corporate/us/en/public-percent20factsheets/Soundscan/Soundscan-U.S.-Sales-Procedure. pdf, accessed 3-18-12.

44. "What the Pros Say about SoundScan and Live Venue Reporting," *Indie Hitmaker*, updated 2011, http://www.indiehitmaker.com/Indiehitmaker_Testimonials.html, accessed 3-18-12.

45. Ibid.

46. Billboard.biz chart search results, http://www.billboard.biz/bbbiz/charts/chart-search-results/1?orderBy=chartDate&orderType=a, accessed 8-27-12; "Atlanta Rockers, State Of Man, Tops Billboard Magazines Hot Singles Chart!" http://top40-charts.com/news.php?nid=24977, accessed 8-27-12.

47. "What the Pros Say about SoundScan and Live Venue Reporting" *Indie Hitmaker*, http://www.indiehitmaker.com/Indiehitmaker_Testimonials.html, accessed 3-18-12.

48. Ibid.

Conclusion

1. Teo Macero, "Teo Macero on Working with John Hammond and on *The Graduate* Soundtrack," http://www.artistshousemusic.org/videos/teo+macero+on+working+with+john+hammond+and+on+the+graduate+soundtrack, accessed 12-17-11.

2. Eds. Aviezer Tucker and Elazar Weinryb, "Historiographic Counterfactuals," in *A Companion to the Philosophy of History and Historiography* (Oxford, UK: Blackwell, 2009), 109–118.

3. David Nathan, "Quincy Jones: The Producer," *Billboard*, Dec. 16, 1995, 28.

GLOSSARY

A2IM American Association for Independent Music

A&R Artist and repertoire—the department in a record company that signs artists and supervises the making of records.

AAC Advanced audio coding—a lossy digital compression algorithm. Generally considered to be better quality than MP3s at comparable bit rates. Adopted by Apple for iTunes files.

A-D, A-to-D, A/D, ADC Analog-to-digital converters

ADSR Attack, decay, sustain, release, usually in reference to the sound-shaping module of a synthesizer.

adds An "add" in radio promotion means that a radio station has added a track to their official playlist. The number of adds is the number of stations that are playing the track on a regular basis. Stations can have several levels of playlists, which can relate to light, medium, and heavy rotations.

advance Money paid by a record company or publisher to an artist or writer in anticipation of sales. The advance is recouped from future royalties.

A.E.S. Audio Engineering Society

AFM American Federation of Musicians

album A collection of tracks on vinyl, cassette, CD, in the digital domain, or future format.

alternative Typically guitar-based rock, also known as indie rock and modern rock, which grew in response to the mainstream rock of the 1970s. During the '90s, alternative rock became a mainstream format.

AM Amplitude modulation

ambience The acoustic characteristics of a real or imaginary space in which a sound occurs.

analog or analogue In the case of recorded music, audio that is represented by a continuously variable electrical signal.

analog or analogue console An audio mixer with input and output channels that uses analog technology (as opposed to digital). Also known as a board, recording console, or desk (U.K.).

arrangement The adaptation of a piece of music for performance by a particular set of voices or instruments.

ASCAP The American Society of Composers, Authors and Publishers, a U.S. performing rights organization, www.ascap.com

B2B Business to business

B2C Business to consumer

B.B.C. British Broadcasting Corporation

BDS Broadcast Data System—collects airplay data off the air from U.S. radio stations.

big band Large dance or jazz band sometimes featuring vocalists and improvised instrumental solos.

Billboard Weekly U.S. music industry trade magazine, www.billboard.com

bit Short for binary bit, it refers to the smallest unit of data with a value of 0 or 1. In music, often seen in the context of 16-bit or 24-bit, the bit depth or number of bits recorded for each sample. In practical terms, it designates the dynamic range or signal-to-noise ratio. 16-bit audio has a theoretical maximum S/N of 96dB, and 24-bit has 144dB. As a guideline, each increase in bit depth of 1 represents an additional 6dB in S/N.

BMI Broadcast Music, Inc. is a U.S. performing rights organization, www.bmi.com

board U.S. term for an audio mixer with input and output channels. Also known as a console, recording console, or desk (U.K.).

business manager Professional who helps the artist with tax matters, monitoring of income from contracts, and other financial matters. Preferably a different person than the personal manager who oversees the artist's general career strategies and day-to-day activities.

caesura or cesura Musical term meaning a complete pause of the music. Designated by two parallel lines known as railroad tracks or tramlines. Mostly used in non-popular music and differing from a stop in that the meter is not counted through a caesura.

C.C.I.R./I.E.C. Comité Consultatif International des Radio Communications

channel The end-to-end transmission path connecting any two points in which specific equipment is connected.

chorus Modulated delays that can add a sense of depth or thickness to a sound.

class A circuitry Considered to be the best-sounding circuitry, it is an active device such as a vacuum tube or transistor biased to conduct through the whole of the waveform, giving the best possible linearity at the expense of efficiency.

Clear Channel The largest single corporate owner of radio stations in the U.S. They also own and operate billboards, venues, and promote concerts.

codecs Short for compressor/decompressor, any technology for compressing and decompressing data.

compression The automatic reduction of output gain by a variable amount when the input begins to exceed some preset maximum.

console A device used to modify and blend audio signals. Also known as a board, recording console, or desk (U.K.).

controlled composition A composition that the artist or producer wrote, usually used in conjunction with a royalty-reducing provision that contractually reduces the mechanical rate for a songwriter/producer (or artist) and publisher on songs written or otherwise "controlled" by them.

copyrights The rights that permit the various owner(s) of a musical work to restrict others from reproducing, displaying, performing, or distributing that work.

CPA A certified public accountant is a person who has passed the Uniform Certified Public Accountant Exam and met state educational and certification requirements.

cross-patch or cross-patching Using the patchbay to move audio from its "normal" position to a different or more convenient one on the console. Most studios have the multitrack recording device "normaled" to the console so that track 1 comes up on channel 1 and so forth. This might, for instance, position the drums at the far left of the console, and the producer or engineer may prefer them nearer the center for the mix and thus "cross-patch" them. DAWs allow dragging and dropping of tracks for repositioning, and digital consoles are digitally re-assignable, making physical cross-patching much less common today.

cut As in "let's cut a take," same derivation as cutting.

cutout bins Dump bins or "for sale" bins in record stores containing low-priced cutouts.

cutouts CDs, cassettes, or LPs marked, notched, drilled, or punched to prevent them from being resold or returned at full value. The record company is usually, by contract, not obligated to pay artist or producer royalties on cutouts. The term comes from a customary method of cutting a slot (~1/8" x 1/8") in the rear spine of the packaging.

cutting These days a generic term usually used to mean "make a recording." It dates back to the days of vinyl, 78s, and cylinders when the music was encoded into the media using a cutting lathe. In the vinyl mastering process, the lathe uses a slightly heated sapphire- or diamond- tipped stylus that etches the groove into a soft oil-based lacquer.

D-to-A, D/A, D-A, DAC Digital-to-analog converters.

Deal Short for record deal—a contract to make an album for a record label.

delay A single or multiple discrete echo that can occur naturally by reflection off of a hard surface or be created by analog or digital signal processing. Delays form the basis of many other effects such as filters, reverbs, and flangers, and can also be used to synchronize out-of-phase signals. Delay can also be the unwanted byproduct of other acoustic or electronic signal processes.

demos Low-budget recordings created as rough sketches of the final audio production.

desk U.K. term for an audio mixing console. Also known as a board, recording console, or console.

digital Digital recording technology utilizes information encoded using binary code of zeroes and ones—discrete, non-continuous values—to represent the audio information.

digital formats Recording formats that use digital technology as opposed to analog.

Digital Millennium Copyright Act (DMCA) Provides for revenue for sound recording copyright holders from digital cable, satellite, and online transmissions.

digital workstations, digital audio workstations, DAWs Self-contained computer-based recording devices using digital technology.

discrete A discrete circuit is an electronic circuit comprised of individual components such as transistors, capacitors, and resistors, unlike integrated circuits (ICs) where all the parts are contained within one chip.

distorted Used to describe a sound that contains distortion (see below).

distortion Any change, during recording or playback, of an audio waveform from that of the original wave form. Usually used to describe an overdriven sound that occurs when an audio signal is pushed above nominal limits for the device it is driving.

DMCA See Digital Millennium Copyright Act

double opt-in Where a user has requested a subscription and separately confirmed their e-mail address. Usually done by checking a box to opt-in and also clicking on a link sent in an e-mail to confirm the opt-in choice.

drop-in U.K. terminology for commencing recording part way through a performance on one or multiple tracks; see punch-in.

radical dance mix A remix of a track (aimed at a specific type of club DJ) that uses little or no material from the original recording.

R&D Research and development

random access The ability of a storage device to read or write material directly from or to the required location within a constant period of time. This is one of the characteristics of disk-type recording media. LPs and CDs can be thought of as random access; cassette tapes are sequential or linear access.

R.C.A. Radio Corporation of America

recording console An audio mixing device with input and output channels. Also known as a board, mixing console, or desk (U.K.).

recording media The physical materials on which the audio data are stored, such as hard disks, CD-ROMs, floppy disks, and tape.

residential studio A recording studio that has accommodations for the artist, musicians, engineer, and producer.

reverb Multiple reflections of delayed and attenuated sound waves against room boundaries and objects within the room persisting after the original sound has ceased, creating a sense of spaciousness in the room.

RIAA Recording Industry Association of America, www.riaa.com

riding the levels Changing levels relative to time and the other instruments and vocals. Rides are used to both improve the dynamic flow of the track and to draw attention to different facets of the orchestration at different points in the song.

rights clearances The process of obtaining permissions from the various copyright owners.

rotation On radio or TV, rotations are a measure of how many times a track or program airs. They are often referred to in terms of light, medium, and heavy or power rotations.

SCMS Serial copy management system, an anti-copying chip that the RIAA required manufacturers to put in their digital machines to allow one copy from an original and to deny the consumer the ability to copy a copy.

scratch vocals A quickly done rough vocal take, often recorded at the same time as the basic track. Scratch vocals are usually discarded later, but because of the casual atmosphere when they are recorded, they sometimes have a special quality that cannot be reproduced or improved upon.

screen See gobo, also called a baffle. Also, screen/pop-screen/pop-shield can refer to the sonically transparent mesh that is placed in front of a microphone to minimize vocal pops and moisture accumulation on the diaphragm of the mic.

SESAC U.S. performing rights organization, www.sesac.com

single Any format that primarily features one song.

SM58/SM57 Widely used multipurpose Shure dynamic microphones.

SMPTE Society of Motion Picture and Television Engineers is the leading technical society for the motion imaging industry. When used in the context of recorded music it usually refers to one of several synchronization codes according to their standards. www.smpte.org

solid state Electronic devices made from solid semiconductor materials (as opposed to vacuum tubes).

sound field The recording area detected by the microphone(s).

SoundScan Sales data collection service for the recording industry, owned by Neilsen.

sound-on-sound A method in which new material is superimposed over previously recorded material.

sounds Used to describe the individual recorded sounds before or after the addition of effects. See also tones.

spec As in the spec of a piece of equipment. Shorthand for "specification," meaning the manufacturers detailed description of the operational parameters.

spec As in a spec deal. Shorthand for "speculative," meaning that the producer will only be paid if a certain pre-agreed result happens, such as the production generates a record deal or earns revenues from sales.

spins A spin is a single airing of a track on a radio station. The number of spins is the number of times that track was aired. Typically (depending on the format of the station), light rotation is in the single digits per week, medium might be 10 to 20 spins per week, and heavy up to 50 or more spins a week.

staff producer A music producer who is employed on staff at a record label.

state-of-the-art The most advanced level of knowledge and technology currently achieved.

story Statistics and information about an artist that can stimulate industry or media interest.

Synclavier Early digital synthesizer developed at Dartmouth College, New Hampshire, in the '70s, www.synclavier.com

tacet Musical term for silence, as when an instrument stops playing.

talkback The system, usually located on the recording console, that enables the engineer and producer to speak to the musicians in the studio through their headphones or the studio speaker system.

Technics SP1200 For many years the most commonly used professional DJ turntable.

terrestrial right Public performance right that would require terrestrial broadcast (such as AM and FM) stations to pay royalties to performers and sound recording copyright owners for the broadcast of sound recordings.

tone Can be used to refer to lineup tones that are single-frequency signals used to ensure that the frequency response of the various recording machines is consistent from day to day and studio to studio. Also used interchangeably with the term "sounds," meaning the particular timbral qualities of an instrument or voice.

tones Sometimes used to describe the individual recorded sounds before or after the addition of effects. See also sounds.

tracking The process of recording sounds to tracks on an audio recorder. Also known as laying down tracks or recording. Tracking is generally used to refer to the first stage of the multitrack recording process.

TV advertising clause A provision in the producer and/or artist contract that modifies their royalties when TV advertising is used to promote the sale of the recording.

two-inch tape machines Multitrack analog recording machine that uses two-inch wide magnetic tape. The recording and erase heads (headstack) are usually configured to record 24 tracks across the width of the tape, but they can be configured in other ways, the most common alternative being 16 tracks. Some other configurations, such as 32-track machines, were manufactured. These machines are being made obsolete by DAWs.

valve U.K. term. The U.S. term is vacuum tube or tube. A valve or tube can amplify AC voltage. The key element in early electronic recording technology, largely replaced by transistor technology but still beloved by audiophiles.

VCA Voltage controlled amplifier

VCF Voltage controlled filter

VCO Voltage controlled oscillator

VCR Videocassette recorder such as VHS or Betamax machines.

vertical integration Companies that own multiple stages of their value/supply chain such as major labels that create artistic content and own the manufacturing, distribution, and marketing elements.

WMA Windows media audio, the windows compression algorithm for digital audio.

BIBLIOGRAPHY

For full transcripts of some of the interviews in this book, more information, and further reading, please visit www.burgessworldco.com.

"120 Years of Electronic Music, Electronic Musical Instrument 1870–1990, William Du Bois Duddell and the 'Singing Arc' (1899)," http://www.mathieubosi.com/zikprojects/120YearsOfElectronicMusic.pdf, accessed 5-18-12.

"1940 Walter Weber AC Tape Bias," *Mix*, Sept. 1, 2007, http://mixonline.com/TECnology-Hall-of-Fame/1940-tape-bias/.

"1950s: Radio Reinvents Itself," Michigan Department of Natural Resources, http://www.hal.state.mi.us/mhc/museum/explore/museums/hismus/special/ontheair/tour50s.html, accessed 8-19-12.

"1951 Pulse Techniques Pultec EQP-1 Program Equalizer," *Mix*, Sept. 1, 2006, http://mixonline.com/TECnology-Hall-of-Fame/pulse-pultec-equalizer-090106/, accessed 5-2-12.

"1957 EMT Model 140 Plate Reverb," *Mix*, Sept. 1, 2006, http://mixonline.com/TECnology-Hall-of-Fame/EMT-140-reverb-090106/, accessed 5-4-12.

"1971 Lexicon/Gotham Delta T-101 Digital Delay," *Mix*, Sept. 1, 2006, http://mixonline.com/TECnology-Hall-of-Fame/lexicon-digital-delay-090106/, accessed 5-26-12.

"1977 Thomas Stockham Soundstream Digital Recording System," *Mix*, Sept. 1, 2006, http://mixonline.com/TECnology-Hall-of-Fame/thomas-stockham-sound-stream-090106/, accessed 5-27-12.

"2011 Year-End Shipment Statistics," RIAA, http://76.74.24.142/FA8A2072-6BF8-D44D-B9C8-CE5F55BBC050.pdf, accessed 8-3-12.

"25 Years of Storage Technology Leadership," http://www.iomega.com/25years/index.html, accessed 5-17-12.

"706 Union Avenue Sessions," http://www.706unionavenue.nl/64258514, accessed 8-20-12.

93.3 WMAR Rocks, "Slipknot/Stone Sour Frontman Blasts Rick Rubin," updated Nov. 23, 2011, http:// wmmr.com/music/news/story.aspx?ID=1576293, accessed 12-12-11.

"About Telarc: Telarc and the Dawn of Digital," http://www.telarc.com/about/Digital.aspx, accessed 8-13-12.

Ackerman, Paul. "*Sholes: Dicoverer and Developer*," *Billboard*, June 3, 1967.

———. "*Shole Dies; Trade Catalyst*," *Billboard*, May 4, 1968.

Adam, Nathan Adan. "*The Times They Are a Changin': The Impact of Digital Editing Techniques on Modern Country Music*," Art of Record Production 2006 Conference, Edinburgh University, UK, attended by author.

Adelson, Martin, and Lisa Adelman. "*The Shadows*," Penguin Diaries, http://www.fleetwoodmac.net/penguin/shadows.htm, accessed 5-21-12.

Adlers, Frederik "Freddan," and James Garfield. "Fender Rhodes: The Piano that Changed the History of Music," http://www.fenderrhodes.com/history/narrative.php, accessed 6-4-12, translation of "The Rhodes Electric Piano: Against All Odds," from the Swedish magazine *MM*, Sept. 1996.

Aerosmith and Stephen Davis. *Walk This Way: The Autobiography of Aerosmith* (New York: Dogeared, 1997).

Afsari, Camran. *"Brian Eno: Mixing the Ingredients of Pop in Culture's Cauldron,"* Mix, July 1993.

———. "Jack Endino: The Godfather of Grunge," *Mix*, Dec. 1993.

———. "Steve Albini: Nemesis of Corporate Rock," *Mix*, March 1994.

Ahrens, Frank. "Technology Repaves Road to Stardom: Internet Gives Music Business Cheap New Avenue to Find Talent," *Washington Post*, May 2, 2004, http://pqasb.pqa-rchiver.com/washingtonpost/access/626283021.html?FMT=ABS&FMTS=ABS:FT& date=May+2-percent2C+2004&author=Frank+Ahrens&pub=The+Washington+Po st&edition=&startpage=A.01&desc=Technology+Repaves+Road+to+Stardom-per cent3B+Internet+Gives+Music+Business+Cheap+New+Avenue+to+Find+Talent, accessed 3-19-12.

"Alan Blumlein: The man who invented stereo," Abbey Road Studios, interview by author, Aug. 4, 2008, http://www.abbeyroad.com/News/Article/22/Alan-Blumlein-the-man-who-invented-stereo, accessed 5-15-12.

"Alan Lomax Collection," American Folklife Center, http://www.loc.gov/folklife/lomax/, accessed 8-18-12.

Alexander, Peter. "New Technology and Market Structure: Evidence from the Music Recording Industry," *Journal of Cultural Economics*, vol. 18 (1994), 113–123, http:// www.peterjalexander.com/images/New_Technology_and_Market_Structure.pdf, accessed 4-13-12.

"Ampex History," http://www.ampex.com/l-history.html?start=30, accessed 5-20-12.

"AMS Neve History: The 80s," http://www.ams-neve.com/about-us/ams-neve-history/80s, accessed 5-28-12.

Anderson, Kyle. RIAA says Jackson classic is poised to surpass Eagles' greatest-hits collection in U.S. sales," July 20, 2009, http://www.mtv.com/news/articles/1616537/thriller-set-overtake-eagles-top-selling-lp.jhtml, accessed 6-16-12.

Andrews, Frank. *"Zonophone" (Label), Encyclopedia of Recorded Sound*, vol. 1, second ed., ed. Frank Hoffmann (New York: Routledge, 2004).

Appleberry, Bill. *"Producer/Mixer/Engineer/Songwriter/Musician,"* http://www.blog.music180.com/pros/3490, accessed 6-16-12.

Araica, Marcella. E-mail interview with Katia Isakoff, Oct. 2011.

———. Panel on Women in Producing that both Araica and the author participated in at San Francisco University for the Art of Record Production Conference, Dec. 3, 2011.

Armington, Nick, Lars Lofas, and Barbara Schultz, eds. *"Bruce Fairbairn,"* in *Music Producers: Conversations with Today's Top Hit Makers* (Emeryville, CA: Intertec, 2000).

"The Art of Record Production," http://www.artofrecordproduction.com/.

Artistshouse Music, *"Teo Macero on Working with John Hammond and on The Graduate Soundtrack,"* http://www.artistshousemusic.org/videos/teo+macero+on+working+wi th+john+hammond+and+on+the+graduate+soundtrack, accessed 12-17-11.

"Atlantic Leads the Field in Rhythm and Blues," http://www.flickr.com/photos/elmcityminusone/6071580709/, accessed 6-3-12.

"AT&T Announces FOX's Seventh Season Breaks All-Time Record for Text Messaging: AT&T Records More than 78 million 'American Idol'-Related Text Messages," May 22, 2008, http://www.att.com/gen/press-room?pid=4800&cdvn=news&newsarticleid=25731, accessed 8-25-09.

"Audio Highway Announces the Listen Up Player—A New Device that Delivers Personalized Audio Content to Information-Hungry, On-the-Go Consumers," Audio Highway Press Release, http://www.tedrichards.me/ahway/news/Press/p5.html, accessed 5-17-12.

"Audio Pioneer Dr. H. C. Willi Studer," http://www.studer.ch/news/willistuder.aspx, accessed 5-2-12.

"An Audio Timeline," Audio Engineering Society, http://www.aes.org/aeshc/docs/audio.history.timeline.html, accessed 5-20-12.

B, Benji. *Tony Visconti: Be sure he knows what he's talking about—part 2*, http://www.redbullmusicacademy.com/lectures/tony-visconti-2, accessed 4-14-12.

Babiuk, Andy, and Tony Bacon. *Beatles Gear* (San Francisco: Backbeat, 2002).

Badenhausen, Rolf. "The Genesis of Vinyl Stereo Record," http://www.badenhausen.com/VSR_History.htm, accessed 5-15-12.

Baines, Anthony, and Klaus P. Wachsmann. "Classification of Musical Instruments: Translated from the Original German" (from the original by Erich M. von Hornbostel and Curt Sachs), *Galpin Society Journal*, vol. 14 (Mar. 1961), 3–29, http://www.jstor.org/stable/842168, accessed 5-18-12.

Baker, Steven. ABC Nightline News, "Meet Dr. Luke, Pop Music's Maestro," Feb. 17, 2011, http://abcnews.go.com/Entertainment/lukasz-dr-luke-gottwald-produced-songs-britney-spears/story?id=12943564#.UAaozO6iG5J, accessed 7-18-12.

Barnes, J. A. "Class and Committees in a Norwegian Island Parish," *Human Relations* 7 (1954), 39–58.

Bates, Benjamin J. "Do Radio and TV compete with, or augment, each other?" *Media Business and the Future of Journalism* (JEM499), posted Aug. 21, 2011, http://jem499.blogspot.com/2011/08/do-radio-and-tv-compete-with-or-augment.html, accessed 8-6-12.

Battier, Marc. "What the GRM brought to music: from musique concrète to acousmatic music," quoting interview of Pierre Henry with Richard S. James, http://music.arts.uci.edu/dobrian/CMC2009/OS12.3.Battier.pdf, accessed 6-1-12.

The-Beatles-History.Com, http://www.the-beatles-history.com/abbey-road.html, accessed 5-26-12.

"Behind the Dial: Radio in the 1930s," Zenith Stratosphere, http://radiostratosphere.com/zsite/behind-the-dial/radio-in-1930.html, accessed 4-13-12.

Benjamin, Brad Leigh, and Barbara Schultz, eds. *"Walter Afanasieff," Music Producers: Conversations with Today's Top Hit Makers* (Emeryville, CA: Intertec, 2000) (originally sourced from *Mix*).

Benson, Allan L. "Edison's Dream of New Music," *Cosmopolitan* 54, no. 5 (May 1913), 797–800, quoted from Library of Congress, http://memory.loc.gov/ammem/edhtml/edgenre.html, accessed 5-12-12.

Bernstein, Adam. "Mitch Miller Dies: Musical Industry Innovator (For Better and Worse)," *Washington Post*, Aug. 2, 2010, http://voices.washingtonpost.com/postmortem/2010/08/mitch-miller-dies-musical-indu.html.

"Bessie Smith–'Empress of the Blues,'" Bessie Smith Cultural Center, http://www.bessiesmithcc.org/about/bessie-smith, accessed 4-23-12.

Beyda, Adam, and Barbara Schultz, eds., *"Flood Rising," Music Producers: Conversations with Today's Top Hit Makers* (Emeryville, CA: Intertec, 2000) (originally sourced from 1995 *Mix* article).

Billboard.biz, chart search results, http://www.billboard.biz/bbbiz/charts/chart-search-results/1?orderBy=chartDate&orderType=a, accessed 8-27-12; and "Atlanta Rockers, State of Man, Tops *Billboard* Magazine's Hot Singles Chart!" Top40-charts.com, http://top40-charts.com/news.php?nid=24977, accessed 8-27-12.

Billboard.biz, posted Feb. 18, 2011, http://www.billboard.biz/bbbiz/industry/record-labels/business-matters-75-000-albums-released-1005042392.story, accessed 8-9-12.

"Biography: Quincy Jones, Music Impresario," Academy of Achievement, http://www.achievement.org/autodoc/printmember/jon0bio-1, accessed 5-26-12.

Blades, James. *Percussion Instruments and Their History* (Westport, CT: Bold Strummer, 2005).

Block, Peter. *Flawless Consulting: A Guide to Getting Your Expertise Used* (Hoboken, NJ: Jossey-Bass/Pfeiffer, 2000), 1–6.

Blumberg, Alex. "An Internet Rock Star Tells All," Planet Money, May 13, 2011, http://www.npr.org/blogs/money/2011/05/14/136279162/an-internet-rock-star-tells-all, accessed 3-17-12.

Boffey, Daniel. "Apple admits Briton DID invent iPod, but he's still not getting any money," http://www.dailymail.co.uk/news/article-1053152/Apple-admit-Briton-DID-invent-iPod-hes-getting-money, accessed 4-28-12.

Bonaguro, Alison. *"Producer Dann Huff: The Man behind the Hits,"* April 22, 2009, http://blog.cmt.com/2009-04-22/producer-dann-huff-the-man-behind-the-hits/, accessed 6-16-12.

Bonzai, Mr. "Lunching with Bonzai: Al Schmitt: The Unforgettable Touch," *Mix*, Oct. 1993, 298.

———. "Lunching with Bonzai: Global INXS," *Mix*, Jan. 1994, 156–158.

———. "Lunching with Bonzai: Albhy Galuten," *Mix*, vol. 19, issues 7–12, 1995, 100.

———. "Lunching with the Lords: The Lord-Alge Brothers," *Mix*, Sept. 1993, 42.

———. "John Alagia," *Mix*, updated Aug. 1, 2005, mixonline.com/mag/audio_john_alagia/, accessed 3-8-12.

———. "Russ Titelman: Warner Bro'," *Mix*, Sept. 1994.

———. "Tony Visconti: A Brilliant Career," *Mix*, Oct. 1993.

Bordo, Michael. *Stock Market Crashes, Productivity Boom Busts and Recessions: Some Historical Evidence* (Newark, NJ: Rutgers University Press, 2003), http://www.cfr.org/content/thinktank/Depression/Bordo_2.pdf, accessed 5-3-12.

Boucher, Geoff. *Practicing the Fine Art of Production*, Cyptron Industries, http://www.maxmartinfansite.com/CyptronLATimes.htm, accessed 6-8-12.

Bowen, Jimmy. "Nashville Here They Come," originally sourced from *EQ Magazine*, April 1992. Also appears in Anthony Savona, ed., *Console Confessions: The Great Music Producers in Their Own Words* (San Francisco: Backbeat, 2005), 78.

Bowman, John S. *The Cambridge Dictionary of American Biography* (Cambridge, UK: Cambridge University Press, 1995), http://encyclopedia2.thefreedictionary.com/ Pridham,+Edwin+S., accessed 5-19-12.

Boyk, James. "There's Life Above 20 Kilohertz! A Survey of Musical Instrument Spectra to 102.4 KHz," 1992, http://www.cco.caltech.edu/~boyk/spectra/spectra.htm, accessed 7-30-12.

Brecht, Bertolt (English version by Eric Bentley). *Mother Courage and Her Children* (New York: Grove, 1996), scene 3, 43.

Breen, Bill. "What's Your Intuition?" Fast Company, posted Aug. 31, 2000, http://www. fastcompany.com/magazine/38/klein.html?page=0-percent2C1, accessed 2-25-12.

"A Brief History of Audio Formats," http://www.mp3developments.com/article1.php, accessed 5-5-12.

"A brief history of Pro Tools: We investigate one of the most successful pieces of software ever made," *Future Music*, May 30, 2011 (some material gleaned or confirmed from http://www.musicradar.com/tuition/tech/a-brief-history-of-pro-tools-45296), accessed 4-19-12.

Brown, Jake. *Rick Rubin: In the Studio* (Toronto: ECW, 2009).

Brown, Jennifer M. *"De-gendering the electronic soundscape: Women, power and technology in contemporary music,"* Southern Cross University, Lismore, NSW, AU (masters thesis, 1996), citing S. D. Potts, "Women in Audio: The TechNet Survey," *EQ Magazine*, May 1993, 57; and Dunstan Prial, *The Producer: John Hammond and the Soul of American Music* (New York: Farrar, Straus and Giraud, 2006).

Burgess, Richard James. Derived from material in the author's Ph.D. dissertation, "Structural Change in the Music Industry: The Evolving Role of the Musician," University of Glamorgan, UK, 2010.

Buskin, Richard. "Classic Tracks: Les Paul & Mary Ford 'How High the Moon,'" http:// www.soundonsound.com/sos/jan07/articles/classictracks_0107.htm, accessed 2-24-12.

———. "Racking Up the Hits," *Studio Sound*, Aug. 1998, 41–46.

Caramanica, Jon. "Pitched to Perfection: Pop Star's Silent Partner," *New York Times*, June 29, 2012, http://www.nytimes.com/2012/06/30/arts/music/kuk-harrell-justin-biebers-vocal-producer.html?pagewanted=all, accessed 8-21-12.

Chaitovitz, Ann. Music on the Internet, Hearing before the Subcommittee on Courts, the Internet, and Intellectual Property of the Committee on the Judiciary House 0f Representatives 107th Congress First Session, May 17, 2001, 90 (attended by author).

"Charles Sumner Tainter Papers," 1878–1919, Archives Center, National Museum of American History, Smithsonian Institution, http://americanhistory.si.edu/archives/ AC0124.htm, accessed 4-4-12.

Chen, Christine Y. "The Bad Boys of Radio, Lowry Mays and sons made enemies building ClearChannel into an empire. Now they want to tell the world they're not…," *Fortune*, updated March 3, 2003, http://money.cnn.com/magazines/fortune/fortune_ archive/2003/03/03/338343/index.htm, accessed 2-12-12.

Christman, Ed. "Exclusive: Clear Channel, Big Machine Strike Deal to Pay Sound-Recording Performance Royalties to Label, Artists," *Billboard*, posted June 5, 2012, http://www.billboard.biz/bbbiz/industry/legal-and-management/exclusive-clear-channel-big-machine-strike-1007226762.story, accessed 7-20-12.

Chu, Jeff. "Top of the Pops," *Time*, posted March 19, 2001, http://www.time.com/time/
magazine/article/0,9171,102126,00.html#ixzz23eOjy5Ig, accessed 8-15-12.

Clark, Rick. "Gehman's New Budget Multiplatinums," *Billboard*, July 15, 1995, 76.

———. "Jim Dickinson: Memphis Maverick," *Mix*, Oct. 1992, 186–187.

———. "Barry Beckett: From Muscle Shoals to Nashville," *Mix*, July 1994, 125.

"Conflict Resolution," Office of Human Resource Development, University of Wisconsin,
http://www.ohrd.wisc.edu/onlinetraining/resolution/index.asp, accessed 9-14-12.

Continuum Encyclopedia of Popular Music of the World: Performance and Production, s.v.
"Arrangement," http://ezproxy.aacc.edu/login?url=http://www.credoreference.com.
ezproxy.aacc.edu/entry/contpmwpp/arrangement, accessed 2-19-12.

Cooper, Anderson. *Simon Cowell interview*, "60 Minutes," March 18, 2007, http://www.
youtube.com/watch?v=IPx_bX5_T70, accessed 8-25-09.

"Counterfactual Thinking," *Encyclopedia of Cognitive Science* (Hoboken, NJ: Wiley, 2005),
http://ezproxy.aacc.edu/login?url=http://www.credoreference.com.ezproxy.aacc.edu/
entry/wileycs/counterfactual_thinking, accessed 3-2-12.

"Credits," Directors Guild of America, http://www.dga.org/The-Guild/Departments/
Credits.aspx, accessed 3-2-12.

Crews, Andrew D. "From Poulsen to Plastic: A Survey of Recordable Magnetic Media,"
Cochineal, 2006, http://www.ischool.utexas.edu/~cochinea/html-paper/a-crews-03-
magnetic-media.html, accessed 5-12-12.

Cromelin, Richard. "Arif Mardin, 74; Record Producer and Arranger Had Hits Over 4
Decades," *Los Angeles Times*, obituaries, June 27, 2006.

Culshaw, John. *Putting the Record Straight: The Autobiography of John Culshaw*
(New York: Viking Adult, 1982), 52, 82–83.

Daley, Dan, and Barbara Schultz, eds. "James Stroud," *Music Producers: Conversations
with Today's Top Hit Makers* (Emeryville, CA, Intertec, 2000), 162 (originally sourced
from June 1993 *Mix*).

Dance, Francis J. "Helen Oakley Dance, Writer, Producer, Publicist," Jazzhouse.org, http://
www.jazzhouse.org/gone/lastpost2.php3?edit=991165404, accessed 7-23-12.

DAT Technology, http://www.dat-mgm.com/about-percent20DAT/DAT-percent20technol-
ogy/, accessed 5-5-12.

Davis, Marc. "Hit music producer's studio for sale in Virginia Beach," *Virginian-Pilot*, Feb.
2, 2008, http://hamptonroads.com/2008/02/hit-music-producers-studio-sale-virginia-
beach, accessed 7-6-12.

Dawson, Jim. *Rock around the Clock: The Record that Started the Rock Revolution* (San
Francisco: Backbeat, 2005).

DelNero, Mathew S. "Long Overdue? An Exploration of the Status and Merit of a General
Public Performance Right in Sound Recordings," http://www.jetlaw.org/wp-content/
journal-pdfs/MatthewDelNero-LongOverdue.pdf, accessed 4-29-12 (1978 report original source).

Denisoff, R. Serge, and William L. Schurk. *Tarnished Gold: The Record Industry Revisited*
(New Brunswick, NJ: Transaction, 1997).

"Digidesign Past & Present: Interview with the President: Peter Gotcher of Digidesign,"
Sound On Sound, March 1995, http://www.soundonsound.com/sos/1995_articles/
mar95/digidesign.html, accessed 2-24-12.

Digital music report 2009—quotes, http://www.ifpi.org/content/library/DMR2009-quotes. pdf, accessed 3-25-12.

Dissman, Michelle Lea. "America and the Automobile, Cars and Culture: The Cultural Impact of the American Automobile 1946–1974," 5–6, www.honors.ufl.edu/apps/Thesis.aspx/Download/457, accessed 5-12-12.

Dixon, Willie, and Don Snowden. *I Am The Blues: The Willie Dixon Story* (Cambridge, MA: Da Capo, 1989).

"Dolby History," http://www.dolby.com/us/en/about-us/who-we-are/dolby-history/index. html, accessed 5-26-12.

"Doug Morris: Record company executive, songwriter, and producer," *Encyclopedia of World Biography*, http://www.notablebiographies.com/newsmakers2/2005-La-Pr/Morris-Doug. html#ixzz227Zc8oxF, accessed 7-30-12.

Doyle, Tom. "Foo Fighters: Recording *Wasting Light*," *Sound On Sound*, June 2011, http:// www.soundonsound.com/sos/jun11/articles/foo-fighters.htm, accessed 8-3-12.

Dylan, Bob. *Chronicles: Volume One* (New York: Simon & Schuster, 2004).

"Dynamic Range of Hearing," http://hyperphysics.phy-astr.gsu.edu/Hbase/sound/earsens. html, accessed 7-30-12.

"Edgar Vilchur: American Inventor, Educator, and Writer," http://edgarvilchur.com/, accessed 5-20-12.

"Edison, Thomas Alva [1847-1931]," New Netherland Institute, Albany, NY, http://www. nnp.org/nni/Publications/Dutch-American/edison.html, accessed 8-20-12.

Edison, Thomas Alva. "Genius is one percent inspiration, ninety-nine percent perspiration," *Harper's Monthly*, Sept. 1932, http://www.phrases.org.uk/meanings/genius-is-one-percent-perspiration-ninety-nine-percent-perspiration.html, accessed 8-27-12.

"Edison Tone Test Demonstration Program," http://www.nipperhead.com/old/tonetest01. htm, accessed 5-19-12.

"Electrical Recording," IEEE Global History Network, http://www.ieeeghn.org/wiki/index. php/Electrical_Recording, accessed 4-24-12.

"Elvis Presley, Biography, 1937-1957," http://www.elvis.com/about-the-king/biography_/1935_1954/1935-1957_page_2.aspx, accessed 5-12-12.

Elyea, Jim, ed. "The History of Vox," http://www.voxamps.com/history/, accessed 5-20-12.

Encyclopedia of Applied Psychology, s.v. "Intrinsic and Extrinsic Motivation in Sport," http://ezproxy.aacc.edu/login?url=http://www.credoreference.com.ezproxy.aacc.edu/entry/estappliedpsyc/intrinsic_and_extrinsic_motivation_in_sport, accessed 2-24-12.

Encyclopedia of Archaeology: History and Discoveries, s.v. "Classification," http://ezproxy. aacc.edu/login?url=http://www.credoreference.com.ezproxy.aacc.edu/entry/abcarch/classification, accessed 3-24-12.

Engel, Friedrich. "Walter Weber's Technical Innovation at the Reichs-Rundfunk-Gesellschaft," http://www.richardhess.com/tape/history/Engel—Walter_Weber_2006. pdf, accessed 5-12-12.

"Engineer Grammy® Award Eligibility, Crediting Definitions" (approved May 2008), http:// www.grammy.org/files/pages/Engineer_Definitions.pdf, accessed 3-25-12.

Englund, Björn. "Gennett Numerical Series," http://www.vjm.biz/new_page_6.htm, accessed 5-3-12.

Eno, Brian, and Peter Schmidt. "The Oblique Strategies," edition 1 (1975), http://www.rtqe. net/ObliqueStrategies/Ed1.html, accessed 8-12-12.

Ericsson, K. Anders, Michael J. Prietula, and Edward T. Cokely. "The Making of an Expert: New research shows that outstanding performance is the product of years of deliberate practice and coaching, not of any innate talent or skill," *Harvard Business Review*, July 2007, http://hbr.org/2007/07/the-making-of-an-expert/ar/1, accessed 8-27-12.

Espacenet patent search (accessed 4-5-12), http://worldwide.espacenet.com/publicationDetails/originalDocument?CC=GB&NR=189612039A&KC=A&FT=D&ND=&date=18970702&DB=&locale=en_EP.

"Essays on Ancient Greek Philosophy," http://faculty.evansville.edu/tb2/courses/phil211/burnet/ch3.htm, quote from Heraclitus, accessed 12-29-11.

Ewing, Jack. "How MP3 Was Born," *Business Week*, March 5, 2007, http://www.businessweek.com/globalbiz/content/mar2007/gb20070305_707122.htm, accessed 4-28-12.

"Famed producer now operates his own office," *Nashville City Paper*, Sept. 23, 2007, http://nashvillecitypaper.com/content/city-business/famed-producer-now-operates-his-own-office, accessed 8-6-12.

Farnsworth, Kent. http://www.byhigh.org/History/Farnsworth/PhiloT1924.html, accessed 3-10-12.

"Fiddlin' John Carson (ca. 1868–1949)," in *The New Georgia Encyclopedia*, http://www.georgiaencyclopedia.org/nge/Article.jsp?id=h-892.

Fildes, Jonathan. "Oldest computer music unveiled," BBC News, http://news.bbc.co.uk/2/hi/7458479.stm, accessed 4-15-12.

Fine, Thomas. "The Dawn of Commercial Digital Recording," *ARSC Journal*, vol. 39, no. 1, Spring 2008.

Firecloud, Johnny. "Corey Taylor Calls Producer Rick Rubin 'Overrated, Overpaid,'" http://www.craveonline.com/music/articles/178639-corey-taylor-calls-producer-rick-rubin-overrated-overpaid, accessed 6-10-12.

"The First Outside Broadcast 1915," http://www.historyofpa.co.uk/pages/history.htm, accessed 5-19-12.

Fischer, Paul D. "The Sooy Dynasty of Camden, New Jersey: Victor's First Family of Recording" (paper presented at the second Art of Record Production Conference, Edinburgh, UK), interview by author, Sept. 8–10, 2006.

Florent, Denis. "How jukeboxes invented CHR radio," http://www.denisflorent.fr/how-jukeboxes-invented-chr-radio/, accessed 5-1-12.

"FM Radio & the Counterculture," http://www.revolutionsinradio.com/fm.html, accessed 8-3-12, citing Susan J. Douglas, *Listening In: Radio and the American Imagination, from Amos 'n' Andy and Edward R. Murrow to Wolfman Jack and Howard Stern* (New York: Times Books, 1999), 263.

Freimuth, Bill. VP of Awards, Recording Academy, quoted via e-mail by Marina Martinez of the Recording Academy.

"Frequently Asked Questions," http://ir.timewarner.com/phoenix.zhtml?c=70972&p=irol-faq_pf, accessed 5-5-12.

"Funding Universe," http://www.fundinguniverse.com/company-histories/koss-corporation-history/, accessed 8-19-12.

Garay, Val. Statement during plenary presentation at the Art of Record Production Conference, 2011, San Francisco State University.

Gelatt, Roland. *The Fabulous Phonograph* (London: Cassell, 1977), 44.

"Georg Neumann: An Inventor and His Life's Work," www.neumann. com/?lang=en&id=about_us_history_part_1, accessed 4-30-12.

Gilbert, Calvin. "Sun Records Founder Sam Phillips Dies," *CMT News*, July 31, 2003, http://www.cmt.com/news/country-music/1475109/sun-records-founder-sam-phillips-dies.jhtml, accessed 7-30-12.

Gillaland, John. "The Pop Chronicles, Show 21—Forty Miles of Bad Road: Some of the best from rock 'n' roll's dark ages" (part 2), University of North Texas Digital Library, http://digital.library.unt.edu/ark:/67531/metadc19772/m1/, accessed 5-14-12.

Gilmour, Alexander. "Masterclass: Joe Boyd," arts section, *Financial Times*, Aug. 22, 2012, 9.

Gitlin, Martin. *The Baby Boomer Encyclopedia* (Santa Barbara, CA: ABC-CLIO/ Greenwood, 2011), 96; and Malcolm Gladwell, *Outliers: The Story of Success* (New York: Little, Brown, 2008).

Goldman, David. "Music's lost decade: Sales cut in half," Feb. 3, 2010, http://money.cnn. com/2010/02/02/news/companies/napster_music_industry/, accessed 5-15-12.

Goldsmith, Charles, William Boston, and Martin Peers. "EMI, Bertelsmann Unit End Merger Talks—Deal Might Have Altered Face of Music Industry; What Now for the Two?" *Wall Street Journal*, May 2, 2001, A25.

Goleman, Daniel. *Emotional Intelligence: Why It Can Matter More than IQ* (New York: Bantam, 1995).

—— —. "Leadership that Gets Results," *Harvard Business Review*, March–April 2000, 82–83.

———. *Working with Emotional Intelligence* (New York: Bantam, 2000).

Gracyk, Tim. "Edison Diamond Discs: 1912–1929," Tim's Phonographs and Old Records, http://www.gracyk.com/diamonddisc.shtml, accessed 8-30-12.

"Gramophone," http://memory.loc.gov/ammem/berlhtml/berlgramo.html, accessed 4-5-12.

Grimes, William. "Raymond Scott, 85, a Composer for Cartoons and the Stage, Dies," *New York Times*, obituaries, Feb. 9, 1994, http://www.nytimes.com/1994/02/09/obituaries/raymond-scott-85-a-composer-for-cartoons-and-the-stage-dies.html, accessed 3-9-12.

Gronow, Pekka, and Ilpo Saunio. *An International History of the Recording Industry* (London: Continuum, 1999).

Gross, Leah, Jeff Place, and Stephanie Smith. "Emory and Martha Cook Collection Finding Aid," Ralph Rinzler Archives, Center for Folklife and Cultural Heritage, www.folklife.si.edu/archives_resources/collections/cook.aspx, accessed 5-20-12.

Guetta, David. Conversation with Gilles Babinet at MIDEM 2011 (author present).

Guttenberg, Steve. "The 'groovy' highway hi-fis of the 1950s: Turntables in cars looked like the next big thing in 1956," CNET News, Audiophiliac, Sept. 21, 2011, http://news.cnet.com/8301-13645_3-20108785-47/the-groovy-highway-hi-fis-of-the-1950s/, accessed 5-12-12.

Ha, Peter. "All-TIME 100 Gadgets, Regency TR-1," Oct. 25, 2010, http://www.time.com/time/specials/packages/article/0,28804,2023689_2023681_2023664,00.html, accessed 5-12-12.

Hafner, Arthur. "Pareto's Principle: The 80-20 Rule," Ball State University, updated March 31, 2001, http://www.bsu.edu/libraries/ahafner/awh-th-math-pareto.html, accessed 3-16-12.

Hammond, Jeanne. "The Father of FM: The Tragic Story of Major E. H. Armstrong," http://www.yonkershistory.org/arms.html, accessed 5-2-12.

Hammond, Laurens. http://www.hammond-organ.com/History/hammond_story1.htm, accessed 5-24-12.

Harmony: International Music Magazine, http://harmony.musigi-dunya.az/rus/archivereader. asp?s=1&txtid=84, accessed 4-1-12.

Hartley, H. A. *Audio Design Handbook* (New York: Gernsback Library, Inc., 1958).

Hawken, Dominic. "Yamaha Promix 01: Automated Digital Mixer," *Sound On Sound*, http://www.soundonsound.com/sos/1995_articles/jan95/yamahapromix01.html, accessed 5-17-12.

"HDRadio: A Very Short History," How HDRadio Works, http://wpr.org/hd/hd_technical. cfm, accessed 6-1-12.

"Helen Keane: Biography," Jan. 1992, http://www.pitt.edu/~pittjazz/individual_htmls/ helen_keane.html.

Henderson, David R. "Opportunity Cost," Library of Economics and Liberty, http://www. econlib.org/library/Enc/OpportunityCost.html, accessed 6-16-12.

Heraclitus. Quoted from Heikki Hyötyniemi, "Emformation Theory: Theory of Emergent (In)Formation," Presentation for Natural Philosophers, Helsinki University of Technology, Nov. 1, 2011, http://neocybernetics.com/publications/pdf/natphi2011. pdf, accessed 12-29-11.

Hevesi, Dennis. "Bebe Barron, 82, Pioneer of Electronic Scores, Is Dead," *New York Times*, April 25, 2008, http://www.nytimes.com/2008/04/25/movies/25barron.html?_r=3&ref =obituaries&oref=slogin, accessed 5-4-12.

"The History of House: The Roots to 1985," http://music.hyperreal.org/library/history_of_ house.html, accessed 5-28-12.

"The History of Taiyo Yuden CD-R," http://www.edocpublish.com/history_of_taiyo_ yuden_cdr.htm, accessed 5-28-12.

"The history of the CD—The introduction," Philips Research, http://www.research.philips. com/technologies/projects/cd/introduction.html, accessed 5-28-12.

"The History of the Edison Cylinder Phonograph," Library of Congress, http://memory. loc.gov/ammem/edhtml/edcyldr.html, accessed 3-31-12.

Hoffmann, Frank, and B. Lee Cooper. *Popular American Recording Pioneers: 1895-1925* (New York: Routledge, 2000).

Hoge, Patrick. "Rhapsody, other streaming services give boost to music industry," *San Francisco Business Times*, March 28, 2012, http://www.techflash.com/seattle/2012/03/ rhapsody-other-streaming-services.html, accessed 6-2-12.

Holiday, Billie, and Arthur Herzog Jr. *God Bless the Child* (New York: Carlin America, 1939).

"Holland, Dozier and Holland: Biography," Rock and Roll Hall of Fame, http://rockhall. com/inductees/holland-dozier-and-holland/, accessed 5-26-12.

Horowitz, Shel. "Emotional Intelligence—Stop Amygdala Hijackings," U. Mass. Family Business Center, http://www.umass.edu/fambiz/articles/values_culture/primal_leader- ship.html, accessed 7-13-12.

Hosokawa, Shuhei. "The Walkman Effect," *Popular Music*, vol. 4, Performers and Audiences (1984), 165–180.

House, Daniel. "Jack Endino," http://www.rocknrolldating.com/interview.php/5, accessed 6-17-12.

Houston, Frank, and Sir George Martin. Updated July 25, 2000, http://www.salon.com/2000/07/25/martin_6/, accessed 8-27-12.

"How the Great Recession Has Changed Life in America, IV. The New Frugality, Making Ends Meet," June 30, 2010, Pew Research Center, http://www.pewsocialtrends.org/2010/06/30/how-the-great-recession-has-changed-life-in-america/4/, accessed 4-13-12.

Hudspeth, Christian. "50 Quotes from the Wealthiest Man in America," July 14, 2011, http://www.investinganswers.com/education/famous-investors/50-quotes-wealthiest-man-america-3088, accessed 8-11-12.

Hurt, "Mississippi" John. "Delta School," http://www.cr.nps.gov/delta/blues/people/msjohn_hurt.htm, accessed 8-18-12.

"IFPI publishes Digital Music Report 2009," Jan. 16, 2009, http://www.ifpi.org/content/section_resources/dmr2009.html, accessed 3-16-12.

"In Memoriam, Peter L. Jensen," *Journal of the Audio Engineering Society*, Jan. 1962, http://www.aes.org/aeshc/docs/jaes.obit/JAES_V10_1_PG096.pdf, accessed 5-19-12.

"Indie Artist Makes $4.2 Million in 2008," Dec. 22, 2008, New Rockstar Philosophy, http://www.newrockstarphilosophy.com/2008/12/indie-artist-makes-42-million-in-2008/, accessed 3-17-12.

"The Invention of the Electric Guitar," Lemelson Center for the Study of Invention and Innovation, Smithsonian Institution, http://invention.smithsonian.org/centerpieces/electricguitar/invention.htm, accessed 5-1-12.

Isakoff, Katia, and Richard James Burgess. Adapted from "Women in Music Production: Education, Representation and Practice," paper presented at Art of Record Production Conference, San Francisco (interview by author, Dec. 3, 2011).

Jackson, Blair. "Ken Scott: New Memoir Sheds Light on an Exceptional Career," *Mix*, vol. 36, no. 7, July 2012.

———. "Tucker Martine: Sonic Experiments in the Great Northwest," *Mix*, June 2012, 52–54, 75.

Jam, Jimmy. "Dynamic Duo," *EQ Magazine*, Feb. 1993.

James, Richard Schmidt. "Expansion of sound resources in France, 1913–1940, and its relationship to electronic music," doctoral thesis, University of Michigan, 1981, note 91.

"Jazz and radical politics," www.marxmail.org, Nov. 30, 2005, http://www.columbia.edu/~lnp3/mydocs/culture/jazz_left.htm, accessed 8-27-12.

"Jesse's Gang—Center of Attraction," http://www.discogs.com/Jesses-Gang-Centre-Of-Attraction/release/1169419, accessed 5-28-12.

"Jim Marshall: The Guv'nor," http://marshallamps.com/welcome/welcome.asp, accessed 5-18-12.

"Joan Deary and Elvis Presley," Elvis Australia, updated April 18, 2012, http://www.elvis.com.au/presley/joan_deary_and_elvis_presley.shtml, accessed 5-4-12.

"John T. 'Jack' Mullin," Museum of Broadcasting, http://www.pavekmuseum.org/jmullin.html, accessed 5-12-12.

"The John T. Mullin Story," *Sound Communications*, Feb. 1989, 42–46, 68.

Johnson, Carolyn Y. "Archaeologists unearth oldest musical instruments ever found," http://www.boston.com/news/health/articles/2009/06/24/archaeologists_unearth_oldest_musical_intstruments_ever_found/, accessed 5-25-12.

Johnson, Heather. "Orrin Keepnews," *Performing Songwriter*, issue 73, Nov. 2003, http://performingsongwriter.com/orrin-keepnews/, accessed 8-10-12.

Jones, Quincy, and Bill Gibson. *Q on Producing* (Milwaukee, WI: Hal Leonard, 2010), 29.

"Judith Sherman Biography," www.banffcentre.ca/faculty/faculty-member/3541/judith-sherman/, accessed 8-13-12.

"Justin Bieber biography," A&E Television Networks, http://www.biography.com/people/justin-bieber-522504, accessed 3-10-12.

Kahn, Ashley. "Jerry Wexler: The Man Who Invented Rhythm & Blues, Aretha Franklin producer, Atlantic Records co-chief and music business pioneer dies at age 91," *Rolling Stone*, Aug. 15, 2008, http://www.rollingstone.com/music/news/jerry-wexler-the-man-who-invented-rhythm-blues-20080815.

Kamina, Pascal. *Film Copyright in the European Union* (Cambridge, UK: Cambridge University Press, 2002), 156.

Karp, Andy. "In Conversation with Rudy Van Gelder," http://www.jazz.com/features-and-interviews/2009/4/11/in-conversation-with-rudy-van-gelder, accessed 8-17-12.

Katz, Mark. *Capturing Sound: How Technology Has Changed Music* (London: University of California Press, 2010), 214.

Kawashima, Dale. "Classic Songwriter Story: How Walter Afanasieff Wrote the Classic Hit, 'Hero,' with Mariah Carey," http://www.songwriteruniverse.com/hero.htm, accessed 8-12-12.

———. "Legendary Trio Holland-Dozier-Holland Talk about Their Motown Hits, and Their New Projects," http://www.songwriteruniverse.com/hdh.htm, accessed 5-26-12.

Kay, Jonathan, Kimber Ghent, Brian Chumney, and Erik Lutkins. "Film Sound History: 40s," How Stuff Works, http://ww2.odu.edu/~kwinters/Courses/Film%20Sound/history%2040s.htm, accessed 6-1-12.

Keener, Roberta. "Ben Selvin's Recordings," http://www.muzakblog.com/new/ben-selvins-recordings/, accessed 5-4-12.

Kennedy, Rick. *Jelly Roll, Bix, and Hoagy: Gennett Studios and the Birth of Recorded Jazz* (Bloomington and Indianapolis: Indiana State University Press, 1999), 20.

Ketchum III, William E. "Producers Corner: Swizz Beatz," May 30, 2007, http://www.hiphopdx.com/index/interviews/id.782/title.producers-corner-swizz-beatz, accessed 6-16-12.

King Jr., Martin Luther. *Strength to Love* (New York: Harper & Row, 1963), 25.

Kingsbury, Paul, ed. *Country Music Hall of Fame® and Museum's Encyclopedia of Country Music* (New York: Oxford University Press, 1998), 431, 483.

"Koss History: About Us," http://www.koss.com/en/about/history, accessed 8-19-12.

Kot, Greg. "Bruce Iglauer interview: 40 years of Alligator Records," Turn it Up, Feb. 16, 2011, http://leisureblogs.chicagotribune.com/turn_it_up/2011/02/bruce-iglauer-interview-40-years-of-alligator-records.html#more, accessed 6-10-12.

KOWH Omaha, "The Birth of Top 40," http://www.davidgleason.com/KOWH_Birth_of_Top-40.htm, accessed 5-20-12.

Krakow, Gary. "New radio formats sacrifice sound quality," March 17, 2005, http://www.msnbc.msn.com/id/7150262/ns/technology_and_science-tech_and_gadgets/t/new-radio-formats-sacrifice-sound-quality/#.T7ZL-uuiG5I, accessed 5-17-12.

Kramer, Eddie. "My Hendrix Experience," *EQ Magazine*, Nov. 1992.

Kuhnke, Klaus, Manfred Miller, and Peter Schulze. *Geschichte der Popmusik Band 1* (Lilienthal/Bremen, DE: Eres-Edition, 1976).

"Kurt Cobain Bio," http://www.moono.com/html/kurt-cobain/kurt-cobain-biography.cfm, accessed 3-10-12.

Lambert, Mel. "George Martin," Electronic Musician, posted Jan. 7, 2009, http://www.emusician.com/news/0766/george-martin/134697, accessed 7-30-12.

Lange, Mutt. "Robert John Mutt Lange Interviews," http://www.muttlange.com/robert_john_mutt_lange_interview_exclusive_interviews/mutt_lange.html (interview by author), accessed 3-2-12.

Lawson, Jake. "Eliminating Passive Aggressiveness," http://www.livestrong.com/article/14713-eliminating-passive-aggressiveness/#ixzz26STSeXxO, accessed 9-14-12.

"Leadership Quotes," Lead Tennessee, http://www.tennessee.gov/dohr/learning/pdf/CoachesCorner/LeadershipQuotes.pdf, accessed 8-27-12.

Leaf, David. "Paul McCartney Comments," http://www.albumlinernotes.com/Paul_McCartney_Comments.html, accessed 5-26-12.

Learning Space: Revolutions in Sound Recording. "Cylinders or plates?: Edison starts with cylinders," http://openlearn.open.ac.uk/mod/oucontent/view.php?id= 397885&section=1.2.1, accessed 5-12-12.

Lebrecht, Norman. "Silent deaths at Decca, Slipped Disc: Norman Lebrecht on shifting sound worlds," Feb. 19, 2009, http://www.artsjournal.com/slippeddisc/2009/02/more_deaths_at_decca.html, accessed 5-20-12.

Lee, Frank. "Sales Is a Numbers Game," Sales Academy Inc., updated Aug. 2001, http://www.irmi.com/expert/articles/2001/lee08.aspx, accessed 12-31-11.

"Leon Theremin (1896–1993): The Theremin," Inventor of the Week Archive, Lemelson-MIT, http://web.mit.edu/invent/iow/theremin.html, accessed 5-19-12.

Levine, Larry. *Da Doo Ron Ron* (film by Binia Tymieniecka), http://www.youtube.com/watch?v=LRmRBrnQq8o, accessed 5-13-12.

Lewisohn, Mark. *The Beatles Recording Sessions: The Official Abbey Road Studio Session Notes 1962–1970* (New York: Harmony, 1988).

Lindvall, Helienne. "David Guetta: the man taking dance music into the U.S. charts," June 1, 2010, http://www.guardian.co.uk/music/2010/jun/01/david-guetta-dance-music, accessed 9-23-11.

Lockwood, Dave. "Bob Clearmountain: Master Mixer," *Sound On Sound*, June 1999, http://www.soundonsound.com/sos/jun99/articles/bobclear.htm, accessed 8-12-12.

Lyons, Nona. *Handbook of Reflection and Reflective Inquiry: Mapping a Way of Knowing for Professional Reflective Inquiry* (New York: Springer, 2010).

Macero, Teo. "Teo Macero on Working with John Hammond and on *The Graduate* Soundtrack," http://www.artistshousemusic.org/videos/teo+macero+on+working+with+john+hammond+and+on+the+graduate+soundtrack, accessed 12-17-11.

Macnab, Geoffrey. "Joe Meek and Telstar's Tragic Tale," *The Independent*, April 18, 2009.

"The Magnetic Tape of Valdemar Poulsen and Fritz Pfleumer," www.history-computer.com/ModernComputer/Basis/tape.html, accessed 4-4-12.

Marmorstein, Gary. *The Label: The Story of Columbia Records* (New York: Thunder's Mouth, 2007).

Marshall, Matt. "*They did it! YouTube bought by Google for $1.65B in less than two years*," *Venture Beat News*, posted Oct. 9, 2006, http://venturebeat.com/2006/10/09/

they-did-it-youtube-gets-bought-by-gooogle-for-165b-in-less-than-two-years/, accessed 8-3-12.

Martin, George, and Jeremy Hornsby. *All You Need Is Ears: The Inside Personal Story of the Genius Who Created the Beatles* (New York: St. Martin's, 1979).

Martin, Shawn C. "Gene Krupa Biography," http://www.drummerman.net/biography.html, accessed 4-24-12.

Massenburg, George. Conversation with author, July 12, 2012.

Masumi podcast, "Producer Judy Sherman," WGBH, undated, http://www.wgbh.org/programs/Inner-Voice-1821/episodes/Producer-Judy-Sherman-37086, accessed 8-13-12.

Mather, Mara, Eldar Shafir, and Marcia K. Johnson. "Remembering chosen and assigned options," *Memory & Cognition*, 2003, 31 (3), 422–433, http://memlab0.eng.yale.edu/PDFs/2003_Mather_Shafir_Johnson_MemCog.pdf, accessed 7-16-12.

Matthews, Gail. "Study Backs up Strategies for Achieving Goals," Dominican University, http://www.dominican.edu/dominicannews/study-backs-up-strategies-for-achieving-goals, 8-27-12.

Matthews, Karen. "Conductor, record exec Mitch Miller dies at age 99," *Washington Times*, http://www.washingtontimes.com/news/2010/aug/2/conductor-record-exec-mitch-miller-dies-age-99/?page=all, accessed 5-20-12.

May, Thomas. "The Producer: Legendary producer Steven Epstein on the art and science of making records sound right," *Listen Music Magazine*, http://www.listenmusicmag.com/music-in-my-life/the-producer.php, accessed 12-8-12.

McKay, Chris. "John Mayer Full-Length Interview: Recorded January 25, 2002," http://concertshots.com/john_mayer_full-percent20interview-percent2012502.htm, accessed 3-8-12.

McKnight, Jay. "AC Bias at Bell Telephone Laboratories, 1936...1939," http://www.aes.org/aeshc/pdf/mcknight_ac-bias-at-btl-1936-1939.pdf, accessed 5-12-12.

McLuhan, Eric. "McLuhan Studies: Issue 2, The source of the term, 'Global Village,'" http://projects.chass.utoronto.ca/mcluhan-studies/v1_iss2/1_2art2.htm, accessed 8-2-12.

McQuown, Dave. "Radio," Chicago School of Media Theory, 2012, citing Jim Cox, *Music Radio: The Great Performers and Programs of the 1920s through Early 1960s* (Jefferson, NC: McFarland, 2005).

MeasuringWorth.com, http://www.measuringworth.com/uscompare/relativevalue.php, accessed 3-16-12; http://www.courierpress.com/news/2008/mar/05/looking-back-at-cost-of-living-in-the-sixties/, accessed 8-3-12; "Money and Inflation 1960s," http://www.thepeoplehistory.com/1960s.html#cost_of_living, accessed 8-3-12.

"A Mellotron History," http://www.mellotron.com/history.htm, accessed 5-26-12.

"Miami hit producer is back after almost losing everything to drug addiction," posted June 11, 2009, http://www.mtv.com/news/articles/1613761/scott-storchs-rise-fall-return.jhtml, accessed 2-09-12.

Michaels, Sean. "Lil Wayne sued for half A Milli, Incarcerated rapper facing another lawsuit for unpaid royalties, with producer Bangladesh claiming he is owed $500,000," guardian.co.uk, posted May 6, 2010, www.guardian.co.uk/music/2010/may/06/lil-wayne-sued-producer, accessed 7-22-12.

Michie, Chris. "Frank Zappa Recording History—Zappa's Music History and Recording Techniques: We are the Mothers...and This Is What We Sound Like!" Jan. 1, 2003, http://mixonline.com/recording/business/audio_mothers_sound/, accessed 5-28-12.

"Mike Pinder: Founder, the Moody Blues," http://wn.com/Streetly_Electronics, accessed 5-26-12.

"Milestones in the Development of the Internet and Its Significance for Education," PBS Net Timeline and Hobbes Internet timeline, http://www.originami.com/sp/milestones. htm, accessed 5-15-12.

"*Milestones in the Evolution of Today's Internet*" (2007), *Congressional Digest*, vol. 86, issue 2, 38.

Millard, Andre. *America on Record: A History of Recorded Sound, second ed.* (New York: Cambridge University Press, 1995).

Mills, Robert. "My Ever Changing Moogs," *Q Magazine*, issue 118, July 1996, http://www. eno-web.co.uk/interviews/qmag96b.html, accessed 3-10-12.

Milner, Greg. *Perfecting Sound Forever: An Aural History of Recorded Music* (New York: Faber and Faber, 2009).

Minnick, Doug. "Ron Fair, Senior VP of A&R, West Coast, RCA Records," undated, http://www.taxi.com/music-business-faq/ar/fair.html, accessed 3-3-12.

"Miss Clara Rockmore Grants an Interview," originally from *Camden Herald* (Maine), Sept. 1936, http://www.theremin.info/-/viewpub/tid/10/pid/13, accessed 5-19-12.

Moody, Rick. "Returning to the Sound of those Golden Years," *New York Times*, Sept. 10, 1995, http://www.nytimes.com/books/97/04/27/reviews/moody-bowie.html.

Moore, Jerrold Northrop. *A Matter of Records: Fred Gaisberg and the Golden Era of the Gramophone* (New York: Taplinger, 1976).

Morton Jr., David L. *Sound Recording: The Life Story of a Technology* (Westport, CT: Greenwood, 2004), 1.

"Motorola Heritage of Innovation, About Motorola," http://www.motorola.com/ Consumers/U.S.-EN/About_Motorola/History, accessed 8-19-12.

Motz, Mark. "What's the Psychology behind American Idol?" Associated Content, Feb. 15, 2007, http://www.associatedcontent.com/article/143981/whats the_psychology_ behind_american.html, accessed August 26, 2009.

Muirhead, Dennis. Author conversation, June 21, 2012, New York; confirmed by Richard Buskin, *Sheryl Crow: No Fool to This Game* (New York: Billboard Books, 2003).

Murray, Alan. "Which of These Six Leadership Styles Works Best?" *Wall Street Journal*, http://online.wsj.com/article/SB10001424052748704041504575045163417674970. html, accessed 6-22-12.

Nathan, David. "Quincy Jones: The Producer," *Billboard*, Dec. 16, 1995.

"Neve, About Us: History: The 70s," http://www.ams-neve.com/about-us/History/ The70s/70s.aspx, accessed 5-17-12.

"A new deal between TuneCore and Universal Music Group Distribution could spell more opportunity for independent musicians," CNet News, July 9, 2009.

Nichols, Roger. "Walter Becker," *EQ Magazine*, Dec. 1994, http://www.steelydan.com/ eq.html, accessed 8-13-12.

"The Nielsen Company & *Billboard*'s 2011 Music Industry Report," Business Wire, updated Jan. 5, 2012, http://www.businesswire.com/news/home/20120105005547/en/Nielsen-Company-Billboard-percentE2-percent80-percent99s-2011-Music-Industry-Report, accessed 9-16-12.

"Nielsen SoundScan U.S. Venue Sales Procedure," http://nielsen.com/content/dam/corpo-rate/us/en/public-percent20factsheets/Soundscan/Soundscan-U.S.-Sales-Procedure. pdf, accessed 3-18-12.

Noble, T. J. Theobald. "The Experiences of a Recorder," *The Talking Machine News And Sidelines*, vol. 8, no.10, Oct. 1912, 331–334, http://www.recordingpioneers.com/docs/NOBLE-191210-The-experiences-NOBLE-t.j.theobald.pdf, accessed 4-1-12.

"Norrie Paramor," *Encyclopedia of Popular Music*, http://www.oxfordmusiconline.com.ezproxy.aacc.edu/subscriber/article/epm/21211?q=Norrie+paramor&search=quick&pos=1&_start=1#firsthit, accessed 5-18-12.

Northouse, Peter G. *Leadership: Theory and Practice*, fifth ed. (Los Angeles: Sage, 2010).

O'Reilly, Tim. "Web 2.0 Compact Definition: Trying Again," http://radar.oreilly.com/2006/12/web-20-compact-definition-tryi.html, accessed 6-2-12.

Padgham, Hugh. Story told to author.

Paradiso, Joseph, "Electronic Music Interfaces," MIT Media Laboratory, March 1998, http://web.media.mit.edu/~joep/SpectrumWeb/SpectrumX.html, accessed 5-18-12.

Paul, Les. "Multitracking: It Wasn't Always This Easy...," *Mix*, May 13, 2005, http://mix-online.com/Multitracking_Wasnt_Always_Easy/, accessed 2-24-12.

Peel, Ian. "Trevor Horn: 25 Years of Hits," *Sound On Sound*, March 2005, http://www.soundonsound.com/sos/mar05/articles/trevorhorn.htm, accessed 3-9-12.

Peoples, Glenn. "Business Matters: 75,000 Albums Released in U.S. in 2010—Down 22 percent from 2009," http://www.billboard.com/biz/articles/news/1179201/business-matters-75000-albums-released-in-us-in-2010-down-22-from-2009, accessed 6-12-12.

Perez, Sarah. "The Number of Mobile Devices Will Exceed World's Population by 2012 (& Other Shocking Figures)," http://techcrunch.com/2012/02/14/the-number-of-mobile-devices-will-exceed-worlds-population-by-2012-other-shocking-figures/, accessed 7-2-12.

"The Performance Rights Act," http://www.grammy.org/recording-academy/producers-and-engineers/advocacy, accessed 2-12-12.

Perlman, David. "Physicists convert first known sound recording," SFGate, *San Francisco Chronicle*, March 29, 2008, http://www.sfgate.com/cgi-bin/article.cgi?f=/c/a/2008/03/28/MNOSVSB9J.DTL#ixzz1q5EDvcKT, accessed 3-24-12.

Perry, Michael R. "What Does Hollywood Know About Atari? Sound Designing with the Mega and ADAP II Sound System," *Start Archive*, vol. 4, no. 10, May 1990, http://www.atarimagazines.com/startv4n10/hollywood.html, accessed 2-24-12,

Petersen, George. 2008 TECnology Hall of Fame, Sept. 1, 2008, http://tecfoundation.com/tec/08mixarticleTEC.html, accessed 5-27-12.

Peterson, Richard A., and David G. Berger. "Cycles in Symbol Production: The Case of Popular Music," *American Sociological Review*, vol. 40, issue 2, April 1975, 158–173.

Pettibone, Shep. "Erotica Diaries, Diary Entry #2," October–November 1991, http://www.sheppettibone.com/sp_erotica_diaries.htm, accessed 8-12-12.

"Phil Spector," *New York Times*, May 29, 2009, http://topics.nytimes.com/topics/reference/timestopics/people/s/phil_spector/index.html, accessed 5-13-12.

Phillips, Mark, and Chris Molanphey. "Charting the Charts: Transcript," Oct. 23, 2009, http://www.onthemedia.org/2009/oct/23/charting-the-charts/transcript/, accessed 5-5-12.

"Phonautograph," http://www.ieeeghn.org/wiki/index.php/Phonautograph, accessed 5-27-12.

"Playback," Bulletin of the National Archive, http://www.bl.uk/reshelp/bldept/soundarch/saplayback/playback23.pdf, accessed 4-1-12.

"Pop to the rescue of the music industry," Music and Copyright's Blog, posted June 13, 2012, http://musicandcopyright.wordpress.com/2012/06/13/pop-to-the-rescue-of-the-music-industry/#more-804, accessed 8-6-12.

Popkin, Matt. "Dr. Luke: A Pop Star's Best Friend," *American Songwriter*, posted May 2, 2011, www.americansongwriter.com/2011/05/dr-luke-a-pop-stars-best-friend/, accessed 8-15-12.

Prensky, Marc. Digital Natives, Digital Immigrants, From On the Horizon (Bingley, UK: MCB University Press, 2001), http://www.marcprensky.com/writing/prensky-percent20—percent20digital-percent20natives,-percent20digital-percent20immi-grants-percent20—percent20part1.pdf, accessed 8-15-12.

Producer Grammy® Award Eligibility Crediting Definitions (approved May 2008), http://www2.grammy.com/PDFs/Recording_Academy/Producers_And_Engineers/Producer_Definitions.pdf, accessed 8-20-12.

Public data, Google, http://www.google.com/publicdata/explore?ds=d5bncppjof8f9_&met_y=sp_pop_totl&tdim=true&dl=en&hl=en&q=current+world+population, accessed 8-2-12.

Pursell, Carroll W., ed. *Technology in America: A History of Individuals and Ideas*, second ed. (Cambridge, MA: MIT Press, 1990).

R&J Records, About, http://www.randjrecords.com/index.cfm?id=3, accessed 8-6-12.

Radio News (a Gernsback popular radio magazine), http://www.magazineart.org/main.php/v/technical/radionews, accessed 4-24-12.

Raeburn, Bruce Boyd. *Jazz: The Smithsonian Anthology* (Washington, DC: Smithsonian Folkways Recordings, 2010), 27.

"Ralph Peer (1892–1960)," People & Events, http://www.pbs.org/wgbh/amex/carterfamily/peopleevents/p_peer.html, accessed 6-4-12.

Ramone, Phil, and Charles Granata. *Making Records: The Scenes behind the Music* (New York: Hyperion, 2007), 8, 155.

Reid, L.A., "Tag Team: How L.A. Reid and Babyface, another dynamic duo, work it out," *EQ Magazine*, Feb. 1993.

Reid, Shaheem, "How Scott Storch's Cocaine Addiction Made Him Spend $30 Million in Six Months," June 11, 2009, http://www.mtv.com/news/articles/1613761/scott-storchs-rise-fall-return.jhtml, accessed 6-16-12.

Reitman, Walter R. *Cognition and Thought* (New York: Wiley, 1965), quoting from James W. Wilson, Maria L. Fernandez, and Nelda Hadaway, *Mathematical Problem Solving*, University of Georgia, http://jwilson.coe.uga.edu/emt725/PSsyn/Pssyn.html, accessed 7-15-12.

Resnikoff, Paul. "Just How Many Releases? These Numbers May Scare You," July 8, 2009, http://digitalmusicnews.com/stories/070809howmany, accessed 4-13-12.

———. "In 2011, 90-percent of New Album Sales Came from 2 percent of Releases," Jan. 12, 2012, http://www.digitalmusicnews.com/permalink/2012/120112, accessed 8-9-12.

———. "Spotify CEO: Profitability Is Absolutely Not a Priority," April 13, 2012, http://www.digitalmusicnews.com/permalink/2012/120413spotify, accessed 8-4-12.

"Revision of the Hornbostel-Sachs Classification of Musical Instruments by the MIMO Consortium," http://www.music.ed.ac.uk/euchmi/cimcim/uymhs02.pdf, accessed 5-18-12.

Reyer, Steve. "1954-2004 The TR-1's Golden Anniversary," http://people.msoe.edu/~reyer/regency/Regency_ad.jpg, accessed 5-12-12.

Rhodes, Henry A. The Evolution of Rap Music in the United States, http://www.yale.edu/ynhti/curriculum/units/1993/4/93.04.04.x.html, accessed 5-28-12.

Ribowsky, Mark. *The Supremes: A Saga of Motown Dreams, Success and Betrayal* (Philadelphia: De Capo, 2009).

"Rickenbacker History: The Earliest Days of the Electric Guitar," http://www.rickenbacker.com/history_early.asp, accessed 5-20-12.

Roland, Tom. "Nashville's New Wave," *Billboard*, Dec. 10, 2011, 10–11.

Rosenthal, David H. *Hard Bop: Jazz and Black Music 1955-1965* (New York: Oxford University Press, 1992).

Rosoff, Matt. "TuneCore ties up with world's largest record label," July 9, 2009, http://news.cnet.com/8301-13526_3-10283224-27.html?tag=mncol;txt, accessed 3-19-12.

Rouse, Margaret. "Enhanced CD (E-CD)," updated Sept. 2005, http://searchstorage.techtarget.com/definition/enhanced-CD, accessed 5-28-12.

Rupert Neve Designs. "A Designer Emerges, 1960s," http://rupertneve.com/company/history/1960/, accessed 5-24-12.

Ryang, Michelle. "Michael Torke: An Interview," http://www.classical.net/music/comp.lst/articles/torke/interview.php, accessed 3-4-12.

Rypens, Arnold. "Vesti La Giubba," The Originals: Arnold Rypens's the Originals Update and Info Site, http://www.originals.be/en/originals.php?id=6614, accessed 4-1-12.

Sachs, Tony, and Sal Nunziato. "Spinning into Oblivion," *New York Times*, April 5, 2007, http://www.nytimes.com/2007/04/05/opinion/05sachsnunziato.html?pagewanted=all, accessed 5-28-12.

Salama, Marc, and James Cote. "Bruce Swedien Interview," http://www.absy.com/ABSMMI/ITV/SWEDIEN/ukitvbsw.html, accessed 8-9-12.

Sarser, David. Letter or e-mail.

Satellite Digital Audio Radio Service (SDARS), GEN Docket No. 89-554; IB Docket No. 95-91, http://transition.fcc.gov/ib/sd/ssr/sdars.html, accessed 5-17-12.

Savage, Jon. "Meek by name, wild by nature," *Observer*, Nov. 11, 2006, http://www.guardian.co.uk/music/2006/nov/12/popandrock28, accessed 5-13-12.

Savage, Steven. "'It could have happened'—the evolution of music construction," originally presented at the 2008 Art of Record Production Conference, University of Massachusetts, Lowell, Nov. 14–16, 2008, http://www.artofrecordproduction.com/content/view/175/109/, accessed 7-15-12.

"The saviour of the 1890s record business—and possibly where Jonathan Ives got his inspiration for the ipod white bud earphones?" http://soundofthehound.com/2011/05/13/the-saviour-of-the-record-business-1890s-stylee-and-possibly-where-jonathan-ives-got-his-inspiration-for-the-ipod-white-bud-earphones/, accessed 3-31-12.

Savona, Anthony, ed. *Console Confessions: The Great Music Producers in Their Own Words* (San Francisco: Backbeat, 2005), 78.

Saxon, Jonathan. "Dave Jerden," *Tape Op Magazine*, issue 86, 2011, http://www.tapeop.com/articles/86/dave-jerden/, accessed 8-11-12.

Schoenherr, Steve. "Recording Technology History," July 6, 2005, http://homepage.mac.com/oldtownman/recording/notes.html, accessed 3-24-12.

Schudel, Matt. "Mitch Miller, record executive and 'Sing Along' host, dies at 99," *Washington Post*, Aug. 3, 2010, http://www.washingtonpost.com/wp-dyn/content/article/2010/08/02/AR2010080202954.html, accessed 12-17-11.

Seay, Davin. "Quincy Jones: Breaking the Soundtrack Barrier," *Billboard*, Dec. 16, 1995, 48.

Seligman, Martin E. P., and Steven F. Maier. "Failure to escape traumatic shock," *Journal of Experimental Psychology*, 74, (1967), 1–9.

Sen, Shourin. "The Denial of a General Performance Right in Sound Recordings: A Policy that Facilitates Our Democratic Civil Society?" *Harvard Journal of Law & Technology*, vol. 21, no. 1, 2007, 241.

Shapiro, Marc. *Creed: From Zero to Platinum* (New York: St. Martin's, 2000).

Shapiro, Nat, and Nat Hentoff. *Hear Me Talkin' to Ya: The Story of Jazz as Told by the Men Who Made It* (New York: Dover, 1966).

Siber, Richard. "Making Mobile Content a Reality," Aug. 22, 2003, http://www.accenture.com/Global/Services/By_Industry/Communications/Access_Newsletter/Article_Index/MakingReality.htm, accessed 8-25-09.

"Sir George Martin: Biography," http://www.wma.com/sir_george_martin/bio/george_martin.pdf, accessed 5-24- 12.

Sisario, Ben. "Eminem Lawsuit May Raise Pay for Older Artists," *New York Times*, March 27, 2011, http://www.nytimes.com/2011/03/28/business/media/28eminem.html?pagewanted=all, accessed 3-16-12.

Smith, Caspar Llewellyn. "Blues greats re-emerge from the pages of history," *Guardian*, June 15, 2011, http://www.guardian.co.uk/music/2011/jun/16/blues-greats-re-emerge, accessed 8-18-12.

Smith, Richard R. *The History of Rickenbacker Guitars* (Anaheim Hills, CA: Centerstream, 1987).

Sooy, Raymond. "Memoirs of My Recording and Traveling Experiences for the Victor Talking Machine Company 1898-1925," David Sarnoff Library, http://www.davidsarnoff.org/soo-maintext.html, accessed 8-18-12.

Sousa, John Philip. "The Menace of Mechanical Music," *Appleton's Magazine*, vol. 8, 1906, http://explorepahistory.com/odocument.php?docId=1-4-1A1, accessed 4-6-12.

Spitz, Bob. *The Beatles: The Biography* (New York: Little, Brown, 2005).

SSL 4000G Console Operator's Manual 1-2, belmont-studios.org/index.php?.../SSL.../SSLConsoleChap1.pdf, accessed 3-9-12.

Sterling, Christopher H., and Michael C. Keith. *Sounds of Change: A History of FM Broadcasting* (Chapel Hill, NC: University of North Carolina Press, 2008).

Stone, Ron. Teleconference and e-mail, April 30, 2012.

"Sun Records," http://www.706unionavenue.nl/76314710, accessed 5-29-12.

Swedien, Bruce. "The Acusonic Recording Process, Tips and Techniques," http://www.gearslutz.com/board/showwiki.php?title=Tips-and-Techniques:Acusonic-Recording-Process-Bruce-Swedien, accessed 5-17-12.

Swedien, Bruce, and Quincy Jones. *Make Mine Music* (New York: Hal Leonard, 2003).

Swenson, Kylee. "Wide-Open Spaces," *Remix*, vol. 5, no. 12, Dec. 2003.

Tagg, Philip. "Melody and Accompaniment," *Encyclopedia of Popular Music of the World* (London: Continuum, 2003), http://www.tagg.org/articles/xpdfs/melodaccU.S.pdf, accessed 7-4-12.

Taraborrelli, J. Randy. *Call Her Miss Ross: The Unauthorized Biography of Diana Ross* (Secaucus, NJ: Carol, 1989).

Taylor, David. "Rudy Van Gelder," *Jazz Listener's Guide*, updated July 27, 2009, http://dave369.wordpress.com/2009/07/27/rudy-van-gelder/, accessed 12-26-11.

Taylor, Jim, Mark R. Johnson, and Charles G. Crawford. *DVD Demystified* (New York: McGraw-Hill, 2006).

Teagle, John. "Antique Guitar Amps 1928-1934: Which came first—electric guitar or amp?" Sept. 5, 2002, http://www.vintageguitar.com/1804/antique-guitar-amps-1928-1934/, accessed 5-20-12.

"Technological Innovations," http://www.lespaulfoundation.org/pages/foundation/seven-pages/page6.htm, accessed 2-24-12.

"Theatrical Motion Pictures—Primary Credit: Produced by, Producers Guild of America," http://www.producersguild.org/default.asp?page=coc_tmp, accessed 3-2-12.

Thomas, Bob. "Record Academy Plans TV Spectacular of its Own," *Ocala Star Banner*, April 8, 1959, 15.

Thompson, Emily. "Machines, Music, and the Quest for Fidelity: Marketing the Edison Phonograph in America, 1877-1925," *Musical Quarterly*, vol. 79, no. 1, 1995, 131.

"Tim McGraw biography," http://www.curb.com/artists/tm/tmbio2.html.

Tingen, Paul. "Benny Blanco, Songwriter and Producer," *Sound On Sound*, www.soundonsound.com/sos/jun12/articles/benny-blanco.htm, accessed 6-16-12.

———. "Kevin 'Caveman' Shirley, Mixing Led Zeppelin's Live DVD & Recording Iron Maiden," *Sound On Sound*, Nov. 2003, http://www.soundonsound.com/sos/nov03/articles/kevinshirley.htm, accessed 8-16-12.

———. "Secrets of the Mix Engineers: Jack Joseph Puig," *Sound On Sound*, Nov. 2007, http://www.soundonsound.com/sos/nov07/articles/insidetrack_1107.htm, accessed 8-12-12.

Tower, Bud. "Seven-Word Lines and Four-Letter Words: The Science of Songwriting," *American Songwriter*, Sept. 15, 2011, americansongwriter.com/2011/09/seven-word-lines-and-four-letter-words-the-science-of-songwriting/, accessed 8-17-12.

Townsend, Pete. *My Generation*, album (London: Decca, 1965).

"The Transistor: The First Transistor," http://www.nobelprize.org/educational/physics/transistor/function/firsttransistor.html, accessed 6-3-12.

"The Truth about the Billable Hour," http://www.law.yale.edu/documents/pdf/CDO_Public/cdo-billable_hour.pdf, accessed 9-14-12.

Tschmuck, Peter. *Creativity and Innovation in the Music Industry* (Dordrecht, NL: Springer, 2006), 79–80.

Tucker, Aviezer, ed., and Elazar Weinryb. "Historiographic Counterfactuals," *A Companion to the Philosophy of History and Historiography* (Oxford, UK: Blackwell, 2009).

Tudor, Alexander. "Radiohead re-issues: new editions of Kid A, Amnesiac and Hail to the Thief assessed," updated Aug. 27, 2009, http://drownedinsound.com/in_depth/4137663-radiohead-re-issues--new-editions-of-kid-a-amnesiac-and-hail-to-the-thief-assessed, accessed 8-27-12.

Tyler, Steven. "Not the Same Old Song and Dance," part 2, *EQ Magazine*, March 1993.

Tynan, Dan. "The 10 Most Disruptive Technology Combinations," *PCWorld*, March 18, 2008, http://www.pcworld.com/printable/article/id,143474/printable.html, accessed 4-28-12.

"U.S. Copyright Office—Online Service Providers," U.S. Copyright Office, http://www.copyright.gov/onlinesp/, accessed 5-17-12.

"U.S. has 33-percent Share of Internet Users Worldwide Year-end 2000, 625 Million Computers-in-Use Year-End 2001," Computer Industry Almanac Inc., http://www.c-i-a.com/pr0701.htm, and http://www.c-i-a.com/pr0401.htm, accessed 4-13-12.

"Valdemar Poulsen: Telegraphone," Inventor of the Week Archive, http://web.mit.edu/invent/iow/poulsen.html, accessed 4-5-12.

Verity, Michael. "The Producers: Steve Sholes," updated June 3, 2011, http://wnew.radio.com/2011/06/03/the-producers-steve-sholes/#ixzz1w67trhxt, accessed 5-29-12.

"Vintage Cassettes," http://vintagecassettes.com/_history/history.htm, accessed 5-26-12.

von Wieser, Friedrich. *Origin of the Idea*, trans. A. Ford Hinrichs (New York: Adelphi, 1927 [1914]), 99–100.

"Vox Pop: How Dartford Powered the British Beat Boom," BBC One, http://www.bbc.co.uk/programmes/b017zwq8, accessed 5-17-12.

Walker, Martin. "The World's New Numbers," *Wilson Quarterly*, Spring 2009, http://www.wilsonquarterly.com/article.cfm?aid=1408, accessed 8-2-12.

"'The Wall of Sound,' an electro-mechanical sequencer designed and built by Raymond Scott, 1950s," http://oldsite.raymondscott.com/1946.htm, accessed 3-9-12.

Wallerstein, Edward. "Narrative about the development of the LP record in 1948," http://www.musicinthemail.com/audiohistoryLP.html, accessed 4-4-12.

Wallop, Harry. "Why I will mourn the death of the Walkman," Oct. 27, 2010, http://www.telegraph.co.uk/comment/personal-view/8088232/Why-I-will-mourn-the-death-of-the-Walkman.html, accessed 5-12-12.

Wang, Pinie. "The Influence of Advertising and the Media on the Development of the Music Industry in the U.S.A," *Music and Advertising*, http://musicbusinessresearch.files.wordpress.com/2012/04/ijmbr_april_2012_pinie_wang1.pdf, accessed 5-19-12.

Ward, Phil. "Brian Eno Interviews and Articles: Ambient Reflections," *Studio Sound*, Oct. 1995, http://www.moredarkthanshark.org/eno_int_studiosound-oct95.html, accessed 8-12-12.

Waterman, Pete. Story told in keynote speech at the Art of Record Production Conference, University of Glamorgan, UK, 2009 (author present).

Waters, Darren. "Napster: 10 years of change," http://news.bbc.co.uk/2/hi/technology/8089221.stm, accessed 4-28-12.

Weber, Jerome F. "Repertory and Marketing," http://www.oxfordmusiconline.com.ezproxy.aacc.edu/subscriber/article/grove/music/26294?q=odeon+nutcracker&search=quick&pos=1&_start=1#firsthit, accessed 4-7-12.

Wexler, Jerry. "Remembering Ray," *Rolling Stone*, July 2004, http://www.rollingstone.com/news/story?id=6214207&rnd=1088673620142&has-player=u\nknown, accessed 8-27-12.

"What the Pros Say about SoundScan and Live Venue Reporting," updated 2011, http://www.indiehitmaker.com/Indiehitmaker_Testimonials.html, accessed 3-18-12.

Whisler, Thomas. Interview by author, *Christian Science Monitor*, April 21, 1964, 61.

White, Forrest. *Fender: The Inside Story* (San Francisco: Miller Freeman, 1994).

White, Thomas H., http://earlyradiohistory.us/sec014.htm, accessed 6-3-12.

Whitson, Signe. "Passive Aggressive Diaries: Understanding passive aggressive behavior in families, schools, and workplaces," *Psychology Today*, http://www.psychologytoday.com/blog/passive-aggressive-diaries/, updated March 25, 2010; accessed 9-14-12.

"William P. Lear (1902–1978), Audio, automotive and aircraft apparatus," Inventor of the Week, Lemelson-MIT, http://web.mit.edu/invent/iow/lear.html, accessed 4-28-12.

Winwood, Muff. Conversation with author, 1993.

Wooley, Bruce, Trevor Horn, and Geoff Downes. "Video Killed the Radio Star," Ackee Music Inc./ASCAP, Carbert Music Inc./BMI.

Worner, Karl H. *Stockhausen: Life and Work* (Berkeley, CA: University of California Press, 1973).

Zollo, Paul. *Songwriters on Songwriting* (Cambridge, MA: Da Capo, 2003).

Zuckerman, Steve. "Beatles Producer George Martin on Record Production: Know What You Are Doing before You Enter the Studio...," http://www.musicdish.com/mag/index.php3?id=5242, accessed 3-2-12.

Zwonitzer, Mark, and Charles Hirshberg. *Will You Miss Me When I'm Gone? The Carter Family* (New York: Simon & Schuster, 2002).

ABOUT THE AUTHOR

Richard James Burgess has produced, engineered, mixed, remixed, and performed on many gold, platinum, and multiplatinum albums. He authored the first three editions of this book, initially entitled *The Art of Record Production* (pub. 1997) and renamed *The Art of Music Production* for the second and third editions. Burgess was an A-list studio drummer and percussionist who has been signed to several major labels as a recording artist and composer, with hit records in his own right. In addition to his production work, he also managed major label artists and producers. He is known for his pioneering work with synthesizers, computers, and sampling in popular music and as an inventor of the SDSV drum synthesizer. He was educated at the Berklee College of Music, Boston; the Guildhall School of Music and Drama, London; and earned his Ph.D. at the University of Glamorgan, Wales. He is joint editor-in-chief of the *Journal on the Art of Record Production* (based in the London College of Music); a member of the national steering committee for the Producer and Engineer Wing of the Recording Academy (U.S.), and a lifetime member of the Music Producer's Guild (U.K.). Burgess played with the National Youth Jazz Orchestra (U.K.) and won Music Week, British Arts Council, Park Lane Group, and Greater London Arts Association awards. He currently works for Smithsonian Folkways Recordings in Washington, D.C., where he was co-producer, co-executive producer, and the project director for *Jazz: The Smithsonian Anthology*, a seven-year project chronicling more than a century of jazz.

INDEX